Producing and Reducing Disaffection

Producing and Reducing Disaffection

Edited by
Tony Booth and David Coulby

Open University Press

Milton Keynes · Philadelphia

Open University Press
Open University Educational Enterprises Limited
12 Cofferidge Close
Stony Stratford
Milton Keynes MK11 1BY, England

and
242 Cherry Street
Philadelphia, PA 19106, USA

First Published 1987

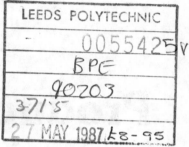
British Library Cataloguing in Publication Data
Producing and reducing disaffection.————
  (Curricula for all)
  1. Problem children————Education
  I. Booth, Tony II. Coulby, David III. Series
  371.8'1   LC4801

  ISBN 0-335-15976-1
  ISBN 0-335-15975-3 Pbk

Library of Congress Cataloging-in-Publication Data
Producing and reducing disaffection.
  (Curricula for all)
  Includes index.
  1. Handicapped children—Education—Great Britain. 2. Classroom management.
3. School discipline—Great Britain. 4. Mainstreaming in education—Great Britain.
I. Booth, Tony. II. Coulby, David. III. Series.
LC4036.G7P76 1986   371.9'046'0941   86–23655

ISBN 0-335-15976-1
ISBN 0-335-15975-3 (pbk.)

Text design by Nicola Sheldon
Typeset by Thomson Litho Ltd
Printed in Great Britain by Thomson Litho Ltd

Contents

We would like to acknowledge the contribution of those teachers and young people whose educational experience has provided the basis for this book.

Acknowledgements

Grateful acknowledgement is made for reproducing the following chapters in this volume: Chapter 2 consists of extracts from Schostak, J., 1986, *Schooling the violent imagination*, Chapter 4 of schooling, community and the emergence of the van-dalised self, reprinted by permission of Routledge and Kegan Paul. Chapter 6 is taken from the *Times Educational Supplement*, 31 January 1986 and consists of Mike Vernon's story as reported by Hazel Shaw. Chapter 8 is an edited version of Ling, R., 1983, A suspended sentence: the role of the LEA in the removal of disruptive pupils from school, *Pastoral care*, 1, 3, 189–199, reprinted by permission of Blackwell. Chapter 9 is an edited version of Ling, R., 1985, Teaching the unteachable: teacher strategies in special units for disruptive pupils, in Walford, G., ed. *Schooling in turmoil*, reprinted by permission of Croom Helm. Chapter 14 is an edited version of Wright, C., 1986, school processes – an ethnographic study, of Eggleston, J., Dunn, D., Anjal, M., Wright, C., *Education for some: the educational and vocational experience of 15–18 year-old members of the minority ehtnic groups* published by Trentham Books, reprinted by permission of the author. Chapter 24 is taken from Sargeant, J., 1985, Tampax and flowers: an approach to pastoral care? in language and gender working party. *Alice in genderland: reflections on language, power and control*, reprinted by permission of the author. Chapter 27 is an edited version of Humphries, S., 1981, *Hooligans or rebels? An oral history of working-class childhood and youth, 1889–1939*, reprinted by permission of Blackwell.

Introduction to the series: curricula for all
Tony Booth

Curricula for All is the general title of a series of three books. The first is entitled *Preventing Difficulties in Learning*, the second, *Producing and Reducing Disaffection*, and the third, *Including Pupils with Disabilities*. They reflect the approach to special needs in education of the special education group of the Open University and are the support material for the project year of our Advanced Diploma. Those familiar with our earlier course E241, *Special Needs in Education* will be aware of its attempt to move the concerns of special education away from a marginal esoteric segment of the education system towards the enhancement of comprehensive nursery, primary and secondary schools and further education colleges. Within that course we examined and developed a concept of integration as the foundation for a philosophy of special education. As the principle was formulated and clarified it merged with a principle of comprehensive, community education. Integration became the process of increasing the participation of pupils, families, school workers and communities in the life of mainstream schools. A focus on one group who experience limited participation, such as pupils with disabilities, naturally leads to an examination of the causes of and possible solutions to the lack of involvement of other groups. The absurdity of finding appropriate forms of schooling for such groups viewed in isolation is emphasised by a pupil's possible multiple membership of disadvantaged groups.

We are concerned, then, to examine the ways in which schools can respond to and reflect the diversity of their pupils. We have come to see how both an integration principle and comprehensive principle can be elucidated by being linked to a principle of equality of value. In schools which operate according to such a principle attempts are made to reduce the devaluation of pupils according to their sex, background, colour, economic or class position, ability, disability or attainment. In fact it can be argued that special education exists as a distinct area of concern for educators because of a particular set of devaluations of pupils on the basis of their disability, ability, attainment or background. If, however, we are to see pupils who gain Oxbridge entry as of no greater value, as no more worthy of congratulation, than pupils with severe mental handicap, then this has far-reaching consequences for what happens in schools and for how we perceive social inequalities outside them. Yet if it is the job of educators to discover and act in the interests of the pupils they serve it is hard to see how those who profess a concern for vulnerable and disadvantaged pupils should take any other view.

For us, the purpose of providing training in 'special needs in education' is to provide support for teachers and others to move away from a system in which large numbers of pupils are thought to be failures and from which pupils are selected out on the grounds of low ability or disability. We argue that the devaluation of pupils within the mainstream and selection out of it are mutually supportive. A training in special education which concentrates on those who fail to adapt to existing mainstream curricula or are excluded from them inevitably helps to perpetuate existing casualty rates. Our concern is with an approach to special needs in education which will enhance rather than undermine the development of comprehensive nursery, primary and secondary provision. We are as much or more concerned with the creation of curricula which cater for diverse groups, as with overcoming the difficulties experienced by particular pupils.

The practical implementation of a principle of equality of value is a thoroughly utopian notion; the possibility of its achievement is remote and partial as long as society and schools continue to provide arenas for competing interests. In such circumstances the advancement of the participation of one group must be at the expense of the re-evaluation of another. We have tried to be clear about the principles which underly this series of books because it is our firm belief that clarity over principles is the best way to facilitate decisions about practice. But the emphasis is on practice rather than principles. We have provided a wide variety of examples of practice concerned with making curricula in schools responsive to all pupils.

Volume One in our series is entitled *Preventing Difficulties in Learning*. This book takes as its starting point a definition of learning difficulty as a mismatch between pupils and tasks. Consequently, the prevention of difficulties in learning involves changing the experiences of pupils in schools so that they are more closely matched to their abilities and interests. The book looks both at the way curricula can be made more generally accessible and at the kinds of organisation and support required within schools to initiate and sustain such changes. It looks at the way existing people and structures concerned with the learning difficulties of pupils can develop a concern for the nature of the whole curriculum. If the problem of learning difficulties cannot be resolved by focusing on groups of pupils who have limited ability or attainment or have disabilities then the job of special or remedial educators becomes a collaborative one and the basis of their expertise has to shift. These issues are carefully examined and exemplified. This book also provides the support material for our pack, EP538 *Teaching for Diversity: Preventing Difficulties in Learning*.

The introduction to Volume Two, *Producing and Reducing Disaffection* follows this series introduction. The third book in the series is entitled *Including Pupils With Disabilities*. We worried about compiling a separately bound book which focuses on curricula for children and young people who have physical or mental or sensory disabilities. It is essential that the pupils which become a focus of concern in this book are also seen as an integral part of the groups who are the recipients of schooling depicted in our first two volumes. At the same time we do not wish to imply that a principle of equality of value means that all pupils should be treated in the same way. Rather, it involves an acceptance or even, dare one say, a celebration of diversity. In this third book we have looked at those aspects of curricula which are related to specific disabilities of pupils such as sign language for deaf pupils, brailling and curriculum conversions for blind pupils. The unifying concern of the book is the participation of pupils with disabilities in ordinary life and ordinary schools. We have examined the power of people with disabilities in society, the nature of current policies and practices, the barriers to increased participation in ordinary schooling and how they can be overcome.

The great majority of the contributions are published for the first time. We have tried to overcome problems of coherence created by having large numbers of contributing authors in part by providing authors with a careful list of suggestions and by negotiating chapters through a process of drafting and redrafting. Our contributors have been wonderfully persevering during these stages and our offices and homes have echoed too with cries of 'never again!' Yet we are well aware of the necessity for allowing many voices to be represented in this enterprise, particularly from practising teachers and others who can tell their experience at first hand. We have also provided each chapter with an introductory paragraph and have written introductory chapters for each book. We do not expect anyone to plough straight through the books. They are a resource for learning and their use should be adapted to the needs of any particular reader. The series is the result of our efforts to reground special education in a body of knowledge which will allow practitioners to begin to implement some of the rhetoric of the last ten years. The abolition of distinctions between special, remedial and mainstream education requires a radical rethink of the work of special educators and, inevitably, new forms of training. The concepts and content of training is one way of assessing whether the rhetoric of change is serious in intent or if what is to be offered is more of the same. The way to avoid a simple backsliding into old ways is to articulate the underlying principles on which a non-selective, non-categorical approach to special education could be based.

To complete our Advanced Diploma students study E241 and a broadening education or social science course. They then produce three projects in conjunction with *Curricula for All*. The first of these is a study of learning from the perspective of pupils, the second a piece of curriculum analysis and development and the third a study of decision and policy making within a school and/or LEA. The demands of these projects have helped to determine the shape of the books and have made us attend carefully to the range of topics we need to cover to provide an adequate basis for training. Perhaps, it is in the third area that we are weakest. Partly this is because policy making was a particular concern of our earlier course but largely it is because the level of discussion about decisions and developments in schools which we would like to include is very difficult to find in already published form and very difficult to persuade others to write. It is honest reporting and discussion about practice and the many slips between policy as rhetoric or intention and its practical implementation from which others can best learn. Perhaps our course will begin to break down the formidable barriers to sharing such information which many find to be excessively threatening.

There are a few final things which have to be made clear. Firstly we do not want our ready use of the word 'curriculum' to imply that we believe what pupils are offered in school can be written down on a bit of paper and handed out or down in staffroom and classroom. Our notion of curriculum encompasses the experiences of pupils, teachers and others in school and the interactions between school and community rather than being reserved for the written intentions of departmental heads. The kind of community a school provides is as important a feature of the curriculum as the words transmitted in formal lessons. Nor do we think it is unproblematic to match curricula to the backgrounds, interests and capacities of pupils. Understanding the needs and interests of others is complex and problematic but it becomes slightly less so if we listen to the voices of those whose interests we claim to serve.

Most importantly, we do not argue that a relocation of the problem of difficulties in learning from inside the child or the child's background or culture or family to the curriculum in school can cause problems within schools to evaporate, nor that teachers can be held personally responsible for the difficulties which do arise. Teachers are under massive pressures within a shrinking education system which is in turn adapting to shrinking employment opportunities for school leavers. There is a definite danger that a new focus on the curriculum within schools will deflect attention from the handicapping economic and social conditions outside them or even hold schools responsible for such conditions. This is a clear strand in attempts to vocationalise the curriculum in secondary schools where high unemployment is blamed, in part, on the inappropriateness of the training given to the workforce which is offered vocational training after school and prevocational training within it. Schooling is not created anew by each generation of teachers; they operate within institutional constraints not of their choosing. But having said this we would argue that viewing difficulties in learning as arising from the relationship between pupils and curricula can enhance the contribution of teachers to their own working lives, as well as to the lives of their pupils.

Introduction to this volume: understanding disaffection
Tony Booth

Prologue

1)   Are you sitting comfortably? Ready to learn? Minds clear of distractions? Sitting still are we...? Then I'll begin.

But perhaps this doesn't strike the right note. Is it just a bit patronising? You see, I want your attention and I am afraid it might wander. Forgive me for applying just a little bit of pressure. Try to concentrate. Look at the words. Now, shall I continue?

Get on with it

2)   It is a Friday morning and I have gone to an assembly at my daughter's school. The junior choir is performing. The children sit on the floor, parents line the walls, the teachers stand at the front facing the pupils. There is perfect silence. Mr Elvis, headteacher, steps forward:

'A hearty good morning to you, children.'

The children respond in unison:

'A hearty good morning to you, Mr Elvis.'

Here is a slight twist to the familiar routine. The pupils acknowledge his authority and demonstrate obedience. But why the extra word 'hearty'? It is a joke of course. It's amusing to hear a hundred pupils uttering that quaint phrase and there is a ripple of laughter from the parents. Mr Elvis notices and faintly smiles himself. Yes, there's another message for us too. He has made the pupils perform a little trick. *He* is in control.

Any one of thousands of incidents inside or outside schools can serve as a starting point for an understanding of disaffection or disruption in school. My opening to this chapter was intended to provoke a hint of disaffection in the reader though hopefully it was not sufficient to prevent you from reading on. Feelings of disaffection, experiences of control, are part of the lives of all of us. An understanding of disaffection and disruption depends on a degree of awareness of our own feelings. When an activity is described, commonly, in negative terms it is tempting to see it as exhibited only by others and to be understood in terms which could not include ourselves. They are the disruptives, we are the mature, law-abiding citizens. In such circumstances we need both imagination and honesty. We have to be willing to see the world from the point of view of others. We also have to admit that, whatever the present purity of our thoughts and behaviour, a range of human emotion and action is, nevertheless, open to us all. A certain self-consciousness is required.

The contribution of this book

This is the second book in the series *Curricula for All*. It continues the attempt to integrate discussion of problems in school with an understanding of the construction and teaching of mainstream curricula. The first book was concerned, primarily, with the 'problem' of learning difficulties. The notion of the 'child with learning difficulties' was seen to be based on a definition of the normal learner and normal curriculum. We advocated a non-normative definition of learning difficulties which reflected the degree of match between a learner and a task and in this way attempted to provide a common basis for considering the learning needs of all pupils. The book was concerned to reconnect remedial education and integrate special education by supporting the diversification of mainstream curricula. But in some ways there was an air of unreality about the approach we took. In focusing on the construction of curricula there was little emphasis on the dominant concerns of many teachers, with classroom control and pupil behaviour. Yet if teachers are occupied with controlling pupils how can they have time and space to diversify curricula?

If the issues are separate, then we may have our books round the wrong way. In a recent book, *Disruptive Children – Disruptive Schools*, the authors argue at one point: 'Misbehaviour in a school can be concentrated in the behaviour of relatively few children who present serious problems to the staff. In a difficult school there will be a proportionately larger number of such children' (Lawrence, Steed and Young 1984, p. 148).

Here, though perhaps not elsewhere in their book, these authors imply that the effective control of a few miscreants might resolve the issue of disruption. One teacher in their project objected to this narrow approach:

> The project did not penetrate deeply enough – just dealing with the serious disruptions. The boy who arrives ten to fifteen minutes late, and has a quick cheeky reason for his lateness that makes the rest of the class laugh ... the pupil who perpetually talks, has to be warned, and warned again, then acted upon; the pupil who opens a pot of paint with a chisel has to be reprimanded and the verbal abuse from him has to be dealt with ... stone throwing, vandalism, litter ... one has to have a confrontation which in the main leaves both parties devoid of a friendly relationship. I have in the last year suffered many nights of sleeplessness ...
>
> (Lawrence, Steed and Young 1984, pp. 129–130)

This teacher's perspective broadens the view. For him control and disruption were features of many exchanges with many pupils experienced cumulatively as extremely stressful. Yet if this is our starting point our attention is still riveted to the misbehaviour of pupils. Why do they do it?

Every day in thousands of schools, pupils are interrogated about their actions. Why were you talking? Why did you laugh? Why didn't you finish your work? Why did you stand up? Why did you hit Susan? Pupils may have an answer and say it, they may have an answer and not say it, they may be bewildered and cry or confused and angry. Such question and answer sessions are part of the culture of schools and may borrow their shape from our knowledge of court procedures where life may be centred for days on a search for motives. Though even here answers are rarely satisfactory even where the crime itself is dramatic. In her

Portraits of Children Who Kill Muriel Gardiner had this to say of the search for explanation:

> Why did he do it?
>
> This is the question asked by every relative, friend, enemy, or judge of the young offender. And by the offender himself. Why?
>
> There is no single explanation of any crime, or indeed of any act, momentous or trivial...
>
> (Gardiner 1985, p. xix)

Absorbing as these questions are, in trying to add to an understanding of disaffection and disruption we have attempted to tear ourselves away from the point of confrontation and follow through a line of reasoning from the earlier volume. We argued that the moral basis for the desire to respond appropriately to the diversity of pupils within a school rested on the application of a principle of equality of value (see series introduction). But failure to apply such a principle will have a series of consequences. Not only will it lead us to neglect certain groups of pupils and take insufficient care over the nature of their curricula, the devaluation of some pupils within a school also creates a pool of potential disaffection. At any time this can feed an apparently impulsive or angry response in a classroom or lead to withdrawal or disinterest. There may exist what John Schostak has called 'a climate of hostility, resentment and suspicion' (Schostak 1983, p. 69).

An understanding of disaffection and disruption can be found in part, then, by examining the value placed on pupils within schools. This includes the extent of the efforts of a school to provide curricula relevant to the capacities and interests of all pupils. The contribution of this book to approaching the reduction of disaffection should be set beside the development of inclusive curricula outlined in *Preventing Difficulties in Learning* (Booth, Potts and Swann 1986).

We have gathered together issues, in this volume, which are commonly left as separate areas of study. As time goes by ways of understanding schooling become rigid. 'Topics' become defined by precedent and the arrangement of books on library shelves. Discussions about them are couched in their own languages and references are made to a limited set of experts, books and journal articles. Thus links may be made between topics represented by the following headings:

Behaviour
Classroom management
Control
Counselling
Disaffection
Discipline
Disruption
Pastoral care
Punishment.

But these may be separated from a consideration of:

Disruptive units
Maladjusted schooling
Child psychiatry
Special education.

Though possibly the first of these may oscillate between both groups depending on whether pupils who are seen as candidates for disruptive units are considered as having behavioural or emotional defects and hence the province of special education or as wilfully undisciplined and hence still within the boundaries of normality (see Chapters 5, 7, 9, 10, 11). Special provision associated with education is commonly separated from social service projects such as intermediate treatment or placement in Community Homes with Education and Remand or Assessment Centres, following court appearance. Whatever the nature of their funding, the overt rationale for special schools and units may lead one to think that they cater for a particular and exotic species of child. Yet whenever we look in detail at the way pupils fall foul of the care and control of the mainstream the group can be seen to be varied and the referral procedures haphazard (Galloway 1982; Ford, Mongon and Whelan 1982). Neither of the above lists are usually considered alongside discussions of the content of curricula, their rationale and the organization of schools; the non-racist or non-sexist curriculum; the organization of groups with diverse abilities or the integration of pupils with disabilities and how these might affect the teaching of mathematics, science, history, the development of project and topic work or the integration of areas of study (see Section 3, this volume, and *Preventing Difficulties in Learning*).

We are attempting to put a consideration of the behaviour of pupils back into its context in the curriculum in schools. Whilst such a task may seem to be vast and to run counter to preprepared topic lists we cannot see how else to make sense of the issues involved.

The devaluation of pupils

The way in which some people are devalued in schools as well as suggestions for countering such processes is the major concern of Section 3 of this book. If you have doubts that such processes occur I suggest that you read through the chapters carefully and then reassess your position. Some readers will be in no doubt of the legitimacy of such ideas from the start. As reported by one teacher:

> I remember walking into a class on my first day of teaching. It was a group of third year, low ability children and the first comment I had was: 'You're a new one are you? They seem to leave every year. I wonder how long you will last. Well, the other one had bigger tits than you ...'

There is a double devaluation here, of the pupils, ranked according to ability, and of women. This particular teacher found sexism an oppressive and pervasive feature of her school:

> From the start it was evident that if you were male you were given more credibility than if you were female. Women teachers have to prove themselves doubly – you have to create an image of almost executive like efficiency or a very 'macho' image and be 'dead butch.' If you step out of role then you are in trouble. Many of the older women have problems perhaps because their style is gentler, they don't have a brittle career woman image. We did meet to discuss this but nothing came of it. We were labelled as neurotic and having problems and were generally put down.

In another school some women teachers and girl pupils got together to discuss the problem of sexism. The pupils decided to keep a record of the sexist comments teachers made to them: 'They made quite a collection. Like the teacher who said: "This will be useful for you as housewives," or "It's a pity you're a girl, because you're quite good at chemistry."'

Lynn Davies (see Chapter 16 and Davies 1984) in her research collected many such examples, including some which combined sexism with divisions along ability and possibly class lines:

> If they're not going to do examinations, if they're not capable, then we should be fitting them for something else. The obvious thing is wife and mother, because they probably will be wives and mothers. So the syllabus should be tailored with that in mind.
>
> (Woman – Home Economics Teacher)

This teacher retained for some girls what the Newsom Report had advocated for all of them: 'Our girls should be educated in terms of their main social function – which is to make for themselves, their children and their husbands a secure and suitable home and to be mothers' (Ministry of Education 1963, quoted in Mahoney 1985, p. 9).

The accumulated evidence of sexism in our schools is there for anyone with the eyes to look. Pat Mahoney provides a good starting place in her book 'Schools for the Boys' as do Chapters 16, 17, 25, in this book. Many girls and women teachers suffer regular sexual harassment too and this has led some to challenge the safety of mixed-sex schooling for them (see Chapter 25, Jones (1985), Hey (1985)). It is not just through looking at what texts are used or what is said that sexism is revealed. The way in which promotions are made according to sex appears to be a major scandal of our educational system and one reproduced in education authority after education authority. Pat Mahoney reported that the position was getting worse; whilst 25 per cent of all headteachers were women in 1963 this had dropped to 16 per cent in 1983. Women still predominate as headteachers in infant schools but only 17 per cent are heads of juniors. Government statistics for 1982 reported that 61 per cent of all scale one posts were occupied by women, 45 per cent of scale two posts, 35 per cent of scale three, 21 per cent of scale four and 18 per cent of senior positions as heads and deputies (DES 1982). Hilda Davidson did a painstaking study of opportunities in Clwyd secondary schools. She found the national picture to be strikingly reproduced there and showed how suggestions that women lacked competence or ambition were myths used to blame women for their own failure to rise (Davidson 1985). The constant representation of women in schools as a relatively powerless group provides a bitter and overwhelming lesson to girl pupils about their own expectations.

The presence of racism in schools is eloquently illustrated in Chapters 14 and 20. Those who deny the existence of racism should ponder on the fact that Chapter 14 is taken from the Eggleston Report (Eggleston, Dunn, Anjali and Wright 1986) which was commissioned by the Department of Education and Science. The report found evidence for systematic discrimination against black young people. The Department of Education and Science failed to publish it themselves but it has now been published independently under the title 'Education For Some.' John Schostak found in his research that racism could be expressed and received at times as a natural occurrence in school:

A head of department, for example, Mr Stone, enters the staffroom doing his 'sambo' impression – 'Hey ma-a-an, how de do' – making 'rubber lips', palmed hands flapping. Everyone laughs . . . The humour defuses his racism. His 'rubber lip' impressions, however, are also carried out in front of black children who can do little else but sheepishly laugh – after all, what harm is there in a little humour?

(Schostak 1983, p. 79)

Perhaps one might concede that sexism and racism exist in school but what about discrimination according to social class? Surely the age has gone when Bertrand Russell could describe a major barrier to the happiness of women as 'the paucity and bad quality of domestic service' (Russell 1930, p. 188). Yet, how much change has there been? The Newbolt Report of 1921 had argued in terms, familiar in the ensuing years, of the need to eradicate working class styles of speech:

Speech training must be undertaken from the outset . . . Teachers of infants sometimes complain that when the children come to school they can scarely speak at all. They should regard this as an advantage . . . It is emphatically the business of the elementary school to teach all its pupils who either speak a definite dialect or whose speech is disfigured by vulgarisms, to speak standard English, and to speak it clearly.

(Ministry of Education 1921, pp. 59, 64)

One of the informants for Stephen Humphries' oral history explained the light one teacher had thrown on the validity of school history and its preoccupation with the wars and achievements of eminent persons:

Now if you got hold of all those history books we had at the time, they was all a load of flannel, about Edward the Peacemaker, Queen Victoria and Elizabeth the First. When he did give us history the way he did give it, he did show us that they wasn't as glorious as what they made out, how we lost the American colonies and in India and places like that. He gave us a truer picture because all the books were glorifying the monarchy and I used to honestly think as a lad that there was nobody like the British. All the rest, if he was a foreigner, that was it, he was a load of rubbish. Well, you can tell by the way they did call 'em 'Froggies' and 'Eyties' and 'Dagoes' and things like that. I mean, the only way you'd describe them was that they were beneath you. But he started me on the trail, that bloke, that teacher. And later on, when I was getting on to fourteen, I started to read these historical books an' I took an interest in 'em. An I thought to myself at the time, well, what a load of rubbish we've been taught in the past.

(Fred Mattock in Stephen Humphries 1981, p. 43)

Such criticisms of the curriculum are still familiar (see Chapter 19). The idea that pupils might shed their background at the classroom door has persisted too. Ronald King describes a teacher referring to the fact that his pupils had nothing 'useful in the way of experience' to bring into school from their homes (King 1979, p. 91). A teacher spoke to me of the way the nursery class in her school was 'an extension of home' but it was clear that she was not necessarily referring to a home extension of the pupils.

Most of our homes are not how I would want a home to be. But when a child's been three years in that home you're not going to say immediately 'you're wrong, your mother is wrong, don't do it like that'...his self-image will fall, he'll get two conflicting standards, but if we can gradually ask him to conform to our standards rather than immediately...

Within schools, as outside them, people are often obsessed with differences in status and class and this can come over most clearly when future occupations are assigned priorities. The contradictions in providing a comprehensive education whilst devaluing the work of pupils' parents is neatly illustrated in the 1985 Richard Dimbleby lecture where Mary Warnock expressed concern at the damage that was being done to the status of teachers by industrial action:

> Nowadays, teachers go in for 'industrial action.' Teachers on strike get little sympathy, however reasonable their case; and they do their image irreparable harm. They are thought to put themselves on a level with other wage earners – miners, car workers and those whose jobs are concerned with the production of goods.
>
> (Warnock 1985, p. 10)

The notion that classism does not flourish is a game sometimes played in writings about education when other writers have no such qualms. Thus, coincidentally, in a thriller I have picked up in the house at which I am staying 'class differences' are used as a theme to provide a familiar line of interest:

> Dominic, Barnabus, Samantha and Georgina were sitting on the kerb poking sticks through the drain cover. Wexford...couldn't help being faintly touched that they who were poor in everything had been affluent, extravagant and imaginative in one respect. If they never gave their children another thing, they had at least endowed them with names usually reserved to the upper classes.
>
> (Rendell 1969, p. 54)

This particular book is littered with unpleasant and dehumanising remarks about people who are seen to comprise the bulk of the population but clearly, are not intended readers. (Incidentally, I feel under no obligation to desist from revealing that it was the dentist who did it!)

The way in which pupils are evaluated according to their ability has been alluded to earlier. Categorisation by ability is a major preoccupation of our culture and of our schools and many in education are well aware of the way pupils in the lowest sets often feel the most disaffected. Many of the chapters in our earlier volume are concerned with describing alternatives to such categorisation. I cannot see how it is possible to select, stream, band or set pupils according to ability without assigning them differences in value. I have discussed this in relation to selection for special schooling elsewhere (see *Preventing Difficulties in Learning*, Chapters 24, 25, 27). The reduction of selection by disability is the subject of the third book of this series: *Including Pupils with Disabilities*. Mark, one of the pupils interviewed for Chapter 5 of this book described the emphasis at his school:

> Everything was geared to exams and the schools showed more interest in the brighter pupils. Prize-giving was only concerned with them, which led to a lot of ill-feeling amongst other pupils. The system wasn't designed for them and they wanted to get out just as soon as they could.
>
> (Chapter 5, p. 32)

In the 'Harpole Report' J. L. Carr describes an entry in the fictional head's journal which humorously summarises some people's feelings about streamed groups. The teacher of the 'backward' class had hung a wreath on her door which Mr Harpole goes to investigate:

Journal

Visited Miss Tollemache's classroom and, after ascertaining that Theaker was at the other end of the building, closely examined the wreath. I shook it but no dust or vermin were dislodged. In fact it appeared to be in unusually good condition and without odour.

In casual conversation with children, I learnt that, besides the usual milk, needlework, pencil, painting etc. monitors, there is a Special Flower Monitor whose duty it is to 'gently' dust *it* each second day.

All else having failed, decided to come right out with it. '*Must* you have that wreath in your classroom?', I said.

'I *must*,' she said, 'and I will tell you why. It symbolises the graveyard of the bright hopes I once had of being given a proper class like everybody else. Ever since I came here, which was before even Mr Chadband, I have been landed with "The Backwards"! There was a time when, in my ignorance, I felt only sorry for *myself*. But now it is for them – "The Backwards"! I have come to abhor streaming: it shows such a crude lack of respect. They know what C means alright – even before As and Bs and disappointed parents translate it. We teach children not to complain, so all they've left is to cry into their pillow and, when they're big enough, kick in the windows of telephone booths. I did think when *you* took over that you'd abolish it.' I went away utterly astonished and chastened.

(Carr 1972, pp. 88–9)

Miss Tollemache would however get little sympathy from the Education Minister, Mr Chris Patten who at the 1986 Annual Conference of the Professional Association of Teachers argued for streaming according to ability and aptitudes:

I understand that many teachers feel uncomfortable about appearing to put a label on pupils in this way. But I believe that what matters is not how you appear to label children but how you actually treat them...

(*Guardian* Wednesday 30 July, 1986)

DEVALUATION AND THE CONSTRUCTION OF NORMALITY

There is another way of approaching the devaluations which occur in schools apart from through the familiar categories of sex, race, class and ability. One can ask: 'how is normality defined in the school?' What picture of normal family life or job or income or set of interests or feelings of sexuality or body shape and physical prowess are conveyed in the school? One can think of the image of normality in a school as both a potential source of disaffection and as a system of social control.

RESPONDING TO DEVALUATIONS

Doubts about the potential for disaffection to be transmuted to disruption might be removed by a reading of *Woman at Point Zero*, the account of a woman who killed a man as recorded by Nawal El Saadawi (1978). It traces which frightening clarity the connection between sexual oppression and one woman's violent response:

> With each of the men I ever knew, I was always overcome by a strong desire to lift my arm high up over my head and bring my hand smashing down on his face. Yet because I was afraid I was never able to lift my hand. Fear made me see this movement as being something very difficult to carry out. I did not know how to get rid of this fear, until the moment when I raised my hand for the first time. The movement of my hand upwards and then downwards destroyed my fear... the movement of my hand had become very easy, and everything in my hand could be moved with a natural ease even if it were a sharp knife which I thrust into a chest and then withdrew... I am speaking the truth now without any difficulty... When I killed I did it with truth and not with a knife... That is why they are afraid and in a hurry to execute me. They do not fear my knife. It is my truth which frightens them.
>
> (El Saadawi 1978, p. 102)

I am not suggesting that oppression always does or should lead to violence. I have included this extract because I found that this book (which incidentally was banned in Egypt, its setting, after publication) contained a compelling lesson of the way oppression can provide a source of simmering motives for reaction.

If there are connections between devaluation, dissatisfaction, disaffection and disruption in schools then one might wish to intervene at the start of such a chain purely for pragmatic reasons; one might want to avoid trouble. Yet many of the pupils whose worth is undervalued may not be disruptive at all. It might be simpler, in any case, to attempt to obscure the processes of devaluation. For the effect of increasing the awareness of any group of their oppression may lead them to be more actively resistant to what they perceive as its source. Some people have argued that multicultural curricula have been used in this way to reduce the opposition of pupils: 'The 3 Ss (saris, samosas and steel bands)... was advanced as the operational mode through which the 3 Rs (resistance, rejection and rebellion) would be contained and defused' (Troyna and Williams 1986, p. 24)

Of course, there are some people who do deny the occurrence of devaluation of groups within society and in our schools. Others express concern at the particular form any countervailing curricula might take. As expressed by Margaret Thatcher, British Prime Minister and ex-Secretary of State for Education:

> Look at Bernie Grant in Haringey. What they are doing to the syllabus in schools, what they are insisting is being taught to the children... We have got to get in many places, particularly in inner cities, alternative schools to some of those the local authorities are running. You know about political indoctrination in some of the inner cities. Well, I could show you examination papers, I could show you books. They come to me. Parents come to one, they dare not talk about it. They say please do not talk about it because they will take it out on my child at school.
>
> (*Guardian* 10 July, 1986)

Presumably, with her reference to Bernie Grant, black leader of Haringey Council, the Prime Minister is referring to anti-racist education. Jonathan Savery, writing in the *Salisbury Review,* dismissed anti-racist education in the following way:

> The anti-racists' apparent interest in education rarely seems to extend beyond the stage of parading the underachievement of certain groups as 'proof' of racism.

Indeed their interest in pupils' schooling seems a mere contrivance. For their true concerns are political rather than pedagogical.

(Savery 1985, p. 41)

I suggest that you evaluate such statements in the light of Chapter 20 on the work of the Inner London Education Authority's anti-racist strategies team, or the contributions to Challenging Racism (All London Teachers Against Racism and Facism 1984.) It is interesting that the anti-racist strategies team, which many might believe to be a cornerstone of the 'new' ILEA policies, is run by teachers on temporary secondment from their schools who feel very precarious in their position.

In her Dimbleby Lecture, Mary Warnock argued that the inculcation of a particular view of morality was the responsibility of schools but she was concerned to draw a distinction between morality and politics:

It is desirable that children should be taught to be honest, kind, generous, tolerant and fair, why should it be undesirable that they should be taught that exploitation, greed and aggression are wrong on a political scale?...I think the distinction is more or less the distinction between public and private morality.

(Warnock 1985, p. 11)

The teaching of a distinction between public and private morality could easily provide a lesson in hypocrisy and merge with a distinction between 'what you say' and 'what you do'. Of course there needs to be a dialogue about indoctrination in schools but it cannot be assumed that the inherited curriculum is politically neutral or that the 'middle ground' which should determine the balance of opinion is easy to locate or does not itself involve a moral and political stance. We have offered the principle of 'equality of value' as one starting point for a shared morality in school. To the extent that devaluations are produced in the society of which schools are a part then an aspect of the moral education in school must include efforts to counter them. How else are pupils to be taught to be 'honest, kind, generous, tolerant and *fair*?'

Obedience to authority

An examination of the nature of 'authority' in school provides a further way to consider the origins of disaffection. Authority relationships in school are not disconnected from relationships outside it. They depend on a structure of dominance in society. Some people and some categories of people are more powerful than others. Their positions are sustained by a vision of normality in which a particular hierarchy of power relationships is represented as ordinary life. This normality is policed or enforced by those willing to take on positions of authority. The nature of such a position is itself obscured by the double meaning of the word 'authority'; implying greater knowledge as well as more power. An authority is the person who 'knows best'. This confusion of meaning may mislead both those who aspire to and those who are subjected to authority. It is a familiar enough occurrence and one which has potential for both humour and intense irritation that when someone changes their power position they may not only swagger and strut but also believe that they are the sudden recipients of wisdom. Those in authority also obscure the powers they serve by representing 'obedience to authority' as morally desirable and criticism of current power relationships as an abnormality: 'an authority problem'.

Many teachers are perfectly aware of the structural determinants of their power, as one secondary teacher remarked: 'Moving up the hierarchy counts for an awful lot and the title of head or deputy head brings respect and credibility'. A primary headteacher was alarmed, at first, by the extent of the power her position conferred as well as the wisdom she was expected to display:

> When I became a head I was terrified by how much power you have. People are prepared to give you limitless power. At first it was awful here as the staff were forever asking if they could do things rather than just getting on with it . . .
>
> Even the parents view me as some sort of referee, recently two mothers were fighting outside in the playground. They came into school for me to judge who was right and who was wrong.

The authority invested in teachers, then, is not 'natural'. It is part of a system of power relationships in society. Teachers may find that they are involved in enforcing this system and to the extent that they support existing power relationships they will adopt the mantle of authority with pride, even literally if they wear a gown. Alternatively they may attempt to subvert it. In any case they will usually discover that part of the complexity of understanding their own authority is that their power, whilst there somewhere, is embodied in the teaching profession in a diffuse and even precarious way. Rarely is there a gown-clad silhouette within the system tailored perfectly to their own shape which will merge with their body and instantly confer unquestioned deference. Such a merging of person and structure may be engineered in a few public schools where the immanence of history may give each occupant of the head's office a pope-like infallibility. But for most, whilst the battle may be weighted in their favour, their authority still has to be fought for and once gained, it may be maintained by threat of coercion or the subtle illusion that when their wishes prevail 'all is right with the world'. Yet there is a great temptation for such an illusion to become a delusion of grandeur, or power trip, in which a challenge to the directives of the teacher come to be seen as a personal affront. For if the authority of schooling does not reside within the bodies and minds of individual teachers but has political origins then the challenge to authority is not simply a personal matter.

Explanations and excuses

Yet for some, there is little sense in looking for explanations of disaffection or disruption beyond the moral culpability of the individual. As Joseph Newman has argued:

> Once upon a time, the young had original sin imputed to them. I might have found that interesting at least. It is unoriginal sin that some youngsters go in for that bores me so profoundly. So do many of the reasons which they have learnt to advance for their wickedness. I remember one lad of eleven who had done numerous burglaries and related offences. I asked why he did such things. He said it was because of the broken marriage. I asked if he meant his own. He looked uncertainly at me and then at the door; only a raging nutcase could ask such a damfool question. I pressed him to give me one cogent reason why the discomforts of his parent should impel him to

> I think we can be too understanding. A bit of ferocity suitably applied can be very worthwhile.
>
> (Newman, J. 1979, p. 13)

Mary Warnock argued that it was actually part of the job of teachers to ignore circumstance in this way. She was at pains to separate those explanations which formed part of the professional repertoire of social workers from those which should exercise the minds of teachers:

> A professional social worker must, in the nature of the case, be concerned with the client as part of society . . . Individuals are neither to be praised nor blamed for their condition. They are, for the social worker, products, perhaps victims, of the economic and social forces that govern human life. This is the irreducible determinism, built into the social worker's professional philosophy.
>
> The teacher on the other hand must be, professionally speaking, an optimist, an individualist and a believer in free will . . . The teacher is not obliged to think of the child as formed by his family, or his income bracket, but simply as himself . . . capable of learning that, with effort, he 'could do better'.
>
> (Warnock 1985, p. 11)

I am tempted to ask which set of professional explanations should be applied to this account. Is the author to be understood as embedded in society, a product of her class and economic position or is she to be seen as someone who, with effort, 'could do better'? For example, sexist language does matter. One women headteacher referred to her experience on a panel interviewing six men and three women for a post of deputy head:

> The county's training officer said 'these are all potential deputy headmasters'. He was so insulting, I said 'excuse me, there is such a word as headteacher, could you please use it.' He was frightfully apologetic but it runs off the tongue so easily. How insulting it was to sit there as a female headteacher and hear the implication that the only person who could do the job was a man.

As Jan Reid shows in Chapter 21 social workers are as likely as others to go in for accounts of people's troubles in terms of personal determination. The way one attempts to understand the actions of others should not be prescribed according to the job one does. The social worker, the teacher or the academic are limited in their appreciation if they do not learn to balance the contradiction in the fact that people's actions are both self-determined and physically and socially constrained.

In September 1985 at the outbreak of the riots or rebellions in Handsworth, Brixton and Tottenham, some politicians, newspaper reporters and editors saw the activities as solely the product of an outburst of criminality; they needed no further explanation either in terms of the events which preceded them or in terms of the economic physical and social conditions or the history of the people involved. As put by the *Daily Express*, with reference to the Handsworth Riot: 'Let there be no doubt about one aspect of the bloody Handsworth riot. It was a criminal enterprise, planned and executed for loot and arson'.

Such attempts to curtail and confine explanation are not acts of logic but are themselves psychological and political; removing unwelcome information from the front of one's own and other people's minds. Perhaps the teacher and the social worker in Mary Warnock's caricatures should both retain access to a range of understanding and adopt a similar aim; to enable others to take control over their own lives.

Starting to make changes

In order to change any particular school we have to take it as we find it and recognise the concerns which predominate within that school. This does not mean we should always accept that present dominant concerns *should* have such a position of eminence. I cannot believe that the amount of teacher time and energy expended on checking and correcting pupil dress serves any educational purpose whatsoever. I wish it would stop. Yet its persistence shows it to be a significant and efficiently reproduced feature of our culture. This desire for uniformity must work against a system of education designed to encourage tolerance for diversity. But where the clothing of pupils is the main focus for expressing and controlling disaffection there can be little doubt that something has to be done about it. Many teachers resent the intrusion of such issues into education as the teacher discussion of Chapter 1 suggests. Another teacher mentioned a particular but familiar example: 'In our place, for example, it is coats, carrying them around or wearing them or whatever, and so the beginning and end of every lesson is marred, however brilliant the teaching material is, by somebody nagging about putting on or taking off coats'.

One perennial source of disagreement and discontent in schools actually will stop. On 22 July 1986 parliament voted to abolish corporal punishment in state schools. There was an element of farce about the decision which was opposed by a government with a large majority and given fortuitous support by the monarchy in the week of the royal wedding. As Biddy Passmore reported:

> The Prime Minister's absence at an official dinner for Mrs Nancy Reagan and the problems of a dozen MPs with pre-wedding traffic in Parliament Square may well have been decisive in giving the abolitionists a majority of a single vote. But one vote is enough. As a result, from mid-August 1987, teachers who beat, tawse, cane or slap a state-supported pupil in any part of the United Kingdom will be open to civil proceedings for battery.
>
> (*Times Educational Supplement 25 July 1986*)

But many schools have other major concerns which may seem to obliterate the possibility of looking for deeper curriculum changes. As a further teacher reported:

> In one school I worked in the major area of difficulty was the lockers. They were outside the classrooms and until they were sorted out nothing could be done. The lockers were constantly damaged, the kids had books thrown out of them or they carried all of them around the school and dumped them. You could have any amount of in-service training about how to deal with problems in the classroom but nothing was going to be sorted out until teachers could raise and resolve the problem of the lockers.

One group of teachers, who I asked to describe the major area of difficulty in their comprehensive school came up with a novel problem. They were preoccupied with the school toilets. The caretaker had decided to lock up all toilet paper and soap because, he claimed, too much was going missing. For a while pupils had to request 'a yard of toilet paper' from their teachers. At one point there was only 'one tiny loo in operation for 1100 kids.' One of the teachers resorted to getting a key cut for the caretakers cupboard to ease the situation. As another remarked: 'This is what you called encouraging responsibility in the growing adolescent.'

STYLES OF ORDER

This book is not a manual on the tricks of the trade. There is no doubt that some people have a greater facility for keeping classroom order than others and it is clear that much can be learnt by observing and working with other teachers. However it is also plain that different styles of teaching require different approaches to discipline and we would favour approaches to learning which give pupils a degree of control over curriculum content and where the learning of one individual does not depend on the attention of all to the teachers demands. The project-based humanities curriculum of Bosworth School (Phillips and Jones 1986) involves teachers in very different ways from the science class teaching described by Robert Hull (1985). A particular example of the way an approach to learning can alter the nature of disruption is illustrated in an account by Richard Martin and Jennifer Smith (1979) of the 'mini-schools' formed by teacher teams at their school:

> John arrived with a reputation for being somewhat disruptive. In his past, he had been described as lazy and of very limited ability. He had a reading age of about seven years and some quite severe learning problems, and I viewed his joining my group with some trepidation,, and I confess, with little enthusiasm. At our intitial meeting, before he joined the school, he seemed taciturn and nervous, unlike the group of friends who accompanied him, who seemed relaxed and enthusiastic about the prospect of coming to a new school. I determined over the holiday that I would try to engage him from the beginning as far as possible in activities that would not require much reading or writing, at least for a while.
>
> Our starting point was photography. John talked to me a little about the farm in the village where he lives, some three miles from the school, and about the amount of spare time he spent on the farm. I suggested he take a camera home with him one night in order to record anything he cared to of the farm and his work there. He did not return the next day. I was, not surprisingly, annoyed both with him, for taking advantage of me, as I saw it, and with myself for having encouraged, even authorised apparently, a day off, with camera, and all within the first few days of the school year. On the following day he returned, with the camera mercifully, and a roll of used film. He had, he explained, waited all day for a calf that was due to be born, and which had not made its appearance until the evening. We developed the negatives together, and then I printed them, explaining to John very sketchily the process involved. The photographs were a considerable success, both in terms of their quality – though the calf was a little murky in the twilight – and of the record they provided him with of an event he recalled time and again for himself and his friends.
>
> From these photographs sprang, in the first place, a tape recording which I transcribed for him, describing each picture in some detail, and, later, a series of drawings and paintings produced over a period of weeks, of a tractor. These tractor paintings, based on his own photograph, involved painstaking effort, for John wished for a precise and meticulous representation. There were many versions:

some were abandoned early on, others would be near completion when with a shout of frustration they would end up in the bin, John would assert that they were not up to his standard – and indeed, one could see why when he at last completed a painting to his satisfaction.

(Martin and Smith 1979, pp. 127–8)

John's curriculum was constructed as a 'conversation' between himself and his teacher and became both broad and memorable. Few secondary teachers are in a position to intitiate such a learning style and perhaps few would approve of it. Nevertheless, the point is that there can be no single prescription for 'the managed classroom'. The separation of teaching skills from learning skills has considerable dangers too. As one teacher remarked: 'With a very inexperienced teacher control is to do with the structure and content of the lesson – as you become more experienced you can get away with a badly structured lesson'.

There appears to be an increasing use of managerial metaphors in education with suggestions that the 'good' school is one in which staff develop a consistent corporate identity (see, for example, Rutter *et al* 1979). While a condition of teaching might involve adherence to a core code of ethics, the expectation of an artificial staff conformity may encourage neither honesty nor tolerance in pupils. One pupil was reported to dismiss a teacher as an object of respect simply on the basis of the clothes she wore, telling the head of year, 'well how do you expect me to have respect for a woman who dresses like that?'

WHICH PATH SHOULD YOU FOLLOW?

The appropriate response to any 'problem' within education has to be part of an educational philosophy. We do not argue that education can only be founded on one educational philosophy but do argue that different educational philosophies limit the solution to problems in different ways. Thus Lawrence, Steed and Young (1984, pp. 165–6), attribute the problems in Matchinfold, a 'difficult' school to three main areas; its size, mixed-ability teaching in the lower school and the fact that lesson periods are too long. We would argue that an approach which values pupils equally leads one towards mixed-ability work and one which gives them control over their learning and builds on relationships between pupils and teachers would lead to longer teacher periods and fewer changes. These authors ask 'how, for instance, can children who barely read or write competently be expected to study French, especially if they are in the company of children with excellent communication skills?'

Such rhetorical questions are not meant to be answered but language teachers do use group work and oral methods in mixed-ability groups (see, for example, Steward Reid 1986). In looking at any area of school life we either make assumptions about or pronouncements on the organisation and content of curricula. One may wish to link the control of disruptive pupils to hierarchical forms of grouping but that is not because other strategies are impossible. Further, any system which is based on assigning differences in value to different groups of pupils retains pools of disaffection which can be prevented from spilling over into disruption only by effective forms of coercion. It is an irony that coercive approaches to reducing disruption are sometimes viewed as 'educational' whilst curricular adaptations to avoid disaffection may be seen to involve a 'political' intervention in school

The structure and contents of the book

The book has gone through a number of transformations as it has been developed and its structure is determined both by a wish to follow through a series of arguments and by the needs of our students on a diploma course. We also wanted to avoid overlap with material in our earlier course (e.g. Booth 1982). It might be seen as a mini-series of books in itself. At the outset we produced a detailed plan which attempted to be comprehensive. We set out the issues we hoped would be covered in each chapter and then negotiated with a number of authors whose area of interest these appeared to reflect. As the book developed a number of chapters fell by the wayside and others, some previously published, have been introduced. Of course the idea of comprehensive coverage was an illusion and the book is large as it is, but there is less coherence than we had anticipated.

It is divided into four sections. Section 1, *The experience of schooling*, sets out to establish the concerns of this book with the realities of school and classroom life and the issues of control and discipline which arise. It contains classroom observations, a case study of a disruptive incident, and the views of pupils and teachers.

Section 2, *Responding to trouble*, is concerned with a response to disaffection and disruption through a focus on disruption. It looks at the way pupils may be moved out of schools through suspension procedures, at the variety of special provision and the particular forms it may take. It looks at attempts to reverse the dominance of the model of identification and exclusion of deviant pupils through the reorganization of support services, resources and in-service training and by developing alternative reactions to trouble in school (see also Coulby and Harper 1985).

The descriptions of the system as well as suggestions for intervention within Section 2 are both concerned with defining and redefining trouble. Section 3, *Producing and reducing disaffection*, contains a series of chapters which set out an alternative paradigm. They are concerned with the identification and reduction of the actual and potential pools of disaffection in school. We have brought together chapters which illustrate the process of devaluation of some pupils because of their sex or skin colour or class or family background and which offer suggestions for combatting such tendencies.

Section 4, *Systems of control*, has suffered more than the others from our failure to find time to do everything we intended to do. It is concerned with the systems of controls which operate inside and outside schools; with pastoral care systems, the control of education by central government, organized challenges to school power, the controls on normality through definitions of sexuality and with an alternative approach to control based on shared rights. In addition to the present chapters we had intended to look at teaching as a profession and stratification by ability as well as ideas of management in school, including 'classroom management'. Perhaps it is good to be aware that there are other jobs to be done and, of course, that there are other people to do them.

Section 1: The experience of schooling

For *Chapter 1*, Tony Booth and Di Hesketh have edited a discussion between seven teachers about their experiences with pupils, the difficulties they face and their fears of losing control of the class or of themselves. They express themselves openly, as any group of teachers might, when they are off-duty. They come from secondary, primary, special schools and a special unit in the mainstream. Despite this diversity, they readily respond to each others' concerns as their own. *Chapter 2* is about the origins of control and hence opportunities for deviance in school. In it John Schostak reports his observations of an infant class during their first days at school. This process of changing children into pupils echoes the observations of Tuckwell (1982) or King (1979). It makes apparent the strangeness of the social situation of the classroom and the foundations that may be laid here for future attitudes and reactions to school. *Chapter 3* is an account by Tony Booth of the Poundswick dispute about 'offensive graffitti' which, he argues, places the needs of teachers firmly into the equation for resolving problems of disruption and disaffection. He uses the case as a starting point for reflections on suspension procedures and policies to reverse the increasing exclusion of pupils into disruptive units.

In *Chapter 4*, Tony Booth and Di Hesketh present a single lesson from a day in a residential school for pupils categorised as having moderate learning or emotional and behavioural difficulties. They argue that the transcript provides a rich source of ideas for understanding the aims of this form of schooling as well as aspects of control in the explicit messages in this lesson on social behaviour. In *Chapter 5* Di Hesketh offers a number of pupils the opportunity to comment on control and discipline in their schools. The section ends with *Chapter 6*, an account by Mike Vernon of the pressures which forced him out of teaching. It is a salutary reminder of the difficulties teachers face in being bombarded with change.

Section 2: Responding to trouble

Chapter 7 is an overview by Mel Lloyd-Smith of forms of provision for pupils excluded from the mainstream because of their 'deviant' behaviour. He documents the growth of such provision and argues that this is not to be explained in terms of a growing incidence of problems. *Chapter 8* is an examination by Rod Ling of the way pupils who find their way into disruptive units are treated in suspension procedures in one LEA, 'Wallington'. He suggests that the operation of these procedures becomes part of the process by which the pupils concerned are progressively alienated from school. *Chapter 9*, also by Rod Ling, is a case study of two disruptive units. Here he analyses the ethos of each school and the focus which each places on the control of the misbehaviour of the pupils, on their re-education to the exclusion of any effort at understanding the precipitating conditions in their schools.

Chapter 10 was written and collated by Stewart Butterfield and concerns the school at which he is headteacher. It is an unusual glimpse into the life of a day school for 'maladjusted' pupils which takes the form of a brief introduction followed by the diaries for one day of the school secretary, school social worker, head of primary department, supply class teacher (juniors) and welfare assistant (infants). From these diaries one builds up a picture of the daily concerns and events in the life of such a school. *Chapter 11*, by Dennis Mongon, examines the dominant view of troublesome behaviour in school which he terms the displacement model, which leads to movement of pupils from the mainstream into the units and schools of the previous chapters. He recognizes the attractiveness of such a model but suggests that it is ultimately self-defeating, generating an ever increasing concentration on troublesome pupils. He offers a number of suggestions for replacing it with a series of initiatives aimed at supporting schools in the development of alternative strategies. The remaining two chapters offer examples of such attempts. *Chapter 12* is a report by Neil Toppin of the School Assessment Panels introduced, in the school at which he is the head, to provide a forum where the school can consider a flexible response to pupils as an alternative to suspension. It is also there to consider how St Augustine's can provide an education for pupils returning from special provision. *Chapter 13* is an introduction to the materials developed by Rob Grunsell to enable teachers within schools to explore joint solutions to problems of disaffection and control.

Section 3: Producing and reducing disaffection

In *Chapter 14*, by Cecile Wright, the experience of black young people, particularly those of Afro-Caribbean descent, is recorded from two secondary schools. The evidence of teachers and pupils conveys a picture of racism from some teachers and a feeling of resentment in many black pupils. *Chapter 15* is the story of the research John Schostak undertook into a community, 'Slumptown', and its school. In it he describes the way he built up a picture of life within the school and the community. It is an area of economic depression and one where racism is commonly experienced. In such circumstances, he argues, the school should question the way they prepare students for life. *Chapter 16* by Lynn Davies is a look at sexism in the curriculum and its interaction with deviance in school. She looks at curriculum materials and methods of approach. She examines the way deviance in male and female pupils is predicated on a different view of conforming behaviour. Finally she assesses the extent to which teachers can challenge the stereotyped approaches in their schools. *Chapter 17* is a study by Sheila Cunnison of a single school which fleshes out the observations of the previous chapter. It portrays the way women and girls are reflected in the curriculum and organization of that school and the styles of discipline based on male power.

Chapter 18 by David Coulby is an analysis of the way schools can fail to reflect the interests of working-class pupils. He argues that the reason that the bulk of pupils identified as disruptive or disaffected are working-class is not to be found in their defective culture or child rearing but in their systematic devaluation within the curriculum. In *Chapter 19* David Coulby extends the arguments for curriculum change at the end of the previous chapter by giving two examples of schools which have attempted to prevent disaffection by developing inclusive curricula. *Chapter 20* is an analysis of racism within the curriculum by Europe Singh. He provides us with suggestions for alternative curricula which are anti-racist and socially relevant. In *Chapter 21* Jan Reid examines the reality behind the phrase 'a problem in the family'. Many people pay lip-service to the poverty which underlies family stress and occurs in the background of many pupils said to be causing problems in school. Here Jan Reid provides a detailed examination of the effects of material circumstances on family life, child-rearing and relationships with welfare services.

Section 4: Systems of control

The first three chapters of this section are all concerned with pastoral care which in most secondary schools is the name for the hierarchy of disciplinarians. In *Chapter 22* John Schostak records, literally, a day in the life of a housemaster, consciously aware of the contradictions by which he operates; between disciplining and supporting pupils, between being a teacher and a counsellor, between 'forcing' kids through the system and revealing what is hidden 'once you start lifting up stones'. *Chapter 23* asks a further question of pastoral care, 'who's inside the wooden horse?'. John Quicke describes the hopes of people who went into pastoral care work as a way of humanising the approach to education in secondary schools and how these efforts have been apparently transformed by others. In many schools, he argues, pastoral care now spearheads the introduction of the 'new vocationalism' and its associated behaviourist methods in schools. *Chapter 24* by Jan Sargeant throws a different light on John Quicke's question. She argues that in the past pastoral care offered a niche for women teachers but its increasing professionalisation has been used as a way to provide further career prospects for men. Far from helping to break down subject specialisms the 'skills' of pastoral work have been mystified and adorned with acronyms so that a new specialism has been created.

Chapter 25 is about an aspect of school life rarely considered in the context of disaffection. Here Shirley Prendergast and Alan Prout look at the messages transmitted in schools about 'normal' sexuality and at the way the views of sexuality in school discriminate against girls. They suggest that the controls on sexuality and the possibilities for incorporating it into power relations offer a focus for disruption in school. *Chapter 26*, by Len Barton, moves outside the school to look at some of the current pressures on teachers and schools, particularly those associated with increasingly centralized curriculum control. *Chapter 27* is an extract from Stephen Humphries, (1981) oral history *Hooligans or Rebels?* It is about school strikes and offers a powerful reminder that the power within schools can be shifted, dramatically, in the direction of pupils when they act in concert. School strikes do still occur, of course, and they were a particular feature of the teachers dispute in 1985 in some areas. (e.g. as reported for Nottingham in the *Guardian* October 3rd 1985). *Chapter 28*, which ends this volume, is an argument from Peter Newell for relationships within school to be founded on the rights of all participants. It is control based on the sharing of a common morality rather than obedience to authority which is one of the central messages of this book.

Note

I would like to acknowledge the help of those teachers whose interviews provided the illustrative material for this chapter.

References

All London Teachers Against Racism and Facism, (1984) *Challenging racism*, London, A.L.T.A.R.F.

Booth, T. 1982. Handicap is Social, unit 13 of E241 *Special Needs in Education*, Milton Keynes, Open University Educational Enterprises.

Booth, T., Potts, P. and Swann, W. (eds.), 1986. *Curricula for All: Preventing Difficulties in Learning*, Oxford, Blackwells.

Carr, J. L. 1982. *The Harpole Report*, Harmondsworth, Penguin.

Coulby, D. and Harper, T. 1985. *Preventing Classroom Disruption: Policy, Practice and Evaluation in Urban Schools*, London, Croom Helm.

Davidson, H. 1985. *Teachers in Secondary Education: A Study of Equal Opportunity in the Secondary Schools of Clwyd*, paper presented to Conference on Girl Friendly Schooling, Manchester.

Davies, L. 1984. *Pupil Power, Deviance and Gender in School*, London, The Falmer Press.

Department of Education and Science 1982. *Statistics on Schools*, London, HMSO.

Eggleston, J., Dunn, D., Anjali, M. and Wright, C. 1985. *The Educational and Vocational Experiences of 15- to 18-Year-Old Members of Minority Ethnic Groups*, Stoke-on-Trent, Trentham Books.

El Saadawi, N. 1975. *Women at Point Zero*, London, Zed Books.

Ford, J., Mongon, M., and Whelan, M. 1982. *Special Education and Social Control: Invisible Disasters*, London, Routledge & Kegan Paul.

Galloway, D. 1982. 'A study of pupils suspended from school', *British Journal of Educational Psychology* 52, 205–212.

Gardiner, M. 1985. *The Deadly Innocents: Portraits of Children Who Kill*, New Haven, Yale University Press.

Hey, V. 1985. 'Innocence and Experience: the politics of gender and sexual harassment' in Language and Gender Working Party, *Alice in Genderland* National Association of Teachers of English.

Hull, R. 1985. *The Language Gap*, London, Methuen.

Humphries, S. 1981. *Hooligans or Rebels? An Oral History of Working Class Childhood and Youth 1889–1939*, Oxford, Blackwells.

Jones, C. 1985. 'Sexual tyranny: male violence in a mixed secondary school', in Weiner, G. (ed.) *Just a Bunch of Girls*, Milton Keynes, Open University Press.

King, R. 1979. *All Things Bright and Beautiful: a Sociological Study of Infant Classrooms*, Chichester, John Wiley and Sons.

Lawrence, J., Steed, D. and Young, P. 1984. *Disruptive Children – Disruptive Schools?*, London, Croom Helm.

Mohoney, P. 1985. *Schools for the Boys: Co-education Reassessed*, London, Hutchinson.

Martin, R. and Smith, J. 1979. 'A case for conversation: teams at Countesthorpe', in Haigh, G. (ed.), *On Our Side: Order, Authority and Interaction in School*, London, Temple-Smith.

Ministry of Education 1921. *Report of the Departmental Committee on Teaching in Schools* (Newbolt Report), London, HMSO.

Newman, J. 1979. 'Care and authority in the secondary school', in Haigh, G. (ed.), *On Our Side: Order, Authority and Interaction in School*, London, Temple-Smith.

Phillips, R. and Jones, S. 1986. 'Integrated design and humanities at Bosworth College', in Booth, T., Potts, P. and Swann, W. (eds), *Curricula for All: Preventing Difficulties in Learning*, Oxford, Blackwells.

Reid, S. 1986. 'French for all', in Booth, T., Potts, P. and Swann, W. (eds), *Curricula for All: Preventing Difficulties in Learning*, Oxford, Blackwells.

Rendell, R. 1969. *The Best Man to Die*, London, Arrow.

Russell, B. 1930. *The Conquest of Happiness*, London, George Allen and Unwim.

Rutter, M., Maughan, B., Mortimore, D. and Ouston, J. 1979. *Fifteen Thousand Hours: Secondary Schools and Their Effects on Children*, London, Open Books.

Savery, J. 1985. 'Anti-Racism as Witchcraft', *Salisbury Review*, 3(4), 41–42.

Schostak, J. 1983. *Maladjusted Schooling: Deviance, Social Control and Individuality in Secondary Schooling*, London, The Falmer Press.

Troyna, B. and Williams, J. 1986. *Racism, Education and the State*, London, Croom Helm.

Tuckwell, P. 1982. 'Pleasing teacher', in Booth, T. and Statham, J. (eds.), *The Nature of Special Education*, London, Croom Helm.

Warnock, M. 1985. 'Teacher teach myself', *The Listener*, 28 March 1985, 9–13.

SECTION I

The experience of schooling

1   Losing and keeping control: a teacher discussion

Edited by
Tony Booth and Di Hesketh

This chapter contains the edited discussion of a small group of teachers who came together for an evening to talk about disaffection and control in schools. The idea was to reproduce some of the nagging concerns of every staffroom. In a group like this, meeting in a relaxed way after school, it is not possible to reproduce the intense irritation, frustration or hurt which a breakdown in relationships can engender. But this discussion may serve as a reminder of these feelings and their part in the common experience of all teachers.

The teachers involved came from a variety of schools. Helen taught in an assessment unit in a special school. Margaret has taught in a junior school and a special school and currently works with pupils who have physical disabilities within a mainstream comprehensive. Claire spent seven years teaching in secondary schools, has worked with pupils with severe learning difficulties and now teaches children with moderate learning difficulties. Martin teaches history in a secondary school. Mary teaches in a junior school and is responsible for children with special needs. Sarah teaches in an area special education class based in a mainstream school. Simon has taught in a comprehensive school.

'There is that moment when you want to wring their necks!'

Mary: I taught a boy Richard last year who I really felt, I never got anywhere with at all. He really didn't seem to be interested in anything despite all my efforts. Even when he settled for an odd moment and you were so ill-advised as to praise him he would look at you and say 'I hate you' and rip up his work and throw it in the bin. He couldn't even take praise. He just wanted to do nothing at all except aggravate other children. He didn't want any attention from me one way or another. I found it very difficult. I just felt a failure with him . . . I just felt I hadn't got anywhere with him . . . I hadn't communicated. My only moment of gratification with him was when he said to me one day '*I hate you*' – and then added 'but I don't hate you as much as I hate Mr Reynolds.' He didn't make a relationship with any of the staff. In the end Mr Reynolds who was a very forceful character managed to keep him in check but he said he never got him to learn anything. He felt a failure too, he didn't want that solution but was reduced to it in the end.

Martin: In a Secondary School you see any one troublesome person much less, unless you are on the pastoral side when you're likely to be sent certain pupils regularly. There are frequently cases when I find a certain child exasperating and I am very glad to say goodbye to that child until next Tuesday afternoon or whenever it will be . . . Sometimes children's behaviour is so out of the ordinary that it is like something you have read about in textbooks but never actually experienced, even with your own family problems etc. They have serious problems, they just don't respond to all the manoeuvres you have learnt . . . There is that moment when you want to wring their neck! Then you remember that you shouldn't wring their neck, so you try to be persuasive and kindly and yielding and firm and a whole battery of other things. But you get a wall-like face or a face full of anger and you are absolutely baffled. You realize that instead of you, just an ordinary classroom teacher, who has their work cut out just to teach anybody anything, the child needs that plus a social worker, and a little bit of a saint thrown in. That sort of person might well cope but most teachers actually can't...

This evening we had a meeting to discuss the possibility of a pupil being sent to another school. She comes from their catchment area but they won't take her. We've been discussing tactics to try to get her pushed over there. She wrecks class after class and when you try to stop her you realize you are talking to someone who isn't on the same wavelength at all... She doesn't work but you feel if she just snoozed quietly in a corner that wouldn't be too bad. She shouts, she jumps up, she has a certain charm and has quite a following and so she feeds off this.

Mary: That wasn't the case with Richard. The other pupils disliked him too. It's much worse when they seem to gang up in support.

Martin: She gets an adrenalin flow when she sees everyone grinning, she just can't turn off. I've had others who wreck lessons. Usually you can negotiate with children individually but she is beyond my powers of persuasion. Judging from our meeting it seems I am not the only one.

Helen: When I was working in a school for children with physical handicaps I got to the point when I simply didn't know what to do. I had to put a child out of my reach. We were eating our dinner and this child was continually spitting his dinner in my face. It got to the sixth or seventh time and I really started to lose my temper. He wasn't safe to be left, so I took him out of his wheelchair, layed him on the floor and told another teacher I was going. I went into the staffroom for ten minutes to cool off. It was a horrible feeling.

Margaret: But sometimes we really hang on for too long. There was one kid with whom I hung on and in the end after I finally blew up we started to have a fantastic relationship. But I'm not saying it is the right thing for all kids. I'm talking about when you *really* go out of control like I've done with my own kids. You don't want to but occasionally it does happen. Perhaps the hanging on to being so calm and so nice and so everything... sometimes *is the problem*.

It all comes back to relationships ...

Simon: Coming back into a teaching situation the other day reminded me very forcibly of the mental contortions you go through as a teacher. I was helping in my daughter's school with a cookery group. They sent me two girls and two boys who I knew from Rosy were the 'naughtiest' in the class. One of them she told me had 'tried to strangle her twice.' Well, the other one spent the entire time sticking his fingers in the ingredients and licking them including the flour and the egg white. After a while I felt like doing him grievous bodily harm. It reminded me how as a teacher one couldn't allow oneself the luxury of anything like one's normal reaction to irritation... as it turned out he opted to stay and chat to me at break and then afterwards he was quite amenable... but I did go through a tricky few minutes.

Margaret: Yes that's one of the most difficult things in teaching, trying to control someone with whom you have no relationship.

Simon: Yes and perhaps even more difficult is having to have a relationship with someone because you know it's your job to get through to them and teach them and have them under control when they're the last person you want a relationship with.

Claire: Yes, it is all down to forming relationships. In my last job I was there for four years. I had the first years all the way through and by the fifth year they were wonderful. I could do anything with them. But starting with a group of fourteen-year-olds at this new place has been hell. Because the kids are trying to test all the time and they get you to that screaming point just to see what your reactions will be. The Wednesday afternoon you came in I'd just reached that point and I'd screamed for the first time at the kids, I'd absolutely lost my cool completely. I was within inches of knocking this kid out of his chair because he'd deliberately sat all lesson and moved his chair backwards and forwards across the floor as I was trying to tell them... get them into groups and I said don't do that Bob there's a good boy and he just grinned at me and then stopped that but started banging continuously [Claire bangs her chair rhythmically] just tapping on the table non-stop as I was trying to talk and then I just blew up and then your lot arrived so it was very quiet and quite calm when you arrived but they were all just totally dumbstruck, that was why. The next day he was exactly the same, the testing goes on and it will go on maybe until I've had them for six or seven months. They'll continue to test because they don't know me, my limits.

Simon: Were you under control when you blew up?

Claire: I wasn't that time, I'd really lost control. Maybe two or three or four years ago I would have lashed out... I can remember picking a kid up by the scruff and pinning her against a wall and absolutely going beserk. So I suppose I was in control but it didn't feel like it... your character is so completely different in the classroom, you're not yourself at all.

Margaret: That's what I'm worried about in a secondary set up. In a physically handicapped school you're relaxed – they're not testing you, they want to learn.

Claire: It was the same teaching pupils with severe learning difficulties.

Margaret: I'm afraid of all that again... It harks on back to my first teaching experience. I was a secretary at the time and I knew I wanted a change and thought my options were teaching or nursing. I became an assistant teacher, completely unqualified in a class in South London. The teacher never turned up again and I had his class. It was in a school where no one seemed able to control their classes. There was no way I could control this class unless I won them. You couldn't read them a story – as soon as your eyes were down you lost them. I used to tell them Grimm's fairy tales and I used to grip them with those but as soon as I said 'Now it's time for something else' they'd be climbing up the walls. I have this fear, and it will never go away I don't think – every time a kid says something in a class that's going to potentially threaten my control. I feel like I felt then, that I'm going to lose them. I know I can do it at one level but there's that fear at the bottom of it all.

Claire: It's almost like being a probationer every time you start. You lose everything. Every time you start a new job you start again. It all comes back to relationships you can't expect a child to trust you or accept you if there's no relationship.

'They seem to react to whatever your power position is ...'

Sarah: But I don't know if it's always alright when they do know you. I take small groups of children out from a special unit attached to a primary school and in the small group they're OK. I do have quite a good relationship with them. But on a few occasions the person in charge of the unit has had to go out and when I've had the whole class, it was totally out of control. That's the first time it's ever happened to me, I've never known it like that. Whatever I said they just laughed. They said they would walk out of the room. If I raised my voice they raised their voices. I had just lost it completely. I don't know if it's because they know I'm not the class teacher. They seem to react to whatever your power position is. If the

Head comes in there's total silence. They know, they daren't...there's not a murmur if the Head's in. He doesn't have to say anything. If the class teacher is in they're quite an ordinary group. But if I'm in it's a riot situation. I'm the second member of staff in a special unit. It's supposed to be team teaching but really she wants to teach on her own. Whether the children can see that I don't know. All the children were already there. The last person who was there left because she had had enough. At first I thought I'll never stick this out, it was totally different to what I'd expected or known before. These children just amazed me. There were sixteen children that I had no control with whatsoever. They were only junior children. In a small group I think they like me, they learn but in the class situation they're very different.

Claire: Kids become so aware of differences in status. For example teachers treat welfare assistants differently. They give them menial tasks or exercises to do with kids that they wouldn't do themselves. I heard a welfare assistant talking to a kid in the hall the other day: 'Please don't swing on the ropes, you'll hurt yourself.' He said, 'You can't tell me what to do you're only a welfare assistant.' So it comes to a respect for power rather than a respect for you as a person...and we reinforce it by saying 'If you don't behave I'll send you to the Head or Deputy Head or Head of Year.'

Margaret: You couldn't say 'Behave or I'll send you to the welfare assistant!' That's the way things are.

'I hope they never say that about me ...'

Mary: We have reached the point in our school where we can admit to another member of staff including classroom assistants when we need a break from a particular pupil. You need to be able to say you have had enough just to diffuse the situation. Some days you're simply on a shorter fuse than others.

Margaret: But it can be so threatening. Of all the things people look at to see whether you're a good teacher or not, the first is always: can you keep control?

Claire: Teachers discuss kids in the staffroom but they also talk about each other: 'Oh she's bloody awful she shouldn't be in teaching.' You hear it being said all the time. You think to yourself I hope they never say that about me. I hope I'm not discussed when I walk out of the door. People are constantly aware of having to be seen to be the all-powerful being when they are in the classroom.

Most secondary schools you are left struggling away on your own. You can send them to the Head but it doesn't usually do you much good. The kids just see you as an idiot: 'Oh she's sent him to Mr so-and-so...' In the school for children with severe learning difficulties there simply wasn't that pressure – there were behaviour problems but no problem of *en-masse* control like you get in secondary schools or primary schools or the school I'm in now. There was a different attitude towards adults from the kind of pupil we had. Their difficult behaviour was something you understood. You didn't get uptight about it.

Mary: And with a better teacher pupil ratio you wouldn't be afraid all the time that one pupil would spark off another.

Claire: That's right, we did have seven kids with three staff. So if a kid decided to throw a wobbly or smear the walls he or she was quietly removed and calmed down and coped with. You can't do that with a class of thirty kids in a secondary school.

Margaret: And also it wasn't seen as a reflection of you.

2   As you mean to go on: first days at school
John Schostak

Issues of control in schools are most salient during the latter years of secondary school when a peak of disruptive incidents and suspensions are recorded. But as John Schostak shows in this chapter the subtle process of transforming a child into a pupil starts from the first day at school. Teachers may have an image of the normal pupil into which a child must fit and they provide a framework of controls to keep their classrooms running smoothly. The deviance of pupils becomes apparent if they violate either of these interconnected sets of norms.

The first day

A dozen children arrive early in the afternoon (the older pupils are still at play), their first experience of school. They are met by the teacher smiling, soft spoken and a welfare assistant in the cloakrooms where they are helped off with their coats. A child edges towards the classroom:

> WA (Welfare Assistant): 'And what's your name? (A whispered reply. Then to another) And what's your name? (Again a whispered reply. Then to another) And what's your name?'
> P: 'Victoria.'
> WA: 'Victoria. Ooh, going to come in and see us?'

With each child entering there is a friendly, 'And what's your name?' One girl says she's got two brothers. The adults appear grateful for any such opening of conversation. The children wander slowly and tentatively through the classroom, past all the polished tables towards the matted area which is divided into a quiet area and a play area. Toys have been left out for them. Overall, what is to be communicated? 'We do this the first day' said the teacher to me, 'It gets them into the place and feeling comfortable and safe very quickly. But then we've got to get them used to the routine and settled in.'

Soon three boys are playing in the toy area and three girls, in the quiet area, are playing with large chunky jigsaws. A boy and a girl holding hands stand shyly, another girl near them. 'You can walk over, I don't mind.' They walk over the mat to the wall benches and sit quietly. The teacher walks from small group to small group encouraging those who are not doing anything to do something and helping those she thinks are having difficulty. The children already know how to address these adults, if somewhat formally 'Teacher, the picture is missing' indicating a missing piece in a jigsaw picture.

Noise from the cloakroom indicates the rest of the class is arriving (composed of children who have already been at school two terms). The new children are asked to put away the toys:

> T: 'Come on then and sit down very, very quietly. Now, here are some more children who are going to be with our class.'

7

Gradually the children are organized until they are all seated as a collection, facing the teacher, beneath her eye-level, most on the floor, the rest on the wall benches. The register is to be called. The headteacher has entered. 'I'm going to listen to learn the new names as well.' The names are called one by one starting with the old boys, the ones who have already had two terms' experience. Then it is the turn of the new boys:

> *T:* 'Now Brian, Brian (looking around and almost whispering). There he is, do you know what you have to say?'

Brian, like all the other new children, has to learn the formula: 'Yes Mrs Andrews.' Brian whispers a reply. Each new boy who gets the right formula is praised with a 'good boy,' a gentle and kindly *training of response*, one example of a gentle but persistent moulding of behaviour towards 'pupil-dom.' When, at last, all the children have been registered, it is found that several have the same Christian names thus:

> *T:* 'Now, you've really got to think hard because, you know, there are two Julias, and two Roberts and four Hannahs.'

Just another Julia, no longer a centre of family attention but another confusing identity, an object of initial curiosity:

> *g:* 'Which is Hannah?'
> *b:* 'That's the Hannah.'
> *g:* 'Where's the other one?'

The teacher is the centre and her authority is always apparent: she leads, organizes, commands. She creates and holds together the class through the kinds of communication she generates and encourages.

> *T:* 'Now I hope everybody is going to listen because there are some different things to do today (. . .) Elaine, sit down please (. . .) Now all those children who've been in school and it isn't their first afternoon this afternoon, have got to listen and . . .' (she pauses expectantly)
> *Pupils with teacher:* 'Think.'
> *T:* 'The tables are set with quite a few little things. On one table there's this shape. Can anybody put their hand up and tell me what this shape is?'
> *Tony* (a new boy): 'Miss.'
> *T:* 'Thank you Tony but Harry had his hand up so let's hear from Harry what it's going to be . . .'
> *Harry* (an 'old' boy): (very quietly) 'A castle.'
> *T:* 'A castle, that's right. They're on the table where you can go. And on the castle. . . This is the shape of the castle but it hasn't got any . . .' (waits expectantly)
> *Pupils:* 'Windows.'
> *T:* 'And it hasn't got a . . .' (waits expectantly)
> *Pupils:* 'Door'

Gradually the children have been sculpted skilfully into an audience. The expert 'old' pupils respond on cue, leading the responses of the 'new' pupils. The key classroom control words 'listen' and 'think' have made their appearance.

At a table where four children are already painting, one boy says to a girl 'we're old at school now, we're used to school now, aren't we?' They too have found a special social standing in relation to the newcomers. The teacher calls on them to show a new child where the toilet is. The new children have to be continually reminded of their responsibilities, and the expectations laid upon them:

> *T:* 'Right now, I'll tell you what we have to do when we do a painting. We have to put an apron on. (...) Mummy would say "Paint on your jumper and on your very first day at school. What was your teacher thinking about?"'

The teacher is continually watchful: looking for moments when she can praise and say 'Oh, that's super' and for those moments when she has to say 'Barry' in that voice which means 'now don't be silly'.

> *T:* 'Lennie, have you made a castle?'
> *Lennie:* 'No.'
> *T:* 'Come on, you must have one Lennie. (...) Billy um, Benny I'd like you to do in five minutes time a castle. You haven't done one have you?' (...)
> *Andrew:* 'I don't want to do one today.'
> *T:* 'Ooh, don't you? Well, what would you think if I said "I don't want to do it today?" We wouldn't get anywhere would we? No. Two more minutes then you make one for me.'
> *Andrew:* 'I don't want to do one. I don't want to do one.'
> *T:* 'Well, if you don't want to do one today it'll have to be done tomorrow. And you won't have a chance to play tomorrow will you? It's best if you do it today and then you've got more chance to play tomorrow.'
> *Andrew:* 'I don't want to do it today.'
> *T:* 'Well, I'd like you to very much.'
> *Andrew:* 'I don't want to.'

The teacher takes on the attributes of censor, judge and motivator. She must find strategies to inhibit some behaviours, advocate others and gradually bring about the behaviours she desires. The problem was returned to at intervals throughout the following half hour. Eventually the teacher decided to give up – there was simply too much to do this first day, and Andrew (an 'old' pupil) was a problem at the best of times. Andrew was expressing his wants, these wants were interpreted as indicating that he was 'an old lazy bones today'.

The teacher, when passing by me, said 'softly, softly, I think today. I've got enough to do...' And at the end of the day she commented: 'It's amazing how nice you can be first day and gradually you sort of (laughs) you sort of lick them into shape.'

Licking children into shape is a gradual process involving being attentive to minutiae as well as the occasional crisis. The teacher was continually conscious of creating a climate of praise (good boy/girl, that is beautiful/good/super) on the one hand as a means of reinforcement and on the other correcting behaviours which fell short of expectation:

> *girl:* 'Can I paint now?'
> *T:* 'Pardon?'
> *girl:* 'Can I paint please?'
> *T:* That's better. I like that magic word.'

All such as these can be called micro-manipulations – they are over in a few seconds; some, like raised eyebrows, can be over in parts of a second. The above micro-manipulation is directed towards an individual. Others are directed towards classes:

> *T:* (claps) 'All children over here please on the carpet area... Benny, Sylvia, *Jane*, come on you heard, didn't you? First time please. Show me your hands (pupils are to stop what they are doing and raise their hands palms towards the teacher)... It means it's time to clear away... So now I want you to put away the toys. (...) Jim, Sam and Billy, it would be nice if I saw you helping to clear away over here instead of just lolling about looking as if you were on holiday (pupils laugh). Wouldn't it? Yes, come on.'

Through gaining control of the children's movements (show me your hands) she reinforces her command; extra attention is given to the three who are lolling about, they are made aware of the distinction between holiday (where you can do as you please) and work. A similar strategy of controlling physical behaviour is in evidence during the story period later. First they all sat in a certain area (the mat) and then, if any are not giving enough attention:

> *T:* 'Once upon a time there were two rows of happy little teeth. Billy – when I tell a story people sit very still and very quiet and they listen. They don't go la-la-la-la when somebody's talking. They use their eyes for watching me.'
> *pupil:* 'La-la-la-la-la'
> *T:* 'And I don't mind sitting here 'til it's time to go home.'

There is no room for a child to say 'I don't want to do this. I don't want to listen to you. I don't want to look at you. Goodbye.' Moreover, the teacher cannot say, 'well do as you wish'; she cannot respond to the boredom, irritation or initiatives of so many without her class disbanding.

With individual relations one could be more responsive and provide more attention but 'Thank goodness for the one or two bright ones one can trust to get on while you are looking after the others.' By dividing the class, mentally, into those who can be trusted to 'get on' and those who cannot, actual class management problems are reduced. When problems arise they can be treated individually if the remainder of the class are 'getting on.' In the crowded classroom, however, 'getting on' frequently becomes problematic.

Two new boys were seen to be involved in trouble. One boy had thumped another because 'he banged my rocket':

> *T:* 'He banged your rocket, yes, but we don't do that to people do we? Mmm? Tell you when you can do that. You can do that when you see me going like that. Do you see me do it? No. So that means I don't really want to see you doing it.'

A little later she approached the other boy:

> *T:* 'Why did Tony get cross, mm? Did you bang his space ship?
> *Tony:* 'No it was' (inaudible).
> *T:* 'Yes, but if you go too near people and bang on their desks they don't like it. You have to learn at school that to just keep away from people when people have a model. And they're not going to get cross with you and you'll not get cross with them. All right?... Have you got a brother at home?'
> *Tony:* 'Yeah, Joey and Mary, she bigger than me.'
> *T:* 'Is she? And what does she do to you if you go too near the things she's making? Does she get cross?'

Tony: 'She don't get cross.'

T: Well, she's very kind to you then isn't she?'

Tony: 'No.'

T: 'No.'

Tony: 'She just kick me.'

T: 'Oh well, you see you don't want people kicking you at school do you? So, you just keep away when people are making models and you make your own. We don't want any, any people getting cross, all right? And sad 'cos their models get broken. All right, can you remember that one for me?'

In the crowded classroom such conflicts occur fairly regularly but are typically soon over, even passing unnoticed by the teacher. Sometimes pupils will bring their conflicts to the teacher for resolution. In these ways aggression and violence are brought under the surveillance and power of the teacher or within the bounds of manageable classroom relationships. The teacher may try to socialize children into accepting some social rationale but in the end it is *power* that counts. She resorts to it whenever she is in danger of not getting her own way 'I don't mind sitting here 'til it's time to go home.' She has the power to detain children against their will. It is a generalizable power, all teachers have this power. And teachers like her, although, kind, quiet spoken, comforting, are *firm* in making use of their power.

3 Sticks and stones: reflections on graffiti at Poundswick School

Tony Booth

In this chapter Tony Booth considers the issues raised by the 'Poundswick dispute' which followed the daubing of offensive graffiti on the school walls. Teachers and Manchester Education Authority were locked into a year-long struggle about the legitimacy of the suspension of the pupils involved. He pieced together the events in the dispute from press cuttings and conversations. He argues that the results of the conflict illuminate both the way in which suspensions should be handled and the extent to which educational decisions can and should be made in the interests of pupils.

Every day in every school in the UK incidents occur which interrupt the flow of education. Pupils may shout out in class, arguments may arise between pupils and between pupils and teachers, property may be damaged or destroyed or stolen. Depending on the degree of disturbance, the approach to discipline by the teacher or school, and the context of the incident, a pupil may be spoken to quietly or fiercely reprimanded, given a detention or extra work, sent to a senior member of staff or suspended from school. If officially suspended it is inevitable that others from outside the school will become involved; parents and school governors and LEA administrators and officials. In most such cases a new routine is devised, the pupil returns to school or transfers to another, a referral is initiated to a disruptive unit or a statement is started with the hope of removal to a 'maladjusted' school. It sometimes happens that suspended pupils remain at home for long periods though again there is usually little fuss; the pupil may be near school-leaving age or the affair may drone on quietly from case conference to committee meeting. Occasionally the reverberations are greater; a case may be taken to the European Court of Human Rights, for example, if a child refuses to accept corporal punishment. But the degree of disturbance occasioned by the suspension of five pupils following the daubing of graffiti at Poundswick High School in Wythenshawe, Manchester, was on an entirely different scale. At one point, it led to the closure for half a day of all of the local authorities' 350 schools when 4,500 teachers went on strike, affecting the education of 74,000 pupils. A dispute arose between councillors, education officers, teachers, parents and pupils which was only finally resolved, almost a year after the incident which sparked it off, and when the five pupils at the centre of the dispute had left school.

The attention focused on the incident and its repercussions raised issues about the status and professional independence of teachers and their relationship with pupils, about the distribution of power between teachers, governors, LEA administrators and Education Committees. It offered insights, too, into the distinctions and contradictions between the procedures for dealing with disaffection in school or incidents of disruption and the statements of educational need leading to special educational provision. Under what circumstances can educational decisions be based on the needs and interests of pupils? It posed questions about the rights of pupils and teachers. It provided a number of clues for other areas on how a policy to reduce suspensions might be handled or mishandled. But there was one aspect of the dispute which received barely a mention. What feelings did the graffiti arouse in the people they depicted? Amongst the plethora of 'official' statements from unions and education committees and teachers is concealed the fact that the pupils and teachers involved have feelings, frailties and limits of tolerance. Whatever other readings are given to the story of the dispute they must share centre stage with our expectations of the participants as ordinary people like ourselves.

The incident

On the evening of Monday 17 June 1985 the back wall of Poundswick High School was covered for 100 yards with graffiti, written with spray cans and felt tip pens which included 'grossly obscene' sexual, sexist and racist remarks about ten named teachers at the school and their families. Whilst the precise content of the graffiti were never made public in the press they were said to contain 'crude drawings' and allusions to 'oral sex and sodomy' (*TES* October 25 1985) and referred to women teachers as 'whores' and 'slags' (*Education* 18 October 1985). The graffiti were quickly removed and following two days of investigations the headteacher suspended five pupils who were said to have 'freely admitted' their guilt although claiming that some other older boys, not at the school, had also contributed to the daubings. The governors of the school met on 1 July and after listening to all the parents and the report of the headteacher they recommended permanent expulsion for all five pupils.

Unlike most local authorities where the school governors are the final arbiters in cases of suspensions, in Manchester, anticipating the provisions of the 1986 Education Bill, the final say rests with the representatives of the LEA. The parents appeal against the suspension was heard by the South Manchester District Appeals Subcommittee meeting to exercise its powers for the first time on Friday 13 September, almost three months after the graffiti were written. The meeting was attended by the five boys and their parents and they were faced by a committee consisting of five councillors and a teacher. A barrister and a solicitor represented one of the pupils. The committee decided to end the suspension of the pupils by a 4–2 majority and the pupils returned to school on the Monday morning (*TES* 18 October 1985).

The Education Committee issued a statement suggesting that the subcommittee's decision 'in no way reflected any lack of concern about the seriousness of the pupils' misbehaviour or about the views of governors and teachers'. But they felt that continued suspension was 'unreasonable' and doubted that these pupils had played the significant role in writing the obscenities claimed by the Poundswick Head (*Guardian* 27 September 1985).

The consequences

It is impossible to assess after precisely which point the long trajectory of the dispute became firmly established, but given the equal determination of teachers not to associate with these pupils and of the education committee that the subcommittee's ruling had to be obeyed the progressive escalation was inevitable. It was exacerbated of course, by the long and bitter teachers' dispute sustained itself by the feelings of teachers that they were grossly undervalued. There were also particular local circumstances; a determination by Manchester LEA to do something about suspensions and what some saw as a centralist tendency, dragging power away from schools. Manchester only introduced governing bodies after the 1980 Education Act and David Hart, general secretary of the National Association of Headteachers argued: 'Manchester Education Committee has never wanted governing bodies to have any power – they believe they are the governing body. They have decided to put their foot down and say we, not the governors are in charge.' He drew a parallel 'in this sense' between the Poundswick case and the dispute between Bradford LEA and Ray Honeyford, the headteacher whose articles in the *Salisbury Review* were alleged to have had racist implications (*Education* 11 October 1985).

Certainly the dispute escalated with remarkable rapidity. After their return (16 September) the boys sat in the hall with books but no teachers. On 18 September the headteacher informed the Chief Education Officer that teachers had collectively decided to refuse to teach the five pupils and had the support of their professional associations. On 24 September the Chief Education Officer visited the school and informed the refusing teachers that they were breaking the law. On 25 September three teachers were suspended without pay for being 'in breach of contract' and the following day thirty-five teachers walked out in their support and by the 27 September only five staff remained. In all forty-seven of the sixty staff at the school were suspended, or in the words of a councillor 'sent home without pay.' The Chief Education Officer claimed that the authority had to observe parents' rights to have children taught at a school of their choice and commented: 'I very much regret any difficulties caused to people but I have to say that in the end there is law, and it must be obeyed.'

The teachers demanded the transfer of the five pupils to other schools or off-site provision but the local authority insisted on their reinstatement. The stand of the teachers drew on unprecedented union unity and support including that of the Secondary Heads Association and National Association of Headteachers, two groups not noted for their militancy. The Manchester branch of the Secondary Heads Association voted for the first strike in its 120-year existence by an overwhelming majority 36 to 2 and passed a vote of no confidence in the city's Chief Education Officer. A spokesperson for the branch recorded that they were 'appalled' by the authority's decision to readmit pupils whose actions were calculated to 'bring the school to the level of the gutter'. They were shocked by the distance the Chief Education Officer placed between himself and the judgement of the heads. As the General Secretary of the Secondary Heads Association put it: 'They feel he has pandered to the prejudices of the extreme left-wing group now running the council' (*Education* 18 October 1985).

Eighty-one per cent of the members of the National Association of Headteachers voted for a half-day strike. David Hart affirmed that this was the first time strike action had been called for over suspensions but claimed it was a response to the 'incomprehensible slap in the face for governors and teachers at Poundswick' (*Daily Telegraph* 8 October 1985).

Parents and pupils also marched in support of the teachers. They formed a Parents Action Committee which demanded the reinstatement of suspended teachers, a reopening of the school and the expulsion of what, with their love for slick phrases, the press were now calling the 'dirty five'. As one parent remarked, 'We will not be satisfied until the teachers are back and the five are expelled. Kids can't be allowed to run schools' (*Guardian* 30 September 1985).

Most of the parents were concerned about the disruption of their pupils education but expected a speedy solution to the dispute. The teachers must have expected that the dramatic show of strength and feeling which closed all of Manchesters schools for the half-day strike on 21 October would have forced the hand of the LEA but they were mistaken. The LEA did not offer to move the pupils but suggested that any teacher who was not happy to teach them could apply for a transfer to another school. There had already been signs of the hardening of attitudes during this period, shown most clearly at the joint public meeting of the Schools and Policy Subcommittees on 10 October. Councillors claimed that they had received obscene and threatening phone calls and letters. Police were guarding the house of one councillor confined to a wheelchair with a broken leg who had received a threat to break the other one. Their response was to dig in their heels and repeat their view that the evidence linking the boys to the graffiti was insufficient. They reiterated their statement of the previous day that: 'The city council do not believe they can acquiesce in any claimed right of teachers to discriminate as to which pupils they are prepared to teach or not to teach' (*Guardian* 10 October 1985). The Liberal and Conservative councillors lined up against the labour majority on the council and on 15 October the Conservatives put forward a motion of no confidence in the education committee.

The general school strike passed, then, with no movement from any side. Although other secondary schools in the area were willing to have them the parents of the five 'reinstated' pupils did not offer to move, one expressing the fear that in a new school his son would be 'bullied and picked on'. The involvement of the Secretary of State for Education produced a statement that in his view Manchester LEA was not acting 'unreasonably'. Various attempts were made to involve conciliators, including ACAS and the Church of England as embodied in the Dean of Manchester, and cracks began to appear in union solidarity. The National Association of School Masters/Union of Women Teachers opposed any negotiations with parents of the pupils and refused to accept the strange deal struck in January 1986 between the city council, the National Union of Teachers and the Assistant Masters and Mistresses Association. The deal involved an agreement to exempt these teachers from classes which in the past contained the five fifth year pupils even though under the agreement these boys were to be taught by a specially seconded tutor. The council was willing to strike a bargain with the union so long as they retained a say in which pupils teachers had to teach. The NAS/UWT argued that this was an immoral compromise which penalized innocent pupils. In effect some fifth year pupils not involved in the incident were to receive only four lessons a week. The NAS/UWT were willing to go back to the school to teach all pupils except the five boys as they had been at the start of the dispute. They remained locked out. The Parents Action Committee, set up to co-ordinate the involvement of parents at the start of the dispute were 'disgusted' by the NUT/AMMA deal. They were also active in scuppering a further attempted compromise by the council who at one point were planning to move the whole of Poundswick fifth year pupils to a neighbouring sixth form college.

The NAS/UWT opted instead for a campaign of selective strikes in Manchester schools to reach a crescendo for the May 1986 elections. By that time however the dispute was virtually settled by default. Two of the five pupils had left school at the Easter break and the other three left at the end of May 1986 during half term. A fifth year cohort at Poundswick had lost virtually a year's schooling. On 3 June, two days before the final end of the dispute, Councillor Nick Harris, Chairperson of Manchester Education Policy Subcommittee, was still adamant: 'I have never had any doubts that the decision to reinstate the five boys, which was made after a whole day hearing the evidence, was the right one' (*Guardian* 3 June 1986).

What was the dispute about?

As the dispute progressed it became linked to a whole range of issues. Parents and teachers marched carrying huge banner appeals to 'Save Our Standards'. The teachers were making a stand against deteriorating discipline as argued by Poundswick Deputy Head, John Hart: 'The return of these five boys would have a disastrous effect on the general ethos of the school ... a number of pupils throughout the city will believe rightly or wrongly, that they have been given carte blanche to behave as they wish' (*Guardian* 5 October). It was reported that on return to the school following their reinstatement the boys had given a clenched fist salute. A view of teachers under siege was conveyed by John Walters, Manchester Divisional Secretary for the National Union of Teachers and a Poundswick teacher:

> There is escalating abuse, assault and foul language and we can only take so much ... The issue is about the rights of teachers to teach and pupils to learn in a sexist-free, racist-free and violence-free environment.
>
> (*The Teacher* 11 October 1985, p. 5)

Nick Harris argued in turn that the visions of violence were motivated by a desire to see the reintroduction of corporal punishment in schools.

At this distance, without the benefit of action replays it is impossible to comment on the precise culpability of each of the five pupils. From the point of view of some teachers and councillors, whilst they may have argued about the extent of guilt, that is not the point. Their argument was about who was the referee in matters of school discipline and hence whose decision should have been taken as final. As mentioned earlier, Manchester is unusual in giving power over suspension to the LEA rather than governors though others will be forced to adopt such a position if the clauses on discipline in the 1986 Education Bill are translated into law. Poundswick may weigh heavily in parliamentary deliberations on that point. As far as some LEAs are concerned, many schools have abused suspension procedures to put pressure on local authorities to provide large numbers of disruptive units and the success of such a strategy has merely fuelled their efforts to get increasing numbers of 'disruptive' pupils out. In order to put a brake on such moves it may be thought necessary to channel suspensions through an LEA committee to which all schools are accountable. But the further reason for providing a forum to consider suspensions outside the school concerns the arguments that some serious activities of schools, including those involving suspensions bring into question the rights of pupils and parents to 'due process'; quasi-legal procedures to ensure that justice is done. Michael Sterne, acting principal of the North Manchester area of community education supported the provision of parents' right of appeal:

> There were 375 reported suspensions in Manchester last year [1984–5] and a great many unreported. The files of any LEA are full of stories of injustice and insensitivity. The line taken is almost always to support the teachers and heads, for administrators and politicians know that teaching and running schools is an arduous and difficult business. A ruined life though, is a ruined life. Some are permanently scarred by their experiences at school...
>   If there is to be a right of appeal, it must be assumed that on occasion the appeal body will make a bad or a wrong decision. Finding the guilty innocent on occasion is an inevitable concomitant of safeguarding against the innocent being found guilty.
>   (*TES* 25 October 1985, p. 4)

In the *TES* for the following week Felicity Taylor acknowledged a shift in her view from giving responsibility for suspensions to governors to establishing independent appeals panels along the lines of those set up by the 1980 Act to contest school choice:

> ...governors are not the best people to hear appeals in suspension cases. For example the governors may be very satisfied on the whole about the way their school is run, yet still feel, perhaps rightly that the head has gone over the top about a particular incident. However when the head, as can often happen, turns the appeal into a vote of confidence, the governors may be very reluctant to allow the appeal... It is surely not in accordance with natural justice that the school should provide prosecutor, judge and jury in its own case.
>   (*TES* 1 November 1985, p. 18)

Other participants in the debate saw such external scrutiny as a failure of trust in teachers and a challenge to their professional judgement:

> In the end it comes to trust. Heads and deputies are appointed to their posts only after the most careful scrutiny of their past records. They are given without question the responsibility for the safety as well as the education of the children, as well as for the running of multi-million pound organizations.
>   They are trusted with all that, and yet the Manchester Authority finds it impossible to trust their integrity in dealing with disciplinary matters.
>   (Peter Snape, General Secretary Secondary Heads Association,
>   *TES* 1 November 1985)

Or as put simply by another union representative, Joan Davenport, 'it is a question of professional judgement. The judgement of teachers is being challenged by people who do not work in schools and do not know schools' (*Teacher*, 25 October 1985).

Given the reputation of some of the councillors as being on the 'hard left' of the Labour Party it was predictable that some would attempt to attribute the stance of the council to their political ideology. The chairperson of Poundswick governors, Les Roberts, thought the council decision was prompted by this bias:

> The LEA has got the balance wrong. They are so concerned that inarticulate parents are well-treated that they forget that schools have to operate as organized and disciplined institutions.
>
> (*TES* 18 October 1985, p. 6)

The father of one of the five pupils, Mr Davenport, argued, in turn, that the teachers action was discriminatory. He claimed that two further pupils involved in the graffiti were let off because they were white and lived in private housing, whilst all those punished were from the council estate and were of immigrant parents or were black (*TES* 25 October 1985, p. 5). However, the teachers were supported by the majority of parents and David Wraxall of the Parent Action Committee made it clear that it was not they who were seen as classist:

> The council say that they are all about giving support to communities. Yet they ignored the views of the community in their decision. This is a working-class area and the dispute has affected the prospects of working-class young people. Many of the fifth year pupils have had their futures destroyed.

Nor was he willing to lend his support to those who saw the school and governors as final arbiters in cases of suspension. He felt that there should be an appeals procedure, but that in this case the committee took insufficient notice of what the head and staff of Poundswick and other parents had to say.

In the long dispute, then, several issues have been said to encapsulate the essence of the disagreement. It has been said to be about standards of discipline, the distribution of power, the professional status of teachers and, even, after the heady days of solidarity, about inter-union rivalry. What has been forgotten in the desire to present an image of disinterested professionals seeking 'an educational solution' to a school problem are the feelings of the teachers involved. The graffiti *were* shocking and because of taboos about publishing them it is easy for them to disappear from the debate. What may be harder to recognize and have discussed is that because of their acutely sexist and racist nature they may even be motivated by sentiments which, in some form, are more prevalent than many would admit. In the absence of a photograph of the 100 yard spread of slogans one has to do a little more to conjure up the impression that the appearance of the graffiti made on both the teachers named and their colleagues, who were expected to teach the pupils responsible. This is a selection of the statements that greeted them:

> I fucked (name of woman teacher).
>
> If you have shagged (name of woman teacher) tick here.
>
> This (name of woman teacher) has been shagged by (name of man teacher).
>
> (Name of man teacher)'s mum sucks niggers cocks.

Now it may be that after an initial period of hurt, upset and anger you might be willing to teach a pupil who had represented you in this way. Yet if you are not it is difficult to see how it could be reasonable to do anything else but respect your feelings. If the five pupils were responsible for writing obscenities, and it does seem that they admitted it, then in this case one might argue the feelings of the teachers should be given a very high priority. The judgement of the appeals committee would imply that it is part of the professional job of teachers to submerge such feelings and the emphasis of the unions on the search for a 'professional' rather than a 'punitive' solution appears to collude in that view. However, perhaps what was required was a human stance rather than a professional one.

The snag here is that, in the interests of fairness towards their pupils, teachers *do* have to suppress their ordinary feelings. In common with other professional groups such as shopkeepers, doctors and social workers they are not free to exhibit preferences for one client over another. They are meant to suppress feelings of dislike and irritation towards pupils inside school who outside the school gates they would be free to shun. Unless you are peculiarly saintly it is extremely difficult to get by in teaching without developing a professional persona to some degree. At the same time, in order to respond to pupils' needs and interests teachers have to develop a genuine involvement and commitment. Because of the degree of continuous contact teachers have with their pupils the contradiction between being a 'professional' and being 'oneself' is more likely to surface than in other comparable occupations. If teachers were only 'professionals' then, whilst this front could always be breeched by physical assault, names might never hurt them. Yet there is always a person behind the working facade and the nature of the Poundswick graffiti, which also involved the families of teachers, made a professional defence mechanism peculiarly difficult to sustain.

One might argue, then, that in this case, insufficient account was taken of human feelings. But there is a lingering problem which forms part of the background of this and every other case of suspension. Although the Poundswick teachers suggested a transfer to another comprehensive school, supposing the pupils had been transferred to an off-site unit for 'disruptive' pupils, do the same conditions apply? If the pupils behave in an offensive way is it reasonable for teachers to refuse to teach them? Or what about at a school for maladjusted pupils? However expert the teachers in such schools are at interesting or controlling their pupils they are likely to face abuse and more likely than most to have to contend with the possibility of physical assault from pupils. One headteacher of a day school for maladjusted pupils replied to the challenge from a governor that he should not consider suspending a pupil by saying 'You give me riot shields and helmets and I'll promise never to suspend anyone'. Whilst in reality there may be no 'end of the line' for pupils in school the idea that there is pervades the consciousness of some teachers and has been promoted by those with an interest in the burgeoning growth of special schools and units (see Chapter 7).

Inferring from these existing trends, if a decision about when pupils' actions have overstepped the mark is left to be determined by each individual school then pupil suspensions and the demand for off-site placements will continue to rise.

A judgement has to be made about whether the increasing segregation of pupils on the grounds of unacceptable behaviour is either the most desirable or the most effective way to make schools easier and pleasanter places in which to teach and learn. Many schools have themselves come to the conclusion that the approach to control which leads to suspension of pupils is actually undermining of discipline. For it ties up the energy of teachers in amassing evidence against miscreants and prevents any possible failings of the school curriculum from coming under scrutiny (see Chapters 11 and 12). Yet because of the attractiveness to schools of removing troublesome pupils any switch in approach has to be co-ordinated by the LEA and has to have the consent of the schools concerned. The absence of such consent appears to have been dramatically illustrated in Manchester schools.

An understanding of responses to disruption is obscured by a confusion of education with care, treatment and punishment. In the Poundswick case some parents, teachers and teacher representatives were mystified by the fact that neither the pupils nor the other young people involved were taken to court and charged with obscene libel. It has been pointed out that the incident took place outside school time at a time when none of those involved were the responsibility of the teachers. Yet the headteacher, Keith Halstead, wanted to focus attention on 'educational' matters:

> Throughout the dispute, I and my colleagues have sought an educational solution and there are tailor-made courses available in other schools which meet the educational needs of the five pupils involved. I continue to expect the support of the Education Department in searching for an educationally acceptable solution which recognizes the needs of the school as a whole.
>
> (*Guardian* 22 November 1985)

Even when a criminal act is committed on the school premises during school time one could argue that the appropriate response initially is to involve the police. Whether one did or not would depend on a number of factors including the severity of the act and the degree of fairness and sensitivity with which any investigation would be conducted.

The Poundswick saga starkly underlined the fact that disruptive incidents involve conflicting interests of pupils and of pupils and teachers. It is rarely feasible in such cases to view 'educational needs' from the perspective of the pupils concerned. Following the 1981 Act the Department of Education and Science, in Circular 1/83, which in common with all circulars is advisory without the force of law, informally encouraged LEAs not to issue statements for pupils when they were sent to disruptive units (DES 1983, para. 15). It is hard to argue that such provision does not fall within the Act's definition of special provision as 'education in addition to, or otherwise different from the educational provision made generally for children of his [or her] age in schools maintained by the local authority concerned' (DES 1981(3)) nor that the pupils who go there are not regarded as having special educational needs. If both conditions hold then legally such pupils should be the subject of statements. There has not yet been a legal challenge of unofficial placements in disruptive units but given the level of feeling about such places, particularly concerning the over-representation of black pupils, that may yet happen. But by avoiding official procedures which make it obligatory to consider the needs of the pupils they describe, it becomes easier to conceal the fact that disruptive units have little to do with pupils' needs and interests. Of course it may be equally implausible to suggest that those pupils sent to 'maladjusted schooling' or, in fact, to any other category of special school, are there in their own interests particularly where sharing a school with other pupils who have experienced difficulties is likely to exacerbate their own problems. Such problems in serving the educational interests of pupils are obscured by characterizing such schools as places of educational treatment. By focusing openly on the legitimate interests of the teachers at Poundswick High School perhaps we will be less likely to obscure the interests that are being served by educational decisions elsewhere.

References

DES 1981. *The Education Act*, London, HMSO.
DES 1983. Circular 1/83 *Assessments and Statements of Special Educational Needs*, London, HMSO.

4   A moral lesson at Marlborough House

Tony Booth and Di Hesketh

In this chapter Tony Booth and Di Hesketh describe a single lesson at a residential and day special school for pupils categorized as having 'moderate learning difficulties' or 'emotional and behavioural difficulties'. The intention had been to observe and record control processes in operation within the lesson but it became clear that the subject matter of the lesson in a course leading to a Certificate of Prevocational Education (CPVE) was itself part of the attempt to inculcate 'acceptable' behaviour and attitudes in these pupils. For these pupils, for this lesson, overt and hidden curricula had become neatly embedded and interchanged. There was the lesson of their attendance at this school as a group categorized in part on the basis of their deviant behaviour. And here was a lesson which moved back and forward from its official subject matter, the behaviour of two groups of young people on videos, to its unofficial subject matter, the use that could be made of such observations in promoting 'good habits' in these pupils.

Marlborough House school is situated on the outskirts of a large village which forms a suburb of a small town. It is a special school for ninety boys aged eleven to sixteen years who are categorized as having moderate learning difficulties or as emotionally or behaviourally disturbed. Over half the pupils are boarders and many of these come to the school because they need a place away from home rather than because there is some educational need for residential schooling. Staff have noticed a change in the labels attached to pupils when they arrive at the school. Many more are sent because of 'difficult behaviour' or 'emotional disturbance' than in the past. There is also a move away from the isolationist policy of former years with contacts being made with the nearest secondary school.

The group we observed consisted of two classes brought together for a one hour lesson on 'communication'. It contained twenty pupils, aged twelve to fourteen, and was taught by two teachers, Mr Grey and Ms Frances, who apart from one of us, was the only female present. The lesson was led by Mr Grey, a teacher with a strong interest in sport which was much appreciated by the pupils. Ms Frances provided occasional support and made attempts to establish a role for herself within the group. There were no major problems of disruption in the lesson and this was not because the pupils were kept on an overtly tight rein. Nevertheless, as the transcript shows, specific matters of the appearance and discipline of these boys were purposefully introduced into the lesson and the general issue of 'good behaviour' was its main theme.

The lesson divided into three main sections. It started with a discussion of a TV programme which the pupils had been watching the previous week. This had been about the exploits of a group of boys from a city on a visit to the countryside. The film had managed to cram a large number of social themes into a half hour and these included the attitudes of people in town and country, racism, bullying and mental handicap. The second phase of the lesson was meant to involve the pupils, in pairs, disclosing aspects of their personalities and interests to their

22

partners, related in some way to the observations they had made on the gang leader in the film. The final part involved the pupils in viewing another film about the changes in the lives of a group of young men in Bristol six years after their common membership of a 'gang'.

There is no single and simple message to be gained from the report of this lesson. In many ways it was highly successful and flowed smoothly from beginning to end. But the recording of any such lesson inevitably throws up many issues about the intended and unintended curriculum content and any of these could form the starting point for further exploration. For example, what messages are the pupils getting about what constitutes 'good' behaviour and the consequences of 'bad' behaviour? What do they learn about methods of controlling others, about the role of male power, and about the space for girls and women? Answers to these questions must take the form of hypotheses derived as they are from the transcript of one lesson lifted out of the context of life in this school.

We have tried to allow the flavour of the lesson to come across without lengthy and frequent interpretive interventions from ourselves though inevitably the clarifications we offer are selective and are our own.

11.00: Getting started

The room was congested with furniture and it took a while for the boys to come in, find chairs and arrange them in a circle in the middle of the room. There were a few minutes of scraping and noise. Mr Grey perched himself on a table and began to ask them to hurry up. Ms Frances left the room for a while. He appeared to have a relaxed easy control of the group and the class were soon settled.

> *Mr Grey:* You're not really involved there James, look there's a chair there. Rat – I know they don't like you but come into the circle. ['Rat' was sitting behind the others trying to look invisible but alas was spotted.]
>   Right, first of all let me have a moan, I don't like to start with a moan, but I will. If you look at your footwear you come in from outside, those of you who have been playing football you usually bring half the field in with you ... [interrupted by a late arrival, no chair, so Mr Grey indicates to get one from the other room] ... half the field in with you. Can you just try and bang your feet or something outside ... [stamp, stamp – dirt flies across the floor] ... Not in here! It does make a difference to the cleaners and everyone else.
> *Boy:* I played football on the playground, sir.
> *Mr Grey:* Yes, I noted yours aren't too bad.

11.05: Lesson Phase 1

> *Mr Grey:* Now listen carefully. For those of you who weren't here last week, rather than me tell you what we did and saw I'll ask one or two people in the group to explain to you what we did. OK ... Not you Mark. James, what did we watch or what talk about last week?
> *James:* We talked about the country – countryside.
> *Mr Grey:* Countryside, do you think that sums up what we saw, that statement? Malcolm?
> *Malcolm:* Four boys, er, they went for this, er, trip to the countryside, and they changed their mind when they got there.

Mr Grey: Right so, Mark... [Points to a boy who was absent the previous week] ... rather than me be the outsider, what have you heard so far? What do you think they've been talking about? Have you got a clear picture? [He leans forward, challenging the group to be more forthcoming.]

Mark: I don't know, I was born in Glasgow, sir.

Mr Grey: Right, let's get a bit more of the picture. Robert? I appreciate what you said Malcolm but...

Robert: Vandalizing everything spraying all over the trees, and being naughty and all that.

Mr Grey: Give me something more about the boys. I want to build up a picture.

Robert: One of them was bossy, a bit of a bully, bullying other people like the handicapped boy...

Mr Grey: Right, so far I've got one of the boys was a bit of a bully, they are in the country, I've got... I think that's all I've got.

Robert: They start teasing, one against the other.

Mr Grey: Right, let's think about it, hold on a sec. If we go a stage further back, where were had they come from and where were they going to?

Boy: From the station.

Mr Grey: What was their home environment? [Most of the group were listening and putting up their hands to get Mr Grey's attention to answer the questions, but calling out was not discouraged. Some kept their heads down hoping not to be noticed, most wriggled uncomfortably on the standard wooden chairs or fiddled with pens or their fingers.]

Boy: Houses and all that and shops. London.

Mr Grey: Yes, a big place – what do you call it?

Boy: London?

Boy: Town.

Mr Grey: Yes, a town or a city. Yes, their home environment, what do we mean by the word environment? [Mostly calling out – several at one time.]

Boy: Things around you.

Mr Grey: Yes, so our environment here is the what?

Boy: Trees, and that.

Boy: People.

Boy: Trees. Classroom.

Mr Grey: What's our immediate environment?

Boy: Class. Classroom.

Mr Grey: Yes, the classroom, the school. We said what was their home environment that they were leaving. The city, noise.

Boy: The smell.

Mr Grey: What word do we use for all...

Boy: Smog.

Mr Grey: Yes, but we had one word.

Boy: Fumes.

Mr Grey: Yes, but one word for all that. [Mr Grey looking round the group – who appeared quite puzzled at his insistence on one word, more clues were necessary.] It began with P, we said.

Boy: Oh... pollution.

Mr Grey: Yes, pollution [sigh of relief]. Yes, it was a very polluted environment. A very sort of smoke... the fast sort of life in the city. [Another teacher, Ms Frances, enters the room and seats herself on a table behind the circle and looks attentively at Mr Grey.] Yes, and these boys were going on bikes ... which we later found out were what?

Boy: Nicked.

Mr Grey: Or borrowed. [Sniggers all round.]

Mr Grey: And they were going to what sort of an environment.

Boy: Countryside.

Mr Grey: Which is we said.

Boy: Nice and quiet.

Boy: Not many houses around.

Boy: Fresh air.

Mr Grey: Fresh air. Not much traffic.

Boy: More hills.

Boy: No smell.

Mr Grey: What did they say, the leader and his sidekick. What did they say when they got to that gate. They leant on the gate.

Boy: Oh, oh.

Boy: It's boring.

Boy: Nothing much to do here.

Mr Grey: That's right, they got out there, and there they were and they said 'What do we do, it's boring.' Right, build the picture up a little bit more. What did the other two ...

Boy: They liked it.

Boy: The other two carried on and said, oh it's boring here, but then the others said, no it isn't and started writing on trees and then they all went to the shops.

Boy: That saddle came off didn't it.

Mr Grey: Alright.

Boy: They went into that shop and mucked about and the lady wouldn't be used to all that, because people down in the country are always nice and quiet.

Mr Grey: Also, there was one other thing the lady wouldn't have been used to.

Boy: Black people.

Boy: Mucking about. [Much of the latter discussion was focused on the same two or three boys who shouted out together.]

Boy: The way they acted and that.

Mr Grey: Well, not people. There was only one – only one black guy. Yes, they didn't think that she would have been used to seeing a black person in that environment, and then the others started taking the mickey then. So far, so good. We've got the picture now, I think, and we said so last week the whole thing was a lot about relationships, and how people see each other. Now they were four lads and in their city environment it was quite clear who was like their boss – who was their leader. Who was the gang leader?

Boy: Steve. Benny.

Mr Grey: Yes, Benny. Benny's sidekick was? [Ms Frances leant forward and answered...]

Ms Frances: Caz!

Mr Grey: Yes, the boy with the horrible laugh, like a little lizard-like creature who came out from under a stone. Now, really it was about relationships I felt, because those four when they were in London and in the city Benny was the leader, if he spoke they listened, if he made a joke they all laughed. If he took the mick ... What did the farmer say? ... no one ... no one ...

Boy: ... 'Stuck up for themselves'.

Mr Grey: Yes, 'you don't stick up for yourselves.' Then when they got to the country the relationships changed, they began to question. To me that was the important bit that came out of it. So how did they change? [Mr Grey looked around the group at this point and picked on one of the quieter members of the class sitting looking at his shoes.] Liam, can you remember? What did Lofty and the coloured chap's name ... [Again Ms Frances joined in at this point by replying with the boys.]

Ms Frances: Omo.

Liam: Omo.

Mr Grey: How did their relationship change?

Liam: They stuck up for themselves.

Mr Grey: Then what happened from then on?

Liam: They gave him that handicapped boy that boy's bike.

Brian: They went down to the shop first and they were outside the shop, and they started to say well right he says where's my bike, I'm going to get it back and he says if you get past me I'll rip you to pieces. [It's not clear who they are referring to at this point, but Mr Grey appeared to understand.]

Mr Grey: Yes, this was the first time they had what?

Boy: Really stuck up for themselves. Then they fighted over the bikes.

Mr Grey: Malcolm [sitting patiently with his hand up].

Malcolm: There's that other time when the girl sticks up for herself. That's the first time a girl was in it then and she stuck up for her brother.

Mr Grey: Yeh, could you relate to that with your brother at all?

Malcolm: [Malcolm blushes a little.] Yeh.

Mr Grey: I thought that, because when your brother was here, yes, because your brother once told me he got very angry when someones was taking the mickey out of you.

Boy: Sidekick, stuck up for himself too in the end, didn't he.

Mr Grey: Quite right, yes he did. Did anyone else remember that? Yes, that last shot ...

Boy: And that boy with the racer when it got stuck in a cow pat he was showing off.

Boy: Yeh.

Mr Grey: The last shot in the film was of the slimey boy, the creature; he wasn't going to listen to the leader either. So really the whole relationship thing of one leader and all the rest knowing their place, it had changed, hadn't it? It had changed. *Different environment, different set of rules, they'd been made aware and that was it.* It changed a lot of things. OK?

11.20: A spot of planning

Mr Grey looks across to Ms Frances and they confer about whether or not they want to show another film. The boys snatch the opportunity to chatter and wriggle, they have been on the whole attentive and co-operative for the past twenty minutes.

Ms Frances: There is another film and it's about the gang six years on but it's not our gang that we saw.

Mr Grey: No.

Ms Frances: It's another gang ...

Mr Grey: If you could set that up for us now I'd like to do some work just to round this off in pairs or threes where they try to work amongst themselves.

Ms Frances: [Not quite understanding her instructions.] When do you want that film shown? Today?

Mr Grey: In about fifteen to twenty minutes because I did promise them they'd be seeing a film today.

Ms Frances: [To Mr Grey and the whole class] This film that you'll see. It starts off and you think er ... I don't know about them six years ago but then it does recap.

Mr Grey: Also with that sort of thing, we could ask them their impression of six years ago. Yeah, I think we'll go for that ...

Ms Frances: I'm a bit divvy with the video ['divvy' means dim or thick – schools like Marlborough House often get labelled 'the divvy school'].

Boys: I'll help you miss. I'll help you.

Ms Frances: I'll try and if I need some help ...

Mr Grey: [At this point Mr Grey takes control and insists that one of the boys accompanies Ms Frances to show her how the video works.] John's quite fluent with the er er video thing.

Ms Frances: Don't you need him in here?

Mr Grey: No, he was away last week, I can pick this up with him later.

11.25: The Lesson Phase II

Mr Grey pairs off the pupils and the one remaining child, Alan, is his partner. He then explains what he wants them to do.

Mr Grey: What I want to do is as follows. Bearing in mind what we said about the gang leader I just want you to chat with the other person. I know you know each other and it's a bit of a false situation. But did like ... In a minute I'm going to ask each person what they think of the other person. We'll use a few key words. Half a minute number one tell number two about themselves then we'll change it round.

Most began to chat immediately, one or two needed to be prompted. Unfortunately several pairs had not picked up the last sentence of Mr Grey's introduction and thought they were to recall their impressions of the boys in the film. Nevertheless some did get the idea. Mr Grey can be heard describing himself in the far corner: 'I'm very sporty. I like running, football. I like teaching. I've applied recently for a job at another school. I like to enjoy myself at weekends, have a drink, go to discos, etc.' There is a general hubbub with some boys prodding, poking and jibing at each other, several boys squirm on their chairs, others look at the floor in embarrassment. When both of the pair have had a turn Mr Grey resumes.

Mr Grey: Right, hold on. Very quickly. Just give me one or two impressions of one another. [Initially the responses are monosyllabic, and stilted but gradually the group gets the idea that in reporting back, at least, they are meant to say something about their partners.] Jason, is Martin a leader, has he a strong personality?

Jason: Yes, he's strong.

Mr Grey: Martin, what did you feel about Jason?

Martin: He came out with stupid things like he's a king and he's married to the Queen and he says he's got 20 BMXs. [Everyone laughs, and someone calls out.] He's an exaggerator!

Mr Grey: Maybe, he's certainly left Martin with the impression that he's a bit of a wally. What's the point of saying you have 20 BMXs?
Mark: He's a bit of a big head. [Silence follows this remark.]
Mr Grey: What about you Liam?
Liam: Well, Mark's alright, he's a good friend. He helps me with work sometimes.
Mr Grey: Now that's nice, that's a nice quality to have in life if you're helpful. That's a good quality to have.
Liam: He's taught me some new breakdance movements too.
Mr Grey: Right Henry, how did Tom come over.
Henry: Polite.
Mr Grey: Polite, that's a good one. Polite, now on first impressions and how you come over to one another I think politeness is important. I like that Henry. Any other qualities?
Henry: Well mannered, well dressed.
Mr Grey: Good, yes. He stays neat and tidy. Such first impressions, neat and tidy, are very important. Yes, anything else? [The boys are largely interested in the comments and the atmosphere is light-hearted and good-humoured. They are momentarily distracted by the arrival of the TV.]
Mr Grey: Right Tony, how did Kevin come over to you?
Tony: He's alright. He's a good football player and cricket and he isn't wearing a tie! [Everyone laughs about the tie, it's obviously not something Mr Grey is going to make an issue of.]
Mr Grey: Philip says a comb through your hair would be a good idea and you oughtn't to be wearing trainers. Shoes would be better. You notice that visually.
Kevin: [who has a strong West Country accent] Tony likes swimming, he likes the countryside and he says he likes girls. [The rest of the group find this very amusing.]
Mr Grey: There is something I always notice when Kevin talks.
Tony and others: His talking, speech – accent.
Mr Grey: Yes, his accent. Kevin always sounds as though he is down on the farm. Right Michael, what about Alan?
Michael: He's nice and interesting, nice and bright, no really bad habits.
Alan: I think Michael's a bit of a bully.
Mr Grey: Did everyone hear that? [The boys are distracted by Ms Frances plugging in the TV and they are beginning to chatter and fidget amongst themselves.] That's interesting, did everyone hear that? Alan is saying that he thinks his great friend there Michael is a bit of a bully. It's worth remembering that Michael and thinking about it. [The last pair is Mr Grey and a quiet lad, Sam.]
Sam: Mr Grey likes having a nice time, likes enjoying himself. Goes to Reynelles and likes all sorts of sports and teaching.
Mr Grey: I got the feeling that Sam was a bit shy and nervous. I felt you didn't have a lot of outside interests and you stayed at home a lot. You don't get out much. Am I right? Also I picked up you are not very keen on school – but perhaps I knew that from before.

Mr Grey draws this part of the lesson together by mentioning some of the keywords that he felt were important such as 'politeness' and 'helpful.' One lad, Liam, points out, however, that some of the boys might be very different outside school, polite in school but causing trouble in gangs outside. With this comment, as if miraculously Liam has linked the lesson back to Mr Grey's summary of the first film: 'Different environment, different set of rules, they'd been made aware and that was it.' We only discovered this ourselves after studying the transcript several times and had struggled to understand the extent of the connections between Phase I and Phase II of the lesson. Mr Grey appears to forget his earlier point but uses Liam's comment to remark that he is well aware some of the boys might be angels in the classroom but that once they were outside they 'take on a different role'.

11.40: The Lesson Phase III

Mr Grey tells the boys they can now watch another film which they will talk about the following week. They all turn their chairs round to face the screen and jostle with one another until they can all see. The film is entitled *The Gang*. It portrays the life of a gang of boys on the South Mead Estate in Bristol, six years previously and how they fared subsequently. Members of the gang now aged 18–20 are interviewed and asked about their life and what they think about the gang that they were in. The message of the film is clear, getting into trouble, mucking about doesn't pay! Several of the lads in the film have been in Borstal or prison and only one has a permanent job.

The film starts.

Commentary: **Six years ago this was the youngest gang of boys on the South Mead Estate in Bristol . . . How do they look back on those days? One gang member has continued to be in and out of difficulties:**

> *Gang member:* I've been unemployed. I've been in Borstal. I've been looking for jobs. I was thinking of going back on the fair because I used to work on the fair before going inside. They try to change you there, you know what I mean? But they can't change you unless you want them to and I didn't want them to, know what I mean? But now I decided that the only way I'll change is to change myself. Know what I mean? People around me aren't going to change me, know what I mean?
> *Interviewer:* **Have you become calmer?**
> *Gang member:* Yeah, 'cos before I used to be, like, violent, a violent person, but I'm not so violent now. Know what I mean? I've calmed down . . . I'm still violent now, like, but I'm not as violent as I used to be.
> *Interviewer:* **Would you say you were happier, a happier person?**
> *Gang member:* No. No. In those days there was always something to do but nowadays it's boring, there's never hardly anything to do. Like, me mates comes over and I go over to their place, playing darts and that, but after a while it gets boring and I can't handle that. Know what I mean?
> *Interviewer:* **Do you have a girlfriend?**
> *Gang member:* On and off. I've been going out with her some three weeks now but I'm getting fed up, like, don't know why, just am.

The gang leader, however, has a job as a postman, a job he has kept since he left school.

> *Gang leader:* I never thought I'd be a postman when I left school I thought that was the last thing I'd do. I didn't take any exams or nothing. I used to mess about at school all the time so it was me own fault. So I was lucky really . . .
> *Interviewer:* **What sort of hopes have you got for the future? What do you dream of?**
> *Gang leader:* Owning a racehorse perhaps . . . I take every day as it comes.

The film ended to loud classical music and the chairs and tables are returned to their original position amongst a lot of talking about gangs and getting into trouble. Most of the boys had watched attentively. Most nodded their approval when Mr Grey asked the group if they had enjoyed it.

Ms Frances: [Talking to the whole group.] Do any of you belong to a gang that size? I'm not just talking about a few. [A number of boys put up their hands including Tony and Peter, a rather small lad.] How many in your gang Tony?

Tony: Six.

Ms Frances: Who else is in a gang? You've got a gang Peter?

Mr Grey: [Drawing attention to Peter's size] What's that, the toddler gang Peter? [The atmosphere has become very informal with the boys wandering around the room and chatting in groups while they get ready to go to lunch. A friendly tap on the head with a rule from Mr Grey enables him to gain the attention of a few as he wants to mention homework.] We'll go over the film next week. There's lots to talk about there. For homework if you think you might forget bits of it, it might be quite helpful to jot one or two bits down.

Mr Grey: One thing to finish on. Have you all handed in your homework sheets? Can I have any outstanding homework sheets now please? You still owe me one . . . get it in . . . [They chat about who is going running or to football training and whether there will be a weights group tomorrow. The bell rings.]

Mr Grey: 4C make your way round to lunch. [A little later] 4F boys follow on.

5 Advice from the shop floor: pupils' views of disaffection

Di Hesketh

This chapter consists of edited conversations about disaffection and disruption between Di Hesketh and five pupils. The first, Mark Edmondson was at sixth form college and reflected on the school rules which provoked indiscipline, the exam orientation of his school and the strategies teachers used to enforce and gain control. Annabel Wilson and Jason Croft both attend an off-site unit and were both suspended from school after fighting with other pupils. They enjoy the freer atmosphere of the unit and a feeling that they are being treated as adults. Sean Smith and Theresa Connor attend the same primary school and compare notes on the rules in their respective classrooms and the personalities, skills and senses of humour of their teachers.

Mark Edmondson

Mark attended Walton Comprehensive School for five years and is now at Sixth Form College studying for his 'A' levels. He had a 'successful' school career and hopes to go to medical school.

I THOUGHT SCHOOL UNIFORM WAS PATHETIC

Di: What sort of behaviour was unacceptable at Walton?
Mark: Not wearing the correct uniform. I thought school uniform was pathetic, a complete waste of time. Certain teachers took it very seriously and some weren't bothered. I could never see how wearing school uniform had anything to do with the way you perform. I remember wearing a light blue jumper instead of a dark blue one and being told off.
Di: Why do you think schools have a uniform?
Mark: Teachers usually said it was so everyone looked the same and it stopped some pupils from buying expensive clothes, supposedly so poor people could not be distinguished. Yet school uniform costs more than anything else we wore. It was just tradition. I think they will give it up eventually. A lot of places don't have it any more and they haven't lost their grip. It gives people a focus for rebelling against the system, so people start doing silly little things like wearing a different tie. The school is providing an automatic way of rebelling really. I suppose that is what punks are doing anyway. I remember there were at least two punks when I was at school who wore punk clothes and the school was too weak to do anything about it so they just carried on. It would have caused more trouble if they had made a fuss about it.

EVERYTHING WAS GEARED TO EXAMS

Di: Were there any other obvious ways of rebelling against the system?

31

Mark: Yes, your general attitude and how you behaved in the classroom. If you insulted teachers, made a fuss in class, skived off or went home. In the higher stream classes there was generally less fuss, because they were more interested in their work. In the first year we were all in the same class, then in the second year for all subjects we were streamed into A, B and C classes.

Di: Was there more disaffection in the lower streams?

Mark: Mostly, but pupils in the higher streams also got fed up. Those who got expelled were generally in the lower streams. Our year was different, because those who were getting into trouble were mainly in the higher streams and the teachers started getting worried because it might affect their 'O' level results. The school might not perform as well. They took a long time to do anything about it, but eventually they kicked out two of the main troublemakers. It didn't really achieve much.

Di: What were these pupils doing?

Mark: Nothing really, sort of trying to destroy the atmosphere in the classroom. Refusing to take it seriously – so teachers failed to create an academic atmosphere in most of the classes.

Di: Was it necessary to expel them?

Mark: One of them is at college with me now and he has no trouble at all. The atmosphere of the sixth form college as opposed to the comprehensive suits him, he is praised by the teachers, whereas before teachers would pull their hair out over him and shout at him all the time. Some teachers got on with him really well, generally the more relaxed teachers.

Di: What sort of an atmosphere should there be in school?

Mark: It's difficult because unlike sixth form college no one chooses to go to secondary school. You can't expect all the pupils to want to be there. You can't be too relaxed but petty things cause trouble. Trying to force pupils to do things that they don't see the meaning of gives them reason to start causing trouble.

Di: What was the school curriculum like at Walton?

Mark: Everything was geared to exams and the school always showed more interest in the brighter pupils. Prize-giving was only concerned with them which led to a lot of ill-feeling amongst other pupils. The system just wasn't designed for them and they wanted to get out just as soon as they could. They weren't interested in exams. Every lesson as you get higher up the school was geared to exams, consequently subjects that we weren't examined in like social and political education, PE and RE, we all felt were a waste of time. I don't feel it was right to have such an emphasis on exams, but that's the way it is. You tended to choose subjects depending on the style of the different teachers, I gave up geography because I found the lessons boring and now I know I would really like to have done it.

OTHERS WOULDN'T EVEN SAY HELLO

Di: How do you think disruptive behaviour should be dealt with in school?

Mark: At Walton we had a pathetic system of punishment where there was a list of the school rules which you had to write out if you were in detention. Silly rules such as, you must wear white PE kit or you must not walk on the grass. Then there was the report book in which your name and misdemeanour were recorded and you usually got a detention. They have given up the book now. The fifth form report book used to get flushed down the toilet or ripped into tatters every week. Most pupils didn't take it seriously, they just regarded it as a waste of time. It would have been better for teachers to talk to pupils rather than report them.

Di: What do you consider a 'good' teacher to be?

Mark: I didn't like work sheets or loads of questions on the boards. I think a good teacher talks and discusses the topic with the class and then gives them notes at the end of the discussion. Worksheets are really boring. If you just sit all lesson doing that, you end up chatting to your friends and they are the sort of lesson where the teacher doesn't even learn everyone's name. If you get involved in the subject it's much more interesting. At sixth form college at the moment, biology is discussed and you can argue with the teacher. But in chemistry the atmosphere is really boring. We just copy off the board.

Some teachers seemed very cut off, others were really good people. Teachers who did extra courses like the Duke of Edinburgh and took us on hikes, they would buy you a drink in the pub, whereas others wouldn't even say hello. I would have thought people who go into teaching ought to be genuinely interested in kids but a lot are more interested in their subject and have fallen back on teaching.

NOT BEING CHAUVINIST OR ANYTHING...

Di: Do you think teachers can be themselves in the classroom?

Mark: It depends on the school. If it is a school where all the teachers put on an act and pretend everything is OK, then if a teacher said I don't feel too good today, they would be asking for trouble. If the school was run differently then teachers could say how they feel. At Walton, especially in the lower years, they would be taken advantage of. In the fifth year it would be OK. Some teachers were open, but never suggested that they couldn't cope, just that they didn't want any trouble. I don't think teachers should really lose their temper, I think that's a weakness, it's a sign that they are losing control of the situation. Not being chauvinist or anything but I do think that the teachers who lost their temper more, were women teachers who couldn't control their class. There were male teachers who did the same thing but I wasn't taught by any of them. They tended to get nervous when there was any trouble in the class and started shouting. You can speak sternly to someone without losing your temper and still maintain control or ask to see the person later. If they started losing their temper they would fall back on the report book, or say go and see the head of year or leave the class which means they have totally given up.

Di: So you feel it is up to each individual class teacher to control their class?

Mark: The school provided the report book as a support for the teacher but some never needed to use it and just didn't believe in it, but maintained control by having pupils respect them. Many teachers left the school as they became disenchanted with the system themselves. You do get the impression that there is a lot of competition between teachers and you get to know which teachers are unpopular with the other ones.

I USED TO GET REALLY ANNOYED WITH THE ROUTINE

Sometimes you could see that a teacher just couldn't get on with a certain pupil but managed to have a good relationship with other pupils. Teachers used to end up gritting their teeth and banging their hands on the desk and shouting, *'Why, why are you doing this?'* Eventually the child might be removed from the class. I think it is a failure on the pupils' part, a failure to respect a teacher who is trying to do his or her best.

In the lower years it was fun when someone made a fuss or shouted at the teacher. The favourite sport at secondary school was trying to destroy a student teacher but in the sixth form you are often pleased to see a different face and they are often better than the usual teacher.

Di: Do pupils make a distinction between probationary teachers and those who are more experienced?

Mark: Established teachers are accepted by the pupils but if you have a new teacher, you have to test them, push them to see how strict they are and whether they can control the class. It happens to all new teachers when they join the school. They get taken in in the first few terms and a lot of them just don't survive it and leave.

Di: Why does it happen?

Mark: Boredom, I think. It's more fun to take a teacher to pieces now and again. Every single day when the bell goes you have got to go into a lesson and you have to sit down and work. I used to get really annoyed with the routine, I used to hate the week. You had a timetable which revolved around the bell ringing at the same time every day. After a few terms of that you get really bored.

Annabel Wilson and Jason Croft

Annabel and Jason are both fifteen years old and have been attending an out-of-school unit for the past two terms. They both enjoy the unit but admit they will be ready to leave as soon as they are sixteen. Annabel, who I spoke to first, spent three years at Ridgmont Secondary School before being expelled for fighting. She was transferred to an alternative comprehensive, Downend before her arrival at the 'unit.'

ONE DAY I LOST MY TEMPER

Di: Tell me about Ridgmont.

Annabel: My first year was alright but in the second year I started getting suspended. I was mixing with the wrong crowd and I got into fights. In the third year there was a fight between me and another girl in the cookery class. The teacher was quite old and didn't really know what to do. She ran to get help from another teacher. Meantime I ran out and ran home and my mum said it was the last time I was going to go to that school. There was a meeting at school and it was all finalized. I got an Education Welfare Officer, Mrs Davies. She came round and asked me if I would like to go to Downend.

I liked Downend and started there in the fourth year. It was very friendly and there were some really nice teachers. But one day I lost my temper with this girl.

Di: What makes you lose your temper?

Annabel: I don't like people laughing at me. If something has happened at home little things will start me off. I hit this girl and she fell and hurt her head. I ran off but they came and got me. I was very angry because I felt this girl was a bully and had got what she deserved.

Di: How did the teachers react?

Annabel: They hated me. One called me a bitch and one called me a little slut. I used to argue with the teachers and they would send me out of the door, but I would come back in again and say you can't throw me out. So they got cross because I was interrupting their lesson.

I WANTED TO GO BACK TO AN ORDINARY SCHOOL

Di: Did you enjoy your lessons?

Annabel: Some of them. I was often naughty in some of my best lessons, I don't know why. I feel I was often blamed for things I never did. But I have done a lot of things wrong and my mum's got a stack of letters all about it.

I was suspended from Downend for fighting and my mum and dad were really cross with me. I wanted to go back because I did like that school. I was just left, there was no meeting, nothing. Then a few months later there was a meeting up at the Education Office. They didn't say very much. They put down boarding school and I cried my eyes out. I didn't want to go to boarding school, I wanted to go back to an ordinary school.

Di: Why was that?

Annabel: Because of my education. You don't get any exams anywhere else. I didn't want to stay away from home so I didn't want to go to boarding school. I'm not very brainy but I can get through. I knew I wouldn't have any friends either. I didn't want to come to this unit either because it was only for a few hours each day and I didn't know what I would do with myself for the rest of the day. I knew I'd been naughty and I knew I'd got to have a punishment. When I was at Ridgmont this unit used to be the 'dumbest' place you could go and so I used to worry about what people would think of me. I was told the unit was the only place I could go, so I decided to give it a try. I like it here, it's a nice small group and I get on with everyone. When I was in a big school I got into fights. I don't here and on my work experience I get on fine.

IF THEY WEREN'T SO MUCH OF A TEACHER ALL THE TIME

Di: You say you wanted to stay at Downend. How could life have been improved for you at Downend?

Annabel: There were some people who were worse than me at school and I couldn't believe that I could only be given two school chances. They said to me when I started at Downend: 'One incident here and that's it, you are out.' They did let me off one incident so I did deserve to be punished but not like that and not so hastily. There was no meeting and I was off school for six months. No one from school ever came to talk to us.

It's more practical here, they try to get you ready for the outside world. I've made a jumper here and a grey cord skirt. I couldn't have done that at Downend. I haven't written for ages. At other schools, like Downend, they think you are still kids.

Di: What should teachers do about fighting?

Annabel: I don't know really. You see fighting a lot. I don't think they should punish fighting as much as they do, certainly swearing at a teacher I think is worse.

Di: How should teachers punish you?

Annabel: I've known teachers hit people but they never hit me. I know they can't control themselves all of the time but I don't think a teacher should hit a pupil because the pupil is younger. They can tell you off but they mustn't keep on at you. My mum went up to school because a teacher there called me a bitch. My mum don't think a teacher should do that. I didn't take offence, but it's not like a teacher to do it. If they weren't so much of a teacher all the time, you know: 'sit down, do this, do that' but talked to you instead, it would be better.

Jason attended Greenways Comprehensive for four years but was unhappy from the beginning. He was finally expelled for fighting and a history of disruptive behaviour.

I WAS PICKED ON FOR MESSING ABOUT

Di: What did you do at Greenways?

Jason: History, English, geography, mathematics, French, classics. I was in the second to top group for English, maths and French but because I messed about I got sent down to the bottom set for all my subjects. It wasn't fair. The teachers didn't talk to us and if they did they talked to us like we were rubbish, or a stone statue. They weren't polite.

Di: Would you have liked to choose what subjects you did?

Jason: Yes, sort of, but you've got to do English and maths, then you could pick other subjects. But I didn't get on with the teachers. They used to pick on one person and I was picked on for messing about. I would talk and make fun of people and the teacher would send me out of the room.

Di: What do you think teachers should do when you are mucking about?

Jason: They used to tell you to shut up as soon as you started. It shouldn't be like that. It makes you worse and you leap out at them. They should say, 'Can you please be quiet.' Instead they just say, 'shut up.' They think they are high and mighty.

Di: Should teachers lose their temper?

Jason: Yes if they send you out of the room, but not if they hit you over the back of the head, or slap you round the face. That just makes you worse and you get up and hit them back. You think, I'm not going to let them push me around, so you hit back and then you get done for it.

Di: Why did you have to leave Greenways?

Jason: I was messing around and I'd get lines or a detention, then I wouldn't turn up for that. So I got in deeper and deeper trouble. Anything done in school was blamed on a few people; me and four others. We were taken to the headmaster's office for tippex sniffing, but I was expelled for fighting with another kid. It was dinner time and nothing really to do with the school. We all got marched into the hall and they found all these things about who was fighting. We just didn't like each other.

A FAIR FIGHT IS A FAIR FIGHT

Di: What should teachers do about fighting?

Jason: It's fair enough to let you get on with it, so long as one person isn't on the floor getting their head kicked in or something. A fair fight is a fair fight, and teachers shouldn't butt in. The two boys might just start on the teacher. If they caught you they just took you down to the headmaster's office and then you got a detention, which seemed pretty stupid. I got suspended twice for skiving off school once and messing about in lessons. I felt it was really stupid to get expelled for fighting and a few months later they had the cheek to ask me back and my dad just turned it down.

I stayed off school for 3–4 months and then I came here. It's been quite different here. They talk to you like adults and you've got a choice of what you want to do. I've done a lot of sport here, gone out with the head, and it's been fun.

Di: Were you sad when you left Greenways?

Jason: No, not really. I wanted to go in the first year anyway and I kept asking my mum and dad if I could leave and go to another school. Most of my friends went to a different school.

Di: What would have made Greenways better for you?

Jason: You should be able to talk in lessons providing you get on with a reasonable amount of work. The teachers expect too much of you, like four to five pages of writing and four sets of homework each night. In maths they would tell you a page that you had to do but you wouldn't know anything about it. So sometimes you couldn't do your homework and they wouldn't go through it with you. When I first came here you had a choice about whether you did your homework. I used to take maths and English home. The teachers talk to you like adults and treat you like adults. If you are angry you can say you will go outside until you calm down and the teacher can wait until the end of the lesson and then come and talk to you.

SHE STAYS CALM AND TALKS TO YOU LIKE AN ADULT

Di: Do you think the teachers here would like to teach in an ordinary school?

Jason: Maybe, they have more experience than other teachers. Kathy, if she was teaching an English lesson and a couple of kids were being disruptive, she would say, 'can you calm down, please'. Then wait until the end of the lesson and we would have a talk. Instead of shouting at you, she stays calm and talks to you like an adult. You get teachers who shout at you and you find you just stand there and don't listen to a word they say.

Di: Do you think teachers have a difficult job to do?

Jason: If it's impossible, if they feel it's too much of a strain they shouldn't be there in the first place. I wouldn't mind being a teacher but not in English, in sport or something. I go to this special school for sport and have fun with the teachers. If you swear you might get a slap around the face and one kid threw the ball and it hit the teacher in the face. So he got hit but it was his own fault. Those teachers are trained specially to deal with kids like us.

Di: Do you think teachers enjoy their work?

Jason: Some do, some don't. If they are bored they ought to get out of the profession because it just bores the kids too. Teachers might have arguments at home with their husband or wife but they bring it to school with them and take it out on the kids.

Di: But a teacher like anyone else has good days and bad days. If they are feeling in a really bad mood what should they do then?

Jason: They should be able to tell you. They are alright in the staffroom aren't they, drinking, and talking, smoking and laughing, but when they get into a lesson they change completely. If I don't like someone I tell them but teachers just hide it. If they don't like you they should tell you straight away, because you can always change class.

Di: What would you do if you were a teacher and someone was mucking about?

Jason: I'd ignore it and in the end the kid would probably calm down. I'd ask the kid to stay behind at the end of the lesson so we could talk. You need to treat them as adults. They had the cheek to suggest I saw a psychiatrist because I was messing about in lessons. There are loads of people all over the world who mess about in lessons.

Di: Why do kids mess around?

Jason: Because they think school is one big joke, they do it for a laugh.

Sean Smith and Theresa Connor

Sean and Theresa talk about life at their primary school in the centre of a small city. Theresa is ten and Sean is eight years old.

SHE WOULD BE BETTER WITH THE YOUNGER CHILDREN

Di: What happens when you're naughty in school?

Sean: Writing lines at playtime is really boring especially in Mr Martin's class because he only gives you lines, he hardly gives you any work. I think my teacher Miss Walters always picks on the same people, even if it isn't them. My teacher is sort of old and old-fashioned. I don't think she is very good and she is not suited to a class like ours, she would be better with the younger children.

Theresa: There is this boy Tom who has been picked on all through the school. He used to be really naughty in the infants and all the teachers knew about that. He calls out a lot, and my teacher picks on him. He is not really naughty, he just messes about a bit. Once a boy swore at the headmistress and he got suspended.

Sean: Sometimes you just have to stay in and put your hands on your head for a whole playtime, and I don't think that does you any good.

Di: Tell me why you have to stay in and put your hands on your head.

Sean: Because we've been very noisy.

Theresa: You don't always have to put your hands on your head but you have to sit still. Sometimes it's because the boys have been running in and out at playtime. My teacher is OK but if you haven't finished your work by playtime you have to stay in and finish it. It's usually just the boys because they mess about and talk too much, and walk around the classroom. Sometimes they get sent down to the infants to do infant work. When we were in the infants you got sent to the head if you were naughty and your name was put in this book and sometimes you got smacked.

Sean: There is this big enormous book and when you are sent to her your name is put in it.

Theresa: If your name is put in three times or more then a letter is sent to your parents.

Sean: We have monitors who are in the top class and they have to supervise the class at wet playtime and if anyone is naughty they have to write their name on the board. We usually rub the names off before anyone sees them.

Theresa: Some boys in our class have been told if their names go up on the board again they won't be able to go on our school trip.

BUT YOU MUSTN'T STEAL ANYWHERE

Di: Are there any rules in school about what you can and can't do?

Sean: You can't eat sweets in class.

Theresa: You can't go in certain places. You mustn't run down the corridors. You mustn't come in too many times at playtime, or go into the classroom.

Sean: Stealing. You mustn't steal.

Theresa: But you mustn't steal anywhere. The rules are in a big book and sometimes you have to write them out if you have been naughty, or she reads them out to us, but not very often.

Di: What sort of things do teachers dislike.

Sean: Being cheeky.

Theresa: Shouting out when she is in the middle of talking, or talking when she is talking. Not working enough and talking instead so sometimes we have to work in silence. But she can't really keep us quiet for long.

Sean: I think of Friday when Miss Walters was in a really bad mood, she made us all read in silence because we were being too loud. Also she had seen us running up and down the stairs earlier on.

I WISH WE COULD DO FOOTBALL...

Di: Tell me about the work you do at school and what you enjoy and what you dislike.

Theresa: Well I like art, and English is OK, and reading providing you have a good book to read. I don't like maths at the moment because we have been doing fractions for weeks and it was really boring. We do history with our headteacher and that is good. I'm doing a project at the moment on Florence Nightingale and we have to go to the library and look things up. We mess around a bit but it's good fun.

Sean: Art is OK, even though I'm not very good at it, it's better than doing work. Maths is OK when it's easy, maths and English is OK. But reading is good because I've got a good book. I like sport.

Theresa: So do I. But I wish we could do football, or cross country, or cricket.

Sean: Yes and the boys can't do netball. We are doing a project on space and about what it would be like to live on an island.

MISS WALTERS DOESN'T REALLY KNOW WHAT A JOKE IS

Theresa: My teacher is quite interesting. She talks to us about racism, and the nuclear bomb and Martin Luther King and South Africa, but she talks and talks.

Sean: Yes and they found out how many boy friends she had when she was little.

Di: What do you think makes a teacher good?

Theresa: Someone who does interesting work and doesn't pick on people and doesn't give you long lectures on how to behave. The teacher we have got now is good fun.

Sean: Someone who doesn't go on about things, gives you interesting work to do and gives you quite a lot of treats, like sweets. Miss Walters gives out sweets. At the end of each week you get team points. You can get them for good work and lose them for bad work. When our team wins you get two sweets each. In our class we have a shield and you can stick badges on it at the end of the week for good work and doing jobs.

Theresa: There is a new teacher who does lots of music and she hasn't got a sense of humour at all. She can't control us, if anyone talks she tells them to be quiet, and she is always threatening us. If another teacher walks by they usually have to come in and tell us off.

Sean: She needs other teachers to help her.

Theresa: But she's alright with her own class, I think.

Di: Do many of the teachers share a joke with you?

Theresa: Mine does if she is in a good mood, usually on a Friday afternoon.

Sean: Miss Walters doesn't really know what a joke is.

6   A burnt out case

Mike Vernon

Mike Vernon worked as a teacher for twenty years. In this chapter he talks of the period when, although teaching was something he had been good at and had enjoyed, he found he had simply had enough. The peculiar pressures of facing class after class meant that there was no respite from his difficulties and eventually he left teaching with an invalidity pension. He attributes his problems to the conflicts and stresses of the job and suggests his disaffection is shared by many.

It was a Thursday afternoon (in October 1984) and I was teaching a fairly bottom-heavy CSE group. I had a good relationship with them and they were behaving no better or worse than they had done before, but you know, there was a constant level of chatter, and one had to work very hard to keep their concentration. I had every confidence in them and I am sure they would have done reasonably well at the end of the course, but I remember thinking to myself 'you can't go on putting in this amount of effort, year after year'.

Earlier that afternoon I had taken the sixth form, one of the brightest and nicest I have ever known. They were very demanding and I enjoyed the lesson, but by the end of the day I was in a dreadful state, utterly exhausted. I was in the habit of marking books after tea, but on this occasion, I just fell into bed.

I awoke about nine o'clock sweating like a pig and trembling. I was in a panic about the marking and started getting the files out, but my wife, who is also a teacher, took one look at me and said 'you simply can't go on like this, it's bloody silly'. I think I made a conscious decision then, not to return to teaching.

The next morning I went to see my GP expecting him to be impatient as I had been to see him fairly frequently with trivial complaints, but he wasn't. He listened carefully and didn't seem at all surprised at what had happened. He suggested various forms of help: drugs, group therapy and so on, but I chose to talk to my friends and colleagues instead, backed up by weekly visits to him. I was dreadfully ill and disturbed for several weeks.

I suppose it was a nervous breakdown although nobody actually called it that. I used to sit in the chair for hours thinking about what had happened. Trying to find some justification for it, I suppose. Remember, I had been a responsible, caring teacher for twenty years and I think people saw me as a pleasant, genial sort of chap, not given to worrying overmuch. One thing that I found very hard to understand was that I wasn't at all concerned about the children. In one way it was a relief, but I felt guilty about it.

It was difficult to accept what had happened because it was just two weeks into the new autumn term, and as an NUT representative I had just been away on a week's residential training course following the long summer holiday. I felt pretty good when I returned, although there was the usual accumulation of marking and general backlog of work to deal with. Before the holidays things hadn't been too good.

I remember a woman colleague telling me that she thought I was very ill because I 'went over the top' in front of two officials from County Hall when she was told at very short notice that she was to be made redundant, although she was not in my union and my job was in no way threatened.

I think I have been very lucky in the close support I have had from colleagues. Many of them would like to do what I have done, because they are under stress, but for various reasons they are afraid to leave teaching. I have seen them work day in and day out, year after year with love, and yes, compassion, as the kids come up with one problem after another. It's like parenthood; you can't distance yourself if you are a really caring teacher and want to create a warm and receptive atmosphere.

There has been much debate lately about what teachers should and shouldn't be doing, and implicit in it is the suggestion that they should be in tune with the children, listening to them, and caring about their needs. Yet the way to survive in the present school situation is the reverse. Many teachers build great walls of defence around themselves, teaching subjects in a cold and formal way, year after year, and distancing themselves from the children. They 'survive' and one is tempted to admire them in an awful twisted sort of way. But the thought of becoming like them, brings you to your senses. There is no doubt at all that it is the caring teacher who is most vulnerable to stress.

The school I left was a very energetic and thrusting comprehensive, in which there were some hard-working and lively-minded individuals, but we had all been caught up in the comprehensive debate and long drawn-out sagas of reorganization and the battle to implement it and justify it to parents and others.

Although we eventually became fully comprehensive and developed a flourishing sixth form, we were then told to prepare for yet another policy change – the sixth form which we had built up was to be disbanded and the pupils were to attend a sixth form college. Not only were we to lose our brightest children, but we actually had to help with the plans for their removal.

I don't believe that people are generally aware of just how much effort, planning and organization goes into building up a sixth form. So many of the teachers behaved unselfishly over plans for the dispersal, but I know that it left them emotionally exhausted. All these things add up to stress, and in my own case I would add to it the unsympathetic remarks that some parents and others make such as 'well you have longer holidays than anyone else, and you only work from nine to four'. I remember one colleague who left the profession in a rather alarming manner, saying that the turning point for her was when she no longer found the summer break long enough to 're-charge' the batteries.

During the last eight years I know of ten teachers who either were admitted to hospital as a result of stress or went right out of the profession. Other people I know are still unsettled but hesitate to make their feelings known for fear of being thought inefficient and inadequate.

I can remember a visit from the English adviser, a great guy with whom I had an excellent relationship, and who I was usually delighted to welcome into the school, turning into something of a nightmare. For some reason I felt very threatened as he sat at the back of the room while I took a third year group who were being very noisy and bobbling around in the way that third years bobble.

I am not one who insists on an oppressive silence, but I don't work in a noisy environment either, and I knew that I needed to bring them to heel, but I simply couldn't do it with him in the room. It was ridiculous. I knew it then and I know it now. I remember thinking at the time: 'I never want to put myself in this situation again'.

I went through a period when I couldn't plan even the next day's work and when teachers were away I was incapable of providing work for their pupils or assisting the supply teachers. I'm sure I looked calm but inwardly I was screaming hysterically.

I was, in general, unable to cope with administration. When I had a free period I wasted it by pursuing trivia. I became worked up about a newsletter I had edited and in which nobody seemed interested. This again was ridiculous because many teachers pushed themselves to do extra-curricular activities which were rarely praised, or recognized, but at the time I minded.

The most useful thing which happened to me directly after leaving the school was a visit by two NUT officials. They didn't treat me like a screwball who had just done something unbelievable – walked out of a good secure job and plunged into chaos – but as one of very many teachers in the same situation.

They were not at all surprised at what had taken place, and immediately started to sketch out an application for a 'breakdown' pension. They informed me that it would be necessary to be examined by several doctors before my condition could be verified. It might be possible, they said, to go gracefully out of teaching with some money – if I was lucky.

I saw a variety of doctors: my own doctor, a local authority doctor and one from the DES before my condition was confirmed and I was declared 'unfit to teach'. It was a terribly difficult time. I used to come down and look on the mat every day hoping for a letter from the DES and worrying about what I was going to live on if I didn't get a pension. I knew that I couldn't have gone back to teaching even if they had said that I was well because I certainly didn't feel up to it. But there were days when I would have little 'highs' and I had no idea what impression I was making or what kind of assessment the doctors would make.

I had to hope that they would be skilled and understanding enough to recognize my true condition. They were, and in June 1985 I received a letter from the DES informing me that I had been awarded an invalidity pension of £4,200 based on my twenty years teaching. By a weird twist of fate twenty years is a very crucial landmark. They enhanced it to twenty-seven so that I get 27/40 of a full teaching pension, plus a lump sum.

Although I can't go back to teaching, I feel very fortunate and cushioned. I am no longer threatened like those caught up in the day-to-day battle, although even now I feel there is a danger in exposing myself, and that some people will consider me 'inefficient' because I dropped out.

I feel desperately angry that society and the Government don't understand what the present demands are doing to teachers. I want my children to go to a school where the teachers are fairly happy and ready to work and where they are not under exceptional stress and have the time and resources to do the job properly. I believe that a very large number of people around the country want this, too.

SECTION 2

Responding to trouble

7   Sorting them out: provision for young 'deviants'

Mel Lloyd-Smith

In this chapter Mel Lloyd-Smith provides an overview of the nature of provision for young people whose behaviour is seen as a source of conflict within and outside schools. He discusses provision variously administered by local education authorities, social services departments, health authorities and the Home Office. He details the changes in extent of provision and analyses the attitudes to deviance which provoke changes in the amount and form of placements.

Among society's foremost images of deviance, groups of young people have always featured prominently. In recent times there has been unprecedented concern and debate about the extent and explanation of deviant behaviour amongst the young, which in various manifestations, is said to be dramatically increasing. At one end of the scale, inner-city riots, violence at football grounds and drug abuse are currently high-profile social and political issues. A number of less dramatic, though nonetheless disturbing phenomena such as delinquency, solvent abuse, vandalism and classroom disruption likewise provide the stimulus for continuing debates about the reasons for these features of modern life and about the nature of the responses they call for.

Broadly speaking, it is possible to see two dichotomous standpoints on deviance among the young reflected in these debates. In one, to take the case of delinquency, for example, deviance is perceived as evidence of insufficiently effective mechanisms for enforcing law and order while in the other, it is seen as the result of social change and the creation of conditions such as urban deprivation and unemployment. Variations in the nature and severity of sentences imposed by the courts for particular types of offence reflect shifting stances on this issue. At times an emphasis on punishment and deterrence has led to calls for the 'short, sharp shock', while at other times the alternative perspective has encouraged responses in which treatment, re-socialisation and rehabilitation have been the overriding aims. Similarly, in the case of disruptive school pupils, differing interpretations of the meaning of this behaviour have led to different approaches to formal responses to it. Thus in the regimes of special units it is possible to discern differing emphases on the aims of care and control.

While beliefs about the reasons for deviance and the meaning of particular forms of deviant behaviour have fluctuated over the years, there has been a steady increase in the number and range of services catering for deviant young people. This trend is quite independent of the prevailing ideology – whether emphasising punishment rather than reform, control rather than care.

This fact raises the important question of whether it is possible that the expansion of provision for deviant youngsters has itself contributed to the increased incidence of deviance. Superficially, the expansion would seem to be a simple response to increased demand but there are two ways in which the reverse relationship might operate. Firstly, the very existence of a form of provision, coupled with increasing capacity, might discourage the use of alternative ways of dealing with a problem which may not have led to formal identification. Therefore, the statistics of deviance reflect a change in response to certain behaviour, not necessarily an increase in the incidence of such behaviour. Secondly, the facilities themselves may unintentionally constitute part of a socialization process which confirms and stengthens a young person's deviant identity and makes the further expression of deviance more, rather than less, likely.

In the light of theoretical possibilities such as these, Schur (1973) has developed a critique of traditional theories and policies relating to delinquency which leads him to advocate what he terms 'radical nonintervention' as a means of reducing the problem of delinquency. This requires a basic change in social values: less fear of youthful 'misconduct', greater concentration on socioeconomic reform and less on measures designed to force individuals to 'adjust' to alleged commonly accepted standards of behaviour. In practice it would mean that only in very extreme cases should young people be allowed to become enmeshed in the formal processes which make up the juvenile justice system.

Although this approach is so fundamentally divergent from traditional ones, it has been reflected in some recent changes of policy, particularly in the field of mental health and, to a lesser extent, in delinquency. A recognition of the damaging effects of institutionalization is seen in the increased provision of community care for the mentally ill, while various forms of community service have been introduced as alternatives to custodial sentences for offenders.

The extent of this trend has been greater in America than in the UK (see Bakal 1973) and Scull (1984) has subjected the policy, which he refers to as 'decarceration', to critical scrutiny. He concludes that in the case of the mentally ill, such policies are not necessarily more effective or even more humane than former institution-based ones and in the case of juvenile justice, the provision of community-based correction programmes can ironically lead to heightened, not reduced, control.

These conclusions should properly inspire a degree of scepticism when trying to assess the relative merits of different responses to deviance. It is an attitude which Topping (1983) also encourages having reviewed the literature evaluating a range of provision for disruptive adolescents. He argues that if the phenomenon of 'spontaneous remission' is taken into account, very few responses to disruptive behaviour can lay claim to spectacular success. Indeed some forms of intervention would seem to make matters worse and, in general, the more elaborate (and expensive) the intervention, the less effective it is likely to be.

When viewing the range of provision for young deviants, therefore, such reservations as these should be borne in mind and the constant debates about how to increase the effectiveness of the various regimes, should not be allowed to obscure the fundamental question about the unintended, negative consequences to which any form of intervention might lead.

LEA provision

In educational, as in other social contexts, labels abound. In institutions with explicit rule systems, processes exist by means of which transgressors of the rules become labelled and 'typed'. Hargreaves *et al* (1975) have illuminated such processes in the context of schools and classrooms.

A label may be a simple description based on observed behaviour, such as 'truant' or 'disruptive', or it may be a judgement inferred from observed behaviour, such as 'disaffected', 'disturbed' or 'maladjusted'. One purpose of labels is to give specific meaning to the behaviour, another is to ascribe membership to groups seen as requiring schooling in establishments separated from mainstream provision. The most common form of segregated provision for pupils categorized in terms of their deviant behaviour are special schools or units for maladjusted pupils and off-site units for disruptive pupils.

SPECIAL PROVISION FOR MALADJUSTED PUPILS

The concept of maladjustment is notoriously vague, criteria for allocation to this category are wide-ranging, theories about 'causes' and philosophies of treatment are likewise diverse (see Galloway and Goodwin 1979, Ford *et al* 1982, Laslett 1983). This, however, has not been an impediment to the development and expansion of provision for pupils so labelled.

The term was first brought into the vocabulary of statutory provision by the 1945 Regulations relating to the 1944 Education Act. During the Second World War, the phenomenon of the 'unbilletable evacuee' had helped to bring the problem of 'difficult' children to the fore and a new category for children who were seen as not well adjusted to their social environment was included in the new framework for 'special educational treatment'.

The statistics of maladjustment as reflected in the population of special schools reveal a remarkable rise from about 500 in 1950 to more than 13,000 in 1983; the sharpest increase came in the period from the mid-1960s to the mid-1970s when numbers increased by a factor of four.

Pupils are placed in these special schools following formal assessment and completion of a statement as required by the Education Act 1981. This procedure will usually involve documentation about disturbed and disturbing behaviour and in most cases will have been initiated by teachers in the mainstream school which the pupil has hitherto attended. Nevertheless, the pupils who arrive at special schools are a varied group and the neatness of forms can obscure an untidy process of negotiations and bargaining, conflict and the exercise of power. The majority of those in schools for maladjusted children are of secondary age, about three-quarters are boys and almost all come from working-class families.

The schools themselves are small, with an average of between forty and fifty pupils on roll, and have a high staff–pupil ratio, one teacher to 6 or 7 pupils, for instance. There are 89 day schools and 131 residential schools in England and Wales (1983 figures). Increasingly attendance at the latter is on the basis of two-weekly or weekly boarding.

It is difficult to generalize about the nature of the pupils' problems or about treatment approaches adopted in the schools. Despite many attempts to provide sophisticated analyses of the nature and manifestations of maladjustment, a simple typology persists in the literature: that of children experiencing either acute emotional disturbance or severe behavioural problems (or a combination of the two). Accordingly, appropriate treatment is often assumed to occupy a place on a continuum ranging from psychotherapy to behaviour modification. This, however, does not seem to be reflected in practice. A Schools' Council study carried out between 1975 and 1978 (Wilson and Evans 1980 and Dawson 1980) collected data from 114 special schools and found a clear agreement regarding the six most effective treatment approaches: warm, caring attitudes in adult–child relationships, improvement of self-image through success, firm consistent discipline, a varied and stimulating educational programme, continuity of child–adult relationships and individual counselling and discussion. Methods based on psychotherapy, group therapy and behaviour management were, in this sample of schools, low on the list of treatments used.

These features of 'treatment' are clearly echoed in the methods advocated for disruptive pupils which is not surprising since the only clear division between the two groups is administrative and legal. Whether a pupil is labelled maladjusted or disruptive and whether he or she is sent to a special school, a special unit or remains in a mainstream school can depend on arbitrary factors as Galloway (1985) points out.

OFF-SITE UNITS FOR DISRUPTIVE OR DISAFFECTED PUPILS

The 1970s saw the sudden advent of the special unit as the preferred solution to the problems posed by pupils whose attitudes and behaviour were regarded as unacceptable in schools. The proliferation of units, with their wide range of euphemistic titles, has been a striking development during the last decade. Since there has been no routine, centralized collection of statistics relating to this new category of pupil, it is difficult to obtain accurate figures. Some indication of the rapid growth, however, can be seen in the findings of a series of national surveys. In 1977 the DES obtained information from 69 local education authorities showing that there were then 239 units with a joint population of 3,962 pupils (DES 1978). In 1980 ACE published the results of its survey which indicated a unit population of 5,957 (ACE 1980). The Social Education Research Project (Ling and Davies 1984) provided data on off-site units in England and Wales indicating a population of about seven thousand pupils. The majority of unit pupils are in the final two years of compulsory schooling, boys outnumber girls by three to two.

As the numbers of pupils referred to special units continue to rise, it is becoming evident that this new form of provision has not had the benign influence on behaviour in schools which many had hoped for. It has not, for example, reduced the use of the sanction of suspension even where units have been set up with this specific intention (Lloyd-Smith *et al* 1985). Such indications as this, together with evidence of the lack of effectiveness of units (Topping *op cit*) and arguments in favour of strengthening internal school structures to accommodate and deal with disruptiveness (Steed 1985), are leading to a change of emphasis. There are signs that many local authorities are now seeking to develop strategies for dealing with problem pupils, which do not rely on removal to an off-site unit (Lloyd-Smith *op cit*, Coulby and Harper 1985).

Court sanctions

The minimum age of criminal responsibility in England and Wales is 10 years and the juvenile justice system makes a distinction between 'children,' aged 10–14, and 'young persons', age 14–17. The courts have a number of sanctions at their disposal: there are various non-custodial orders, including absolute discharge, conditional discharge, fines and deferred sentences, as well as custodial sentences which are principally detention centre orders and youth custody centre orders. Other sanctions include the requirement to spend time at an attendance centre, the supervision order, which may involve attendance at an intermediate treatment centre, and the care order which may entail removal to a foster home or community home.

The tension between care and control referred to earlier can be clearly seen in the operation of this system. In 1969 a new Children and Young Persons Act was introduced with decriminalization as one of its intentions. It shifted the emphasis in juvenile courts from criminal to care proceedings, it introduced a greater stress on prevention measures and opened the way for the greater use of community-based measures for young offenders. The Act was, however, received with suspicion, it was criticized as being 'too soft' and some of its key provisions have never been implemented. In the courts, its effect on the sentencing policy of the magistracy was the opposite of that intended by its sponsors. The number of custodial sentences meted out in the 1970s and 1980s has risen more sharply than the number of offences. The preventive aspects have led to increasing numbers of younger children being identified as 'at risk' and subsequently drawn into the control mechanisms of the juvenile justice system.

The backlash against the ostensibly liberal and reformist features of the 1969 Act, found strong expression in the most recent piece of legislation relating to young offenders, the Criminal Justice Act 1982. Although this encouraged the use of non-custodial sentences and, incidentally – like much recent educational legislation – emphasized parental responsibility, the Act also shortened the length of custodial sentences. The purpose of this was to make more places available in the overcrowded detention centres and borstals, (which the Act renamed youth custody centres). The overall effect of the latter measure, however, is to encourage the greater use of these shorter custodial sentences which will inevitably provide reduced scope for rehabilitation work and Muncie (1984) predicts that 'the 1980s are likely to see more working-class young people having a "taste" of custody, as welfarism recedes and state authoritarianism becomes more strident' (p. 155).

ATTENDANCE CENTRES

Among the non-custodial sanctions representing the trend for community-based and preventive measures, the network of attendance centres has expanded in recent years. In 1984 there were 127 altogether, 109 junior centres for 10–16 year olds and eighteen senior centres for 17–20 year olds. An attendance centre order can only be made in respect of an offender who has not previously served a custodial sentence. It specifies a number of hours, usually twelve to fourteen, which have to be spent in a series of Saturday afternoon sessions consisting typically of physical education followed by recreational activities. The centres are run by police officers in their own time who attempt to 'strike a balance between the punitive and rehabilitation objectives of the attendance centre order' (Home Office 1984a, p. 55).

INTERMEDIATE TREATMENT

Intermediate Treatment came into existence as a result of the Children and Young Persons' Act 1969, providing a court sanction which was 'intermediate' between supervision at home and custody. The term 'treatment' implied the aim of improvement rather than punishment though the validity of the concept of treatment in relation to what is actually carried out has been questioned (McCabe and Treitel 1983). Intermediate Treatment (IT) is often included as a condition in a supervision order, in which case the duration of attendance is determined by the court, generally on the advice of a social worker. It will usually last for the equivalent of thirty days; the time in some cases may involve attendance in out of school hours, while in others day-time attendance is required.

Many young people are referred by agencies other than the courts: by schools, educational welfare officers, the police, the probation service. In many cases, school-related problems feature as important reasons for referral. Kenny (1981) found in a survey of IT centres in the London Boroughs that underachievement, non-attendance and behaviour problems were commonly cited criteria. The increasing use of these centres as an alternative to mainstream schooling has been noted and they have been criticized for their limited educational programmes and for the possible effect they have of drawing attention away from fundamental problems in schools (Beresford and Croft 1981 and 1982).

Intermediate Treatment centres are in the main run by Social Services Departments and the form the 'treatment' takes can vary greatly from one centre to another. While it may incorporate trips to pursue activities of the outward-bound type, it is essentially community-based, the main emphasis being on 'constructive activity' and preventive work with young people who are seen as being 'at risk'.

COMMUNITY HOMES

In 1982 there were 93,200 children in England and Wales who were in the care of a local authority, which represents one in every 133 young people below the age of eighteen. About 35,000 were in some form of residential home, though the current trend is for the greater use of 'boarding out' with foster parents as an alternative to institutional placement.

The majority of children in residential care are in community homes which were created following the Children and Young Persons' Act 1969, replacing the old 'approved school' system. Most receive their education in ordinary schools but those considered to need care and control throughout twenty-four hours will attend a 'community home with education on the premises' (CHE). The respective populations of CHs and CHEs in 1982 were 16,700 and 4,500. Despite the direct descent of community homes from the pre-1930s juvenile reformatories, via 'approved schools', only a minority of their combined population is admitted as a result of criminal proceedings: less than 10 per cent in the case of CHs and 50 per cent in CHEs. As Muncie (1984) indicates, it is evident that there are problems in determining suitable aims and regimes for the mixed occupants of these institutions and the House of Commons Social Services Committee in a recent report (1984) say that CHEs 'still seem uneasily poised between their essentially punitive past and their supposedly therapeutic future' (p. lxxxvii).

The more disturbed and disturbing children in residential care are likely to be found in the CHEs. An HMI survey of fifteen boys' and six girls' CHEs (DES 1980) found a high incidence of health and behaviour problems, emotional disturbance and violent and disruptive behaviour; almost all were said to be underachievers. The most common age of entry was between fourteen and fifteen years and the lengths of stay were from 10½ months to 2 years for girls and from 14 months to 2 years 11 months for boys. It was reported that return to ordinary school was rare, schools being reluctant to re-admit pupils.

OBSERVATION AND ASSESSMENT CENTRES

O and A centres were also set up in response to the 1969 Act. Their purpose was to provide a means of carrying out a multiprofessional assessment of juvenile offenders, prior to making a decision about placement. The centres are also used for non-offenders for whom a place of safety order has been made (for a maximum of twenty-eight days). Though the intention was that attendance at these centres was to be short-term, many young people remain for longer than the period required for assessment. It has been suggested that in practice O and A centres have become dumping grounds for young offenders regarded as unacceptable by other institutions (Taylor *et al* 1979). A major government report has recently commented on these centres and their 4,500 occupants, remarking that 'Observation and Assessment Centres are in a sense the waiting-rooms of care: too often they have become the sidings' (House of Commons Social Services Committee 1983–4, p. lxxxvi).

DETENTION CENTRES

Detention centres for young male offenders were first introduced in 1948; they are part of the Home Office Prison Department provision and cater for either 14–16 year olds (junior detention centres) or 17–20 years olds (senior detention centres). A detention centre order can be made by the courts for a minimum of three weeks and a maximum of four months. The total number of receptions in the year ending 30 June 1984 was 11,790 and the average length of sentence was ten or eleven weeks. A recent report (Home Office 1984b) shows that of inmates in JDCs, 20 per cent had no previous convictions, the figure for SCDs being 10 per cent. Burglary and theft are the most common offences leading to conviction, motor vehicle offences coming next. About half of JDC trainees had previously been in local authority residential care and a similar proportion of SDC inmates were unemployed prior to committal.

The regime is intended to be a punitive one, incorporating the notion of the 'short, sharp shock' and reflecting aspects of military training: drill, parades and physical education, as well as outdoor work. The percentages of DC inmates who are reconvicted within two years of release are 72 per cent of 14–16 year olds and 59 per cent of 17–20 year olds (Home Office 1985). In an attempt to enhance the ability of this sentence to deter young offenders, the Home Office introduced an experimental tougher regime at two centres in 1980 and evaluated its effect on the reconviction rate (Home Office 1984b). Despite the fact that this showed the new 'rigorous and demanding' regime to be no more of a deterrent than the old one, nor to have any appreciable influence on the conduct of inmates, it has now been decided to introduce it generally throughout the DC system. It is characterized by more parades and inspections, more physical education with the emphasis on effort rather than skill and reduced privileges and association.

YOUTH CUSTODY CENTRES

The youth custody order for young offenders between the ages of fifteen and twenty was introduced following the 1982 Criminal Justice Act to replace the former sentence of 'borstal training'. This had been an indeterminate sentence (six months to two years), where trainees had earned their release by progressing through a series of grades. Under the new arrangement, the sentence length is fixed by the court within the range of four months to one year.

There are 33 youth custody centres, 9 'open' and 20 'closed' establishments for males and two of each type for young female offenders. The average population in 1984 was 7,534 boys and 217 girls, the number of receptions during that year being 11,305 and 844, respectively (Home Office 1985).

Among the effects of the new sentencing structure has been an increase in the numbers sent to these centres, 41 per cent more in 1982 than the previous year's male borstal admissions, and a reduction in the numbers of young offenders sentenced to detention centre (a drop of 16 per cent between 1982 and 1984). The average lengths of sentences in youth custody centres in 1983–84 is shown below; the first column gives the average length of sentence (to the nearest month), while the second shows the average lengths of time served, taking remission into account:

	Age range	Average length of sentence in months	Average length of time served in months
males	15–16	8	5
	17–20	12	8
females	15–16	5½	3½
	17–20	6	4

It remains to be seen whether these shorter periods of incarceration will have any effect on the reconviction rate. The percentages of those discharged from borstals in 1981 who were reconvicted within two years were 80 per cent of 15–16 year old males, 65 per cent of 17–20 year olds and 45 per cent of all females. Anticipating the shorter sentences, the Prison Department Report of 1981 (Home Office 1982) described the new regimes as having a strong educational and training ethos based on modular courses in which stress would be laid on social and life skills. One of the sacrifices will be the former emphasis in borstals on vocational preparation which was the means for many trainees of taking public examinations and gaining certificates such as those of the City and Guilds Institute.

SECURE ACCOMMODATION AND YOUTH TREATMENT CENTRES

Among the children and young people in residential care or in custody following conviction there are some (approximately five hundred) who are regarded as being so disturbed or disruptive that the normal forms of residential provision are considered inadequate or unsuitable. Those who are severely emotionally disturbed, who exhibit extreme anti-social behaviour, who repeatedly abscond or who are thought to be a danger to themselves or others are likely to be admitted into 'secure accommodation'. This is provided in certain local authority social services establishments: selected community homes with education for longer-term placements and some observation and assessment centres for shorter periods. In 1984 there were 364 approved secure places, on 31 March 241 were occupied (by 196 boys and 45 girls) (House of Commons 1985–6). The majority of inmates (70 per cent) had been in for less than three months but approximately 12 per cent had been there for a period between six and twelve months.

In addition to these units, there are four 'youth treatment centres' administered by the DHSS. These establishments, the first of which was opened in 1971, are for the long-term care and treatment of boys and girls between 12 and 19 who are severely disturbed or who have committed grave crimes.

Serious concern has been expressed about the growth of secure accommodation in its various forms. A DHSS research report in 1979 pointed out that there was no evidence of an increase in disturbed or violent behaviour among children in care and no evidence that secure units were effective in reducing such behaviour (Cawson and Martell 1979, Muncie 1984). Despite this, despite allegations that their use may sometimes infringe children's rights (Children's Legal Centre 1982) and despite the extemely high cost of such provision, as much as £1,200 per inmate per week in a youth treatment centre (House of Commons 1985–6), the creation of more places is currently being planned.

Conclusions

The development of this diverse system for disposing of young people who attract labels of deviance is striking for the extent of its growth in recent decades. There are many social factors, structural and cultural, which might account for this but it seems clear that although the incidence of certain forms of deviance may have increased, the capacity of the social control institutions has grown at a faster rate in a seemingly ineluctable trend. Attempts to reverse this and divert deviants into less stigmatizing and more constructive forms of treatment and training have so far made little real impact. The rhetoric of prevention has not reduced the numbers of young people coming within the ambit of welfare and justice agencies, the system has merely expanded to accommodate new clients (those 'at risk'), who then have an increased likelihood of promotion in a deviant career. The rhetoric of care has not succeeded in decriminalizing juvenile offenders, the new strategies have been only grudgingly used for recipients of the traditional measures. And these measures have continued to emphasize punishment and deterrence despite evidence of the failure of these aims. The rhetoric of 'special' provision for disaffected pupils has sometimes been a thinly disguised justification for ridding schools of their most troublesome pupils.

There has been constant agonizing and argument about the various programmes and institutions provided by society for its young deviants and the debate has principally been concerned with issues such as working philosophies, types of regime, duration of intervention, location and resourcing. The pursuit of these surface issues can easily cause us to overlook a fundamental truth, the implications of which are seldom explicitly recognized. Each of these forms of social control, however justified or necessary – whether punitive or caring, custodial or community-based, segregated or integrated, preventive or deterrent, long-term or short-term – constitutes a stage within a deviant career. It can never be an alternative to such a career and rarely an escape route from one.

References

Advisory centre for education 1980. Disruptive units – ACE survey, *Where*, 58, 6–7.

Bakal, Y. (ed.), 1973. *Closing correctional institutions*, Lexington, Lexington Books.

Beresford, P. and Croft, S. 1981. 'Intermediate treatment, special education and the personalisation of urban problems', in Swann, W. (ed.) *The practice of special education*, Oxford, Blackwell.

Beresford, P. and Croft, S. 1982. *Intermediate treatment: radical alternative, palliative or extension of social control?* London, Battersea Community Action.

Cawson, P. and Martell, M. 1979. *Children referred to closed units*, DHSS Research Report No. 5, London, HMSO.

Children's Legal Centre 1982. *Locked up in care*, London, Children's Legal Centre.

Coulby, D. and Harper, T. 1985. *Preventing classroom disruption*, London, Croom Helm.

Dawson, R. 1980. *Special provision for disturbed pupils: a survey*, London, Macmillan.

Department of Education and Science 1978. *Behavioural units: a Survey of Special Units for Pupils with Behavioural Problems*, London, HMSO.

Department of Education and Science 1980. *Community homes with education*, London, HMSO.

Ford, J., Mongon, D. and Whelan, M. 1982. *Special education and social control*, London, Routledge & Kegan Paul.

Galloway, D. 1985. *Schools, pupils and special educational needs*, London, Croom Helm.

Galloway, D. and Goodwin, C. 1979. *Educating slow-learning and maladjusted children: integration or segregation?* London, Longman.

Hargreaves, D. H., Hester, S. K. and Mellow, F. J. 1975. *Deviance in classrooms*, London, Routledge & Kegan Paul.

Home Office 1982. *Report of the prison department 1981*, London, HMSO.

Home Office 1984a. *Report of Her Majesty's chief inspector of constabulary*, London, HMSO.

Home Office 1984b. *Tougher regimes in detention centres*, London, HMSO.

Home Office 1985. *Prison statistics: England and Wales 1984*, London, HMSO.

House of Commons 1985–6. *Social services for children in England and Wales 1982–1984*, HC90, London, HMSO.

House of Commons Social Services Committee 1983–4. *Children in care Vol. I*, London, HMSO.

Kenny, D. 1981. *Intermediate treatment: review of policies and practices in the London Boroughs*, London, GLC Central Policy Unit.

Laslett, R. 1983. *Changing perceptions of maladjusted children 1945–1981*, Portishead, Association of Workers with Maladjusted Children.

Ling, R. and Davies, G. 1984. *A survey of off-site units in England and Wales*, Birmingham, City of Birmingham Polytechnic.

Lloyd-Smith, M., West, J. and Richmond, J. 1985. *A Review of suspension and guidance units in Birmingham*, University of Warwick.

Muncie, J. 1984. *The trouble with kids today*, London, Hutchinson.

McCabe, S. and Treitel P. 1983. *Juvenile justice in the UK: comparison and suggestions for change*, London, New Approaches to Juvenile Crime.

Schur, E. 1973. *Radical non-intervention – rethinking the delinquency problem*, Englewood Cliffs, Prentice-Hall.

Scull, A. 1984. *Decarceration – community treatment and the deviant*, (2nd edn), Cambridge, Polity Press.

Steed, D. 1985. 'Disruptive pupils, disruptive schools: Which is the chicken? Which is the egg?', *Education Research*, 27, 1, 3–8

Taylor, L., Lacey, R. and Bracken, D. 1979. *In whose best interests? The unjust treatment of children in courts and institutions*, London, Cobden Trust/MIND.

Topping, K. 1983. *Educational Systems for disruptive adolescents*, London, Croom Helm.

Wilson, M. and Evans, M. 1980. *Education of disturbed pupils*, London, Methuen.

8 Cutting adrift or building bridges? The role of LEA suspension procedures
Rod Ling

In this chapter Rod Ling reports on his investigation of suspension procedures in Wallington Local Education Authority. He was concerned, in particular, with the experiences of pupils who ended up in that authority's off-site units. In the course of their movement from school to unit these pupils commonly attended a suspension panel established by the LEA to confirm or otherwise deal with suspensions from schools. Such panels, operating in august municipal surroundings, seemed alien to parents and pupils who only had dim recollections of what they were for. Rod Ling argues for this system to be replaced by another based within schools that is preventative in intent rather than judicial and punitive.

Not all disruptive pupils, as any teacher will confirm, are attending special units nor are all those in such units suspended from their schools. Nevertheless the phenomena of special units and suspension are indissolubly linked in many local authorities either because units were established to cater for these pupils when other schools proved reluctant to take them on or because an early referral to such a setting was intended to obviate the need for suspension by modifying behaviour and remediating learning difficulties.

In Wallington suspended pupils are likely to be found in each of the thirteen units established by the Education and Social Services departments sometimes with the assistance of voluntary agencies. Three of these have however been designed to cater exclusively for suspended pupils who are nearly always in their final year of compulsory schooling. In the course of the last two years, in a qualitative study of the practice of some of these units I have informally interviewed a large number of suspended pupils. I have also had the opportunity to examine the, often voluminous, documentation that accompanies them on their transfer from one institution to another. On the basis of this data it is possible to make a number of qualified statements about the nature of suspension procedures in Wallington but which might also be expected to have, to a greater or lesser degree, wider currency and application.

The majority of suspended pupils do not in fact attend special units and thus no claim is made for the 'representativeness' of those interviewed. Most suspended pupils are transferred to other schools with the assistance of the LEA officer with responsibility for placement. Moreover because the majority of suspensions occur within the last twelve months of compulsory schooling and because recommendation and placement procedures often take months to operate, a number of pupils are 'lost' from the processes for long enough to make energetic efforts on the part of the LEA unlikely. The LEA must tread a delicate path between its legal responsibility to provide continuous schooling and the reluctance of schools to accept difficult pupils who in turn, perhaps together with their parents, may well be antipathetic to the efforts being made on their behalf. It is my contention that some of this pupil (and parental) antipathy may well have been generated by the operation of the procedures employed and directed by the LEA and it is to an outline of these procedures that we must now turn.

Suspension procedures in Wallington

In recent years, as the number of suspensions has grown, many LEAs have reviewed their procedures in this area. This process of 'tightening up' may well have contributed to a further increase in that schools which previously preferred to avoid the use of formal measures are now required to employ them (Grunsell 1980).

In Wallington the most recent review was in 1980 and all schools were informed of the steps to be taken by the school, the governing body and the LEA in the event of suspension. The procedures also outline the grounds upon which suspension should be based and the measures schools might be expected to have taken before resorting to this 'final solution'.

Considerable variation exists across the country in the usage of the terms suspension, exclusion and expulsion. In this authority the term suspension is employed to include both those who are temporarily removed from school and those for whom return is extremely unlikely. In fact in the procedural guidelines the latter group is defined out of existence through the implication that suspension is always an emergency measure and of a temporary nature.

Now it may well be the case that headteachers do employ suspension most frequently as a means of ensuring that a 'cooling off' period elapses before the pupil's return to school. Its use in this way also emphasizes the seriousness of the offending behaviour in the school's view and brings pressure to bear on otherwise reluctant parents to visit the school. However, permanent suspension as we have seen is not an infrequent occurrence and in everyday usage the distinction between these forms of suspension are denoted by the addition of the adjective 'temporary' or 'full'.

When a school moves to fully suspend a pupil it marks the end of a process that may well have been lengthy and complex. Schools employ a variety of strategies (see, for example, Bird *et al* 1981) to manage the behaviour of disaffected pupils and they are unlikely to suspend before these strategies have been exhausted. Undoubtedly it is the case that some headteachers will suspend far more frequently and more swiftly than others but no head is likely to do so without careful consideration. This is because this action is recognized as having potentially serious implications not simply for the pupil and his or her parent but also for the head and the LEA charged with the responsibility of providing an alternative placement. Thus once the decision has been taken by the senior staff they are thereby stating their unwillingness to work any further with the pupil and as such will expect their decision to be endorsed.

Those involved in the endorsement or confirmation process are firstly the chairman of the governing or managing body and secondly the LEA through the deliberations of the Standing Suspension Panel.

THE STANDING SUSPENSION PANEL

The support of the chairman of the governing body, given the practice if not the theory of their role in relation to schools, is usually beyond doubt. Similarly, the suspension panel is equally unlikely to fail to confirm the suspension but this stage in the procedures is one that headteachers must approach in a prepared manner. It should be noted at this point that although the meeting of the panel is understood to involve the ratification or confirmation of the school's decision to suspend this is not acknowledged in the documentation. Under the Articles of Government for Secondary Schools and Rules of Management for Primary Schools (made in compliance with Section 17 of the 1944 Education Act) this local authority has no legal authority to lift suspension and return a pupil to school. Nevertheless, headteachers do submit themselves to the deliberations of this body and must therefore take due care to marshall the kind of argument that will leave the panel with little option but to confirm their decision.

The panel must be convened and meet within three weeks of the Chief Education Officer receiving notification of the suspension (which in turn should be within twenty-four hours of the act). The panel comprises the chairman of the governing body or his/her alternate and a representative of the Education Committee to act as chairperson. The latter are selected from a small number of councillors and co-opted members nominated by other members of the Education Committee.

Others obliged to attend the meeting are the headteacher and the CEO or their representatives. In Wallington the latter representative is usually a liaison officer appointed to oversee the placement of 'marginal' pupils. Where other agencies have been involved their representatives will also be invited to attend in an advisory capacity or to submit a written report.

In the procedural guidelines the function of the panel is to determine either the date at which the suspension will be terminated by the pupil's return to school 'subject to any conditions agreed by the Head and the authority' or the recommendation of an alternative placement. The latter represents confirmation and amongst the options open to the panel in its recommendations are the transfer to another orthodox school, to a special school, to a special unit or to the Home Teaching Service.

PUPIL PERSPECTIVES

The outline of the procedures given above represents the 'bare bones', the skeleton, on which the experiences of the participants are fashioned. The skeleton gives this body of experience its basic form and stature but tells us little of its meaning and emotional impact for the pupils and their parents.

Pupils' recall of the manner in which they approached the meeting varies. Some claimed to be indifferent, some hostile and others nervous. Almost invariably however they were and are confused as to the meaning of suspension. Amongst pupils and their parents the term 'expelled' is preferred in that it better expresses the force and finality of the removal of a pupil from school.

Almost all those pupils who could recollect their visit to the Education Offices for the panel meeting (and a few found this difficult) were very unclear as to its stated purpose. Most suspended pupils and often their parents do not understand local government structures and their impression is one of confronting an undifferentiated authority inimical to their interests. None of the pupils I spoke to shared the view that one of the major functions of the meeting was to review the details of the case and come to a conclusion that met not only the wishes of the school but also the educational needs of the child.

The most common analogy made by the pupils in recounting the events is of the resemblance borne by the meeting to a court of law. Some pupils have already had direct experience as a basis for comparison while others might have framed their accounts in the light of subsequent events. Whatever the case the force of the analogy remains:

> It was up town . . . that place . . . big it was and like being in a court. The bloke was like the judge, sitting there. There was lots of people. I only knowed two of them; my social worker and Smith (headteacher). I spent most of the time outside waiting for them. They asked me if I liked small schools better than big ones. I said 'yes'.

Pupils can often identify the features they feel are designed to impress and intimidate; the wait while the headteacher 'fixes' the panel, the imposing array of self-assured and articulate adults whose differing roles might be explained but are seldom comprehended and the municipal grandeur of the building and its furnishings. The rooms used for these meetings are large with ornately moulded ceilings, marble fire surrounds and panelled walls decorated with the portraits of civic dignitaries. The following pupil was particularly struck by the arrangement of the polished tables,

> We had to wait in this long hall for them . . . me and mum . . . dad wouldn't come. When we went in there was all these long shiny tables put together . . . huge they was . . . (turning to a friend) must have been four or five of them! They wanted to know if I felt like going back to Greystones (the pupil's school). I told them I wasn't going back there.

Inevitably, then, whatever might be said about the concern of the panel with the pupil's educational needs and welfare the fact that they and their parents feel themselves to be on trial (one particularly distressed mother referred in a letter to a 'kangaroo court') means that they often behave in ways that only serve to confirm the intractable nature of the problem as described by the school. When pupils are invited by the panel chairman to put 'their side of the story' it is unsurprising if they respond in a surly and unco-operative manner: 'I didn't say nothing to them; not to that stuck up old pig'.

One girl I spoke to told me of how she had a fit of giggles, an outstandingly inappropriate piece of behaviour:

> It was so embarrassing . . . and when I get embarrassed I start laughing, I can't help it. They kept asking me what was so funny, why I was laughing.

Interestingly, the judicial nature of the panel meeting has been recognized in Wallington by the development within the Educational Welfare Service of an advocacy role on behalf of the pupil and parents. A senior Educational Social Worker presents a Social Enquiry Report to the panel (unless another agency is better placed to do this) and generally adopts a supportive role for the family. There are however real limitations to this approach. Firstly the Educational

Social Worker does not have the school's lengthy first-hand experience of the way the pupil behaves in school. Secondly they do not have the same status as the senior school staff and they are well aware of the necessity to ensure that, as a service, they continue to enjoy the goodwill of headteachers. In so far as this move within the authority has resulted in the kind of more open contestation that the term 'advocacy' implies, some headteachers, active in their associations, have begun to question the undoubtedly shaky assumptions upon which the panel meetings are founded. One concerned headteacher has categorically stated that: 'A suspension is a suspension is a suspension'.

HEADTEACHER PERSPECTIVES AND THE SUSPENDED PUPILS' REPORTS

The most influential person in the deliberations of the Standing Suspension Panel is the headteacher. It is upon his or her account that the panel must depend for an understanding of the nature of the problem before them. This account will have already been submitted to them in the form of a report outlining the pupil's educational record, relationships with teachers and peers, home circumstances and, in most detail, the behavioural patterns that have brought about the suspension.

It is my intention here to consider these reports in the light of the function for which they must be seen as being primarily employed: the persuading of the panel members of the justification of suspension. This is not to say that such reports do not contain objective information nor that the accounts of pupil behaviour have been deliberately distorted. This is no more the case than the equally absurd assertion that there is no such thing as problem behaviour or that certain children do not exhibit such behaviour more frequently and severely than others. Nevertheless, it is to say that reports must first be viewed in the social context in which they arise and have creative meaning; that is the public and legally bounded arena in which local authority sanctions are imposed upon parents and their children.

In this light the report forms reveal that there are fundamentally two distinct and separate organizing principles upon which a case for suspension might be founded. These principles might usefully be conceived as ideal types, conceptually distinct but often interwoven in individual accounts.

The first of these and that most frequently employed, particularly in the last few years, may be termed the 'camel's back' principle. Here the intention is to demonstrate that the disruptive and problematic behaviour of the pupil has a long and complex history. Exhaustive efforts are shown to have been made, usually through the imposition of sanctions, although reference may also be made to other pastoral measures such as counselling, for instance. Occasionally, schools present some of the apparent contradictions between these disciplinary and welfare approaches in quite stark terms. One form recorded:

> Pupil seen by head and counselled. Boy reported that there were domestic problems. Counselled and told to avoid bringing his feelings into school.

Another report listed no less than seventeen separate incidents each of which had resulted in the boy being caned:

This list shows only the major offences for which Paul was punished. Many hours have also been spent in counselling Paul – especially since he joined the upper school.

Reports of this kind stress the long-standing and irremediable nature of the child's behaviour. Very often they consist of lists of incidents and the actions taken by the staff. The incidents themselves may not be regarded as particularly serious in their own right (they most frequently stem from matters of dress, smoking, writing graffiti, 'cutting lessons') but when presented in a tabulated and condensed form testify to the persistent nature of the problem. It is not unusual to read of between twenty and thirty such incidents and on a few notable occasions of more than fifty.

In presenting material in this way the school must be viewed as acknowledging the point expressed in the LEA procedural guidelines that behavioural difficulties do not develop 'overnight'. Suspension in these cases is justified because the school has struggled over a considerable period of time to remediate the problems. It has issued ultimatums and final warnings, exhausted its range of sanctions and limited resources of time, energy and expertise (and those of hard-pressed support agencies). The school is, in effect, claiming that the time has now come for the LEA to place the pupil in a different setting preferably one where new skills and techniques can be brought to bear.

If the school is to present the case for suspension on these grounds then the staff must begin the process of compiling a 'suspendable profile' at an early stage. Indeed some lists of incidents go back to the pupil's first year of secondary school. It is possible, however, for schools to reconstruct a record of misbehaviour from the recall of staff and some report forms exhibit evidence of this. The following example describes not simply the recall of events but the redefinition of behaviour which at the time was not thought to be disruptive but which, in retrospect might lend support to a suspension. A girl who had adopted a 'punk style' was found to be responsible for some 'obscene writing on the toilet walls'.

> Subsequent conversation with the staff revealed that whilst individually they felt no need to complain of Geraldine's behaviour in class, collectively they recognized, with hindsight, that she had been quietly simmering on the edge of a verbal outburst for some time – this they had 'read' as being very reserved and slightly defensive.

Most report forms that adopt the 'camel's back' approach however do so by reference to pre-existing records. This raises the possibility, and I would put it no stronger, that suspension might arise at the point when senior staff feel they have an 'open and shut' case rather than when they feel unable to manage or respond to a pupil's misbehaviour. This may also mean that where schools are concerned about a group of pupils, and some reports specifically refer to peer group influences, they may not always move to suspend the major source of disruption. Instead they may decide to remove the pupil against whom they have the strongest case (or who might be expected to present the weakest defence).

The second organizing principle employed by headteachers in the presentation of documentary accounts is that which might be termed the 'outrage' approach. In such cases the task confronting the school is to convey the extreme nature of the pupil behaviour. Great emphasis is usually placed upon a single incident and it is recounted in terms that may be expected to elicit instant opprobrium. Often the persuasive power of these accounts is confirmed by the fact that no other detail is felt to be worthy of inclusion apart from the barest information required by the proforma.

Cases of 'outrage' often involve the touchstone of teacher attitudes, pupil violence towards a member of staff. Occasionally they may involve an assault on another pupil, most frequently of a sexual nature. Incidents of this kind may well be additionally described by accounts from those members of staff who witnessed or were the subject of the attack. Once again it is necessary to point out that I am not suggesting such assaults do not take place nor that they are unimportant. Rather it is my claim that the necessity for headteachers to enlist the support of the LEA in moving for a suspension means that they are induced to present the case in a manner that readily connects with the 'commonsense' sympathies of the panel members. As a result the suspension of the pupil is often accompanied by the suspension of critical judgement on the part of those who are almost certainly in the best position to assess the pupil's needs.

In seeking to communicate the requisite sense of extremity and abnormality of behaviour (or the sense on the part of the staff of powerlessness and exhaustion) measured descriptive analysis is replaced by a retreat to stereotypical portrayals and the emotive language of terms like 'beserk', 'villainous' and 'incurable'.

It would be possible to give a number of examples where teachers have, no doubt unconsciously, obscured their understanding of a pupil's emotional and educational needs in favour of a lack of it. At this point two such examples will suffice. The first concerns a dramatic account by a headmistress of the way in which a boy loses self-control whilst in her office. The boy believes (mistakenly) that she is writing a letter of protest to his father and physically seeks to prevent her from doing so. The headmistress is undoubtedly intimidated by his behaviour:

> I went towards the entrance and George came towards me. He was shouting and screaming at the top of his voice and hitting out wildly.

The extraordinary feature of this account is the fact that at no point is any reference made to the nature of the boy's relationship with his father. From my conversations with this pupil after he had been suspended and went on to attend a special unit (where he was considered to be a good example to his peers, presenting no behavioural problems and attending regularly) it was clear that this subject, of obvious emotional significance, received no consideration whatsoever.

The second example is perhaps even more revealing in that it involves the suspension of a pupil from one of the city's special units for children in the lower secondary school age range who, usually, have not been suspended and are expected to return to their original schools in due course. The staff in this unit adopt a very positive and welfare-oriented approach to their pupils but even in this setting felt unable to cater for a boy prone to violent outbursts. The incidents in which this boy was involved are described in terms that reveal little of the understanding they might have been expected to have gained. Instead the necessity to seek confirmation of suspension results in a portrayal which stresses the insolubility of the 'problem' and the need to refer onto another setting.

It is on these occasions when a personal knowledge of the teachers and pupils involved can be set alongside the Suspended Pupil Reports that the persuasive function of these accounts becomes apparent. Information which on one level appears to promote insight may in fact subtly (or not so subtly) be designed to do the reverse, to close down and channel interpretation in a specific direction that serves the immediate needs of the staff and obscures, in so doing, those of the pupil. Other glimpses of an 'alternative reality' may be provided by heads who candidly concede that an apparently extreme case of pupil disruptiveness was badly handled by the member of staff involved. Nevertheless the headteacher may feel confident of gaining the endorsement of the panel on the grounds that the matter has become a contentious issue amongst the staff. Headteachers it would appear may quite reasonably anticipate confirmation on the grounds that good staff relations are in jeopardy. Even comments which in another context might convey an entirely different meaning can be presented in 'objective' and neutral terms yet at the same time rendered problematic. Consider for instance the following sentence within the context of a Suspended Pupils Report: 'He is of West Indian background. His mother is religious and there are religious messages on the wall'.

The inducement that headteachers are under to communicate the intractability and abnormality of the presenting behaviour helps, I believe, to explain the phenomenon that is often referred to in special school or unit settings. This is the disparity those working in these institutions observe between the documentation concerning the pupil and their direct experience of him or her. This is not to say that teachers and social workers in these settings reject these accounts (though some may well be inclined to do so) but rather that they seek to resolve the contradiction in other ways, perhaps in a comparison of structural differences between the sites which has resulted in behavioural change.

Conclusion

In summary, I would suggest that little is gained by pupils or teachers in the way suspension procedures are currently organized. In effect these arrangements serve the purely administrative ends of ensuring an apparently orderly exit of pupils from school. Headteachers are encouraged by these procedures to adopt stylized modes of presenting accounts which might be expected to secure the endorsement of a supposedly independent body established to safeguard the rights of all parties. The reality is of course that the standing suspension panel invariably serves to rubber stamp decisions taken in school whilst at the same time bestowing on them a new legitimacy. In submitting themselves to the panel's authority the schools are induced to obscure the often extensive understanding they may have gained of the pupil's educational and emotional needs. In these circumstances the panel's references to these needs must be seen as little more than a rhetorical device aimed at engendering compliance and masking the real purpose of the meeting. This is the censuring of the pupil and the parents and a demonstration of the authority that gives this censure its force and meaning.

It might be argued that these procedures do at least inhibit the premature recourse to suspension and provide a final opportunity to challenge an unsubstantiated case. Even if we overlook the fact that this assertion remains unproven it still raises the question of whether this restraint serves the educational needs of the child. Moreover on the two occasions I have come across, over a four-year period, where the headteacher was denied confirmation and the pupil returned to school both were subsequently resuspended. Once a pupil has lost the confidence of the senior school staff a return to school can be little more than a pyrrhic victory. Most parents recognize this and although an appeals procedure does exist for those who feel unfairly treated (and it is not my claim that all do) it is seldom used.

Finally, I would make three points. The first of these would be to assert that a case has been made for Wallington Education Authority and others to consider ways and means of examining the operation of suspension procedures both within and without the school. Any such investigation would best be undertaken by an independent organization.

The second point is that the recommendations of the Taylor Report should be carried out by all LEAs in that the terms *exclusion, suspension* and *expulsion* should be clearly defined and this information made routinely known to parents. In Wallington the term *exclusion* does not appear to be employed at all and the rights of schools to expulsion denied. As a result both the temporary and the permanent removal of pupils from school are described by 'suspension'; a state of affairs which not only serves to confuse but also does violence to the English language.

My third point is that although it is the procedures within one LEA that have been the subject of this paper what is really at stake here are the tensions and contradictions between the responses to deviance that are based upon the notions of 'welfare' and 'justice' and these are common to all parts of the country. It is my contention that in Wallington the justice model comes into play at an early stage although it is disguised by the rhetoric of welfare. Our response however should not be to do away with the rhetoric and provide the pupil with a a defence counsel. If we genuinely believe in welfare, pastoral care and the concept of educational need then we must devise procedures that enable teachers and others to express and then act upon rather than withhold the insights and understanding they have acquired, often painfully and at the cost of much time and effort.

This does not mean retreating to a woolly and open-ended relationship with an ever increasing tolerance of disruptive behaviour. It does mean however making the school rather than the education department offices the site where both pre- and post-suspension procedures can operate. Whilst recognizing that not all suspensions can be prevented, prevention must remain the primary aim. To this end much might be gained by employing a genuinely effective governing body in the bringing together of support agencies, parents and teachers before an irrevocable decision has been taken. Such a role was conceived by the Taylor Committee for governing bodies but their current practice is a pale shadow of that prescription.

References

Bird C., Chessum R., Furlong J., Johnson D. 1981. *Disaffected Pupils,* A report to the Department of Education and Science by the Educational Studies Unit, Brunel University, London, Brunel University.

Grunsell, R. 1980. *Beyond control? Schools and suspension,* London, Writers and Readers in association with Chameleon Books.

9 Teaching the unteachable: teacher strategies in disruptive units

Rod Ling

In this chapter Rod Ling describes two off-site units for 'disruptive' pupils, the Victoria and Delphi centres. He concentrates on the attitudes and personalities of the headteachers. In a centre of twenty or so pupils with three or four teaching staff, heads have tremendous influence even where, as at the Victoria Centre, they espouse democratic principles. The atmosphere and approaches within the two places may appear quite different at first. The Victoria Unit is concerned to reintegrate pupils whilst the head of the Delphi Centre rarely sees this as his aim. However they have much in common. Both start from an acceptance that it is the pupils within their care who have to be changed and the organization of both emphasizes the superior physical strength of male staff. In the report of the macho-methods of staff one is left wondering about the position of women teachers and girl students within these units.

Look Graham no-one objects to you having problems – so long as you're prepared to talk about them!

(Owen, Head of the Victoria Centre)

We get curious pride, you know, working with these kids . . . it's rather like the kind of pride and fascination you get when you persuade a wild animal to eat from your hand . . . a curious feeling.

(Roger, Head of the Delphi Centre)

Introduction

In this redeveloped wedge of the inner city, monotonous tower blocks dominate the skyline and encircle a cluster of public and commercial buildings: the shops, pub, community centre and local primary schools. The latter, built of brick and glass in the functional and unelaborate manner of the early 1970s, were originally planned to occupy adjacent premises but the numbers of infant children were such that another larger building was needed which now stands a few hundred, wind-swept, yards away. The original, redundant infant school comprising two flat-roofed, one-storey blocks subsequently became the home of the city's first disruptive pupils' unit, the Delphi Centre.

Approaching these buildings one begins to notice the signs of wear and tear; the cracked window, peeling paintwork and doors in which the original toughened glass panels have been replaced by more serviceable ones of sturdy plywood. Inside one of the two classrooms in the 'teaching' block, we may see twenty or so young people seated behind individual formica-topped tables. About half these pupils are black and more than a third are girls. They are of different ages and wear a variety of clothing. There is no noise. On the tables lie opened books, magazines, and, in one or two cases, comics. One pupil, sitting in the coveted position alongside the radiator, is gazing through the window and into the distance. The majority however are reading. At a desk by the window the head of the Delphi unit is seated, surveying the classroom.

At the same time, on the other side of the city centre, but still within the inner zone where industry and housing are entangled, other pupils are attending another special unit. The buildings occupied by the Victoria Centre are more typical of special units and have a much longer history. Built in the revivalist Gothic style, popular in the Victorian period as a Board school, they are located on a rise in the manner of the medieval churches the architecture celebrates. Overlooking the railway line, the new dual carriageway that runs alongside it and the surrounding housing development these buildings look even more dishevelled and uncared for than the Delphi Centre. The many tall ogival windows provide the classrooms with a great deal of light but they have proved more difficult to protect. A number of them are patched with squares of the ubiquitous plywood which is also employed to board up the now empty, adjoining, caretaker's house.

Inside the building the atmosphere is more inviting. Pupils are to be found in a number of rooms and there is more noise here. Some children are chatting across the desks whilst working unsupervised in their project folders, a few others are constructing a 'trolley' and making table-tennis bats in the craft room and another group is involved in another classroom in a range of art activities. In the office, some girls have engaged the secretary in conversation. A boy with pool cue in hand is hoping that his presence in the games room will not be noted by the staff.

Scenes such as these may be witnessed in many of the special units for disruptive and disaffected pupils which have been established in the last ten years. There are now more than four hundred off-site units (Ling and Davies 1984) and an unknown, but probably similar, number of on-site units i.e. located on the campus of an orthodox school. Not all of these off-site units are administered and funded exclusively by LEAs although this is so in the majority of cases. In addition referral procedures and working methods exhibit considerable variation. Taken as a group, however, their expansion, in a period of considerable financial difficulty, indicates the 'success' of their operation and, by extension, the 'failure' of popular schooling.

This success raises some important questions. Given the long-standing behavioural problems that the pupils attending these sites have set the teaching staff in schools, how is it that they can be brought together in a seemingly improbable admixture with the results, orderly and controlled, as described above? When each pupil's deviant career embraces many hours of chastising, cajoling and counselling, how do unit teachers succeed in teaching the unteachable? What skills and strategies do they employ and what, if any, are the implications for schools?

It is the purpose of this paper to explore these questions through a detailed examination of the two units to which we have already been introduced. Both units, catering for a similar age-group and facing similar pressures and demands are part of a sizeable unit provision established by education and social services departments in one large urban authority.

Special units do not have the extended hierarchies of schools, the majority having no more than three or four teaching staff and a secretary. A high degree of social and ideological cohesion is made both necessary and possible if the staff are to work closely together. It is this feature that makes the identification of a 'collective strategy' largely shaped by two strong-minded headteachers possible.

Owen and Roger, the two heads of centre, have developed their respective strategies in response to the broadly similar sets of expectations and demands that confront them. I shall argue however that in attempting to satisfy these demands, with all their inherent contradictions, each employs a distinctly different strategy. This comparative analysis is assisted by the fact that although their individual biographies are different, both are motivated by a similar ambition – they wish to secure a position of deputy headteacher in one of the city's comprehensive schools.

Owen and the Victoria Centre

Owen is in his middle thirties and his working background is in education. Over ten years ago he was teaching in a school, that was to become one of the LEA's first comprehensives. Even then his interests lay with the disadvantaged groups. He was active in the fields of multiracial education, pastoral care and curriculum innovation for the 'ROSLA' pupils. After a period teaching abroad he returned to the UK and worked in one of the city's newly opened centres for suspended pupils. Three years later he became the Head of the Victoria Centre.

For Owen the resolution of the conflicting pressures and the demands made of him and the unit staff takes place through an education philosophy that reconciles the interests of the child, the school and the LEA. Such a resolution emphasizes an egalitarian and humanistic view of society and the place of schools within it. Its main contention is that there is no irrevocable conflict of interest between the different parties. Disruption in school is epiphenomenal and dysfunctional. The interests of the child reside in obtaining the best possible education, something that only regular attendance at school can bestow. Certificates are one outcome of schooling and will enable the pupil to compete effectively in the labour market. If children approached schooling in this manner schools would have no wish to 'lose' their pupils, the throughflow of children with genuine adjustment problems in units would be assured and the 'moral order' re-established. A child-centred philosophy which for many free schools in an earlier period, was part of the justification for an alternative educational provision has been transformed. Units, in some ways the descendants of the free schools (Francis 1979, MacBeath 1977), are not seen as alternatives to schools but as supplementary. A child-centred approach has become pupil-centred; the interests of the child, particularly the working-class child, are seen as being compatible with and not antagonistic to, those of the school.

This approach does not reduce to a simple acceptance that the child or the family are deficient and in need of 'treatment.' Schools cannot escape criticism. Many are considered to be ineffective and contribute to the problems of disruptive and disaffected behaviour – but for unstructured and individualized reasons – an uncaring and insensitive teacher here, an inappropriate and irrelevant syllabus there. Owen, significantly, makes repeated reference to the work of those who insist that 'schools do make a difference'. For Owen therefore there is no 'philosophical' objection to the goal of returning a pupil to school in the manner that the LEA is eager to encourage:

> School is where these kids should be. If they are not going to fit into school then they must be placed somewhere more suitable. It makes no sense for them to stay here; that's been tried and it didn't do them any good in the long run.

It is only within the context of this 'world view' that particular features of the Victoria Centre and the attribution of meaning given to them can be understood.

PROCEDURES AND PROCESSES AT THE VICTORIA UNIT

The emphasis upon the consensual nature of school and pupil interests which is symbolized by Owen's adherence to the 'return goal' can create real difficulties for staff–pupil relations within the unit. It means that pupils must both want to come to the unit and eventually, to leave it. Engineering this balance of aspirations is inherently difficult. The former is usually approached by the promotion of close personal relationships, but such relationships may be threatened by an insistence that the placement is temporary. In order to ensure that pupils who have come to enjoy the advantages of the unit do not deliberately fail on a return to school, Owen refuses to readmit them once reintroduction has taken place. Such pupils may then be left outside the school system for a considerable period of time, perhaps indefinitely. This may be distressing not only to the child and his or her parents but also to the unit staff who have got to know the pupil well.

In order to reduce the possibility of failure of this kind, with all its implications for staff and staff–pupil relations, Owen seeks to systematize and formalize the process of referral. He stresses the importance of establishing rules and procedures that will govern unit–school relations. Data is collected with a view to determining which 'kind' of pupil 'succeeds' and which does not. This data is incorporated in publicizing of the unit and its work; in articles, meetings with other professional groups and in a display on the wall of the head's office-cum-staffroom where it is often referred to in the course of interviews with parents and pupils.

> *Owen:* Well Kevin, we are trying, and we'll be working with your parents on this, to get you back to school and up onto that list up there ... see ... that's a list of those who've returned to school. It won't happen until you've done a term here but it will be within the year.

Referring schools are expected to assist in the collation of information by providing a case history, attending meetings and co-operating in assessments (using the Bristol Social Adjustment Guide and the Rutter Scale). This information is supplemented by reports requested from the Education Welfare Service and Schools Psychological Service. Pupil files contain these records together with the brief notes recorded daily by the staff, copies of termly reports, and completed conduct forms which accompany the pupils when they commence a programme of phased re-entry to school.

The collation of this information and its subsequent analysis is seen to be central to the procedures within the unit. In referral meetings attended by all the staff, an educational psychologist, and an education social worker, decisions on particular cases are taken according to a broad consensus which operated around two major and related considerations. The first of these concern a judgement as to the likelihood of the pupil returning to school which in turn is seen to be crucially influenced both by the nature of the pupil's case history and the record of the school in re-admitting pupils. The second entails a projection as to how the pupil will behave in the unit but this is often obliquely expressed and reworked in terms of the first. The 'ideal' pupil is one who is thought to require a period of adjustment coming from a school which has expressed a willingness to take the pupil back.

It is of interest to note that in seeking to systematize referral procedures Owen has begun to undermine the principle of flexibility which was one of the advantages such provision was thought to have over special schools. One senior teacher in a referring school has bluntly informed Owen that if he continues to insist upon the adherence to detailed procedures and referral criteria 'they will be forced to lie.' Though he is aware that there is another, more commonly accepted, way of working Owen is reluctant to compromise

> Some people do this I know; they say 'if you take this one then we'll help you out over another' – deals in other words. I couldn't do that.

Another feature which brings us closer to the issue of the control of pupils within the unit is the 'unit contract'. This arrangement comprises a documented exchange of obligations between the unit staff and the pupil. It is signed by all the parties present at the pupil's initial interview. Whilst the pupil agrees to be polite, attend punctually, behave considerately and ask for permission before leaving the premises the staff agree to provide specific curricular inputs requested by the pupil and to secure a place for him or her back in an orthodox school. Establishing this agreement with its quasi-legal status does not, of course, spare the staff the continual difficulties of maintaining control. Its significance is symbolic; it represents a tangible token of the consensual nature governing the pupil's attendance and in so doing attempts to counter the punitive and coercive meaning which accompanies referral.

These elements are also present in other features and an important one concerns the operation of what Owen terms 'participatory democracy'. Group meetings are a regular daily event. Staff and pupils are usually seated in a circle in the games room. The meetings are often prolonged, ungoverned by the timetable and the bell, ending when the staff feel it to be appropriate. An obvious and important feature of these meetings is the way in which Owen makes the personal and the private, public, and a subject for general discussion. Individual pupils are praised for their achievements and transgressors have their sins exposed.

This is not to say that staff do not seek to ensure that an apparently open exchange concludes with the 'correct' decision. On one occasion the group were being asked about their thoughts on the question of how pupils who disrupt lessons by walking out should be disciplined.

> *Owen:* When George, or you Robert... or you Carol walks out and slams the door that means the teacher has to give up time they could be giving to the others in the class, the ones who need the help. Now how do you think they should pay back the time wasted?
> *Several:* Detention, give 'em detention.
> *Chris* (member of staff): No, not detention.
> *Owen:* Not detention.

[After some conversation and the usual smattering of frivolous suggestions, one pupil interjects]

Steven: Stay in at break.

Owen: That's what we were thinking, not detention ... but why should the people who misbehave have the nice things here like pool and table tennis?

[After further comment Owen sums up]

Owen: It's agreed then people who misbehave and cause the teacher to waste time must pay it back at break.

This notion of 'paying back time' is yet another example of the way in which the pupil–teacher relationship is couched in moral terms, on this occasion in the language of 'consumer ethics'. This leads the staff into some contortions since logic would suggest that those who 'consume' more than their fair share of 'teacher time' should lose some in the future rather than take up still more as the monitoring of the punishment will entail.

The purpose of group meetings is not just the demonstration of those aspects of 'negotiation' and 'making the private public' that have already been referred to. They also function as a focus for the generation of collective values and a group identity which is considered desirable given the fragmented and impermanent nature of pupil attendance. This desire is also reflected in the encouragement given to pupils to undertake group projects, perhaps in making a display, organizing fund-raising events or planning for an excursion or residential experience. Lunch periods are also intended to be a group activity. All pupils and staff are encouraged to eat together around a U-shaped arrangement of tables.

An additional feature of the unit's organization is the administration of a Behaviour Modification or 'points' system. This can be viewed as a fairly powerful mechanism for exerting control over a number, if not all pupils, in a situation where few sanctions exist. In fact, because the pupils have exhausted the range of sanctions available to a school, new and additional ones can only be created by the granting of rewards and privileges. The removal of these then constitutes a sanction. In this sense the privileges and goods that pupils can 'purchase' with the points they earn provide for an effective degree of control. Rhetorically the points system is also designed to reinforce specific identified behaviours that will be 'learnt' and carried over into other (school) situations.

A further feature, implicit in much that has already been said, is the emphasis given by the staff to 'openness' and 'accessibility.' Owen operates what he terms an 'open door' policy that permits pupils access to the staff at all times. Moreover he welcomes the involvement of other agencies in the work of the unit. These and others; schoolteachers, students, the police, media, and even researchers, are welcome, if only, 'to show kids that there are other adults besides teachers around the place prepared to talk with and listen to them'.

THE USE BY STAFF OF PHYSICAL CONTACT

Chris and Owen often indulge in brief physical exchanges apparently designed to communicate acceptance and friendliness and thereby reinforce the consensual nature of social control. These exchanges may take the form of 'mock fighting' in which a clear set of rules may be said to operate. Firstly the teacher must 'win' or at the very least not 'lose' in a manner that would result in a loss of face. No real violence may be done, intentionally, to either party and as accidental injury may cause the definition of the situation to change quite radically, it must be avoided. These encounters are for this reason accompanied by a great deal of laughing, smiling and verbal exchanges. This continuous flow of information may be seen as maintaining the equilibrium in a situation which entails considerable risks, particularly for the teacher.

The secretary at the Victoria Centre in conversation with staff referred to this behaviour as 'joshing' and when questioned confirmed both its frequency and importance, 'Oh yes, they like it – especially the black kids'. Female staff are less likely (though not unknown) to adopt such approaches largely it is assumed, because they have less confidence in their ability to control a potentially hazardous interaction. In this context it is of interest to note that male staff in the city's special units often have sporting interests and a significant number are former PE teachers. Not only then do they come from a professional sub-culture which permits and often encourages a range of physical contact (quite apart from the obvious sporting activity, PE departments in schools often administer their own disciplinary code) but they also have the physical self-confidence to undertake the risks that are present in these encounters.

Physical contact of a different yet similar nature is also entailed in the sporting activity at the Victoria Centre known as 'murderball'. The onset of this 'game' is often triggered by instances of behaviour during the lengthy lunch break which is likely to be seen as 'boisterous' and 'high spirits'. The object of this activity is for one side to carry a 'ball' from one end of the assembly hall to the other. The opposition's task is simple – to prevent this and attempt to 'score' their own 'goals'. Both sides are permitted considerable licence to achieve their aims and in the ensuing melee, where there is little prospect of administering rules, many old scores are settled.

The effect of this activity is cathartic. In an environment where considerable emphasis is placed upon the regulation of behaviour by reference to a moral code the playing of murderball is an anarchic act. Underlying it however is the demonstration by the staff of their superior physical strength. Pupils and staff meet in direct physical confrontation. Pupils may well score goals but the staff assert their strength and in addition their willingness, given the shared knowledge of the event's unusual nature, to indulge in unteacherlike behaviour.

In summary, the use of physical contact in the Victoria Centre, the organization of the daily cycle of activities, the regulation of the pupil's unit career and the attribution of meaning to these events demonstrate continuities which are also evident in the educational philosophy which Owen articulates. The underlying connection reflects an adherence to a moral solution to the configuration of demands which he and the staff must confront. In asserting the common interests of schools, pupils, LEA and parents, Owen does not of course escape the consequences of the inherent tensions and contradictions. In many respects the adoption of this approach increases the problems of containment and control and thereby demands a greater degree of commitment. The 'high profile' that this gives Owen provides the satisfaction that he requires and in addition holds out the prospect of career advancement.

Roger and the Delphi Centre

Within the Delphi Centre, although it is possible to identify the employment by Roger of a distinctive strategy for resolving the demands that are made of him, it is radically different from that of Owen and the Victoria Centre. This alternative strategy is in many respects less coherent than Owen's and it is this which helps to explain the fact that Roger's approach is often misunderstood by those outside the unit. He is seen by colleagues in special units including Owen, as reluctant to pursue the 'return to school goal'. He is considered, partly as a result of this, to be particularly child-centred, willing to keep pupils for longer because he is unwilling to make the potentially painful decision to insist that a child should leave an environment to which he or she has grown accustomed. 'They love him' says Owen ruefully, 'but it's very short sighted.' On this issue Owen and Roger have come into open conflict but, although the observation that Roger lacks commitment to the aim of returning pupils to school is a correct one, the implications drawn from it are not.

Roger's background, unlike Owen's has been in social services establishments. Prior to his appointment as head of the Delphi Centre he taught for a number of years in an Observation and Assessment Centre. Roger sees himself and the unit not as child but as school-centred:

> Only after we have helped the schools are we child-centred. If we can do things for the kids then that's fine, a bonus, but otherwise we are trying to help the system, to respond to what it wants of us.

It is Roger's belief that the cause of a substantial amount of disruptive behaviour is due to the size and impersonal nature of many schools. The solution to this situation revolves around a celebration of 'variety' which contains an element that is hostile to the principle of comprehensive education and considers it ill-conceived.

> There should be a variety of schools. Too often they are forced into being the same. There should be schools of different sizes with different disciplinary procedures; not all children respond to the same approach . . . and even different kinds of curriculum. This would cater for the variety of children that exist.

The argument is extended to the work of the units themselves each of which is felt 'to have its own strengths' and which, at a time when some pressure was being exerted by the LEA, should be permitted to retain its distinctive and separate character. Roger has little interest in the development of a local association for those working in education and social services units. He and his staff rarely attend their meetings which he tends to view as an extension of the interests and personalities of those to which he is, to some degree at least, in opposition. This would include not only Owen but the education officer responsible for the administration of the units. Roger does not share the commitment to a 'return to school' or the educational philosophy on which it is founded.

PROCEDURES AND PROCESSES AT THE DELPHI CENTRE

The processes entailed in referral and admission are less accessible at the Delphi Centre because they tend to be concentrated in the hands of Roger himself;

decisions are often made instantaneously, without consultation and frequently in the course of a telephone conversation. More emphasis must therefore be placed upon Roger's explanation of events.

A feature closely related to the celebration of variety referred to above is Roger's scepticism towards any attempt to systematize the operation of the unit. The identification and espousal of appropriate regulations and procedures is considered to be an illusory goal. It is more important in his view to give unit staff the freedom to respond to the particular circumstances that exist with each pupil. Allied to this is the tendency to work closely with those schools which share this unstructured and flexible approach to referrals.

> We work with kids from schools which treat us properly. I've taken someone this afternoon from Highdown just until the half term when they should go to a special school. Some schools abuse us and once a kid's in, they leave them here – but if I think a school understands us then I'll fit in with them.

For the Delphi as with the Victoria Centre it is important that schools recognize their needs but for Roger this is based upon a mutuality of interest which is unimpeded by the operation of specific criteria. When pupils return to school from the Delphi unit it is because the pupils themselves wish to (in Roger's words 'the problem solves itself') or because the staff are anxious to 'relieve the pressure' in the unit rather than as part of a scheduled policy of reintegration.

The pragmatic nature of this relationship with referred heads is exemplified by the absence of almost any interest in the collation of information about the pupils attending the centre. None is required of schools and only the barest details are maintained on the files:

> We don't believe in keeping information. I tell the kids that they start afresh here. I don't wish to know what has gone wrong in school.

In the almost total absence of information there can be no interest in systematizing procedures in the manner of the Victoria Centre. Similarly other features such as the Behaviour Modification System are considered to be of little value. Roger has also dismissed the use of 'contracts': 'As if you can hope to put relationships down on paper'.

In interviewing pupils and parents Roger is not constrained by the need to ensure that 'acceptance' of a place is conditional upon a future wish to leave. The formal and contractual element between the staff and the pupil is not present; conditions are laid down, but verbally and not on paper. In an interview attended by a newly referred pupil, his parents and the head and year tutor of the referring school Roger was blunt and uncompromising:

> We aren't a unit that believes in giving kids a lot of freedom. They have to follow school routines, can't swear, smoke, or call the staff by their first names and we will use physical means of punishment if we have to, if they're naughty. If they are verbally aggressive to staff they will be dumped unceremoniously in this room. If you don't want me to touch your child then I would not take him.
>
> I should say as well that we are mostly concerned with behaviour here, not academic progress. You must realize that we cannot provide all the subjects when they are all at different stages.

There is no attempt to persuade the pupil that his perception of the experience of schooling is in need of readjustment, only his behaviour.

At the Delphi Centre pupils are told that whatever happens they will never be suspended (except in the case of persistent truancy). The impression given to those outside the unit is that the staff are prepared to tolerate misdemeanours that others would not. The reality is different. In effect the staff, in making this statement, are erecting a 'fence' around the unit which excludes those agencies that might otherwise expect to be involved. There was very little evidence at the Delphi Centre of the involvement of the Education Welfare Service or Schools Psychological Service. The events within the unit are privatized, pupils and staff must be left to establish their own solutions to problems.

> I want my staff to sort out their own difficulties with the kids. Jean Gray (the former head) ran this place like a headmistress. If the teachers had a problem they sent them to her. I won't do that. I won't have staff justifying themselves to me.

This approach means that the task of establishing and maintaining control takes on a different form at the Delphi Centre; the deliberate employment of 'control periods'. Two examples can be given of this.

Lunchtimes at the Victoria Centre are intended to be a communal affair but at the Delphi Centre they are strikingly different. In Roger's words, lunch provides an opportunity in the middle of the day to exercise control over all the pupils in one group. The partaking of the meal is compulsory. Pupils are seated in groups of up to four around a number of evenly spaced tables. Silence is established before the meal is served, the staff patrolling the perimeter of the room, affecting indifference as to how long the pupils continue to talk. Compliance to the often unspoken demand for silence is eventually forthcoming, though the dignity of the pupils necessitates that this is not given immediately.

When Roger feels that the group is sufficiently quiet he will ask for someone to say 'Grace'. This brief ritual has little or no religious significance. It is a symbolic episode echoing the experience of the primary school (an experience which is generally thought to have been more successful and with which all units make connections; most notably in the organization of an 'academic' morning and an 'activities' afternoon). The pupil who says 'Grace' earns for his or her table the privilege of being first in the queue. I asked one pupil if he ever said Grace. He replied, 'sometimes, yeah, if it's fish for dinner'.

The staff have no illusions as to the secular nature of the 'trade' being made here. When the meal is over Roger once again insists upon a 'satisfactory' degree of silence before pupils are dismissed. Compliance on this occasion is advanced by the pupils' desire to enjoy the recreational facilities, most importantly the 'pool' and table tennis.

A further example of the use of 'control periods' is the 'reading lesson'. With all pupils gathered together in one room always with Roger supervising, at the end of the day, control is enforced in a highly visible and audible manner. At the same time Roger demonstrates his unique position in relation to the other staff, a distinction that Owen with his emphasis upon 'staff democracy' attempts, with only limited success, to blur:

> I really don't mind if they're not reading. Graham spent a lot of time staring out of the window – did you see him? – but it was very quiet. It's good to end the day like

this – they often don't get the opportunity to experience this at home. It might be thought of as repressive but they actually enjoy it.

I asked Roger how he managed to establish this kind of control, to reproduce with twenty or more disruptive pupils the semblance of a 'model' lesson.

It was difficult at first. In my first six weeks here I had lots of battles – taking on the bigger ones. But when that was won it was much better. I now occasionally have to look fierce but generally it's fine. The other kids will warn the one who is going too far.

At the Delphi Centre there is no equivalent of the group meeting. Problems are individualized or even suppressed rather than openly explored with all the possible difficulties that this entails.

Race is a real problem amongst the girls at the moment – not with the boys, they are active and have to mix, but with the girls. We try to keep it under the surface but it's definitely become much more of a problem.

Pupils are encouraged to establish their own personal accommodation with each other, the staff and particularly with Roger who will play the major role in the decision-making process. Rules and procedures would interfere with this approach but even in their absence an appeal may be made by pupils to a wider understanding of a moral order. In one conversation Roger was accused of favouritism in the placing of some girls back in school. This pupil went on to criticize him for his lack of 'fairness'. 'Fairness' said Roger, 'doesn't come into it, it's a question of what is best for you'.

That 'fairness doesn't come into it' is of considerable significance for Roger. His view is that pupils at Delphi are 'naughty but normal'. Sometimes pupils react to insensitive or even boorish and bullying behaviour on the part of some teachers, but this has to be accepted by the child. His definition of a Delphi Centre pupil is:

One that can't cope with the fact that some teachers are pretty hopeless. Others see this and they do cope, but keep their heads down.

THE USE BY STAFF OF PHYSICAL CONTACT

Reference has already been made to the preparedness of the staff at the Delphi Centre to use overt forms of control both in terms of language and physical contact. Many such incidents are of a consensual nature as is illustrated in the following example.

In one of the morning's brief, structured lessons the pupils were told to draw a still life composed of cups, a tea pot and a coffee pot. During the lesson the male member of staff was continually engaged in a physical interaction with a number of pupils. The teacher used a stick to repeatedly tap or prod pupils whenever he felt that they had spoken too loudly or obscenely. The pupils were evidently prepared, despite their protests, to accept this physical means of censure in return for the continued excitement of being noisy and abusive. The pupils probed the boundaries of accepted behaviour, trading the acceptance of a physical rebuke for the freedom to enjoy verbal skirmishing of a kind that would be generally unacceptable in school.

When one boy attempted to impart some sense of movement to the still life by pouring himself an imaginary cup of tea the teacher lightly but firmly kicked him back to his seat, smiling and talking in a manner that confirmed for the pupil the 'naturalness' of this action. Physical contact of a different nature was employed by another member of staff when during a break period he enquired disarmingly of a pupil whether he'd ever seen an 'Irish whip'. When the pupil replied in the negative his wrist was seized and swung violently up behind his back. 'You have now' said the teacher.

Roger was observed to favour during one period an indirect form of physical contact but one that remains based upon the demonstration of a superior strength, ability and resolve. At the end of an outdoor games session Roger encouraged the pupils to risk themselves by attempting to catch a cricket ball he would throw into the air. No one could be persuaded to attempt this feat until Roger offered the pupil a monetary inducement. Three or four pupils danced at a distance of thirty or forty yards and occasionally sprang forward to catch the ball. None were successful. The fifty pence went unclaimed and all had been witness to the head's control of events. It appears that underlying these and other instances of physical contact is the staff's preparedness to inflict physical discomfort and to demonstrate quite openly the nature of their authority. This does not mean that they are in continual and open conflict with their pupils. Some pupils did, on occasion, object to the behaviour of the staff but many derived considerable excitement from these exchanges.

Conclusion

In summary, Owen and Roger present fundamentally different approaches to the similar situation in which they find themselves. The difference between them stems from the choices made in the context of organizing a provision for those who have challenged the authority of their schoolteachers. The creation of special units as an administrative response to disaffection heightens the tension between the principles that operate when deviant behaviour is perceived and subsequently acted upon. Owen's aim is to repair the moral order breached by the challenge to the teacher's authority and the assumptions of intrinsic worth upon which it is founded. This repair entails the reconstruction of the child's experience of schooling. Control at this level is likely to be difficult to establish but when it is achieved it will be deep and self-sustaining. Roger on the other hand does not attempt any such reconstruction. Those who contest authority may be genuinely unable to 'cope' in school and may therefore need alternative provision. The majority, however, are simply in need of a demonstration that 'authority' cannot be challenged with impunity. The acknowledged and exclusive aim of the unit is to control and contain. In many respects this releases the staff and pupils from the moral imperative and may well come closer to an authentic understanding of the pupil's experience. It provides for a sense of continuity and is not invasive of the pupils private and meaningful 'worldview'. It permits the pupil to derive unfettered satisfaction from the excitement of 'skirmishing' and the release from school-like demands. The paradox is, of course, that this may well enable the staff to establish relationships with some pupils which would not be possible in school or in the Victoria unit. Although control is, in these circumstances, more easily established it is unlikely that it will be generalized to other sites. The reintroduction of pupils to school is therefore given less emphasis in the Delphi Centre.

It is not my intention to argue that the strategies identified here are necessarily exhaustive of those that pertain in other units. They are shaped by the nature of the particular circumstances in these two units and the biographies of the staff and particularly their heads. Nevertheless it is hoped that this analysis will provide a framework within which the detailed practice of other unit staff can be examined. The other aim is to suggest that in order to understand 'how teachers teach the unteachable' one must recognize the manner in which they are engaged in managing a delicate balance of perceptions – that they be like and unlike schools.

References

Francis, M. 1979. 'Disruptive pupils: labelling a new generation,' *New approaches in multiracial education*, 8, 1, 6–9.

Ling, R. and Davies, G. 1984. *A survey of off-site units in England and Wales*, Birmingham, City of Birmingham Polytechnic.

MacBeath, J. 1977. 'Goodbye free school, hello special unit,' *Times Educational Supplement*, 9 December, p. 3.

10   November 27th: a day in a 'maladjusted' school
Stewart Butterfield

The headteacher of a day school for maladjusted pupils asked the staff of his school to keep a diary on one day, 27 November 1985, to try to record an impression of the activities, concerns and pressures which make up daily routine. Of course, no day is typical and there are particular tensions which emerge in the few weeks before the Christmas break. Yet the extracts from the diaries of staff contained in this account demonstrate the stress and emotional intensity encountered in working in a small school of this kind. The amount of time and energy staff need to spend in communicating (and sometimes miscommunicating) with each other comes over very strongly, and one can see how easily misunderstanding, resentment or perhaps even hostility can develop when individuals work in close proximity under pressure, even where channels of communication may seem open and well defined. In this school there is a staff code of practice agreed by all, and working procedures are continuously reviewed at regular staff meetings.

After a brief description of the nature of the school and the order the staff attempt to impose, Stewart Butterfield lets the diaries speak for themselves of the way this order appeared on one day.

The school in question offers day provision for children with emotional and behavioural difficulties, and is the only one of its kind in its Inner City Borough. Internally the school is organized into separate departments, primary and secondary, which between them cover the entire school age range. The five classes are of mixed ability and each has up to eight children of similar age and/or developmental level. Three classes make up the primary department, while there are two in the secondary department.

There is a head of department for each side of the school, who has particular responsibilities for the curriculum, and each teaching group has a teacher and a welfare assistant. These assistants undertake a wide range of duties under the supervision of the class teacher, from working with individual children to preparing classroom materials, and are invaluable in enabling the school to more closely meet the needs of individual children in a variety of ways.

The school aims whenever possible to reintegrate children back into mainstream schools, and is reasonably successful at doing so, especially in the case of primary aged children. At any given time then, a number of pupils may be involved in supported full-time or part-time placements at other schools in the borough. The deputy head has a particular responsibility for supporting children in mainstream schools with the aim of obviating the need for special school placement.

A high but realistic standard of work and behaviour is expected from all pupils, and generally the response is positive. Parental support and co-operation are regarded as of paramount importance and to facilitate this the school is open until 9 p.m. on one evening each week during term, when parents meet heads of departments and/or class teachers according to a system of appointments. We try to see parents at least once every half-term to discuss children's progress.

Transport is provided for those parents who require it, either by the caretaker using the school's mini-bus or by the part-time school social worker.

The great majority of the children were recommended to the school because they presented severe management difficulties to teachers in mainstream schools and many of them experience a multiplicity of adversities in their personal lives. A majority of children have intractable learning difficulties, and few of them have responded to conventional interventions by members of child guidance clinic teams or remedial services before admission.

The school attempts to provide a positively structured learning environment where sound appropriate educational opportunities are available, together with suitable attention to individual difficulties. It is considered that in the past the children's learning in crucial areas of their lives may have been either insufficient or inappropriate. Reinforcement of appropriate behaviour is seen as a key issue pervading the work of the school, as is enabling the children to experience regular feedback concerning their performance in any given area. Children are encouraged to assume as much responsibility as possible regarding their own learning, and to be involved in setting their own personal goals when appropriate. We focus on the need for change in a way which does not regard the child as being 'damaged' or having something 'wrong' with him or her.

In order to maximize consistency of management at the school, and to ensure regular positive, feedback to pupils, the deputy head set up a reward system some five years ago, when the primary department was first established as a separate department. This has enabled staff to match their management techniques to an agreed standard and children have thereby experienced a more consistent approach. The system has been continuously discussed and amended in the light of experience and has also thereby provided a most valuable focus for staff support and development.

The diaries

For reasons of space the diaries are limited to those of the school secretary, school social worker, head of primary department, supply class teacher (juniors) and welfare assistant (infants).

SCHOOL SECRETARY: 25 HOURS PER WEEK

Arrived for work at 9.30. First job is to check that Tony, a boy who is brought to school by mini-cab is in. Then search for the Junior bus list. Infant teacher has it and asks me to make sure that the Head of Primary knows that one of the children had a fit on the bus this morning. Also sort out the dinner money!

9.40: Phone call from Education Office re. Petty Cash Account. I still have nightmares about this! They want to know why we have to send in so often for reimbursment. I explain to them that the local garage which supplied us with petrol has closed and we therefore no longer have an account. We now have to buy it from our petty cash. Obviously we use up the money more quickly. I don't think they really understand, so I suggest sending them a copy of the bank statement.

10.00: I complete the dinner and attendance registers. Then I sort the internal mail for the office. Phone call from our School Nurse to let us know that the School Doctor, who had to cancel medicals because of illness, is out of hospital but will not be back to work for some time. We must get him a card. Head comes in, has already thought of this, and agrees to organize a collection from staff for fruit or whatever. Type some letters for parental appointments. Phone call from a parent saying she cannot make next week's appointment. Could we postpone it until the following week? Juggle the appointments around and manage to fit her in. (Her husband works shifts and they have a small baby.)

Next I photocopy the bank statements for the Office. Start typing a letter for Head of Primary who is trying to sell some raffle tickets to raise funds for a new mini-bus. Another parent phones. She is going off to work, but in the meantime we have had to send her son home with the Head of Primary Department (*see his diary*). He arrives just before she leaves. Head of Secondary explains why he was sent home.

11.00: Break for five minutes for a cup of coffee.

11.05: Back to typing letter. Phone call from Education Office, re. dinner money summary sheets. We get them to balance over the phone. Discuss the possibility of getting a £51 school meals debt taken off our books. Am advised to let the School Meals Organizer deal with it. I don't think we will get this money from this particular Mum. We have tried repeatedly.

11.30: I phone the School Meals Organizer. She tells me that the Mum has applied for free meals but should really pay back the money owed. Agrees to write it off for me. At least I don't have to keep carrying it forward any more.

11.40: Continue typing letter. I'll finish it eventually. Phone again! (This time for the Deputy Head.) Phone – Office again to let me know that free school meals have been confirmed for pupil B. Back to typing.

12.10: Discussion with Head about a suspected case of head lice in the juniors. How shall we word a letter so as not to offend the parents? Head starts scratching himself! Type the letter (see appendix letter 1) and look up information on Head Lice (no pun intended!) Send a precautionary letter to all the parents in the class concerned. Also the Head discusses the problem with the School Nurse who agrees to do a home visit to the child in question.

12.45 to 1.15: Lunch Break.

1.15: Work on my favourite book – the Petty Cash Account. Enter receipts, work out VAT, deduct from our own books and dole out the money. Phone call for Head of Secondary. Phone calls for Head who has gone to visit a school where one of our pupils now attends full time. Take messages.

2.00: Video comes back from the repair shop. I have to search for a two-way adaptor and a tape to try it out. Engineer tests it out. Working OK now.

2.10: Careers Officer pops in to say goodbye. She has been talking to the Seniors about working on Saturdays.

2.15: Type the Agenda for tonight's Primary Department staff meeting. Looks like quite a long meeting.

2.30: Class Teacher comes to have a word about the 'Head Lice' letter. Could I retype it? (See appendix letter 2.)

2.35: Public works section arrive to repair a fence which has been causing a lot of problems. Have to find the caretaker for them. At the same time our School

Social Worker arrives back in school. Had a brief discussion about B's dinner money owing.

2.55: Internal Audit Officer phoned. Could I make an appointment to see her at the Education Office to sort out the dinner money debts once and for all – hopefully. She also needs a list of equipment that we transferred to another school. She suggests next Monday afternoon might be a good time.

3.00: Typed a third letter for child to take home re the Head Lice problem. Hope this one will do. (See Appendix, letter 3.)

3.05: Typed letter to parent about child's fit on the bus this morning, he has had two more fits during the day. Tidy up, lock the safe, time to go.

SCHOOL SOCIAL WORKER: SPLIT POST – 20 HOURS SCHOOL, 15 HOURS AREA TEAM

Arrived Area Office 9.05 a.m. having spent fifteen minutes trying to park car.

9.10: Collected eight urgent messages from reception left from yesterday. Make coffee.

9.15: Confronted by Admin Worker with case file problems re Senior Social Worker last week.

9.20: Telephone call to Work Supervisor of ex pupil of School. Very angry with me as he had not got his cheque for £82 for ex pupil's tools. Stated I had done report to justify it and had the expenditure approved – not my fault. Would ring back.

9.26: Telephone call to Finance Section. Cheques have been delayed.

9.30: Telephone call back to Work Supervisor explaining cheque delay. Also asked him for report which I needed for Statutory Review. (One message dealt with.)

9.40: Ten minutes late for meeting of Area Team. Difficult meeting as some Social Workers are refusing to work with colleagues and have taken steps to frustrate the function of the Area Team. I supported my Senior and therefore have been 'sent to Coventry' by my peer group.

11.20: Meeting finished.

11.30: Talk with Student Social Worker about three cases of children at School.

11.55: Make telephone call (answering second message) to Rowntree Family Fund re pupil C.

12.10: Telephone call to boy's mother to reassure her.

12.15: Telephone call to check if pupil B is in school (engaged).

12.20: Another Social Worker asks me to arrange half-day visit to the School.

12.30: Student Social Worker worried. Late for appointment at School with Deputy Head. School numbers still engaged.

12.40: Psychiatrist on phone to confirm meeting with him for December 3rd. (Told by receptionist three more messages in.)

12.45: Telephone call to Rowntree Family Fund re pupil A for holiday September 1986. Discussed. Call back to mother to discuss. (Three messages dealt with now – five to go still from yesterday.)

12.50: Urgent telephone call from IT (Intermediate Treatment). Told I have broken Borough policy by recommending custodial maximum on lad. Telephone call took twenty minutes and had to explain how I had arrived at such a decision.

Resolved by arranging case conference. Left message with reception that I had only dealt with three calls – no more time to deal with any others. Will deal with rest of calls tomorrow.

1.30: Allocation meeting. Long time in discussion about moving desks – needless waste of time. Feel very frustrated. Called out of meeting – dispute between Admin Officer and Social Worker re my cases at School. Admin Clerk burst into tears, could not cope with situation. Back to desk to prepare letter and telephone call to arrange Statutory Review on ex pupil 7.30 next Thursday.

2.20: Reminded Senior to check with Area 4 re. NAI (Non Accidental Injury) personnel to be at case conference at School next month. Leave office for School. (Two clients waiting to see me.) Late for appointment with Student for 2.30 at school.

2.44: Arrive at School. Secretary mentions pupil's dinner money. Discuss.

2.50: Try to find Head of Primary Department to confirm collection of parents for appointment at School at 4.15.

3.00: Told by School Secretary not to pick up parents.

3.05 to 4.15: Supervise Student Social Worker.

4.15 to 4.45: Discuss four pupils with Head. Lots of worrying developments in home circumstances of two of them. Can't get much co-operation from parents of another. It's not been the most satisfying of days.

HEAD OF PRIMARY DEPARTMENT

8.40: Arrived at school with Welfare Assistant to whom I give lift each morning. Greet other staff and have a coffee in Staff Room.

8.55: Begin preparing materials for pupil at a local Junior School who is having difficulties with reading. This help is being offered during my visits to see one of our children who is attending the same school for one day a week.

9.05: Gave Welfare Assistant permission to take her car to garage for minor repairs before children arrive.

9.10: One of the three coaches arrive at School earlier than usual. Go out to supervise children into playground and check with Coach Guide about any absences or misbehaviour on journey home yesterday or to school today. Saw children into playground and checked for staff on duty. Returned bus list to Office.

9.15: Checked with supply teacher if she needed my help while Welfare Assistant was out. Supply said she would not start cookery lesson until she returned.

9.30: Children brought into classes.

9.35: Check money and ticket stubs returned from parents for the Christmas Draw to take place at the school social evening next month. We still need £3,000 more to replace our ageing mini-bus.

9.50: Rang Supplies Office to cancel enquiry about monitor shelf for new computer trolley. Have at last worked out how it fits on to the trolley.

9.55: Looked for Social Worker's copy of Directory of Charities. Found local Handbook of Voluntary Organizations and Community Groups to which I will send begging letters.

10.00: Was informed that a child on the small coach had an epileptic fit on the way to school this morning and that Coach Guide was very upset. Should I have been told before this?

10.15: Completed materials needed for pupil at the mainstream school. B (secondary pupil) on bench outside Office refusing to work in class and otherwise being totally uncommunicative. Has been given notice by Head that he will be returned home if he continues to refuse to co-operate.

10.25: Check with class teacher who is covering my playground duty this morning in my absence.

10.30: Prepared to leave for the junior school. Secondary pupil still not communicating and has to be taken home. Begin to look for route to his home in A–Z. Interrupted by other senior pupil asking for materials.

10.35: Leave school in mini-bus with B as passenger.

10.40: Tried to engage B in conversation but this proved useless. Decided to play him at his own game. Drove for fifteen minutes in silence. Now in right locality and have just realized I did not finish looking up where he lived in A–Z. Will look silly if I have to spend time driving around in circles to find it. See diversion sign and ask B if he knows the best way around it. He directs me. Breathe sigh of relief.

10.55: Arrived at B's home. Spoke to mother who as we arrived was holding a conversation with Head of Senior Department over the telephone.

11.00: Left for the junior school.

11.10: Arrived at junior school just as driver of one of the coaches which brings our children was delivering dinners. Spoke to him about child who had epileptic fit in coach on journey to School this morning and he supplied further details.

11.15: Dashed into the junior school. Met Headteacher and asked if he would be willing to extend the time our pupil spent with them from one day to three after Christmas. No problem; Wednesdays, Thursdays and Fridays agreed. Head will write to mother arranging a meeting during last week of term to inform her of details, also Social Worker. Passed on friendly reminder about forthcoming Christmas social at our school and sale of Christmas draw tickets.

11.20: Left for Annexe where our part-time pupil and his class teacher are located.

11.25: Arrived Annexe – children were in school hall for 'International' activity. Spoke to class teacher in corridor about work I proposed to do with one of his children. Spoke to Acting Head of school where Annexe located. Managed to let him know about our Social and sold him a book of Christmas Draw tickets. Continued discussion with J's teacher about how he could extend the work I would be doing with his pupil during week before my next visit.

11.35: Spent time with J. Talked about how his day was going, what work he had done etc. He has settled well and is enjoying his time here.

11.45: Worked with nine-year-old girl. Left materials plus work to be getting on with next week. Told Class Teacher about arrangement with Head to extend J's time after Christmas – no problems.

12.02: Left to return to my own school.

12.10: Stopped at Petrol Station to give our old mini-bus a drink and some air.

12.28: Arrived back at School. Met Head in corridor who wished to see me urgently regarding an incident which occurred when I was out.

Head informs me that after play this morning a Welfare Assistant asked

Deputy Head for assistance to bring a child into school who was refusing to move. Welfare Assistant tried again but child still refused. Deputy Head brought child into school and was dealing with the incident in his office when the child's Class Teacher burst in in a frenzied manner shouting that this was what she didn't want to happen and the child was getting too much attention. Deputy Head would like a meeting with me and Class Teacher to discuss the matter. Would I please see Deputy Head before dinner.

12.40: Saw Deputy Head re incident and arranged to see him with Class Teacher in his office when I have completed my dinner duty.

12.48: Started Dinner Duty in hall. Had school dinner with children. It was a mistake. I think I ate the courses in the right order!

13.14: Finished Dinner Duty. Made a cup of coffee.

13.16: Started meeting with Deputy Head and Class Teacher who has since apologised. Discussed the incident and clarified the need to have clearer lines of communication. Apparently the Class Teacher has been unaware that the Welfare Assistant asked the Deputy Head for help.

13.30: Took class for the afternoon.

13.45: Prepared to go out to collect leaf specimens.

13.50: Loaded children onto coach and left for woods.

13.54: S has a mild epileptic fit on coach. Dealt with by Welfare Assistant. (Second today.) Turn back.

14.00: Return to classroom. Welfare Assistant takes S to medical room.

14.03: Took remainder of class to small woods next to School. Collected examples of evergreen leaves. One or two of the children have not really understood the concept of evergreen. I found one carrying an old umbrella and another a length of old rope!

14.40: Returned to classroom. Informed that S had a third fit while we were out. Left Welfare Assistant with class to go to see about Junior Staff Meeting Agenda.

14.45: Secretary informed me that Class Teacher had written a letter to parent of child with Head Lice to replace one written by Head. Told her she must send out the original.

14.50: Teacher sees me about letter. Checked pupil for Head Lice and tried to unscramble the situation.

15.00: Dictated letter for parent almost word for word as Head's letter. (See appendix letter 3 and letter 4 which shows the reply which came back from the parents.)

15.05: Dictated letter to S's parent about fits on coach and in school.

15.10: Gave letter to coach guide and checked children onto coach.

15.15: Told Social Worker not to pick up parent as previously arranged. Asked Caretaker to collect parents who have confirmed appointments.

15.20: Started Junior Staff Meeting. Discussed:

1   Christmas decorations and other arrangements.
2   Children (3).
3   Reports to parents for the end of term.
4   Timetable changes.
5   Playground behaviour.
6   Next week's agenda.

16.10: Meeting ended.

16.15: Quick word with Class Teacher about parent coming to School this evening.

16.20: Made a cup of coffee which I hope to finish.

16.30: Write up part of diary.

16.55: Parent arrives. Introduce her to Class Teacher who begins meeting.

17.00: Discussed traffic delays with Caretaker.

17.01: Address envelopes for begging letters to charities etc.

17.15: Head asks me to tell Class Teacher that he would like to see her after meeting with parent is over.

17.20: Join Class Teacher and parent in meeting and discuss child's progress so far and our hopes for the future.

17.45: End meeting. Class Teacher goes to see Head. Write up diary. Check up on possible sales of raffle tickets. Grade a number of reading books. Clear tray of work pending.

18.28: Head ends meeting with Class Teacher. Go for drink with Head to discuss plans for sale of raffle tickets on Saturday morning. Approach barman to try to sell some tickets in pub.

19.15: Leave pub.

19.30: Call at another pub to give raffle tickets to Head of a Junior School. Meet Head of PE at Secondary School and arrange to collect spare PE clothing for some of our children.

20.20: Arrive home.

SUPPLY TEACHER (JUNIOR CLASS)

Arrived at school (8.50 a.m.) – ten minutes later than usual because I overslept. Still had time for the essential cup of coffee! Welfare Assistant arrived and then disappeared! Maybe I'll abandon cookery lessons if she's not back in time. (I obviously rely on her very much for this.)

9.20: Kids arrived. S had a fit (epileptic) on the bus so I took him to lie down. He insisted on staying in the class with me and the others. He enjoys colouring and drawing when he's had a fit. I question my medical knowledge for looking after a child that fits.

9.40: We start to write out diary for OU. Welfare Assistant returns. Hooray! We can make chocolate crispies as we planned.

Children are vey well behaved this morning in cookery room. S does lots of pacing. M forgets to be grumpy (angry) and is so helpful and capable. They love making chocolate crispies.

10.50: We've nearly finished making the cakes. Deputy Head arrives to chat and have a cake. D wants to share his cakes with the little ones. They all go very quietly to play.

11.00: Art students are here today one day a week this term from the local Poly. Ask me if I did 'marbling' with kids last week. Had to admit I was not ambitious and did pasta/bean collage instead.

Deputy Head arrives in staffroom with Swann Report. I take one look and think how uninspired I'd be to read that. Welfare Assistant with Infants class gave me her telephone number so that I can arrange to have my hair highlighted by her daughter.

11.20: End of playtime. Two minutes silence in class with children. Explain it is clearing up time in the cookery room. M and J always tidy up well, so did not let them do the washing/drying up. R and N worked together – D and A did the same. A, who shows so little spark, proved to be slow but a very good washer-upper. I was really pleased to see the eight of them clearing up so well and independently. Welfare Assistant and I chatted about life (i.e. something outside of school) whilst they busied themselves around us. They must have done this for at least ten minutes. (A time when there was no 'lid on' – they controlled themselves – very exciting feeling. What I'd like to achieve with them all the time).

12.00: Back to classroom. Time for them to write their diary. Each person gave one thought about the day. I wrote them down for each person. They copied down their sentence and then illustrated it. Meanwhile I started my diary. Most of them left me alone whilst I wrote and if they did want something they waited till I looked up. I read my diary (not the part about S's fits) to them. No one listened except D, who was really interested. He has such potential which is not being used. How can I help him to achieve this? So far he has done very little 'work' for me. Then they all drew pictures till lunch.

12.55: I sat down and had lunch with the kids. Sat next to M in infant class. This lot really are a challenge. I decided to eat with them as Head of Primary Department is giving me this afternoon off and therefore I don't need a break from the kids. It's hard not to get indigestion when eating with them as you are constantly chatting with them. Back to staffroom for a cup of coffee. Chatted about the diary. I really enjoy this – usually I'd never make time for it.

1.25: Afternoon free. Head of Department has the kids. Spend time mounting pasta/bean collages from last week to make calendars for Christmas. It's now 2.18 and this is near the end of my diary. Must dash at end of school to meet Tom, David and John from school (my own boy and two of his friends). I'm now going to think about tomorrow. Must buy calendars for the kids' work.

2.50: Am in staffroom. Had some thoughts for tomorrow. School Social Worker is here and has had a bad day. He's discussing this with Student Social Worker. Two art students wonder if they should be writing diaries too. School Secretary has shown me hers. She hasn't put any personal thoughts into hers. I just can't stop chatting to the paper. Must go back to the kids and see them to the bus. Will I be working here tomorrow?

3.05: They're on the bus. S had two more fits this afternoon. Still haven't asked if I am here tomorrow!

CLASSROOM ASSISTANT (INFANTS)

9 a.m.: Prepared an assault course with apparatus. Fed and watered birds, checked for bread for chidren's toast just before break.

9.30: Helped T with house picture (drawing by numbers).

9.45: Help A with colouring of shapes.

10.05: T undressed ready for PE.

10.10: T redresses himself (too noisy). G has chocolate button, reward, for being the only boy undressed and sitting quietly.

10.15: T undresses again. I remained in class with A and P to finish their work.

10.25: Work completed go into hall.

10.27: Brought P back to class (behaviour unsatisfactory in hall). Ah, well! I did have two minutes to see A do his ladder climb, and T's climbing feat.

10.28: Persuaded P to get dressed and beat the clock – 3½ minutes, then back to coaxing him to finish some colouring.

10.40: A returned to class announcing he felt unwell. Chatted with him and found he'd missed breakfast. Helped him dress, then we made tea and toast. Whilst doing so he managed to chomp his way through several broken biscuits. Not altogether sure he didn't break them deliberately! Colour now back in his cheeks. So...

11.00: Playtime.

11.20: Photocopying for Deputy Head.

11.50: Returned to class. Sorted out some more work to be photocopied.

12.00: My lunch break.

12.30: Back to class. Storytime before dinner.

12.40: Hands washed for...*lunch*. R (part time pupil who comes in at lunch time) seemed quite placid, so was easier to control; alas when dinner was presented he announced it was 'finished' without tasting it. He seemed keen to try the jelly and oranges for pudding, but ended up choosing to give me a cuddle after fingering it all. Meanwhile, G was playing for attention, so I was haggling with him over how many forkfuls he was to eat. (He said four I said five he said five I said six...) With the hassle, I somehow missed out on the pudding, but G assured me he'd had the usual number of five. (I had my doubts after seeing the squashy mess left on the table where he'd sat.)

1.15: The rest of my lunch break.

1.25: Got R to take off his coat and hang it up but I wasn't quick enough for him as he removed his shoes and socks in a flash too. Then into the playroom for a chat with the birds, numerous visits to the corridor to talk to the fish and feed it two grains of fish food at a time. We looked through several books, did puzzles, played cars. I would turn my back a second and find him sitting in the sand tray. There were other climbing feats, like into the sink and on top of the wendy house furniture.

2.00: Another Welfare Assistant takes over with R from me at this time. Back into class to help the boys make surprise birthday cards for her birthday (today). Got out assortment of crayons, pencils, coloured paper. Boys very excited.

2.30: Called her into class and sang 'Happy Birthday'. Gave her cards and boys all got a kiss on cheek.

2.35: 'Faces' time. (System of reporting to parents via 'Smiley Face' stickers, which we send home with our younger children each day. Children can earn smiles when they do well by their own standards.) Put faces on sheets, then folded and put into covers ready for going home. Coats on and out for bikes etc. R wanted to talk to the birds (yet again). Oh! and see the fish.

2.50: Boys come in for orange and cornflake cakes (made by boys in next class).

3.00: Assisted with lining up boys for bus. Tidied up classroom and playroom.

3.20: Staff meeting.

4.15: Home time.

Postcript

Although only about one third of staff are represented by their diaries, the reader can still perhaps get a 'feel' of how some parts of the school operate, and may on occasion be able to read between the lines.

One might focus particular attention on stress points in the day, perhaps where a mismatch of perception between individuals or even outright conflict occurred. On this particualr day such differences were resolved through later discussion, but how could conflict have been avoided altogether? The day was chosen at random, and although subjectively it felt like quite a difficult one, apart from the fact that staff were asked to complete personal diaries, it was potentially just like any other.

Appendix

LETTER 1   27th November 1985

Dear Mr and Mrs Williamson,

It appears that Thomas has head lice and I enclose some information that we have in school relating to this.

Nurse Buckle intends to visit you this afternoon to advise you further.

Obviously Thomas should not be in school if his head is in an infested condition.

Yours sincerely,

School Secretary.

LETTER 2   27th November 1985

Dear Mr and Mrs Williamson,

Thomas has been scratching his head a lot and appears to have nits in his hair. Please could you have this checked by a Doctor and treat him with the appropriate shampoo before sending him back to school.

Nurse Buckle may visit you this afternoon to check Thomas's head herself.

Yours sincerely,

Class Teacher.

LETTER 3   27th November 1985

Dear Mr and Mrs Jones,

Thomas has been scratching his head a lot and appears to have head lice in this hair. Nurse Buckle may visit you this afternoon to check Thomas's head herself and advise you further. Obviously Thomas should not be in school if his head is in an infested condition.

Yours sincerely,

Head of Junior Department.

LETTER 4

Tom has no more flees I done her hair 4 Times

11 Going against the grain: alternatives to exclusion

Denis Mongon

In this chapter Denis Mongon argues that the predominant approach to disruptive incidents in school is through the displacement model whereby pupils are increasingly subjected to negative sanctions until they are finally excluded. He contrasts this with an approach to education said to characterize 'effective schools' and argues that this is undermined when schools are preoccupied with removing troublesome pupils. He attempts to account for the prevalence of the placement model despite its lack of apparent success and offers a number of suggestions for reversing the trend to identify and exclude ever-increasing numbers of pupils as deviant.

The displacement model

Central government, local authority and academic reports (e.g. Department of Education and Science 1978a, Inner London Education Authority 1986, Rutter, *et al* 1979) answer the question 'What processes contribute to effective schooling?' with elements of a consensus along the following lines. Schools tend to be more effective when the relationship between the teachers and pupils is 'good' and when the latter are offered status and respect; when expectations are high; when there is an emphasis on rewarding good, rather than punishing bad, behaviour; when there is an overall approach characteristically described as neither permissive nor authoritarian. Schools which do not adopt these processes tend to have greater difficulties than those which do.

However, it is fair to claim that the common response to individual instances of difficulty in the classroom is the antithesis of what seems to be known about the more effective school. Table 11.1 illustrates how poor behaviour provokes ever-more interest and attention as, paradoxically, pupils become literally and metaphorically isolated – the educational equivalent of irresistibly poking a sore tooth with your tongue. The language and procedures for dealing with that alienation encompass conflict and confrontation at the expense of planned purposeful strategies.

Table 11.1   Sanctions employed: a composite list indicating a trend in seriousness

1   Non-verbal cues, silences, disapproving gestures.
2   Rebukes, tellings off, to individual, group, class.
3   Lines, extra homework, punishment exercises, unproductive writing.
4   Threat of movement to other seat in class.
5   Movement of seat.
6   Threat of isolation in another class.
7   Time-out, 'on-assignment,' isolation.

8   Detention, unofficial, in class teacher's room.
9   Corporal punishment.
10 Threat of report, oral or in writing, to guidance or Year Head or 'Office.'
11 Report and possible intervention by Year Head and guidance.
12 Withdrawal of privilege.
13 Official detention, school-organized.
14 Threat of parental involvement.
15 On report: behaviour timetables with or without parental knowledge.
16 Letter or telephone call to parents informing of problem.
17 Pupil sent home for clarification (a pre-suspension warning).
18 Parental involvement through visit to school.
19 Withdrawal to Special Unit.
20 Tactical or unofficial suspension.
21 Suspension, exclusion – official.

(Cumming *et al* 1981, p. 6)

The dominant approach to behaviour problems in schools is based on identifying and categorizing individual pupils with a view to removing some of them from mainstream schools. Although it would be glib to presume that the removal of a pupil from his or her usual classes is necessarily the wrong strategy, there are obvious contradictions in operating a system based on negative sanctions and the off-loading of responsibility for one group whilst attempting to accept and cater for the diversity of the rest. Moreover, when the dominant approach to problems of behaviour is to remove the pupils it is not surprising that an increasing proportion of the school population is drawn into that model.

The growth of the 'displacement' model would be understandable if it resolved individual difficulties or reduced the general incidence of difficulty. The available evidence suggests otherwise. In fact no one argues that the marked increase in provision to service this model (Department of Education and Science 1978b Ling and Davies 1984) has led to a marked improvement in pupils' behaviour. Lloyd-Smith (1984) provides a telling summary of the shortcomings of the 'displacement' model in his account of three 'Guidance Centres' established by a West Midlands Local Education Authority. These were opened for the temporary short-term placement of pupils in danger of suspension, with the expectation that suspension rates would be reduced. Ten years later, after a 17 per cent drop in the secondary school population of the area, suspensions are up 230 per cent, the centres admit suspended as well as pre-suspension pupils and a fourth centre has been opened.

The adversarial 'displacement' model, whatever occasional, temporary relief it offers, is having little if any positive impact on underlying patterns. Instead it is associated with unforeseen increases in rates of difficulty and displacement. Despite this, the model has a grip on our imagination which inhibits enquiry. It does so by providing scapegoats – 'the disruptive pupil' and 'the parsimonious LEA' which have sufficient reality and credibility to bear a disproportionate blame for the ills of present-day schools. As a result, difficulties in the education service can be explained as the consequence of incidents of which they are probably the cause.

Four notable factors have sustained the model in the absence of supportive evidence: short-term expediency; the idea that a number of pupils are 'irremediable'; the structure of support services and the political context of behaviour.

SHORT-TERM EXPEDIENCY

The simplest explanation for the persistence of the displacement model is that problems arising from pupils' behaviour are so stressful that they provoke an expedient response. In a recent study (Kloska and Ramasut 1985) sources of stress were placed in the following order by teachers:

1   Lack of pupil motivation.
2   Lack of time to resolve problems with individual pupils.
3   Pupil indiscipline.
4   Lack of consensus on discipline by staff.
5   Completion of records and reports.
6   Meetings, during and after school.
7   Marking and preparation time.
8   Lack of resources and equipment.

Kloska's findings echo those in other research (e.g. Docking 1980, Dunham 1977, Kyriacou and Sutcliffe 1981) which record an increasing sense of occupational stress of which the predominant sources are said to be classroom control and pupil misbehaviour. Teachers believe that their interaction with pupils and the disciplinary problems which arise are the greatest source of stress in their work. A consequence of that belief is the pursuit of expedient solutions which remove the problem and therefore, it would be hoped, the stress. Teachers need to feel, and to be seen to be, in control. When their control is threatened it is possible for them to obtain relief by displacing a prominently misbehaving pupil. The existing system for doing so is there to be used, alternative systems are not. In those circumstances, the displacement system provides its own self-fulfilling momentum.

IRREMEDIABILITY

The causes attributed to behaviour problems – and the frequently attendant learning difficulties – are often thought, by teachers, to be beyond their influence. In turn, the problems and difficulties themselves are thought to be irremediable (Hargreaves 1975, Leach 1977), in the sense that they cannot be resolved in the usual school or classroom context. The sample of teachers who identified the causes of learning difficulties and behaviour problems for Croll and Moses (1985) illustrated a common belief that the role of the school is relatively insignificant. In less than 4 per cent of cases did teachers think that teachers and schools contributed to problems of disruption. Almost 40 per cent of such problems were attributed in whole or part to the pupils'.characteristics whilst in about 65 per cent of cases the home was thought to be wholly or partly to blame.

A worrying indicator of teachers' sense of helplessness in dealing with such problems is found too in Kloska and Ramasut's study. Asked to describe their strategies for coping with stress, teachers were concerned 'to focus upon situations or activities well removed from the work place'. There were no sustained views that stress – arising again in the main from discipline issues – could be alleviated by efforts directed at or close to its source. It follows that if teachers believe they are incompetent or impotent in these matters, they will accept and expect that the proper strategy is to pass on the problems to suitably qualified colleagues.

THE STRUCTURE OF SUPPORT SERVICES

A third factor which supports the system for separating teachers and 'uncontrolled' pupils is the recruitment of experts to advise, support and assist in resolving the difficulties. The experts travel in various guises: support teachers, unit teachers, special school teachers, child guidance workers, educational psychologists, special education inspectors and others. What they have in common is that with still rare and recent exceptions their main role has been to consume whatever problem is identified for them. Access to their help, leaving aside the question of whether it employs a separate, distinct expertise, has usually meant passing on pupils from the classroom or the school. This process confirms the belief that many of the difficulties cannot be resolved by teachers in their classrooms and so require specialist services in a specialist context. This, in turn, provides the displacement model with further self-justification.

THE POLITICAL CONTEXT

At the point of referral the system is primarily concerned with pupils whose behaviour is 'aggressive,' 'extrovert' and 'disruptive.' There are many other pupils, of whom a significant number are girls, who are alienated and disaffected but who provoke no response from professional services. Whether pupils' behaviour is itself a political statement or not, the aggressive forms impress themselves onto educational politics. Schools and teachers are part of a wider political arena and it is inevitable that school disruption is sucked into the wider debates about and responses to law and order. Nor can the expectations of senior staff in relation to 'control' be ignored by others looking to the hierarchy for guidance and favour. The politics of law and order and the demands for 'standards,' whatever that means, are consistently presented in ways which undermine the capacity of schools to tolerate any forms of deviance.

An alternative perspective

The displacement model has persisted and expanded in part because of its own self-fulfilling features but also in the absence of credible alternatives. That can now be corrected. The credibility of alternatives depends in a large measure on three factors: a new perspective on disruption and disaffection; support for teachers; a re-alignment of current resources.

There is an increasing amount of evidence (see Galloway 1985, Reynolds and Sullivan 1981) which shows that teachers can make a difference to the levels of disaffection and alienation in their schools. Ouston summarizes such a view:

'Successful schools appear to prevent too many difficulties arising rather than being exceptionally skilled in dealing with them once they have arisen' (Ouston 1981).

To this we can add the cumulative evidence that school-focused approaches to problem behaviour can be effective (e.g. Kolvin *et al* 1981, Coulby and Harper 1985). Behaviour problems are not the inevitable product of pupils' characters or home backgrounds, nor are they irremediable in classroom or school contexts. Instances in which they are 'irremediable' or 'inevitable' are a mere residue of the much larger number of cases currently treated *as if* they are.

In the face of this evidence there is no sense in continuing to rely on the pathological or medical model as the main basis for the development of additional or specialist services. That model was consistent with the view that the only factor in the equation which was not reasonable, constant and satisfactory was the pupils. Any element of the curriculum and organization of schooling can contribute to the production of difficulties and is therefore a reasonable subject for intervention. That is the basis for a new rationale which services should reflect.

Many teachers feel that their training inadequately prepares them for dealing with behaviour problems in schools (Mongon 1984). There is a need to offer them opportunities in initial and in-service professional development to acquire or improve relevant skills. That in itself would not reduce the stress which teachers report unless they could also be allowed to tolerate the normality of some problems. It would, for example, be an extraordinary institution which could encompass a thousand or so adolescents and not encounter some difficulty. So long as teachers are made to feel guilty about such difficulties in a negative and personal manner then they will be susceptible to short-term placebos. If they are encouraged to be analytical in a positive and practical sense they will be more able to take a longer-term and reforming perspective. Such change will not come about by chance but it is now possible to describe the ways in which it can be brought about.

REALIGNING RESOURCES

The common belief that resources are not available to implement the necessary changes is a major obstacle to the development of a new service delivery pattern. More resources are required and one has to acknowledge that because of their absence the teaching profession is wary of accepting additional responsibilities. However, present resources *can* be better deployed. A campaign for the effective use of current resources is not at all incompatible with a campaign for additional ones and may enhance the clarity with which the shortfall in support for teachers is expressed.

Three areas of potential development within current resources, outlined below, are familiar propositions and can be dealt with quite briefly. The fourth, liaison between Local Education Authorities and teacher training establishments will be considered in a little more detail.

Developing a unified service Ling and Davies' (1984) questionnaire survey of a sample of 132 off-site units found that 16 per cent operated under the auspices of social service departments or voluntary agencies, 56 per cent were said to be part of the special education sector and 27 per cent had some other administrative background. Whatever its historical justification, this diversity now reflects ad hoc developments lacking in central direction leading to a chaotic, patchwork pattern (Inner London Education Authority 1985, see also Chapter 7). If we add to that the distinct empires which units and special schools often constitute and whose border crossings have indeterminate customs regulations, then there is scope for duplication and confusion in most LEAs' provision.

The first steps to remedy this can be taken by an LEA prepared to think of its specialist services as a coherent structure. It may well then have to face the vested interest of different institutions and organizations and there may be difficulties defining where some provision could fit in. That in itself would only be a further illustration of the need for an innovative, coherent plan.

A single service with a unified management structure for on-site, off-site and what is currently special school provision would considerably enhance the professional opportunities of its staff and reduce to a minimum the duplication or even rivalry that exists. Its chief asset in the longer term would be flexibility. From one post within the service a teacher could at different times within the week or year act in a range of teaching or advisory roles. Conversely, using a negotiated, contractual approach with schools, the head of this service can respond more directly to expressed local need. A school with, for example, a difficult second year might need and could be offered a selection from in-service training for staff, an analysis/assessment exercise focused on the whole or particular parts of the school, a support teacher for particular departments, some kind of on-site unit, some share in off-site provision. The negotiation and offer would be limited on the one hand by the school's ability/willingness to use different initiatives and on the other by the head of service's management of his or her total team resource and his or her balance of support to all the schools in the team's catchment area. This also provides an instant monitor of the distribution of actual and/or perceived problems presented by schools.

Redirecting off-site staff Although it would be wrong to presume that teachers who are excellent in their off-site unit work with small groups of pupils could necessarily become the vanguard of a new service they can provide the focus for some initial developments. An increasing number of these teachers already have experience of peripatetic, school-based work on behaviour problems (Lane 1978, Coulby and Harper 1985). In addition, the number of people involved – usually as few as two, three or four adults with pupils at a ratio around 6 to 1 – provides a more manageable unit for change than special schools of at least twice that size.

This is not to underestimate the possibility that for many of these staff this work is a consciously chosen alternative to teaching in primary or secondary schools. However there are, perhaps, an increasing number who recognize some of the contradictions in the outward referral model and are looking for alternatives. These changes can be encouraged and supported by an alert LEA. The authority will not only need to provide opportunities for development in schools in the form of in-service training opportunities and 'non-contract' periods but also to anticipate an adverse reaction from schools who believe that the outward referral of their pupils is the only acceptable solution to their troubles.

Because LEAs are not required to provide data on units to the DES as they are, for example, in respect of special schools, it is impossible to say how many teachers work in them. Surveys are faced with the limitations of non-response rates and unreliable respondents. Nevertheless there are some clues. The HMI finding of 321 teachers in 108 visited units (Department of Education and Science 1978b) is consistent with Ling and Davies' (1984) finding that three-quarters of the units in their survey had between two and four teachers. They identified about four hundred units and suggested that they accommodate over seven thousand pupils at ratios rarely exceeding 6 to 1. It seems reasonable to draw these strands together and to presume that considerably more than a thousand teachers are now working in off-site units. These are in effect posts withdrawn from primary and secondary schools where difficulties with troublesome pupils persist despite the removal of the 'worst' cases. A realignment of the work of those thousand teachers aimed as much at servicing teachers and schools as at treating individual pupils is a realistic consideration.

Bringing in the special schools The latest available DES figures (DES 1983), probably the last to list schools by 'categories,' identify 200 maintained schools for maladjusted pupils. There were 8,576 pupils in these schools. If the staffing ratio of seven pupils to each teacher, recommended in circular 4/73 (DES 1973), is accepted as a basis for calculating the necessary teaching force for this group, then 1,225 teachers would be required. In 1983 the figure was 1,424 plus 39 full-time equivalents made up by part-time appointments. Heads are excluded from all these calculations. Staffing standards therefore exceed the 4/73 baseline by a fifth and that should be welcomed so far as it is an attempt to provide favourably for a group in need. What should be questioned is the use to which that additional staffing is put. If it is used only to improve the pupil–teacher ratio within special schools then its value is limited. It is difficult to believe that pupils gain a great deal more from being in a group of six rather than seven pupils; or that the curriculum of a 43-pupil school (the average size derived from these statistics), can be much more enriched by seven rather than six teachers. If, however, the staffing improvement can be imaginatively exploited to create links between the special school provision, other special provision and primary or secondary schools then it could create the first stages of a unified, coherent service whose institutional boundaries are eroded.

If life could be as readily organized as statistics can, then the additional staff would be spread fairly evenly at about one teacher for each of the 200 schools for the maladjusted. Inevitably that will not be the case; areas and individual schools within areas will be in quite different positions with regard to their staffing. For some, the ratios mentioned and the ideas which followed will seem pious and wishful. The corollary is that some areas will be better placed to initiate a shift away from the isolated role of special schools. Whether they do so or not depends simply on the decisions which teachers, headteachers, local authority officers and elected members choose to make. The statistical data points unequivocally to the potential within some, if not many, LEAs, for the special schools for maladjusted pupils to transfer staff away from the immediate treatment/curricular activities without unduly diminishing the quality of that work. These teachers could become the seminal elements of a newly aligned service.

What is at issue is whether improved resource levels should be used to make special schools internally more satisfactory, doing what they have historically done but doing it in some sense more efficiently, or whether those resources are used in an attempt to improve the general education service in ways which might reduce its need for transferring pupils to special schools.

Using the potential of in-service training Although the resources allocated to in-service training are numerically small it is a potential source of notable innovation. There is an analogy between teachers' in-service development and the mounting evidence that intervention in pupils' careers which take place away from their school have limited value for either pupil rehabilitation or for changes in school ethos (Topping 1983). The further in-service training occurs, literally and metaphorically, from their school base the less likely it is that teachers will be able to sustain personal changes and motivation for innovation. It is therefore remarkable that the amount of co-operation and collaborative work between local authorities and higher education institutions has been so limited and only shows recent signs of expansion. Those signs have included Open University distance-teaching approaches, the development of modular courses in the North West of England and the school-based element of courses funded by the DES under its Circular 3/83 and subsequent arrangements. However, it is not only in these but also in most longer courses that there is scope for an imaginative alliance between the institutions, authorities and students. It remains to be seen whether the DES's new funding arrangements for in-service training will enhance or inhibit that alliance, despite its avowed intentions to do the former.

Many courses require that some kind of placement project is undertaken by the student. A caricature of this exercise is that the tutor and student agree on a suitable project at a school which has been selected on the basis of its willingness to be disturbed by the student. When the project is completed copies of the project report, written up and assessed, gather dust, one on the tutor's shelf another on the student's. Whenever this happens it is a sad waste of the stimulus which projects can engender.

The alternative approach is for the project to be more explicitly a contract between the LEA or schools concerned, the higher education institution and the student. Schools and LEAs can be invited to tender projects and schemes which reflect their current preoccupations. Within the constraints of their courses the institutions then attempt to match potential projects to the interests and availability of individual students. Some negotiation is required but the outcome is that in exchange for using the schools/LEA, the student/institution provide a service; and vice-versa. The scheme is applicable whether or not the school in question is the student's main base. This is typical of the approach used in a number of the DES funded one-term courses.

A different illustration is provided by the collaboration in 1983–84 between the ILEA and the London Institute of Education, in which one of the former's advisory teachers acted as placement tutor for six students from the emotional/behavioural difficulties option of the latter's Diploma Course. The students were placed in pairs in three secondary comprehensive schools with which the advisory teacher was familiar. The advisory teacher was then well placed to act as broker between the course requirements, the students and the schools. The

Authority, and its schools, were able to draw on the skills of six experienced teachers; the institute and the students were able to use the local knowledge and pragmatic insights of the schools' staff and the advisory teacher.

The success of that initial project has encouraged the establishment of similar schemes in following years. Other LEAs and colleges have taken different collaborative steps, including the creation of joint lecturer/advisory appointments.

The approaches taken by, for example, Lawrence (1980) and Taylor (1985) have also shown how school staffs can rationalize their approach to disruption. It is quite clear that some need to do this. In one school senior members of staff sat in rotation in a room to which disruptive pupils could be promptly sent from the classroom. The rule was that three referrals there led to an automatic three day 'cooling off' suspension but in the absence of agreed criteria the referral rationales varied wildly. The PE department sent pupils who turned up with inadequate kit, by contrast, other teachers would not send even obviously disruptive pupils for fear of causing their suspension. Use of the facility was bound to be capricious until there was some agreement about the intent and purpose in committing the equivalent of a full-time senior post in this way.

The absence of a thoughtful approach blights this area of schools' work. It is difficult to imagine a school appointing a Head of French or Science without having either a fair idea of what a French or Science curriculum should be or a commitment to quickly devise one. Yet schools are prepared to tie up the time of senior staff, in effect the resource equivalent of at least a full-time head of department post, with the vaguest responsibilities for taking difficult pupils away from classrooms.

Conclusion

The displacement model which has historically prevailed in schools' responses to troublesome children has failed to show a satisfactory effectiveness either in terms of outcome for identified pupils or in terms of relieving pressure on teachers. The belief that there is no real alternative is being challenged by the activities of teachers working in consultative/support roles and by an increasing body of research. The pursuit of the alternatives can be inhibited by the view that little if anything can be achieved within present resource limits. Although improved resources are a pre-requisite for the necessary level of services, a start can and should be made to adapt service delivery models within present levels. The deployment of current resources within a coherent, unified service, the adaptation of the use to which off-site units are put, the mobilization of resources from within the special schools sector and the imaginative employment of in-service training each provide some opportunity for developments in the very immediate future.

References

Coulby, D., and Harper, T. 1985. *Preventing classroom disruption: policy practice and evaluation in urban schools*, London, Croom Helm.

Croll, P. and Moses, D. 1985. *'One in five': the assessment and incidence of special educational needs*, London, Routledge and Kegan Paul.

Cumming, C. E., Lowe, T., Tulips, J. and Wakeling, C. 1981. *Making the change: a study of the process of the abolition of corporal punishment*, Edinburgh, Hodder and Stoughton for the Scottish Council for Research in Education.

Department of Education and Science. 1973. *Circular No. 4/73: Staffing of special schools and classes*, London, HMSO.

Department of Education and Science. 1978a. *Truancy and behavioural problems in some urban schools*. (A report by Her Majesty's Inspectorate of Schools), London, HMSO.

Department of Education and Science. 1978b. *Behavioural units: a survey of special units for pupils with behavioural problems*. (A report by Her Majesty's Inspectorate of Schools), London, HMSO.

Docking, J. W. 1980. *Control and Discipline in Schools*, London, Harper & Row.

Dunham, J. 1977. 'The effects of disruptive behaviour on teachers', *Educational Review*, 29, 3, 181–187.

Galloway, D. 1985. 'Meeting special educational needs in the ordinary school? Or creating them?' *Maladjustment and Therapeutic Education*,' 3, 3, 3–10.

Hargreaves, D. H. 1975. *Interpersonal Relations and Education*, London, Routledge and Kegan Paul.

Inner London Education Authority 1985. *Working Party on Off-site Centres*, London, ILEA.

ILEA 1986. *The Junior School Project*, Research and Statistics Branch, London, ILEA.

Kloska, A., and Ramasut, A. 1985. 'Teacher stress', *Maladjustment and Therapeutic Education*, 3, 2, 19–26.

Kolvin, I., Garside, R. F., Nicol, A. R., Macmillan, A., Wolstenhome, F., and Leitch, I. M. 1981. *Help starts here*, London Tavistock.

Kyriacou, C., and Sutcliffe, J. 1978. 'Teacher stress: prevalence, source and symptoms', *British Journal of Educational Psychology*, 48, 2 159–167.

Lane, D. 1978. *The impossible child, 1* and *2*, London, ILEA.

Lawrence, J. 1980. *Exploring Techniques for Coping with Disruptive Behaviour in School*, Educational Studies Monograph, London, Goldsmiths College.

Leach D. 1977. 'Teachers perceptions and "problem" pupils', *Educational Review* 2 3. 188–203.

Ling, R. and Davies, G. 1984. *A survey of off-site units in England and Wales*, Birmingham, Birmingham Polytechnic.

Lloyd-Smith, M. (ed.), 1984. *Disruptive schooling*, London, John Murray.

Mongon, D. 1984. *An analysis of the process through which pupils become classified as 'maladjusted'*, Ph.D. thesis, Polytechnic of the South Bank.

Ouston, J. 1981. 'Differences between schools: the implications for school practice', in Gillham, B. (ed.), *Problem behaviour in secondary school*, London, Croom Helm.

Reynolds, D. and Sullivan M. 1981. 'The effects of school: a radical faith restated', in Gillham, B. (ed.), *Problem behaviour in secondary school*, London, Croom Helm.

Rutter, M., Maughan, B., Mortimore, P., and Ouston, J. *Fifteen thousand hours: secondary schools and their effects on children*, London, Open Books.

Taylor, D. 1985. 'Schools as a target for change . . .', in Dowling, E. and Osborne, E. (eds.), *The family and the school*, London, Routledge and Kegan Paul.

Topping, K. 1983. *Educational systems for disruptive adolescents*, London, Croom Helm.

12 School assessment panels at St Augustine's School

Neil Toppin

In this chapter Neil Toppin describes the assessment panels at his school in Scotland, which were established to attempt a flexible response to problems of disruption within the school and to offer pupils excluded from other schools or returning from special provision another chance in the mainstream. He and his staff reject the option of off-site provision and argue for an individually tailored solution involving guidance (pastoral) and curricular staff. They see the assessment panel as providing an alternative, non-punitive role, for guidance teachers. The chapter contains an outline of the panels, case studies of three boy pupils and Neil Toppin's evaluation of the successes and problems they have met.

School-based assessment panels were established in St Augustine's in 1979–80 for a number of reasons. The school's philosophy of child-centred education required that an individual-based assessment of problems and difficulties be attempted. The panels therefore are a contribution by the guidance staff to a total school philosophy which includes continuous assessment, a school-based certificate in years three and four which covers both the cognitive and affective domains and which is wholly positive in its comments, and mixed-ability teaching in years one and two. They were also set up as a way of avoiding off-site referral. It was the school's belief that the creation of special units would not solve the behavioural problems which we encounter and furthermore there was little likelihood of re-integration into mainstream schooling (a view largely substantiated by the available evidence of many of the existing units). Finally, we were supported in our approach by the social work department's growing emphasis on trying to deal with problems in the context of the local community and where possible through mainstream schooling rather than any other provision such as residential schools.

We identified several aims for the panels:

1 To identify the nature and causes of behavioural difficulties of each pupil referred to a panel.
2 To establish an integrated approach incorporating teachers, social workers, child psychologists, pupils and parents plus any other relevant people.
3 To establish if a pupil can be sustained within St Augustine's (to date only one panel declined to accept a pupil).
4 To be flexible in devising ways of suporting pupils.
5 To ensure that all those involved fully understand their contribution.

The panels in practice

Every panel has two permanent members, the assistant headteacher (guidance) and the school psychologist. Other members include the pupil, the parent(s), the appropriate member of the guidance staff and, where appropriate, other members of the teaching staff such as the principal remedial teacher or form teacher, social worker and staff from other educational establishments such as an assessment centre or residential care. The meetings are informal. All participants are encouraged to contribute to the definition of the problem and its solution. A minute is kept of the meeting and everyone present receives a copy.

Referral to an assessment panel may come from staff or parents or external agencies. To date there have been almost two hundred. Of these about 25 per cent have been from outside St Augustine's, including referrals from List D,[1] school psychologists in other areas and special education. Many of the external referrals have been exclusions from other schools.

While the panels normally take place in St Augustine's in many instances it has been judged more beneficial to hold the meetings outside school (e.g. in the secure wing of St Mary's List D, at Rosevale school and at Larchgrove Assessment Centre). Staff have also found it necessary to attend children's hearings[2] both before and after an assessment panel. As a result a strong working relationship has been established with the reporter's department.

TONY

Tony was in Larchgrove Assessment Centre when his case was first referred to St Augustine's. He had been involved in housebreaking and an assessment had been requested. At fourteen, Tony got on well with his peer group and had settled quickly into the assessment centre routine. His educational attainments, however, rang alarm bells. He had a measured reading age of only seven years and could cope with only the most basic calculations. His educational problems were aggravated by his refusal to wear glasses, without which his eyesight was very poor. At Larchgrove some expressed the view that the remedial input necessary to develop Tony's literacy and numeracy could be provided best at a residential school, but there was a stronger view that it would not be to his benefit to remove him from a secure and caring home.

The children's panel hearing which followed the assessment period concentrated on Tony's brushes with authority both in and out of school and his learning difficulties. They went along with the feeling that Tony should have a non-residential supervision order but strongly recommended that he should change his school.

An approach was made to St Augustine's and an assessment panel was held to consider Tony's enrolment in the school. Represented at the meeting were Tony and his mother and sister, assessment centre staff, social work, child guidance and three members of St Augustine's staff, including the assistant head (guidance) and the member of the guidance team that would look after Tony. The other member of the school staff was the principal teacher of the remedial department who it was felt would play a key role in Tony's remaining time at school.

---

[1] Schools similar to the Community Homes with Education in England and Wales (see Chapter 7).
[2] The Children's Hearing Panels were set up in 1971 and act as a sorting point for young people who have been in trouble with the law or who are said to be 'at risk.'

The assessment panel agreed to Tony's enrolment in St Augustine's and attempted to co-ordinate the help which could be provided by the different agencies. With the agreement of Tony's parents, Tony would follow a partial timetable for between two and three weeks, allowing him to phase himself into full attendance at the school. This arrangement received the full blessing of the children's panel who agreed that 'too much, too soon' might be a retrograde step. Tony himself suggested attending at different times each week in order to familiarize himself with different subject areas of the curriculum. In light of Tony's learning difficulties, Tony was to attend the assessment centre two evenings a week for help with basic reading and writing. The principal teacher of remedial education at the school agreed to accompany Tony to the assessment centre after school in order to get the arrangement off the ground. A review of these arrangements would be held in the assessment centre after a suitably short period. With the help of his mother and sister, he agreed to continue this work at home which would be set by the school and assessment centre jointly. A review of the assessment panel was to be held within one month of Tony's enrolment and thereafter when deemed necessary.

Tony remained at St Augustine's for the remainder of his schooldays, a period of eighteen months. By the terms of his enrolment, there is little doubt that the provision of regular review assessment panels helped him by offering support, encouragement and occasionally chastisement for letting himself down. Where previously Tony had struggled to accept even basic school discipline, he was able to survive St Augustine's with only the occasional small-scale disagreements with a minority of staff. In terms of the development of social skills, Tony undoubtedly was a success story.

Tony's learning difficulties and in particular his own attitude to them, proved more intractable. A series of review panels wrestled with the problem and provided a series of responses. Child guidance offered two half days a week for half his final year. Under the supervision of the principal teacher of remedial education, he received an extraordinary degree of help with basic reading, writing and arithmetic. Arrangements were made for a voluntary tutor to visit his home to supplement his studies. His attitude to all these arrangements was somewhat cavalier. It was with disappointment that a final review assessment panel decided that, despite the earnest efforts of all concerned, Tony would leave school with a limited ability to read and write.

However, since he left school he has been in no further trouble with the police and, although unemployed, remains happily at home with his family.

JIM

Jim is the second youngest of five children and the only boy. Jim's father has a chronic drink problem and he eventually put the family out of their house. They went to live elsewhere in Easterhouse in very poor accommodation. Jim was an extremely nervous child and was subjected to bullying, both by his family and by his peer group. As a result he early on developed the habit of staying out of the house as much as possible.

In December 1982 Jim's family started squatting in council housing and were referred to the social work department by the housing department. Bedsitter accommodation was eventually provided but in the course of the investigation by the social work department it was discovered that in addition to Jim's persistent truancy, he was also staying away from home, sleeping rough for days at a time. The children were eventually admitted into care as a result of neglect. (One of Jim's sisters had to be rushed to hospital with a critical diabetic condition.) Within a short time, however, the children were allowed to return home. Jim was described by his social worker as 'looking haggard, dirty and withdrawing more and more into his old ways again'.

Jim was due to leave another school in the area at Christmas 1984 and shortly before summer 1984 a panel hearing was requested due to Jim's non-attendance at school and the theft of a pushbike. The children's panel noted the family problems and Jim's increasingly introspective nature. The panel accepted the social work argument that if there was a high degree of Social Work input to the family home, and that if Jim could be placed in a new school for his remaining few months of statutory attendance, then this might be the most suitable response.

In the course of the assessment panel, several salient points were made. Jim had little or no support at home apart from that provided through social work. He had a long history of truancy. He had few friends. He enjoyed good relationships with adults especially on a one-to-one basis. He said he wanted to attend school and had a particular liking for technical subjects.

It was the view of the assessment panel that a few months of reasonably stable attendance could be of great help to Jim when he left school and they decided that a flexible arrangement might encourage attendance where previous efforts had failed. Jim was therefore enrolled at St Augustine's. He was given a flexible timetable which, in terms of classes, could be built up as seemed appropriate. The technical department provided a base for him in order that he could pursue Technical Studies over and above normal classes. The assistant headteacher agreed to see him every day, on an informal basis, to get a chance to talk to him about home, family and school and to offer support where possible. He also arranged with the school resource centre for him to have access to the library area at certain periods, during which he could relax with a book or magazine. The social worker and the assistant headteacher agreed to meet regularly to discuss his progress.

In the event Jim completed his schooling at St Augustine's with little difficulty. He certainly had a number of absences, but all were explained with notes from his mother or from his doctor. He enjoyed his final few months at school and even returned after Christmas to visit and to say hello to members of staff. He had, meantime, managed to get himself a job on a building site.

WILLIAM

William is at present completing his third year at St Augustine's. He lives at home with his mother and stepfather and younger sister. His behaviour at school, and apparently outside school, alternates between the 'angelic' and the 'diabolical'. His parents alternate between feelings of pride and moments of frustration and desperation. Unfortunately, as William's behaviour deteriorates, so does his relationship with his parents

Early in the first year his behaviour pattern was showing dips and troughs. Money problems at home led to a temporary fragmentation of the family and a new school for William but when the family got back together and William returned to St Augustine's, reports from the other school followed the previous pattern at St Augustine's.

This pattern of behaviour could be described as generally good with occasional bouts of attention seeking. However, what was particularly worrying, was that William was becoming more and more involved in solvent abuse, and as the abuse became more frequent, so the behaviour both at home and in school, became more extreme. On one occasion William catapulted a lump of metal into a classroom full of pupils and a girl was quite badly injured. On another occasion he kicked in the glass in a series of school doors. On neither occasion could he say why he had done what he did, nor had he done it in the company of other pupils he wanted to impress.

In the wake of this behaviour, which resulted in the police pressing charges, William was placed in Larchgrove for a 21-day assessment. The children's panel hearing which followed this assessment felt that he should be placed on home supervision, given the generally supportive nature of the family home, but that he should attend a privately-run child guidance facility in Glasgow, instead of mainstream schooling, for long-term assessment, as a day-pupil.

Following a period of many months, William expressed a desire to return to mainstream schooling and approaches were made to St Augustine's by the educational psychologist concerned. An assessment panel was convened and all the relevant agencies were invited. At the assessment panel it was pointed out that William was doing very well. He had seemingly conquered his solvent abuse problem and his relationship with mother, stepfather and sister were good. He was genuinely keen to return to St Augustine's where his sister was now a pupil and both social work and child guidance were keen to see him return to mainstream schooling.

In light of this, St Augustine's was prepared to accept his re-enrolment in the school, although the assessment panel expressed a strong wish to keep his case under constant review. The panel also arranged for William to spend two half-days a week at child guidance. In addition, the psychologist from child guidance arranged with the assistant head (guidance) in the school to meet every three weeks to discuss William's progress. At the time of writing these provisions have been in operation for nearly six months and appear to be effective.

The children's panel met four months ago to consider the termination of William's home supervision order. Prior to this, an assessment panel review meeting was held in the school to consider a submission to the children's panel. Acting jointly, William's parents, the social worker concerned, child guidance and the school all advised against terminating the supervision requirement as all felt William needed the joint supervision. William, who attended the meeting, also agreed that he behaved better when the eyes of the world were upon him.

Not only, therefore, was William party to the decision to request continuation of the supervision order, but he now looks back and agrees it was the right decision. He certainly has not become an angel overnight, but his more extreme behaviour has been left behind and usually he can be relied upon to be helpful and co-operative.

Our conclusions

A review of the assessments to date shows we cannot claim total success. We have had partial successes and failures. We have had to adjust and re-assess the format, aims and processes of the panels. But in a majority of cases there has been some success, and in many instances the outcome has been very successful. In general we have been most successful with pupils excluded from other schools and returning from special provision. We have been less successful where the difficulty already has a long-standing history in our own school.

The assessment panels have contributed to the development of the general idea that, within reasonable constraints and parameters, schools should be sufficiently flexible to adjust to defined needs and problems rather than impose rigid, homogeneous solutions to particular and individual problems. That is what the guidance staff of St Augustine's believe to be the essence of their role and work. In the light of the experience of two hundred assessment panels, it is our confirmed view that an approach in which a whole school can and will adjust to individual need, without prejudice to majority rights, can offer a viable alternative to 'sin bins' or the like.

All teachers are or should take responsibility for guidance work. The assessment panels have contributed to a better working relationship between guidance staff and other members of staff. The fact that such a relationship has been established in a difficult but rewarding area is of significance to all staff. The willingness of all staff to co-operate and contribute serves as a useful counterpoint to the divisive and negative views which are commonly expressed elsewhere. This is helped by the fact that all teachers involved with pupils from an assessment panel receive full and positive information. The support of the staff and their willingness to adjust their provision and their reaction, clearly demonstrates that given the proper approach teachers are in both principle and practice more willing to review their methods and sustain alternatives than is usually acknowledged.

The value of a co-ordinated approach is without question the most significant conclusion. The improved relationships between the school, the parents, the child guidance service, social work and others has been of immense and profound benefit. The creation of a more positive and co-operative attitude by all involved, based on an appreciation of the legitimate areas of parental and professional responsibility and competence, has proved beneficial not only at assessment panels but in the total life of the school. The removal of barriers between services, the removal of traditional doubts and reservations and the acceptance of disagreement and dissent has contributed greatly to realistic and constructive relationships.

The amount of time required to pursue a highly individualized approach cannot be discounted. The time required for arranging meetings, preparing reports, attending assessment panels, producing and circulating minutes, contacting relevant staff and monitoring induction and/or progress is considerable. Yet had the assessment panel system not existed in most cases equal amounts of time would have been occupied later but in the negative cycle of suspensions, parental interviews, referral procedures and the preparation of reports.

We have learnt much about the possible pitfalls of a flexible approach. For example, if pupils are on part-time timetables some staff must accept that a pupil will not attend their class for a period of time. This also requires a good working relationship with the attendance department. Where a personality clash exists between a pupil and a teacher and the obvious solution is a change of teacher this must be achieved without demoralizing the teacher or reducing his or her personal and professional status. Equally, it must be ensured that other pupils do not see such a change as a precedent which they can then seek to exploit.

Assessment panels cannot produce all the answers. They do, however, produce a forum in which all of the questions will be asked, where all who should be listening and responding are present, and where all those involved in the 'total child' can contribute to an individualized solution. Perhaps the most important aspect of the scheme is that it ensures that guidance staff are not deployed as disciplinarians. Rather it is an opportunity for them to contribute positively to the educational, social and personal support which many pupils do need but often do not receive.

13 Discussion as a basis for action
Rob Grunsell

In this chapter Rob Grunsell gives a brief outline of his approach to in-service training which he developed at the schools council and published in Finding Answers to Disruption *(Grunsell 1985). It involved identifying common concerns of teachers and then producing stimulus materials to initiate and focus discussion and trigger groups working on them to devise their own plans of action. Rob Grunsell encourages teachers to adapt his materials to their own needs or use them as a source of ideas for devising their own training. He stresses the participatory nature of training and the need for it to be grounded in teachers' own priorities.*

'To produce in-service training materials which will help teachers respond more effectively to problems of disruption in schools.' That was the brief for a one-person project I took on with the late schools council some four years ago. This is an account of how I reacted to that very tall order. I came to the project from a background in and around off-site education, convinced that while removing a disaffected minority from the mainstream might give those pupils a better chance of survival and their teachers relief from extreme disruption, it did nothing to change the factors which produced that disaffection. I believed then and still believe now that schools make a difference. Features of background experience and personality may create potential in pupils for disaffection; 'disruptive' or 'passive.' How far and in what form that potential is realized depends on where they go to school. There is a wealth of evidence to say so. 'Disruption' is not an objectively definable illness suffered by a precise percentage of youth, nor a given set of behaviours. It's what teachers individually and collectively define it to be: the limits of their tolerance, moral and personal. It's the expression of a negative dynamic, in which the cycle of action and reaction between teacher and pupil seems only to confirm the pupil in the disruptive role and of escalating sanctions which consume energy, time and morale in large amounts.

So what could in-service training offer teachers in locating and treating the causes of this dynamic? Looking around I had to conclude that if the training has no roots in the 'real life' of school then the answer is bound to be – not very much. Thus many techniques for analysis and reaction presented through in-service training as 'cut flowers', have failed to grow in schools because they do not make sense to the teachers once back in their schools.

All too typically I saw enthused teachers returning from training, armed with new perspectives who became progressively drained of optimism as they faced non-understanding in colleagues, shortage of resources, lack of follow-up support, and who ended up despairing and cynical about possibilities of real change. But, if the methods of delivery were frequently inappropriate so, I felt, was the content of training. Talking about disruption involves admitting and examining failure, professional and personal. It's a difficult, demanding and, at times, painful process. The doctrine of 'coping', keeping the classroom door shut, is still very heavily entrenched in the teaching profession. It is unsurprising, therefore, to find that the great majority of training about disruption places the problems firmly within the child, their family, their background, their learning difficulties. There would seem to be little incentive for teachers to examine the problem in dynamic terms, as a product of interaction; everyone's or no one's fault.

I decided that what was urgently required was a method and content which didn't place either the problem or the expertise 'out there', which helped teachers to share and analyse their own experience, define their problems and priorities, identify their own routes to solutions. Whatever I designed would have to take account of circumstances as they are for the hard-pressed teaching population. They have very little time to talk; our education services allow scant space for the education of its own workers. The overload of urgent daily business constantly distracts teachers in their attempts to step back to examine underlying causes and long-term problems. And the difficulty of starting that examination is compounded by the existence of a bewildering range of equally valid starting points for explanation.

I have travelled round England and Wales listening to many teachers who had much to say. I constructed a map of their principal starting points for concern; teacher stress and the need for support, the social dynamics of the classroom, the efficiency of sanctions and rewards, the school's relationship with parents and outside agencies and many more. For each of these I then evolved time-limited discussion structures applying to the subject of disruption a simple group-interaction method (for which I would make no claims of originality), a process intended to maximize the chances of 'on-task' participation leading to clear definition and appreciation of areas of agreement and divergence and needs for further analysis or action.

The group is invited to start at a common point: response to a specific trigger – a research quote, a statement about opinions to be completed, a range of factors to be ranked for importance, a role play. Responses have to be shared, first, in the relative safety of small numbers in order to enable participants to build up confidence in coping with the frequently painful nature of talk about disruption. Group members have to co-operate within the disciplines of time and equal opportunities for participation. So much discussion of disruption loses its way with attention wandering from one priority to another. Here people are asked to focus upon one topic only.

An example of the way activity sheets are used to structure discussion is given below. It is a 'unit' entitled *Everyone a winner*, taken from the pack I developed (Grunsell 1985) (see Fig. 13.1).

Stage 1 invites group members to spend five minutes in quiet reflection, a space in which to clear minds crowded with concerns of the teaching day, to focus on the cartoon and commit their first reactions to paper. Moving into their stage 2 sub-groups they are asked to share and relate these reactions. There is safety in numbers but less risk of embarrassment when the numbers are small. Whatever response is formed, is fed into a second round of sharing, this time with the whole group in stage 3. In pooling their ideas the group can work towards establishing by the end of the session, a prioritized agenda for further discussion, enquiry or action. There is no unrealistic assumption that one hour of talk will produce any

B1   Everyone a winner?

This unit asks you to look at confrontation where both teacher and pupil feel they have 'won'.

* Are some pupils bound to use conflict with staff as a means of enhancing their status among classmates?
* What can teachers do to avoid such conflicts?

Time: 1 hour

STAGE 1 — *Individually* — *5 minutes*

Look at the cartoon below

Complete the following statement:

When teachers and pupils end up having this kind of confrontation it may be because

. . . .

. . . .

. . . .

or because   . . . .

. . . .

. . . .

or because   . . . .

. . . .

. . . .

B1

STAGE 2 – *In groups of 4 to 5 – 30 minutes*

Share your completed statements

List all the reasons you have identified

Discuss in detail those reasons you feel to be most significant.

STAGE 3 – *As a whole group – 25 minutes*

Share the lists compiled in stage 2 and the main points arising from discussion

Ask:

* Can you identify certain types of pupil who will tend to use any conflict to boost their status in the eyes of their classmates?

* Are particular types of punishment likely to produce this kind of confrontation?

* Are there general attitudes or specific strategies which staff can adopt to avoid counterproductive conflict?

Next steps? Section M; units D1, K1, L2.

---

definitive solutions. Rather the aim is to help people bring their specific and collective perceptions about the problems quickly into focus – a basis from which a course to direct action can be plotted.

Over four years, through a process of trialling of exercises with teacher groups and much instructive error, I have evolved some forty discussion units which are presented in sections organized according to areas of concern – for example *'Problems with the whole class'*; *'Describing disruptive behaviour for yourself and others'*; *'Support: what you want and where you get it'*; *'Schools and parents'*. Because every teacher group which decides to discuss disruption will need to find its own starting point, its own trigger for concern or anxiety, the materials are offered, not as a prescribed course of discussion, but as a resource bank from which groups are invited to select discussion units appropriate to their needs.

The pack is fronted by user notes which offer advice on how to set up working parties, the pitfalls and key points in locating 'appropriate' school and teacher groups, how to narrow the choice of relevant issues, to find exercises which match urgent concerns. The exercises are aimed at a common denominator of concerns amongst secondary school staff but their value lies, not in specific content, but in the process they demonstrate for the structuring of discussion. Users can hang their own content on the framework. They can modify, adapt, improve, the existing units. They can write their own. They can be primary or special schools, mixed groups of teaching and outside agency staff. The process can be relevant and effective for all these groups.

That, then, is the theory – but how does it work out in practice? Describing what is demonstrated in practice needs a careful preamble. No single teaching strategy, set of interpersonal techniques, no one package of in-service training materials can produce nationwide and instant results. That seems too obvious to be worth raising, but it isn't. The history of our education service is littered with burnt-out bandwagons. The pursuit of fantasy solutions has repeatedly drained energy from the much more difficult business of pursuing workable models for change which are rooted in what acutally happens and could be made to happen in our schools. I will say very clearly then, that the discussion process I am offering does not work in *all* schools, with any group of teachers. Its a participatory method. It can only realize its full potential when, at a school level, head and senior staff are actively committed to its use and prepared to involve themselves in discussion sessions, demonstrating, by example, allegiance to the notion that talking about areas of personal anxiety, confusion and failure is an essential part of professional development for *all*. And those who take part in groups have to show a parallel commitment to working within the spirit of the process; putting as much energy into listening as in talking, staying on task, collaborating rather than competing in the pursuit of common objectives.

It looks like a great deal to ask of our underpaid and undersupported teachers. But there are many teachers in many schools who feel the need to break out of the cycle of crisis management and low moral so keenly that they *are* prepared to make those commitments. They want to replace ineffective reaction to the symptoms of trouble with positive action aimed at the roots of the problem.

Trialling has been done through weekly after-school sessions, through whole staff conferences in school and weekend courses. The materials have been used as the sole in-service training source and in combinatoin with role-play, the use of outside speakers and video. Predictably the reactions from teachers who have used the exercises have been varied. For a minority there was disappointment: 'Well, it was all very interesting, I found out a lot about what other staff think. But so what. Nothing's *happened*', or, 'It's still just talk'. Significantly others have reacted with ambivalence:

> That exercise on support really took the lid off things in our school. All hell broke loose. Everybody – senior and junior – started talking about how they weren't getting the support they needed. And it hasn't stopped since.

When views and feelings, previously hidden, do get a chance to show themselves, the situation may indeed seem worse. Staff have to face the challenge of turning their honest, even depressing appraisal of difficulties into action. However an encouraging number of teacher groups did find a first step of action to take as a result of using the process. Some of these were minor, others were administrative. A significant number were aimed at positive prevention and these included altering the time allowed for lesson changeover to reduce crowd chaos, a decision to involve all staff in corridor supervision, a move to set up mutual support pairs amongst staff and the creation of a rewards system following the realization that for non-academic pupils the school offered little or no incentives.

A final evaluation of the process will have to wait. The benefits of teachers identifying common problems or feeling solidarity, take time to appear. They are cumulative, subtle and frequently indirect. In one group a discussion on referral procedures may produce a lessening of resentment amongst senior staff. In another school an oppressive staffroom atmosphere may be lightened as a spirit of mutual concern filters in from groups who have shared their needs for support.

I have seen enough to believe that the materials, over time, *will* prove to be of real help to teachers trying to solve their own problems by enabling them to see what support there is in the sharing of difficulties and by strengthening the belief that efficient discussion can lead to effective action.

Reference

Grunsell, R. (1985). *Finding Answers to Disruption: a Discussion Pack for Secondary Teachers*, Schools Council Pamphlet Series, London, Longmans.

SECTION 3

Producing and reducing disaffection

14 'The English culture is being swamped': racism in secondary schools
Cecile Wright

In this chapter Cecile Wright provides an insight into attitudes towards black people in two midland secondary schools ('A' and 'B') based on interviews with staff and pupils. They are both mixed comprehensives. In school A the proportion of pupils of Afro-Caribbean and Asian origin is approximately 25 per cent, whereas for school B the ethnic 'minority' pupils are in the majority, comprising over 60 per cent of the school population. Despite these differences the school experiences of the Afro-Caribbean pupils, on which she concentrates, appear very similar.

School A – 'Everybody just seems so disillusioned'

This was originally a boys' grammar school. It amalgamated with a boys' secondary modern in September 1975 to form a mixed comprehensive but retained a strong grammar school ethos amongst a section of the senior teachers. These teachers exerted considerable influence within the school, because they held positions as heads of departments or as year heads. They saw themselves as wanting to get on with the teaching of their subject. However, they felt frustrated by teaching in a comprehensive school rather than a selective school and by what they saw as the poor quality of the pupils. This in turn led to feelings of disillusionment. As a probationary teacher explained when she talked about the general attitude:

> Everybody just seems so disillusioned ... everybody seems fed up ... the staff as a whole, I mean. I came in as a young teacher, enthusiastic, full of new ideas but you soon find that the old attitudes rub off on you, and so you end up thinking, 'Oh, why am I doing this? Do I want to teach after all?' and this is because of what the others say to you, the more experienced teachers. I think instead of encouraging you to try out new ideas they seem to get some kind of kick out of telling you how bad it is ... I don't think it is a bad school.

The headmaster responded in a similar way when asked if staff portrayed attitudes which are conducive for teaching in 'both a comprehensive and a multiracial school'. His reply was:

> In the positive sense of showing sympathy and understanding and above all, in listening to the children talk, I am not so sure about there being a majority ... In a comprehensive school attitudes conveying sympathy, understanding and concern for the pupils are fundamental. This does not necessarily mean letting everyone do exactly what they want to do ...
>
> I think that attitudes that come from people who are concerned with academic excellence and expect it to be so (remember, it wasn't a dirty word ten years ago, it was what society expected, the school to be achieving), now find themselves faced

with having to turn right around and in many cases, do feel disillusioned, very upset and bitter indeed and honestly, the kinder the system can be in terms of early retirement, the better.

I'LL SEND YOU BACK TO THE CHOCOLATE FACTORY

It is difficult to say conclusively that there are differences in the way in which teachers in the classroom interact with Afro-Caribbean pupils. However, the following dialogue noted during a classroom observation, demonstrates how a teacher's insensitivity can result in conflict with Afro-Caribbean young people. The teacher was talking to the class. Whilst he wrote on the blackboard, a group of four white boys, sat talking to each other in an ordinary tone of voice. The teacher, being annoyed by the noise level in the room, threw a piece of chalk at an Afro-Caribbean boy who was not being particularly noisy.

> *Teacher:* Pay attention [shouted].
> *Teacher:* [To an Asian boy] Could you get me that piece of chalk.
> *Peter:* [Afro-Caribbean] Why don't you use black chalk?
> *Teacher:* [Turning to the researcher] Did you hear that? Then I would be accused of being a racist, take this for example, I was down at lower school, I had a black girl in my class, she did something or another. I said to her, if you're not careful I'll send you back to the chocolate factory. She went home and told her parents, her dad came up to school, and decided to take the matter to the Commission for Racial Equality. It was only said in good fun, nothing malicious.
> *Keith:* [Afro-Caribbean (aggressively)] How do we know that it's a joke, in my opinion that was a disrespectful thing to say.
> *Teacher:* [Raising his voice and pointing his finger at Keith] If I wanted to say something maliciously racist, I wouldn't have to make a joke about it. I'd say it. I've often had a joke with you, haven't I?
> *Keith:* [Angrily] Those so-called jokes, were no joke, you were being cheeky. I went home and told my mum and she said that if you say it again she would come and sort you out. As for that girl, if it was my father, he wouldn't just take you to the CRE, he would also give you a good thump. My father says that a teacher should set a good example for the children, by respecting each one, whether them black or white. He says that any teacher who makes comments like that in front of a class, shouldn't be in school that's why he said to us that if a teacher ever speaks to us like that he would come up to school and sort him out.
> *Harry:* If it was me that you said that to, I wouldn't go home and tell my parents, I would just tell you about your colour.
> *Keith:* Teachers shouldn't make racist jokes.

THEY JUMP TO THESE CONCLUSIONS

One way in which attitudes towards and categorization of black pupils was fostered was through gossip among staff. This is an important medium in the school, since a fair proportion of teachers do not actually teach the pupils they hear talked about. Its effect was described to me by a white probationary teacher:

> A lot of teachers jump to conclusions about pupils before they've even come into contact with them and broken through the pupil's resentment. They jump to these conclusions and these conclusions are passed round in the staffroom. You only have

to sit in there and you hear the rumours and the gossip that's going around and the thing is, in the staffroom it's always the bad kids that are talked about, never the good ones, which I suppose makes sense in a way, but as a new teacher, you come in, you hear these rumours like, I used to hear rumours about Kevin (an Afro-Caribbean pupil) and I thought, 'Oh, God, I'll have to watch out for Kevin, everybody thinks he's a trouble-maker and that means he's bound to be in my class', but I mean it's not as simple as that, it really isn't . . .

There are a few white kids that are talked about but I mean that's inevitable. I think to a certain extent the West Indian kids tend to get labelled and these labels they feel they've got to live up to. I mean, you might think 'well, what goes on in the staffroom doesn't get round to the kids' but it does, it does, even if it is just through the teacher's own attitude. They can sense it, they are not stupid.

This teacher's view that the Afro-Caribbean pupils felt obliged to live up to the labels given them by the school was reiterated by other teachers. A black teacher claimed:

The West Indian pupils, especially the boys, are seen as a problem in this school because they are so 'aggressive'. You see, I am using a quote here, they are so openly aggressive and surly . . . If it is always assumed that they are intellectually inferior, what else is there for them to do . . . every time teachers are constantly amazed by the fact that in the first year they have at the moment there are two or three really bright West Indian boys, and it's of constant amazement to people like Mr G . . . 'my goodness he's bright where does he get it from'. Pupils here in the fifth year are generally thought to be dross.

How might the behaviour and attitudes of the pupils be affected by the organization of the school and the teachers' attitudes and expectations? From discussions within a racially mixed group of sixty pupils, both from the fourth and fifth year, there seems to have been a consensus of opinion that the streaming system does not truly reflect ability. There was also a consensus that the streaming system works more against black pupils, indicated in the following remarks from a white pupil:

I think that black kids are treated rather badly in this school, for example, there are less black kids in the 'A' band. In my opinion it is not because they are not capable, it's because they are not given the opportunity. Teachers generally hold a low opinion of them, for example, I'm in the 'A' band, I'm doing 'O' level English. I find that some of the 'B' band kids are doing the same syllabus, and in some cases they get the same marks or better marks than us, yet they can't do 'O' level and they're in the 'B' band.

Conversations with two black pupils further revealed the dissatisfaction felt about the school's organization:

We came here because our brother and sister went to this school. They got on badly, they were unhappy with the school, so they didn't try. They were also put in the 'B' band. However, they are now at (another school) in the sixth form. The headmaster would not allow them to go into the sixth form here. Anyway, they're better off there. They are both doing 'O' levels and 'A' levels. Since going there my brother has got 'O' level Grade A in Maths. He never did any good here.

THEY DON'T GIVE HALF-CASTE KIDS NO HASSLE

Further conversations with black pupils revealed a general belief that the school's organization was against them because of its attitude towards their colour. They saw little point in trying. School seemed to be a 'battle ground', a hostile environment: rejecting their colour and identity. The dialogues which follow clearly emphasize this. A group of eight black boys in this discussion reveal how they feel about certain teachers making derogatory comments about their skin colour in the form of a joke, and also how it affects them emotionally when this takes place in front of the class.

> *Michael:* It's like once the man (referring to the teacher) come in the class, and ask me in front of the class, 'Why me coffee coloured', he say, 'How come Wallace dark, and Kennedy black and Kevin a bit browner? How come you that, you a half-breed?' Me say, 'No man, me no look like me half-breed'. Me say, 'just like some a una white like a chalk and another couple a una got blond hair, some have black hair, me no come ask wha that!' ... That's how he is, he just come around, crack him few sarcastic jokes about black kids.
>
> *Paul:* But they're not nice at all. They're not nice. The jokes aren't nice. The jokes are disrespectful.
>
> *Kevin:* They're not jokes man.
>
> *Errol:* You can't call them jokes. When he cracks a joke or whatever he does in front of the class, he just turn round and laugh. You get him and the class laughing at you.
>
> *Kevin:* What he is doing is running you down. He's just bringing you down like dirt. Nobody is bring me down (said with anger). Every time I'm chuck out of (subject) completely man, because every time in (subject) he always keep calling me something about me colour and I answer back.
>
> *Errol:* The teachers are forever picking on the black boys.
>
> *Michael:* Like me now, them no too bother with me because them think, say me a half-breed, you know. Half the teachers in the school think say me a half-breed so they don't too bother me. Just lately they find out, say me black, so they've started bothering me. Like the half-caste kids them they used to left me alone.
>
> *Kevin:* They don't give half-caste kids no hassle, no hassle whatsoever. However, if the half-caste kids act black, they pick on them hassle man.

The boys were asked in what ways they felt that this so-called 'hassle' affected their academic performance. Paul succinctly voiced the views of the group when he said:

> You're not really given the opportunity to learn. Most of the time we're either sitting outside the head's office or we are either fighting or we are either arguing with them. It's just we got no time, as you sit down to work they pin something on you.

WE ARE BEING FACED WITH A BARRAGE OF PATOIS

The above dialogues illustrate the resentment, bitterness and frustration felt by the Afro-Caribbean boys towards the school – as reflected through the attitudes of certain teachers. The kind of social relationship which existed between certain teachers and this group of boys became very apparent when one examined the terms of reference used by the boys when they were referring to the teachers and themselves; 'us' and 'them'. The pupils have developed a sub-cultural adolescent group within the school which is not only anti-school, but is also somewhat anti-white. This 'all-black' group is composed of both boys and girls: pupils from the third, fourth and fifth years. The thirty pupils or more making up the group move around together in the school during the school breaks.

Most teachers were aware of the presence of this group but unaware of the reason for its development, with the notable exceptions of a teacher from South Africa and the deputy headmistress. As the teacher pointed out:

> This group is a reaction to the racism in this school, we have what can be described as a very strong 'black mafia' within the school. They feel that they belong together, so they stick together.

This point was further expressed by the deputy headmistress, who said:

> There is certainly a race problem here at the moment. There is certainly, not so much a race problem between pupils, but there is a great problem here at the moment with the congregation, shall we say, of black pupils. By the time they get to the fourth form there are very few black pupils who are not mingling largely with black pupils. There are identifiable groups of black pupils as they move around the school and we have had problems this last year with a particular large group of black pupils who have set out their stalls to appear aggressive.

The group attempts to assert its presence through both verbal and non-verbal means. As the headmaster points out:

> A number of black children, particularly boys, seem to lose interest in the school's aims (unless they are good at games, then they dissociate that from the rest) in the third year and, from then, become increasingly seen as an anti-culture... probably the most striking manifestation of West Indian pupils, is just that group of large boys, and the sort of threatening physical presence, which you can see consistently around the school.

Even more important than this 'gang' behaviour was the deliberate assertion of 'blackness.' This was done successfully through the use of patois both defensively and offensively by the group. Patois was a success for the group insofar as they used it succinctly to communicate rejection of authority. Although the teachers were aware of this 'weapon' they had great difficulty in finding anything to attack it with. This point was reiterated by the deputy headmistress:

> We've got a problem at the moment, which is very nasty... where we are being faced with a barrage of patois. It is so worrying because you see when that happens we as teachers have a choice. We either ignore it, but if it's done in public you feel threatened, or you feel that you are showing weakness if you just ignore it. You can either react equally aggressively and verbally back in Spanish, or French, which in fact is what is happening, but that is not helpful, or as one member of staff said to me today, 'I came very close to clobbering him today'.

There was a parallel feeling amongst the black pupils that they were under surveillance. As Errol remarked:

> I try to keep out of trouble the best I can. If they cause trouble with me I cause trouble with them it's as simple as that. If you are a troublemaker, right, and you're pretty intelligent, they still keep you down. Look what they've done to Delroy, he's

pretty intelligent, yet they keep him down, no wonder he causes trouble. Because I want to get on I try to keep out of trouble.

School B 'The school never recovered'

School B was originally a girls' grammar school. It became a mixed comprehensive in September 1972 by amalgamating with two single-sex secondary modern schools. Some members of staff at the school felt that it had suffered and was still suffering from the effects of the reorganization. This comment from a senior teacher expresses a general view held by staff:

> When you have a very small, very select, very ladylike grammar school, joined with two rough and ready secondary moderns what basically happened in my view is that when they joined together the grammar school staff, or most of them, couldn't cope with the rough and ready aspect the school they came to have. They were all in positions of heads of department, consequently I got the feeling that the secondary modern staff who could cope with it to a certain extent, withdrew labour. I don't mean that they went on strike, it was well, 'let them buggers do it – they're the ones in the position let them do it'. The school has never recovered from this.

Although many of the original grammar school teachers are no longer at the school there is still a strong academic ethos amongst some of the senior teachers, though this is sometimes more a sense of nostalgia than something realized in their teaching. There is also an element of nostalgia, too, amongst the original secondary modern teachers, in the sense that, 'the staff knew where they stood within a small school', with 'a more traditional authority pattern'.

'THE SCHOOL IS FOR TEACHING ONLY WESTERN WAYS OF LIVING'

Since the reorganization twelve years ago, the ethnic composition of the school has gradually changed until the proportion of black pupils entering the first year is well over half. This intake of children from ethnic minority groups has been associated by some with difficulties within the school, such as 'declining standards' and 'discipline problems'. A year head who originally came from the secondary modern school at the time of reorganisation had this to say on the status of the school:

> This school is a low-ability school because of its catchment area, which consists of a low social class and a high immigrant population. More fundamentally, it is the high proportion of immigrants in this school which is responsible for the lowering of standards.

Many teachers try to obscure the fact that they are teaching in a multiracial school. Little attempt is made to acknowledge the ethnicity of the pupils. However, what is perceived as the belligerent, aggressive, lively, gregarious character of the Afro-Caribbean pupil, cannot be easily ignored by the teachers, and presents a constant reminder of the nature of the school. One teacher remarked on the lack of acceptance of the pupils:

> The pupils in this school come from working class and multi-cultural backgrounds. It seems to me that very few staff are addressing themselves to the kinds of things (e.g. resources, teaching style, subject content, and attitudes and the hidden cur-

riculum) that can be used to bring out the best of the pupils' cultures and backgrounds. The attitudes of teachers to West Indian and Asian cultures is at worst negative, and at best condescending and patronising. These cultures are viewed as remote and distant, and few teachers go out into the community to learn or take part in community activities ... Pupils are seen as recipients, with very little to offer to the curriculum. Teachers view themselves as doing a good job by educating 'these immigrants' in the 'best education system in the world' ... For these 'immigrants' to start demanding having a say in the way their pupils are taught and what they are taught is viewed with great disdain ...

There is so much that pupils can offer to the school if there can be someone to listen and take notice. The end result is that pupils switch off any interest in the school, and how they manage to go through five years of their school years still amazes me. They have a negative view of the school, of the West Indies, Africa and Asia and of themselves and their abilities.

Some of the views of this teacher were echoed by an Asian pupil in a Social Studies lesson, where the class was looking at the issue of 'prejudices in society'. The pupil pointed out to the teacher and the class that she felt that there is pervasive racial prejudice in the school, which the teachers failed to acknowledge. As she says:

We were discussing in form period, Asian languages in this school, about people who want to take it, that it would be a chance for people to learn another language, say, if non-Asian children take it they would come to respect it. The form teacher then was on about that the school is for teaching only Western ways of living, and European ways of living. She said that's what you come to school for. That opinion really shocked me, coming from my own form teacher. She was trying to tell me that we're nobody. She then said that when there was a lot of Polish people in the school, they never practised any of their culture here, they went away to their own community. She also tried to tell me there wasn't any prejudice in the school. And the worst thing is she was trying to tell a coloured person that there wasn't any prejudice, and that you only come to school to learn about the European way of life. That's the thing that needs bucking up in this school ...

I said to her, 'I'm not willing to argue with you here because it would get me into trouble but if I ever saw you on the street I would'. Because I made a mistake once when a teacher told me that there wasn't prejudice in this school. I blew up and I tried to tell her, no you're wrong. I got myself into trouble ... I made a mistake of doing it then in such an organized atmosphere. If I was going to ... I should have done it out of school because in school everything is organized. The teachers are willing to back each other up. I asked another teacher, 'Well, what do you think?' she said 'You were wrong to shout back at her full stop! Never mind what you were saying'.

The following comment from a year head provides direct support for this pupil's observations:

I find it very difficult to accept the immigrant people and children that I come into contact with. I cannot change my feeling because it is part of my upbringing – I feel that the English culture is being swamped. I do not see how the Asian and West

Indian pupils that I am responsible for can take on English behaviour for half a day when they are at school and change to their culture when they are at home.

'GO BACK WHERE YOU CAME FROM'

To what extent then do attitudes of this nature shape the Afro-Caribbean pupil–teacher relationship? Informal discussions with Afro-Caribbean pupils indicated that the pupils felt that certain teachers disrespect them on the basis of their ethnicity and that for these pupils the pupil–teacher relationship was based on conflict, with the pupils attempting to play the teachers at their own 'game' in order to survive. They saw the school as condoning these teachers' attitudes. A discussion with a group of twenty Afro-Caribbean girls illustrates this:

Barbara: The teachers here, them annoy you, too much.
Researcher: In what ways do they annoy you?
Barbara: They irate you in the lesson, so you can't get to work.
Susan: For example in Cookery, there were some knives and forks gone missing, right, and Mrs B goes 'Where's the knives and forks?' looking at us lot (the Afro-Caribbean pupils in the class).
Vera: Yeah, all the blacks.
Sonia: Seriously right, in the past most coloured children that has left school they've all said she's prejudiced.
Jean: She's told some kids to go back to their own country.
Sonia: Seriously right, if you go to another white teacher or somebody, and tell them that they're being prejudiced against you, they'll make out it's not, that it's another reason.
Jean: When Mrs B told Julie to go back to her own country she went and told Mrs C (the deputy headmistress), Mrs C said that Mrs B was depressed because her husband was dying.
Sonia: So why take it out on the black people then, she's told black people to do many things, she's even called them monkey.
Sandra: As for that Mrs C I can't explain my feelings about the woman. Because Mrs B, right she just prejudiced, she comes up to me in the Cookery lesson, tell me to clean out the dustbin, and I was so vexed I started to cry, I was so vexed by it. I didn't come to school for two weeks.
Sonia: You see the thing is, right, they can get away with saying anything to your face, there isn't anything you can do about it.
Susan: Mrs C is prejudiced herself because, I mean, she said to Karen that she is only getting bad because she hangs around with too many black people. It's not as if (shouting in anger) as she says, black people are going to change you to bad.
Researcher: Would you say that the Afro-Caribbean boys have the same experience with the teachers as yourselves?
Vera: The boys I know don't get the same treatment because most of the lads are quicker to box the teachers-dem than the girls, you see.

Assertions from pupils about what teachers call them may not always be believed by sceptical readers. A year head who talks about one of the phrases – 'go back to your own country' – referred to by this group of girls, provides evidence in support of their assertions – but about a different teacher. He reported a familiar parental complaint which began in the following way:

I have come to see you because that Mr R said to my son 'If you don't like it here then go back where you came from and where you belong' and I was so upset at that because my son was born here and I have lived in this country for over twenty years and how *dare* he say that, because my son comes from here. I came from Jamaica over twenty years ago and I got married in this country and I have stayed here ever since and although perhaps *I* might want to go back to Jamaica it's not home to him.

The year head had no doubt that the protest was well-founded

And that lady was quite genuine. The member of staff when I spoke to him about it afterwards – I did not call him in to speak to him about it immediately because I did not think it was either my place or my duty – I told him that she was very concerned about that being said to her son and quite frankly so was I, and really was that the sort of thing to say and he agreed it wasn't the thing to say but he said 'I was so angry at the time. The pupils had been going on at me about "You're always picking on me"' and then finally the boy said to him that he was picking on him because he was black and he said 'That just triggered it off'. He said 'I just turned to him and what I said. Yes, I did say that'.

He also reported times when a parent complained about the way their child was treated when he knew the reason before they did:

I know he said it in anger but you don't even say things in anger if you don't feel them and that really bothers me a bit. But that's not the only one. I have had others who've actually said 'X doesn't like my child', but then of course X doesn't like any black child. And I think we both know who I'm referring to . . . Black children react in a certain way because they feel they are being picked on, and because they react badly then further reaction follows.

HE'S BLACK SO IT'S TO BE EXPECTED

Discussions were also held with Afro-Caribbean boys, particularly with one group of fifteen pupils in this school. In these discussions the boys often voice similar complaints to the girls. In the extract below they refer to the effect the teachers' attitudes have on their behaviour and on the way prejudices appear to match their gradations of colour:

Stephen: I suppose it makes me behave bad, they pick you out, on your colour anyway. They tend to say, oh well, he's black so it's to be expected, they're bound to do that, so when they give you that kind of attitude, you think oh well, blow them, if that's what they think, why not act like that.

David: It's not really as bad for me because they can't really tell that I'm half-caste (this pupil in appearance looks more white than Afro-Caribbean) like the rest of them. But I still feel it the same, but not as much as this lot.

Lee: I haven't experienced any problem in classes, but when I'm in the group hanging about the corridors I do, not really in class, like David. I'm not really full black, I'm half-caste.

From conversations, like this, with Afro-Caribbean pupils it appears that many see a conflict with teachers as an inevitable response to the attitudes held by teachers towards their ethnicity. As one pupil succinctly put it 'you then treat them without any respect because they don't give you any, so really it's just a two-way thing'. Nevertheless, the pupils did acknowledge that not all teachers held negative attitudes towards their ethnicity.

WE BEND OVER BACKWARDS TO BE FAIR

A number of senior teachers and other staff were asked whether they acknowledged that an estranged relationship existed between the Afro-Caribbean pupils and teachers, and whether they attributed the nature of the relationship to negative racial attitudes projected by teachers towards these pupils. The deputy headmistress in charge of discipline was categorical that Afro-Caribbean pupils were treated fairly:

> We bend over backwards to be fair, to get to terms with the pupils, to try to get their confidence. And when you do have to grumble about something, they are always asked 'is this fair', 'did you do this?' and only then do you jump. I would never punish any child who didn't agree with me that they had done something . . . That's the important thing about discipline, to make them see themselves as they really are, not as they think they are.

A deputy headmaster similarly attributed problems to the behaviour of pupils:

> There are not many, a tiny minority, who have done outrageous things, who've misbehaved outrageously and who've been allowed to persist in their misbehaviour. For example, two children, Simon a white boy, and Jane, a West Indian girl, are two children who have disturbed and disrupted this school ever since they came. Although we have tried hard with Jane, we have not succeeded . . . in keeping her calm and amenable and pleasant, as she can be. She is capable of a public display of aggression . . .

However, other teachers suggested that 'race' *was* frequently the basis of the conflict between some Afro-Caribbean pupils and their teachers. An Asian teacher who had taught at the school for six years stated:

> There is a lot of racism in the school, and I have often believed that a lot of multicultural talk should start with the staff before it starts with the pupils. There is little racism amongst the children . . . I, even as a friend and a colleague of the staff notice it strongly in little points of racism, all the time constantly there, it gets beyond a joke, I've lost friends in the school or I don't associate with certain members of staff purely because of the constant jibing which eventually gets beyond a joke.

This teacher's annoyance was reiterated by a white teacher who related his experience of the school when he took up his post seven years before:

> I had kept fairly quiet while I tried to establish myself and gauge the atmosphere of the school. Even so, I had some fairly sharp differences with several members over their attitude towards the coloured pupils. There were fairly frequent serious and 'humorous' comments made in the staffroom and at the dinner table that I sometimes challenged. One or two other teachers were encouraged by my willingness to argue against racial prejudice and became more vocal themselves. On reflection, racialist comments are much less common now, in my presence at least.

Comments from a teacher who had been at the school for two years added credence to the points raised in the above dialogues stating that there is 'racism' amongst staff within the school:

> *Teacher:* Definitely I have come across incidents where I have actually seen teachers pick on children for no other reasons than the colour of their skin.

Researcher: What evidence have you to support this claim?

Teacher: Mr Y (year head) for example, I had a great verbal battle with him over a West Indian girl called June Green who I teach. She was a bit troublesome and still is to some teachers. She was a bit troublesome to me to begin with but I soon cottoned on to the fact that it wasn't her but the girl she was sitting next to within the class. When I cottoned on to that I started to encourage June, sitting her on her own, it took me a long, long time, she is a very sensitive girl. Now I can get her to virtually do anything for me. She's great. She is still a bit shy but she's tremendous with me. Mr Y wrote me a note, 'would I make some notes on her, there is a possibility of her going into the unit' (withdrawal unit for disruptive pupils). I wrote back and said no way did I think that she ought to go into the unit. He came back to me, went on about her being West Indian and all that. I said to him on what grounds did you want to put her in the unit. He said 'she's a troublemaker'. I said to him you just don't go and put a child in the unit because she is a troublemaker. Of course, she has not been the only case. In each case it has been a West Indian pupil rather than an Asian child.

Researcher: Well, you have only referred to one teacher.

Teacher: I have not come across such blatant attitudes amongst other members of staff but I would get that feeling and if I can, being white, feel an atmosphere like that then the children can too, especially if their skins are black.

THEY DON'T REALLY TALK TO YOU AS A PERSON

So far we have reported Afro-Caribbean pupils' perception of the attitudes held by certain teachers and how this may influence their behaviour. How does their experience affect their educational opportunities? There is concern within the school about the relative underachievement of pupils – especially amongst the Afro-Caribbean group. This point is illustrated by the head of the sixth form, who describes its composition:

Head of sixth: This year they're mostly Indians, that is the largest ethnic group of people who stay on to the sixth form, followed by the white children, then the Pakistani and West Indian in very small numbers.

Researcher: Why is the percentage of Afro-Caribbean pupils staying on in the sixth form so low?

Head of sixth: Now I was asked this at my interview and what was I going to do about it. I don't know. I think to try and break down the barriers that some of the West Indian children have against teachers and academic things... I find them all delightful in the first and second year, something happens between the second year and the fourth year, and in the fourth year they seem to have lost interest in academic things. I don't find them any less delightful, but they don't seem as interested in academic things.

This observation was further expressed by another teacher who stated:

There's no specific area that I can lay my finger on to explain why West Indian kids underachieve... what is inevitable is that a lot of West Indian children particularly the bright ones will do fairly well up to either the beginning or the middle of the fourth year, and for some peculiar reason their progress will fall off towards the end of the fifth year. There's no deterioration in intelligence or anything like that, the intelligence is there. The hard work is missing, the motivation is missing, the need to get on is missing and the exam results inevitably suffer from that.

Conversations with Afro-Caribbean pupils suggest that, like the Afro-Caribbean pupils at school A, they believe that teachers held low academic expectations of their performance. However, unlike the pupils at school A they saw the organization of the school as having little influence on their educational opportunities, rather they saw the attitudes of the teachers as being paramount, concluding that the prevailing attitudes held by certain teachers would undermine the organization of any school. This point is suggested by the following comment made by a pupil:

> Some coloured children in this school are getting bad because of the way they get treated, and they make out as if we're just doing it because we get low examination grades so we start getting bad with the teachers. They think it is because we got no sense. We're acting like that because of the way we've been treated in the past throughout the school. See if you know that Mrs L and Mrs T can get away with talking about your colour and that knowing there's not a thing you can do about it because they don't believe you.

Another pupil points to the subtleties of a process which strikes at a pupil's identity:

> When you know that they are sort of negative and they don't really talk to you as a person, you know that they're not really bothered about what happens to you. Whether you pass an exam or not and you think to yourself, well they're not really bothered about what you do, so that means you don't really think of it in terms of, oh well, he is really taking pride in me or her and really want me to do well, it goes beyond just teaching me, it's something personal as well.

A further comment from an Afro-Caribbean boy indicates the way the label of 'troublemaker' interferes with academic success, just as earlier at school A a teacher had seen 'trouble' as the avenue pupils were pushed towards when they were viewed as 'intellectually inferior':

> A teacher called Mrs C she has even said it to us herself that she wants all the black people out of the school. If a black pupil comes to see her a few times she automatically labels them as troublemakers. If anything happens in a crowd their names are always shouted out, so they're labelled in front of all the teachers as a bad person. So then the teachers think if he is like that he's not worth the trouble.

A concluding remark

From such observations and discussions in both schools, it seemed that the relationship between Afro-Caribbean pupils and teachers was often one of conflict and that the issue of race was frequently central to this conflict. In school A from about the third form (as the headmaster pointed out) black pupils became aware of negative attitudes they felt that the school held towards them. Similarly in school B teachers became aware of the barriers between the pupils and the teachers from the second year onwards. The perceived attitudes of teachers seemed to convince them that the school system was 'rigged': some saw very little point in trying. Many were still frustrated by what they saw as not 'getting on' academically. From conversations, it appeared that they were not against education *per se*; in fact a number of them had left school to go to further education. However, in school their energy was not always tapped and was sometimes directed towards disrupting the school or, as one pupil said: 'to get our own back on them for the way they have treated us'.

15   Slumptown: a community and its school
John Schostak

This chapter presents a series of cameos which together begin to sketch in aspects of life in a northern town and its comprehensive school. It is also the story of John Schostak's research on which he based his book, Maladjusted Schooling *(Schostak 1983). Slumptown is a community which experienced a brief period of industrial expansion before a rapid economic decline. It is also an area to which black people immigrated with positive expectations only to experience racism and to bear a disproportionate burden of hard times. This is the context in which John Schostak interrogates the school. How could it enable pupils to contest their lives?*

They're spendin' a few thousand on the Town Centre plantin' all trees 'n' things. They'll all be torn down when the bizzies get fed up patrollin'. Spendin' thousands on trees when there's all this unemployment round 'ere. If I can't get a job I won't stay in Slumptown – I don't want benefit or a Youth Scheme an' all that crap.
(Darren Baily, fifth form)

What contribution may education make towards the development of a sense of individuality, a sense of identity and a sense of community? To what extent does schooling reinforce the structures of inequality which produce feelings of valuelessness and which in turn contribute to problems of deviancy? What would be an adequate educational response?

I did not commence my research with these questions firmly in mind. They emerged as I began thinking about and writing about the data I collected. Initially, I simply wanted to 'do a case study', a study in depth of a school. At first I tried to make a comparison between a large northern comprehensive school and a smaller London church school. But this aim proved to be too large and the northern comprehensive school, as it were, took over my interests.

For years I have had an interest in phenomenology, the attempt to get behind, understand and interpret the way others see the world. This interest drove me to inquire in depth into the experiences and feelings of individuals and to try and identify the processes by which they came to define themselves and other people under one set of categories rather than another. The only way I could do this was to make myself as familiar as I could to the members of the schools. This involved being around, or hanging around, just watching, recording, holding conversations. Obviously, the volume of data by making notes and by taperecording that I acquired made it sensible for me to concentrate on the one school rather than the other. However, I continued to collect data from the church school.

I was permitted to use the office of one of the deputy heads in the comprehensive school as my base. I could enter and leave at will. I roamed the school. After gaining the necessary permissions to enter classrooms my freedom to follow up themes and issues discussed in interviews was very great. In this free and easy style, I accustomed myself to the rhythms of school life. I had agreed to do a study of the pastoral care system for the school as the 'price' for this freedom to roam. I spent a great deal of time with housemasters (see Chapter 22) and hence I became interested in the kinds of problems they encountered and began to follow-up the children I saw regularly in their offices. Most noticeable were the 'naughty' children, the ones who had been sent to be told off, or who in some way had become 'cases'. I thus became interested in the school's notion of 'deviance'. I heard such children contest the view of themselves as being deviant. I wondered what would count as an adequate educational response to individuals being labelled deviant, a response which would not simply take for granted that certain acts were or were not deviant but would look at the whole context of the interaction. This would include, not simply, the immediate members of a particular drama or interaction – the teacher and the pupil – but would extend outwards towards parents, friends, enemies, those in authority, the community at large, the historical structures of schooling.

To compel a pupil to obey a teacher makes no sense without placing it in the context of compulsory schooling enforced legally. Any single act is embedded in historical events which preceded the act, making such an act possible. I decided to try and sketch out such contexts in the book I wrote about my research. However, I did not want to write about one single instance, one particular community. I wanted to create a symbol of all such communities. Hence I 'invented' Slumptown and its comprehensive.

The community

No one individual statistic or set of statistics holds the key to describing any community. A community reveals itself gradually through a multiplicity of voices. The unities, and disunities, commonalities and eccentricities of these voices mark out the divisions and the degree of integration within the community, those qualities which are rich and those which stagnate and fester. The mother of Debbie Graves says of her home:

> When I first came to Slumptown which is twenty-one years ago, this street was one of the quietest streets in Slumptown. My sister came here and she said 'It's like walking down a grave yard'. Now this house had been standing empty when I came in it, for twelve months. There wasn't a window smashed, no boards up outside. Look at it now. I mean I don't know what's happened to Slumptown.

It is a semi-detached council house. There is a small overgrown garden in the front. 'I planted a rose bush', said Debbie's mother, nodding towards the front garden. 'Someone had taken it by morning.'

Sharon, Debbie's friend, lives in a newer council house about half a mile away. They are concerned that people condemn Slumptown without actually going there. Her mother says, 'Don't judge before you've not actually been and don't believe everything you read 'cos you can read the same stories about every town in England, good and bad.' Sharon's father says:

> There was nothing at all, just woods and empty fields, you know. We had to build our own church, St Lawrence's. We thought it was a barn at first. And we gradually done our own church and things have gone on from there. But they still haven't kept pace with the population even though it is slowing down now. They're even thinking

of closing schools down. But they, they never catered – just threw people out and said, 'well, get on with it'.

This, refers to Slumptown's 'new' face, they feel there were not enough facilities to cater for the young population of the town. Sharon's father blames it all upon the economic climate. 'Everything's against us.' He goes on to say:

> They've killed the place. A lot of it was new estates – Well, same as Newtown. Government give them a grant (i.e. 'new' industries), cut the rent and all the rest and once the period of, you know, free rent period, free taxes . . . they move out. This has happened all round here.
> The whole top and bottom is unemployment. Kids have got no money, so they get bored. They see other people who have got money so they're taking it . . .

Sharon's father has been unemployed for the last three years. His wife has a job and it hurts his pride, although he is grateful for the money. Of Sharon and her future he says:

> Here children like her and others are studying for 'O' and 'A' levels knowing that soon as they leave school they go right on the dole. And surely this is not conducive to kids really studying?

Of 354 fifth- and sixth-formers who left Sharon's school in the summer of 1981 forty had found real jobs by 18 November, four of these having entered military service. The remainder were either on Youth Opportunity schemes, the dole, or had re-entered education.

Sharon's father talked to me both of the building and the killing of a community. In the building was pride, and at its death sadness, bitterness, helplessness.

To Slumptown have also been attracted many from other countries who during the 1950s were drawn by the glittering promises of prosperity diligently advertised by Great Britain. British industry needed cheap labour. Indeed, the West Indians originally thought that they had much in common with British people and expected to be able to identify with the British way of life (PEP 1976). However, many saw the 1962 Commonwealth Immigrants Act as ending 'the "Mother Country" hallucination' (Kapo 1981). A similar reaction followed the publication of the British Nationality Bill in 1981. This Bill redefined British nationality, excluding perhaps millions who previously would have been able to claim citizenship.

It all adds, little by little, to a climate of resentment which at street level may be interpreted as by this black girl (Lucy):

> . . . she call us in to do 'er dirty work for her, build 'er up, she wants us out again 'cos she see that we're gettin' education and we're gettin' brainy, and we're comin' into power so she wants us all out before we reach too high. That's why she wants us out.

So-called 'structural racism' is experienced personally. In the end it come down to the individual's sense of being violated and the individual's reassertion of his or her pride. Lucy describes her feelings:

> *Lucy:* You're not safe in Babylon. *This* is what we call Babylon – you know, England. Babylon, y'know. To we blacks, it is Babylon.
> *JFS:* Why?

Lucy: Why? Because there's so much tribulation goin' on now. I mean, so much racism by the police against black people ... I've gotta carry a 'dool' around with me, right, that's a knife. Got to carry a knife to protect myself. 'Cos I know I ain't lettin' police 'old me up 'cos they disgrace me. They 'urt my pride. An' I'm aware of them so much now that I'd do anyfink in my power to do somefink to them to get self-satisfaction.

Growing up black involves asserting an individual identity, and an ethnic identity. Establishing an ethnic identity itself facilitates the assertion of an individual identity. A black identity allows the individual to oppose white authority; to assert the image of Babylon. At every turn friendship is violated by the divisive image, an image which serves to predict and to explain. When Babylon rules there can be no brotherhood and sisterhood between black and white, any apparent friendship does not deceive. In one context a person may be a friend. Yet in another context the 'friend' will shout, 'You black bastard.' Why? According to Lucy: 'It's a fing like, I'd be talking to Carol, right, and she's with Ann ...' And Carol and Ann are white and all it needs is for one of them to lead the other, censoring friendship, arousing hostility. Thus the other follows because she does not want to lose face with her white friend. Allegiances are formed according to colour and group censorship demands conformity as ritualized insults fly:

Lucy: (At school) there used to be a group of white girls and a group of black girls, right and y'know, they start ... once they're on their own they're alright but once they're with their people they get a bit lippy so they start callin' me black bastard – 'Look at you you mother fucker' – an' all that fing. An' I tell ya I, it really got to me. It burnt my feelings an' I went over there an' I just hit her. An' I kick her down. She had to go to 'ospital, right. But I also was injured 'cos her friends were hittin' me. But yet I was suspended, right, for a long time and she after she came back all she had is a little scratch there but they took 'er to 'ospital just to make it seem serious and she come back in school the next day. I said, 'Oh that's fuckery,' you know, 'Oh, that's nice init?'

In response, a white friend of Lucy's says, 'There's too much 'ate in this world an' not enough love'. But in the group the love, if any, is inhibited. The group censors any expression which would break solidarity within the group. Violence as 'fighting back' and 'standing up' becomes a way of regaining dignity:

Lucy: ... I'm black. I'm proud of it, right? But I know, it's a strain to be black. It's a strain. You could be proud of it or not proud of it. It's a strain. It's a damn strain because I mean, I could be talkin' to 'er (Lucy's white friend) an' that, at the end of the day she can say, 'You fuckin' black bastard'. She can say it but, you know what I mean, it can 'appen ...
Friend: Yeah.
Lucy: An' I can take that. I've gotta take that. An' I ain't gonna take it! I'll kick 'er down! An' I feel a, I won't feel no way for 'er. I'll feel good inside me 'cos she shouldn't dare to talk to me like that 'cos I've never said to 'er noffink like that, you know. But that's 'ow it 'appened. It always works that way you know.

Unemployment in the area amongst black people is high – perhaps 60 per cent. Amongst black school leavers, finding a job is practically impossible. Unemployment becomes a symbol of the neglect by the authorities of the black people.

Lucy's black friend Yvonne puts it this way; 'On the whole right, it's the people in authority what brings that tension around, you know, 'cos the black people are thinkin' 'ow comes they not gettin' all the jobs, you know.' And the lack of money and lack of things to do may lead towards thoughts of crime:

> *Lucy:* They have nothin' to do so all they're thinkin' about is crime 'cos that's the only way we can live, nowadays, to be frank wiv you that's the only way you can live. To feel nice, to have a little nice time. 'Cos you're on the dole, as soon as your money comes – I mean you're prayin' for your money to come – as soon as it comes it goes. You know, an' you're wonderin' what 'ave you done wiv it.

Lucy and Yvonne point to two distinct sources in explaining deviant behaviour: (1) racism and (2) those pressures, such as unemployment, also faced by white people.

Each individual within each community has a monetary value – the current market price at which he or she can sell his or her labour. Some individuals are worth a great deal, some very little. Some individuals have advantages heaped upon them (for they are so valuable), while others have disadvantages heaped upon them (for they are so valueless). Individuals develop a sense of worth to themselves and to others by the ways in which people treat them and their communities. These experiences and these senses of self valuation are carried by each individual into school.

The school

How does one suspend one's prejudices about a place so familiar as a school? In my research I deliberately sought out alternative interpretations. I would hear a teacher's viewpoint. Then I would go and ask pupils for their viewpoint. I tried not to give any extra weight to the explanations or justifications made by one individual rather than another. As a parent, and as an experienced teacher, I sympathized with teachers, and recognized similar attitudes in myself. But it is all too easy to accept one version of reality as opposed to another version, particularly if one version is backed up by authority or power. The social reality, for me, resided in the complex of interpretations, which could not be reduced to any one of the interpretations which composed it. To illustrate this, I will take the example of Nicky Wragg.

A student teacher, during dinner time, asked a boy, Nicky Wragg, to take the teacher's dinner tray of dirty dishes back to the kitchen hatch for him. The boy refused. The teacher insisted. A confrontation developed and the aggrieved boy decided to take the matter to the headmaster. The question was, did the student teacher have the right to compel Nicky Wragg to do something he did not want to do during what was supposed to be the boy's free time?

The headmaster was not a sympathetic audience. Throughout the incident he spoke with an air of exaggerated outrage and disbelief. The boy when I saw him was sobbing hysterically. The deputy headmaster arrived on the scene and the headmaster proceeded to explain to him the cause of the fuss:

> '...He'd come to complain to me because our student (teacher) had asked him to take a tray back to the (dinner) hatch. And having this, this *enormous* insult and indignity, injustice thrust upon him, he wanted to complain to, to a headmaster. I'm

not yet sorting out exactly why but within half-a-minute of my arriving here he'd been *extremely* rude to me as well . . .'

Nicky sobbing heavily gasps out,

'. . . 'Cos he was tryin' to f' force me.'
'Because what?'
'He was tryin' to f' force me.'
'He was trying to force you?'
'Yeah.'

The head lets out a high-pitched 'Wellll' and proceeds to present his case, voice grating,

'You see you have to have a situation in schools where in the end teachers – and this gentleman is a visiting teacher – can give reasonable orders to people just as you do in a home. Now your problem is young man – is that you really don't believe that teachers ought to have authority, ought to be able to say "do this" and you do it. And until you do understand that you're just going to get into more and more trouble.'

Theoretically, in a free democratic society, especially in an academic community, it is open to dispute and argumentation as to what constitutes a 'reasonable order' in a given situation. Schools are not democratic communities. The headmaster continues by saying:

'You're trying to fight a war old boy. And rather a silly war to fight. It's a bit like the Isle of Man declaring war on the United States or something like that . . .'

The deputy head supports him

'You know, the headmaster is quite right, you can't tell a teacher what you're going to do . . . for your own good some time son you're going to have to learn the lesson that there are people who can force you to do things and you're going to have to do them and you've got no choice.'

In the opinion of Nicky, 'I'm in the right'. It's a war. Nicky has run up a unilateral declaration of independence. There are two basic strategies with which to fight a war such as this: all-out naked force or subversion of your opponent's will. The latter is the technique used by the deputy head. Nicky sticks to force. He tries to gather reinforcements:

'I'll come with me mum.'
'Well, I'm sure the headmaster would be delighted to see your mum. When is your dad going to call? Is he home?'
'He's in the house.'
'I think it's one of the reasons why you're upset isn't it? That you know that you made such an awful fool of yourself.'
'I've not.'
'Oh yes you have.'
'I'm right, everyone is . . .'
'But Nicky, you're not right. This is the thing. You're not right. You're *quite* wrong. And you're going to have to learn that you're quite wrong. One way or another son you're going to have to learn. I'm confident . . . I know you pretty well by now Nick Wragg don't I?'
'Sir, yeah.'

'Yeah. And I'm confident that I know that one reason why you are so upset at this moment is because you realize you made such an *awful* fool of yourself, haven't you?'

'Sir, no.'

'Yes you have Nick.'

'I'm in the right.'

'Well that's just you dreaming and I'm not going to argue with you. I'm not going to argue with you at all . . . sit there until you've calmed down.'

The deputy head is trying to define the situation and the role of the boy in the situation. The situation is defined as one where 'you can't tell a teacher what you're going to do,' the child who resists must face up to the consequence that 'you've got to accept that you're going to get into more and more trouble.' This definition is backed up by power. It is the power to apply punishments as well as the power to control any discussion of rights and wrongs, the power to say 'that's just you dreaming and I'm not going to argue with you'. The child's point of view is relegated to 'dreaming'; it is not a real and valid point of view at all. Indeed, the deputy head is able to penetrate whatever act the boy plays because 'I know you pretty well by now Nick Wragg don't I?' It is almost as if the teacher can enter the consciousness of the boy.

Nicky is entangled in a sticky web of subtle rhetoric concerning 'right' and 'wrong', his mother's feelings, his own feelings, and underlying all this is the reality of the force to which he must ultimately submit. Resistance to control makes Nicky a problem, a deviant, a troublemaker.

After reading about this incident in my book the headteacher involved wrote to me saying he felt that teachers do perhaps shout too much but that the issue for him was that the student was a 'guest' in the school which in turn was a family. Nicky Wragg therefore was breaching etiquette. But what kind of guest is it that compels a host to carry dirty dishes? And what kind of family is it that is composed of nearly two thousand members?

However, the dominant issue emerging from this transcript centred on 'force' and upon obedience. Are these truly educational values? Forcing values upon another without full discussion of what are to count as rights and duties appear to me to be anti-educational. Are children, when they grow up, better able to challenge injustices, misinformation and hollow values because of their experiences at school?

The Nicky Wragg incident raised a number of issues and questions for further exploration. One could identify the political and social attitudes or perspectives, and the social structures or historical events which would have to precede such an incident for it to occur at all. Or, one could attempt to see whether the issues raised occur again in the concerns of teachers and pupils as they speak of their experiences of schooling.

The political theme was raised in many different ways. To what extent can a child challenge adults? There is an irony in the way this issue was raised by a housemaster reflecting upon his school and what the school should be doing for children:

I think if I were fourteen or fifteen years old looking towards leaving school, average ability, I'd be thinking to myself 'Well, what's the point of working at school? These teachers are telling us that you've got to work hard if you want a good job but there's no jobs there anyway. So I think we're coming up against . . . And I've noticed it this year more markedly than ever before, a certain resignation to unemployment when they leave school. And I'm almost having to bully kids in the fifth year at present into getting hold of the *Echo* at night and writing off to jobs because they believe they are of no value. And it all comes back to what I was saying earlier about trying to get kids to believe in themselves a little bit. But having said that even if they all believed in themselves we still know that a lot of people wouldn't get a job. Even if they were all trying like mad, a lot of them wouldn't get jobs. And this is what I meant when I said circumstances outside the school over which we have no control, they have no control... So perhaps we should be thinking more about political education and perhaps we should be thinking more about encouraging them to be non-conformist in the sense that they are prepared to ask questions, to challenge and not to accept glib answers that teachers give out willy nilly...

I asked this housemaster to develop this further. 'Suppose the pupils started organizing themselves into writing letters, protest marches – what would happen to the school?' His response was quick:

I think we would oppose it. I think you would get the situation where the teachers would oppose it. I mean, it's happened. It's happened in the past. It's kind of 'quash the rebellion'. Because generally speaking ... when they get a bee in their bonnet, they tend not to write letters. It tends to be 'violent revolution' in inverted commas. And that is unacceptable to teachers. Maybe if we were teaching them properly they would know how to protest without just resorting to violence or vandalism of some type, without the first step being breaking the rules; but we don't. You know, I'm not being just critical of this school. I think it's very difficult to envisage a school of nineteen hundred-and-odd kids where kids are encouraged to disapprove. And what happens, they come to me and they say, as housemaster, they say 'I'm not going to maths because I don't like that maths teacher. He was rude today and I don't want to sit with rude people and I'm not going any more.' It requires a complete turn round in the way that teachers have been trained to think. It requires society to allow us to turn round.

This passage, I believe, points to a basic educational question. He said 'if we were teaching them properly they would know how to protest...' Yet, how possible is it for teachers to take such an educational stance with children towards the immensely depressing social issue of their communities?

Such issues grew out of my reflections upon the images of school which were built up incident by incident, interview by interview, comment by comment. Although each interview, written comment and observation provided details particular to each individual and incident I began to discern commonalities, patterns or regularities. The above housemaster felt that to change certain kinds of a teacher's relationship to children would need a major restructuring of society. Another housemaster in describing what he would ideally like to do also set it in the context of his sense of powerlessness. He expressed a need to talk to the pupils:

... the flotsam and jetsom, the people ... the kids who're failing in the system (and) uh (the) kids who, who're ... probably successful in the system but really just need to talk to somebody occasionally, y' know uh.
J.F.S.: D' you, do you see a complete divorce between that kind of counselling and teaching? ... the academic bit...
Brown: Yeah.
T.F.S.: A complete divorce?

Brown: Uh . . . well yes because I really am talking about one-to-one stuff and that's why I don't think you can do what I'm talking about in a class . . . I mean it crops up occasionally, spontaneously, y' know. But it's so chancy that way uh and I don't think either if you gave y'self the role or y'know, the title, say, of school counsellor or whatever that you . . . it would work. All . . . all that I'm saying is that I would like my job and what I do ideally to be like that. The opportunity and the time to just talk to some kids and sound them out . . . or y' know, listen to what they've got to say – have the time to do that. And we don't. I haven't time to really listen and get good feedback from my kids . . .

In imagination anything is possible. Set against this is the felt reality; the constraining influences of the number of individuals a person has to interact with at any one moment and the problem of time. In addition, schooling he says:

isn't for all kids – some kids find it excruciating; boring, meaningless and fruitless as well 'cos they're not going to get anything. They haven't got the ability . . . y'know, to succeed in a system that by definition says so many will fail.

A conception of a 'system' unifies these experiences and symbolizes this teacher's sense of frustration and powerlessness. He constructs in his mind a sense of the overarching power and obdurateness of the 'system'.

Some personal conclusions

I will not forget the many people I met in the course of developing the many images I now have of *Slumptown Comprehensive*. For a while I became a part of their lives. I learnt something of the joys, frustrations and bitterness of their lives. Most importantly, I have learnt something of the responsibility a researcher has towards these people who have let him or her into their lives. No one can represent fully the lives of those met during a case study; nor can full justice be done to the complexity and the range of issues, interpretations and concerns experienced by each individual.

Some voices do not find it easy to reach the public stage. I listened to many tales of powerlessness, of personal degradation, hopelessness and unhappiness. It is all too easy to emphasize the positive image, the tales of success. These make happier reading and please the powerful. In our concern to manage the lives of others and our intention to do this in the best interests of all, we can too often simply define those who cry out in despair as moaners, as 'deviants', 'defectives', or as the lazy ones who haven't played the game in the way they should. The lives of others, I believe, are not mere management problems, their despairs are not simply amenable to technical solutions which 'repair the system as it is'; they are cries for radical solutions, solutions which go to the root of the problem: the structures of society which gnaw away at their lives, their self-worth. As Darren Bailey who introduced this chapter pointed out, it is no good simply putting a pretty gloss on the environment, the solutions require more than 'spendin' a few thousand on the Town Centre plantin' all trees 'n' things'. Education, I believe as a result of my experience with the people of Slumptown, is a radical solution. Through educational critique the roots of the problems confronting people in their everyday lives can be faced and action can be founded then in educational critique.

Thus, children have the educational right to challenge racism, sexism, material disadvantage and other forms of social inequality and discrimination. If this is so, then the educational role of teachers is to facilitate this. Such an educational role clearly dismantles the authority of the teacher as the custodian of right and wrong answers and as a controller of behaviours. Recall the Nicky Wragg example. The issues raised there not only go to the root of the relationships between adults and children but also raise the issue of political control in general and in particular, the rights and duties of individuals to confront a sense of injustice.

References

Kapo, R. 1981. *A savage culture, racism – A black British view*, London, Quartet.
PEP 1976. 'The facts of racial disadvantage: a national survey', Vol. XLII *Broadsheet* No. 560, London, PEP.
Schostak, J. 1983. *Maladjusted schooling: deviance social control and individuality in secondary schooling*, London, Falmer Press.

16 'Viking wives at home': sexism and deviance in school

Lynn Davies

In this chapter Lynn Davies explores the sexism in the official and hidden curriculum of the school and its relationship to the forms of deviance of boys and girls. She starts by examining sexist assumptions in curriculum materials and considers the possibility that what counts as knowledge in some subjects may also discriminate against girls. She describes the results of her research into those pupils teachers identify as deviants and normal and argues that their typology is discriminatory. She examines the connection between the curriculum and the deviance of boy and girl pupils and looks at the possibilities of combating sexist curricula.

A title which includes *Sexism* and *Deviance* must rate as unparalleled in its 'shock horror' value, combining as it does two of the current ghouls on the contemporary school scene. The connections between sex, sexism and sexuality are easy to conjure up. When I was working at a Polytechnic, we were once required to submit the areas of current research interest for storage on central records. Mine reappeared on the computer printout spelled 'Deviance and Sex Rolls in School.' My colleagues fell about with mirth, demanding to know the nature of the in-depth investigation and whether I was seeking film rights. Yet interestingly, 'deviance' and 'sexism' are not two additive features which together portray the school as a fetid jungle of would-be Tarzans and Janes swinging over the desks and refusing to wear proper clothes. This chapter will argue instead that deviance and sexism act as brakes on each other, and interact in a myriad of fascinating ways to make schools very complex and unpredictable places in which to work out pupil (and teacher) identities.

'Sexism' means setting people at disadvantage because of their sex. It involves making judgements about how people will and should behave on the basis of gender stereotypes believed to be determined by their sex. In the analysis of how schools transmit culture, there has been a swing away from the idea that schools were gender-neutral conveyors of 'objective' knowledge to the view that schools, through the way they structure knowledge, are almost complete reproducers of societal divisions – including sex role stereotypes. Exploration of school deviance, however, indicates that an alternative position is required. For we find, in looking at pupil resistance, that while sex roles may be transmitted, they are by no means always taken on board; and furthermore, that one of the 'causes' of pupil disaffection may be the presence of *contradictions* in gender ideologies – even within one school. Schools are indeed sexist places; but they do not present a unified 'role' for each sex. Instead they make selections amongst the many variations of 'masculinity' and 'feminity' which suit their control purposes. A girl may simultaneously have to wear a masculine tie; show womanly 'maturity'; conceal feminine allure; present a female non-assertive front in the classroom; and read male-oriented textbooks. Teachers in the same breath convey the message that they value 'quiet' pupils (often girls), while patently giving more time and attention to noisy pupils (often boys). Such contradictions may inspire various forms of strategic pupil resistance, and preclude any permanent 'socialisation' into a pre-determined sex role. I have thus found the study of pupil deviance a fertile valley for optimism to set beside the forbidding mountain-like permanence of theories of gender reproduction.

Reflections on curriculum materials

The revelations about sexism within educational materials are now widespread and, I would surmise, relatively well-known. Everything from pre-school picture books to university texts have come under scrutiny, and the detail is still coming in. Whatever age range or subject under review, four main areas appear rife: sex role stereotyping; the under-representation of females; masculinist language; and the omission of gender as an issue in its own right. Much of this is now widely available, and excellent coverage is provided in Janie Whyld's *Sexism in the Secondary Curriculum* (1983); hence a brief review is enough here.

With regard to stereotyping, the justifiable objections are not only that males and females are depicted as occupying separate and 'traditional' spheres, but that the books present an over-exaggerated version of contemporary gender roles. A mother invariably in the kitchen while father is at work or cleaning the car does not in fact represent the actuality of British family life today. The boy always having adventures and escapades while the girl looks on admiringly, tells him to be careful or stays to play with dolls, is by no means automatically true of the day-to-day play activities of young children. Nor, in occupational terms, are men *always* the police officers and lawyers while women are *always* the nurses and the social workers. In direct percentage terms, school books do not on the whole reproduce current gender reality, let alone encourage flexible orientations regarding future career and role planning.

Secondly, and perhaps even more significantly, the studies have demonstrated the basic invisibility of women in a large proportion of published material. Simply counting heads reveals that men appear far more frequently in pictures, illustrations, examples, maths problems and examination questions. History has indeed been history, with its bias towards 'great men' and 'great battles', and its scanty coverage of family or society history and its lack of interest in 'great times of peace'. Geography books may rely on European occupational concepts and, in typically depicting, for example, farmers as male, ignore the centrality of women in the agricultural economy of many countries. The instances of the over-valuation of the male are endless and penetrate the entire curriculum; more disturbing is the corresponding under-valuation of the female, and the fact that when women and girls do appear they often have negative images. One example from a maths textbook analysis will suffice:

> Girls . . . are shown wallpapering across the door of a room . . . as prizes to be won by competing males . . . as onlookers while the boys cheer *Match of the Day* . . . as items to be scaled down from fat to thin, etc. Image is infinitely more powerful than text.
>
> (Sharkey 1983, p. 129)

A third related area of concern is that of language. There is now some controversy over whether attacks on the constant use of 'he,' 'him,' 'Man,' and whether the counter-insistence on 'Ms and 'Chair' are not trivializing the issue. Yet it has been convincingly shown by Spender (1980) and others that 'he' and 'man' do *not* include women as they are supposed to.

> If man can suckle his young (because man includes woman) then man can give birth, become Pope or impregnate man. But this is nonsense, only women can do some of these things and only men others.
>
> (Mahoney 1985, p. 14)

Pupils, especially, appear unaware that man includes woman, for when asked to draw a book cover for 'Man and His World' they draw men, whereas when asked to do the same for 'People and their World' they draw both sexes (Harrison 1975). The effects of girls perceiving that their sex does not figure in a large part of school knowledge is immeasurable. It is obvious, too, that image and language become combined in a more pervasive and subtle way still to give some words a gender – as in European languages – although they appear neutral: I find it a constant effort of will to look at picture books with my three-year-old and say 'That's the farmer and that's the farmer's husband'. Women themselves cannot escape conveying man-made language. I had similar difficulties with the use of phrases like 'working-class youth values' when writing up research on sub-cultures (Davies 1985a): in the singular 'a youth' does mean a young man, and hence while writers may use 'the youth of today' to imply generalizations across male and female, the connotation is still of a masculine prominence and centrality in adolescent affairs.

Finally, it is not just that women are invisible, but that gender itself is. Social studies textbooks have only comparatively recently begun to include gender as an area of study alongside social class or ethnicity. Sociologists, as Oakley (1974) pointed out, have elected to focus on power, particularly as exercised through politics, the law, business etc. – which are 'male dominated arenas'. 'The more sociology is concerned with such areas, the less it is, by definition, likely to include women within its frame of reference.' Economics textbooks may still hold to the notion of 'work' as paid employment and deny the importance of unpaid women's work (in agriculture or the home) in their theories and explanations and their insistence that most countries have moved to a 'monetary economy'. The contribution of different types of gender division to economic 'growth' or 'recession' does not, I would claim, figure largely in economics textbooks. And in educational administration textbooks, of course, written for potential (male?) managers of schools, gender barely even gets a mention in the index (Davies 1985b).

What counts as school knowledge?

Once one is in the right frame of mind, it is a relatively easy exercise to play spot-the-sexism within curriculum materials; indeed both teachers and pupils now use this serious game to highlight gender biases in their books and, rather than toss them out, make the best of distorted material to act as a starter for discussion. More effort is required, however, to begin to question the whole logic on which our selection of school knowledge is based. We have to look at the determination of content *within* each subject, and at the various statuses of separate 'subjects' *across* the curriculum, to unpack any masculinist domination in the framing of school knowledge. In terms of social class, sociologists since the 1970s have successfully revealed the power and class interests behind the acceptance of school art or school music as meaning the classics rather than pop or photography, and have shown that the unquestioned valuation of abstractness, 'pure' knowledge and literacy in school (in preference to immediacy, 'applied' knowledge and practicality) acts to promote the interests and skills of the dominant elite. A similar analysis for gender would begin to question in whose interests 'hard' sciences like physics and chemistry should enjoy higher status than 'soft' sciences like biology and home economics. It would challenge the boundaries *between* subject areas: for example, why science is construed and taught as a totally separate area from social science, when it might be argued that the social effects of science (particularly in our nuclear age) should be given equal weight to the mechanisms of science. It is not, then, just a question of men being over-represented in science textbooks and girls lacking suitable role models; it is also the possibility that what does and does not 'count' as science itself is male-dominated. The idea that science should be expressed in someone else's language, the compulsory 'the test-tube was placed over the bunsen burner', may disadvantage many pupils but especially girls if that other language is seen to be part of the world of men.

The tradition of distancing oneself from knowledge or research begins in school, and the horror of emotional interference or personal feelings is, I submit, a very masculine approach to the study of our world – whether the physical or social world. Analyses of sexism in the curriculum should also include identification of what is left out, either within subject areas, or in terms of potential links between areas of knowledge: my contention is that the higher the prestige, and the more valuable a credential the subject becomes, the more likely it is to exclude issues, themes and approaches which relate to personal and female domains.

Additionally, we might profitably pursue how curriculum is evaluated and assessed. So-called 'objective' tests may hardly be objective at all, for Harding (1980) reports that girls seem to do worse than boys when multiple choice questions are used. They do better than boys, however, on open-ended 'essay' type questions. Whether this relates to the greater verbal fluency of girls or to their being less prone to instant 'right-answerism' remains open. As Kessler *et al* (1985) point out, school curricula often exaggerate the clear-cut distinction between right and wrong, relevant and irrelevant; there is little room for ambiguity, multiple layering of truths or open-ended explorations. They argue that such an approach to knowledge 'is associated with a particular kind of masculinity that is currently hegemonic'.

Typing the deviants

As with the official curriculum, much has been researched and written on the ways teacher–pupil interaction can be different for boys than for girls, and a brief initial summary will suffice. Basically, in a mixed sex classroom, teachers consiously or unconsciously spend about twice as much time with boys than with the girls (Spender and Sarah 1980). Boys monopolize physical space, linguistic space and teacher attention (Mahoney 1985). Teachers may be more chivalrous towards girls (Grant 1983), but be preoccupied with the disruptive behaviour of boys (Buswell 1981). Yet if forced to make a choice, about three-quarters of teachers say they would prefer to teach boys (Davies 1984).

It appears from my own research that while, overall, boys are seen to be less conformist, teachers prefer their type of classroom resistance to that of the girls. Girls are seen to 'bear grudges', to be insolent, sulky, or 'right little madams'. Men teachers in particular find the various feminine strategies used by the girls difficult to cope with; both sexes of teacher deem the boys to 'take their punishment better' and hence teachers prefer the immediate thrust and counter-thrust of the predictable encounters with boys to the longer drawn out 'deviousness' of the girls.

Teacher definitions of 'normality' and 'deviance' are therefore very complex, and something I attempted to explore through stereotype questionnaires (see Davies 1984). In terms of expectations of the 'good' pupil, I found surprizingly few sex differences. However, there were clear differences in expectations of deviant pupils. In fact a continuum of behaviour emerged which explains more fully the teacher preference for boys. I sub-divided deviance into 'normal' and 'abnormal' for each sex (Table 16.1).

Table 16.1   A summary of teachers' perceptions of perfection, normality and deviance

Ideal pupil		Normal deviant		Abnormal deviant	
		male	*female*	*male*	*female*
helpful		*cheeky*	*passive*	*cissy*	*tomboy*
motivated		*rough*	*sulky*	*poof*	*butch*
responsible		*untidy*	*docile*	*violent*	*loud*
hardworking	*terms*	*slapdash*	*over-sensitive*	*over-*	*unladylike*
conscientious	*more often*	*boisterous*	*emotional*	*aggressive*	*slut*
neat	*attributed*	*disruptive*	*shy*	*destructive*	*bitch*
interested in	*to girls*	*rascal*	*coy*	*macho*	*cow*
opposite sex			*concerned*		*flirt*
aware of feel-			*with*		*devious*
ings of others			*appearance*		
mature					
logical					
self-confident					
independent	*terms*				
adventurous	*more often*				
career-oriented	*attributed*				
acting as leader	*to boys*				
never conceited					
keen on sport					

While teachers would presumably like a class of thirty hermaphroditic paragons, they nonetheless expect pupils to 'deviate' from this – and on sex-differentiated lines. Their perception of the 'normal' lad is the Just William type – rough, cheeky and slapdash; the 'normal' Violet is passive, wet and emotional. Boys are 'boisterous' but girls 'sit like puddings.' Hence teachers hold stereo-typical views of normal deviants that correspond to social images outside the school or within the curriculum. They have various strategies to cope with the showy behaviour of boys, such as giving more attention, allotting instant verbal or physical punishment, aligning the curriculum to interest them; the normal deviant girl does not anyway present too many control problems. It is when we reach the realm of 'abnormal deviance' that the teacher's problematic really emerges, for here pupils are not only deviating from the 'good pupil' role, but may be denying or over-exaggerating their gender image as well. In the 'good pupil' list, teachers placed a high priority on 'being interested in the opposite sex', and the pupils who appear to deviate from this ('cissy' boys or 'tomboy' girls) call up spectres of homosexuality uncomfortable for many teachers. Conversely, while pupils are expected to conform to certain role images, pupils who exaggerate these are also problematic. Teachers will apparently expect and condone a certain amount of aggressive behaviour from boys, and even sexual harassment towards the girls, as both Jones (1985) and Mahoney (1985) would concur; but over-exaggeration of this 'machismo' of course is played out in terms of violence and destructive behaviour, which no teacher wants.

Similarly, teachers will expect girls to exhibit the demure, ladylike attributes of the female role, and to be interested in boys and fashion, but they castigate overt expressions of femininity or sexual allure, and are quick to label girls 'sluts' and 'bitches'. Such insults have no masculine equivalent, and arouse great hostility and counter-measures in adolescent girls very concerned to protect their moral identity. The hostility can of course then take the form of 'masculine' behaviour – being aggressive, or 'loud with the mouth'; and we can find girls offending *three* behaviour rules; they infringe the good pupil role, the femininity rule and the girls-are-better-than-boys presupposition. It is no wonder that teachers find 'difficult' girls far harder to cope with than the difficult boy.

What is the effect of the sexist curriculum

In highlighting gender differences in deviance, there is the risk of overplaying such dimensions and of confirming the very stereotypes that one is attacking in curriculum materials. There are many aspects of school disaffection – alienation, boredom, 'mucking about', smoking, refusal to wear uniform – which are com-mon to both sexes. Sex differences are also less in actuality than they are in teachers' perceptions, as self-report schedules demonstrate, and clearly depend on who is defining what as 'deviant,' 'disruptive' or 'disaffected' – that is, what and whose rules of 'normality' are being infringed.

A second problem with attempting to make connections between (sexist) curricula and (sex-typed) deviance is the difficulty of establishing any causal effects. With regard to the norm of 'achievement', Mahoney (1985) writes:

> Distorted and offensive though it may be, riddled with he-man language though it still is, despite the information on the subject . . . no straightforward links can be

made between biased, sexist material and girls' alleged underachievement. First, the same textbooks are used in single-sex schools and the contents are not always challenged by teachers. Second, it is not true that girls underachieve across the board in education. Relative to boys they achieve highly in English and modern languages, yet . . . the curriculum in these areas is no less biased in favour of males.

(Mahoney 1985, p. 14)

Similarly, Hingley (1983) comments on the 'new wave' modern language courses which

. . . settled on the lowest common denominator of European life as their vehicle – the nuclear family. They depict a stereotyped norm where father makes all the decisions, goes out to work and waits for his meals to be prepared by the wife with occasional assistance of the daughter. The son is indulgently allowed to be noisy, greedy and disobedient; the daughters are usually quiet, helpful, punctual, deputy mothers, but in a tight spot they have to be busily frightened while the (otherwise irresponsible) male child takes charge of the situation . . . the first two years of the (Longmans) course revolve around the Marsaud family and a not unreasonable answer to the question 'Where is Madame Marsaud?' might be 'She is under house arrest'. *The one advantage of the Longmans course is that it is rather dull and lifeless and therefore less likely to have any impact on the pupils.*

(Hingley 1983, p. 103, my emphasis)

While the portrayal of both normality and deviance may be stereotyped in curriculum texts, we have no way of quantifying how far they are internalized by pupils. Pupils who are already alienated by school and its artefacts are even less likely to absorb curriculum messages than are 'conformist' pupils. However, it is worth exploring some of the possible effects of sexist curricula.

Firstly they may reinforce a macho, non-caring image for boys. Whether we are talking of the families portrayed in reading schemes and modern languages material, the heroes of novels chosen in English literature, or the personages selected as worthy of interest in history, the picture may be of a male who is larger than life, dominant and personality-projecting. While one cannot say with certainty that such images 'teach' boys to be aggressive in class, there is on the other hand little there which would permit boys to be quiet and accommodating, the attributes valued by the harassed classroom teacher.

Secondly, it is possible that the roles portrayed by women do reinforce passivity and submissiveness from girls. From the teacher's point of view this is acceptable up to a point, but in excess leads to an exasperating lack of response and an apparent stolidity from girls. It does not provoke the adventurous independence favoured by teachers in their ideal pupils. The absence of career models, particularly in maths and science, links of course to another aspect of female deviance – 'underachievement', and intermittent aspiration in certain curriculum areas.

While the above are possibly reinforcing features, school curricula, may also evoke tensions in gender identities. A third area of interest would be the contrast between the values celebrated by the working-class male culture (see Willis 1977) of action, excitement, collectivism and practical displays of hardness, and (whatever the materials portray) the *actual* route to school achievement, which is sedentary, book-based, individualistic learning. While a large proportion of pupils manage to achieve multiple identities and to co-exist in a range of daily cultures, there are some pupils for whom such transitions are problematic, and for whom the inconsistencies in curriculum messages are too great.

A final area of tension would again be for the girls, and relates to the invisibility and marginality of the female in curriculum material mentioned earlier. Whereas boys may become alienated from the *means* of learning, girls would be alienated more swiftly by the *content* of learning. In materials geared to male interest, male definitions and male language, girls seeking involvement and indentification are likely to become disappointed. Girls are supposed to be conformist; but what appealing models are there for them to conform *to*? This explains the joy with which single-sex or girls-only discussion groups plus non-sexist materials are met by girls (Deem 1984), because issues of direct relevance and impact can be raised and addressed without being filtered through male perceptions or boys' scorn. Otherwise the continued experience of sexual discrimination in school and its artefacts may provoke a range of reactions from passive 'opting out' to outright rejection.

Without seeming too deterministic, it would appear then that at least two dimensions in the curriculum-deviance link can be identified in terms of gender. One is the reinforcement of already inherently problematic behaviours for teachers; the other is the creation of sex role contradictions in curriculum transmission or content which, by forcing pupils to manage tensions in their own identity, may lead to alienation or disaffection from school life. There then follows another complication. Delamont (1980) in her case-study of a comprehensive school discovered that 'the more teachers tried to make the lesson material relevant and immediate to the pupils, the more likely they were to make sexist assumptions and remarks' (p. 54). The anecdotes and examples chosen to add colour to strictly academic material revealed highly sexist ideas about history, the pupils' homes or their own knowledge or interests. It could be that such pupil cultures *were* sexist; but an interesting dilemma emerges. Trying to prevent boredom and contain deviance by making the curriculum 'relevant' to pupils' cultures may elicit sexism; yet sexist curricula may exacerbate deviance.

How can sexism be challenged?

I have watched student teachers attempting dramatic role plays of the Vikings, only to come unstuck with parts for girls; not really able to encourage them to be raped or pillaged, the only alternative is, as one student hastily improvised, for them to be 'Viking wives at home'. Yet to challenge conventional curriculum stereotypes is not easy for teachers in co-educational schools, for the boys object and the girls are reluctant (Spender and Sarah 1980, Mahoney 1985). It has even been argued in the US that stereotypes become more extreme in 'progressive' classrooms (Sussman 1977). We cannot accuse teachers of being sole agents of reproduction: they may themselves be considered deviant by the pupils or parents if they try to encourage domestic skills in boys or engineering orientations in girls. Sally Shave's attempt to counter sexism in her junior school invoked headlines in local newspapers such as 'A school recipe to turn boys into pansies'. The chairman of the education committee said 'If boys are to be turned into fairies and girls into butch young maids, it should be for the parent to decide and not the education authorities' (*TES* 13.10.78). The confusion of sex and sexuality, invoking the dread of any deviations from 'normal' heterosexuality, means that anti-sexist curricula may encounter more resistance even than anti-racist measures.

Boys in particular seem to have more control over curricula with teachers making efforts to select materials that will interest them (Shaw 1980). While girls are used to operating within a masculine frame of reference, boys object vociferously if presented with what they deem as 'girls' stuff'.

Organized responses to sexism have involved equal opportunities initiatives or more fundamental efforts to challenge curriculum assumptions through 'girl-friendly' curricula and anti-sexist policies. Attempts to enhance opportunities for girls in traditionally male subject areas include GIST (Girls Into Science and Technology), GATE (Girls and Technology Education), and GAMMA (Girls and Mathematics Association). The development into 'girl-friendly science' or indeed 'girl-friendly schooling' in general, has engendered wide-ranging analyses of the way curricula are constructed, and of how schools could play a transformative rather than a reproductive role in gender indentities for *both* sexes (see for instance Kelly 1985).

The distinction between 'equal opportunities' and 'girl-friendly' approaches has similarities to the 'cultural deprivation/cultural difference' debate about social class. An 'equal opportunities' ideology which focuses purely on girls aims to provide compensatory experiences for the 'problems' ensuing from their (disadvantaged) socialization. It tries to raise their aspirations, alter their attitudes towards science, technology and computers, to 'widen' their horizons – i.e. to make them more like boys. A girl-friendly approach, on the other hand, sees girls inhabiting a different (not deprived) culture, which should be given equal value in school. Girls' educational 'problems' would derive from female devaluation within the school; a girl-friendly school would restore to them through both organization and curriculum the time, space, attention and (sexual) dignity which has been usurped by the males.

Kessler *et al* (1985) has provided a useful recent critique of 'equal opportunities' strategies in Australia:

1   The strategy assumes that educational institutions are neutral, when not only is the education system controlled by men, but it actively constructs gender and actively produces women's subordination.
2   The knowledge sought is itself not neutral.
3   The programmes do not affect boys and need to combat their sexism.
4   They ignore homosexuality and take for granted categories of 'male' and 'female'.
5   They are class-blind, in that the programme may reach only a minority, and separates this elite from the bulk of girls who are defined as failures and frequently pushed into opposition to the school's programme.

The equal opportunities strategy is, the writers claim, likely to be self-defeating. They argue for the empowerment of subordinated groups, rather than giving them selective access to existing hierarchies; for the 'democratization' of the curriculum by reorganizing knowledge to advantage the disadvantaged; and for special teacher training for teachers to assist girls in resisting the sexist demands of their schools.

The debate is therefore about whether 'gender equality' means equal opportunities to study what is to girls a rejecting curriculum, or whether it means changing the curriculum so that boys and girls are equally advantaged (or disadvantaged). If we attack curricula, the next level of debate centres round how fundamental the change needs to be. Just as there is a fundamental difference between 'equal opportunities' and 'girl-friendly' strategies, there is more than a semantic difference between non-sexist and anti-sexist initiatives. Non-sexist material implies some neutral reality 'out there' waiting to replace the old gender biases; anti-sexist indicates a more radical assault on distortions and discrimination. Spender claims that 'if sexism were removed from the curriculum little would remain'. Non-sexism can only be a utopian or post-revolutionary state arrived at after the massive change in social relations and ideas demanded by an aggressive anti-sexist policy. A scissors-and-paste job on the existing curriculum – which removed masculinist language, substituted female examples and models, deleted stereotypes or debasing images – would provide a superficially 'non-sexist' transmission process, but it would not make many inroads into the valuation of, or boundaries around, such knowledge areas at present designated 'home economics' or 'applied maths', or, indeed, have any direct effect on the hidden curriculum.

It is obvious that it would be insufficient and even counter-productive to tackle official curriculum areas in isolation from the rest of school life, from the rest of school-based gender construction. A different direction is taken by projects such as DASI (Developing Anti-Sexist Initiatives) where the aim is 'to give girls a positive self-image, and make them aware of the way society controls them rather than to direct them into "male" areas of study or work' (Whyld 1983, p. 303). Resources of anti-sexist teaching materials across the curriculum are built up, and some introduced *into* the official curriculum; there are courses on sex-role stereotyping, but the work also includes single-sex assertiveness training, and male teachers working with boys to change their attitudes. The number of individual schools developing their own non-sexist and anti-sexist initiatives is increasing continuously, and most tackle far more than just the official curriculum, aiming to provide verbal and physical 'space' for girls, to tackle careers and option choices and to involve parents. There is recognition of the need for realignment for both sexes, to 'offer active support for all students. The non-macho boy probably gets more teasing than the assertive girl' (Mahoney 1985, p. 99). Thus the 'Skills for Living' course at Hackney Downs Boys School encourages boys to think about things such as food preparation, shopping and baby care, to anticipate their future domestic lives, to discuss sexism and 'to treat each other in a caring way' (Arnot 1984).

Conclusion: the effects of change

The question remains as to how far non-sexist or anti-sexist curricula would act to alter amounts and styles of pupil disaffection. Those including single-sex tutoring, courses on sex-role stereotyping and assertiveness training certainly report increased involvement and less truancy by girls. Conversely, projects which encourage a caring attitude in boys and acceptance of 'non-macho' traits would presumably act to deflect the automatic expression of male toughness or aggression – although it is always possible that hostility to the course itself could provoke even more of a 'male backlash'. One thing never to be forgotten is the way social class interacts with gender, and makes for different interpretations in different school milieux. Another is that no school is static, and both before and after the introduction of non-sexist materials will be grappling with a *range* of possibilities for each sex, rather than a unified 'role'. Both teachers and pupils will select and experiment with different styles, depending on their immediate power needs; unless pupil deviance is gender-based, there is no guarantee that sex role shifts will reorient that deviance. If pupils are disaffected with school because they fail to see its relevance to the labour market, then non-sexist curricula may become yet another target for displays of boredom and alienation, yet another part of the school fabric to be attacked.

It clearly depends on how far the 'empowerment' of pupils and 'democratization' of curriculum and pedagogy can be carried out within the political climate deciding school objectives. If power interests are threatened, then new models of conformity may merely provoke new forms of deviance. To prevent male or female backlashes, to stop hostile retreats into conventional gender styles, it is essential for anti-sexist curricula to give pupils the power and courage to select from real alternatives in their future lives. Paradoxically, a true anti-sexist curriculum is one that encourages creative and political resistance – both in and out of school.

References

Arnot, M. 1984. 'How shall we educate our sons?', in Deem, R. (ed.), *Co-education reconsidered*, Milton Keynes Open University Press.

Buswell, C. 1981. 'Sexism in school routines and classroom practices', *Durham and Newcastle Research Review*, Vol. IX, 46. 195–200.

Davies, L. 1984. *Pupil power: deviance and gender in school*, London, Falmer Press.

Davies, L. 1985a. 'Ethnography and status', in Burgess, R. (ed.), *Field methods in the study of education*, London, Falmer Press.

Davies, L. 1985b. 'Towards a gender-inclusive theory of educational administration for the Third World', Paper presented at the Commonwealth Council for Educational Administration Conference, Barbados, August 1985.

Delamont, S. 1980. *Sex roles and the school*, London, Methuen.

Grant, M. 1983. 'Craft, design and technology', in Whyld, J. (ed.), *Sexism in the Secondary Curriculum*, London, Harper and Row.

Harding, J. 1980. 'Sex differences in performance in science examinations', in Deem, R. (ed.), *Schooling for women's work*, Routledge and Kegan Paul.

Harrison, L. 1975. 'Cro-Magnon woman-in eclipse', *The science teacher*, 42, 4, 8–11.

Hingley, P. 1983. 'Modern languages', in Whyld, J. (ed.), *Sexism in the secondary curriculum*, London, Harper and Row.

Jones, C. 1985. 'Sexual tyranny: male violence in a mixed secondary school', in Weiner, G. (ed.), *Just a bunch of girls*, Milton Keynes, Open University Press.

Kelly, A. 1985. 'The construction of masculine science', *British Journal of Sociology of Education*, 6, 2. 133–154.

Kessler, S., Ashenden, D. S., Connell, R. and Dowsett, G. 1985. 'Gender relations in secondary school', *Sociology of education*, 58, 1, 34–48.

Mahoney, P. 1985. *Schools for the boys*, London, Hutchinson.

Oakley, A 1974. *The Sociology of housework*, London, Martin Robertson.

Sharkey, S. 1983. 'Mathematics', in Whyld, J., (ed.), *Sexism in the secondary curriculum*, London, Harper and Row.

Shaw, J. 1980. 'Education and the individual: schooling for girls or mixed schooling – a mixed blessing', in Deem, R. (ed.), *Schooling for women's work*, London, Routledge and Kegan Paul.

Spender, D. 1980. *Man made language*, London, Routledge and Kegan Paul.

Spender, D. and Sarah, E. (eds.), 1980. *Learning to lose*, London, The Women's Press.

Sussman, L. 1977. *Tales out of school*, Philadelphia, Temple University Press.

Whyld, J. (ed.), 1983. *Sexism in the secondary curriculum*, London, Harper and Row.

Willis, P. 1977. *Learning to labour*, Farnborough, Saxon House.

17 'Let us take these thoughts with us into the day': macho culture in the school

Sheila Cunnison

In this chapter, based on three months participant observation carried out in 1978, Sheila Cunnison explores the values assigned to women and girls in a mixed-sex secondary school. The data has been interpreted in the light of interviews with teachers working in fourteen other secondary schools in the same city. She argues that the culture of the school is dominated by men who control the structure of authority and that is expressed in the way aspirations are defined and by styles of discipline which emphasize male strength. It is a macho-culture. After an introduction the chapter falls into three main sections. The first examines images of women and girls portrayed by gender divisions in subject areas, the allocation of seniority and specifically by the content of lessons. The second section looks at the role of the male macho image in the maintenance of control and shows how it undermines the position of women teachers. The third section explores the attempts some women teachers made to challenge and escape from the predominant culture of the school.

School teaching claims for itself the status of a profession. Entry depends, with some exceptions, on the possession of an educational qualification. Within a profession one would expect that status and pay would be determined largely by educational qualifications and experience. Yet analysis of teachers' pay and position on the career ladder shows gender to be of crucial significance. Women earn less and they occupy lower status jobs (National Union of Teachers 1980). School teaching is one of the few professional occupations where women outnumber men. However, the distribution of women and men is uneven. Women are found mainly in the primary sector working with younger children, in smaller schools with fewer opportunities for promotion. Even here men do far better than women: one man in three in primary teaching is a head teacher, one woman in ten. Men gravitate towards the older children. In the profession as a whole women outnumber men by about two to one. In secondary school teaching men outnumber women in the same ratio. In secondary school teaching one man in thirty is a head teacher, but only one woman in a hundred. Nearly forty per cent of women are on the lowest scale, but only twenty per cent of men (National Union of Teachers 1980).

Secondary school teaching is well and truly male-dominated, not only numerically, but also structurally through the system of school management, and culturally through the values and attitudes expressed by teachers and passed on to children. In terms of structure, in the school I studied, men dominated the hierarchies of authority, both academic and pastoral. In terms of culture the dominant values formally supported and rewarded were those consonant with success in the occupational world of work: a clear regard for hierarchy and a positive emphasis on ambition and achievement, competition and winning. These are values more closely associated with men than with women, for it is men rather than women who move up the occupational hierarchies in the world of work. The dominant value system of the culture thus referred to boys and men and can be thought of as part of a male-dominated culture. It is noteworthy that the male head of the school when explaining the promotion process to me reported that he was always on the lookout for the 'good all-round schoolmaster in the public school sense'.

I have chosen to call the school culture 'macho' rather than 'male-dominated' because I want to describe an image of male-dominance in which physical strength and power plays an essential part. Women and girls were largely excluded, not only because the values seemed in some way inappropriate to their experience, but because they were constantly assigned to a different and specific sphere, to the domestic, the soft underbelly of the school culture, the complement to macho. An examination of images of women found within the school culture, both those put before girls and those referring to women teachers, shows a stress on domesticity and family roles. These images combine to support a stereotype of 'the woman teacher' which defines her as inherently domestic, and which over-rides objective assessment of her performance in the school and thus constitutes, for those women with career aspirations, a primary handicap in the competitive race for scale points.

When I worked at the school I was surprised at how easily women teachers accepted what appeared to be their structured disadvantage within the school. I was puzzled by the women's general lack of interest in either their own position in the school or that of their girl pupils. Very few of the women had any conception of the systematic way in which they were subordinated within teaching. Only a very few expressed any concern about the messages of domesticity and inferiority received by the girls, about the effect of so-called subject 'choice' on pupils' future occupations, or about the way many more girls than boys ended up in unskilled and low-paid work. In fact the only skill that sixteen-year-old girl school leavers learned, apart from office work, was hairdressing, one of the lowest paid occupations. Very few entered any other kind of apprenticeship.

Putting the school in its social class context goes some way towards under-standing these attitudes, at least with regard to teachers' expectations of girls. The girls were mainly working-class, the teachers, by standards of education, residence and income, were middle-class. And middle-class women, even teachers, can be expected to be fairly complacent about working-class girls going into dead-end unskilled jobs.

A fuller understanding however comes from looking at the women's attitudes in the context of the culture of the school. Seen thus it becomes clear that women teachers, by virtue of working in the school become part of that culture which reinforces the values of the wider society which define men primarily as occupational achievers and women primarily as wives and mothers whose occupations are a secondary source of income only.

But there are points of tension both within the school system itself and between the school and the wider society where contradictory values about the position of women result in some questioning and even challenging of the school culture and its values. Within this culture, mechanisms had developed for reconciling the stereotype of the domestic dependent woman with the fact that women held, and had for a long time held, a small number of senior posts. Tensions between the values and attitudes about the role of women in the world outside the school and those about women within it were much greater. Younger women in particular were influenced not only by long-term changing demographic and employment patterns (Titmuss 1958) but also by the resurgence of the Women's Movement and by equal opportunity and abortion legislation of the seventies. These women tended to bring into the school views and attitudes which were only barely compatible with the stereotype of the woman teacher. Some of them openly rebelled against this stereotype. Some saw the school culture as being unfair to women as employees, as failing to give them equal career opportunities with men. Of these, a few additionally saw the school system as discriminating against girl pupils, failing to provide them with the same kinds of opportunities that were offered to boys. These rebels constitute the group I term the 'new career teachers' whose challenges I recount later. First, however, I look at the cultural pattern against which they rebelled.

Images of women

Gender is an important principle in the organization of teaching. Some subjects are taught by both men and women: English, history, geography and languages. A few subjects, especially maths and the hard sciences, physics and chemistry, where there are few women graduates, are nearly always taught by men. In certain areas however, where the subjects themselves are strongly associated with one sex or the other, notably domestic science and office practice for women and craft and technical studies for men, teaching has been traditionally regarded as the province of one or the other sex.

These subjects and the physical spaces associated with them carried powerful images about women and men and their appropriate place in society (cf. Whyte 1981, p. 265). In this school the workshops, places for woodwork, metalwork and car maintenance were the preserve of men teachers; few girl pupils crossed the threshold; no women taught there. One image carried by these subjects was that of men as producers, creators and maintainers of artefacts and machines; men as part of the occupational world, part of the physical labour of creation. Another was the male macho image of the use of physical force over people. The workshops were the only part of the school where pupils were believed to be physically assaulted. Teachers told stories of past exploits when boys' heads were said to have been put in vices, and claimed even now that kids were punished by having their heads banged against a wall. Myth no doubt played its part in these tales. But a teacher in the staff room actually demonstrated how he used his own head to bang a kid: he said it left no marks.

Domestic science and office practice carried images of women whose main identity was to be found in domesticity, in housekeeping and childcare and within the occupational sphere in manual service work as cooks, cleaners or – the arch image – secretaries. They were images of dependence and servitude. Like technical studies, domestic science and office practice were located in particular physical spaces. Domestic science was in the cookery rooms with their rows of stoves and sinks, in the needlework room and in the flat. The flat was complete with kitchen, bedroom, bathroom and living area. Here girls could practise *in situ* the 'real' concerns of their lives, homemaking and childcare. Real babies were sometimes brought into school for the childcare courses. The emphasis was inexorably domestic rather than occupational or academic (e.g. a lesson I attended included emulsion painting and the presentation of an afternoon tea tray). A domestic science teacher who attempted to extend her course out of traditional areas to cover the history and international trade of commodities such as cocoa and cotton, was quickly discouraged. Ironically the only domestic science course directed towards an occupation was entitled 'catering for boys', a course designed by a woman and pointed towards the occupation of sea cook. Only very few boys took cookery or childcare. There was one male teacher in this area, a drama teacher, skilled as a tailor. Predictably he came into this female area at management level, as head of needlework, after having threatened to leave the school for a better paying job.

The teaching of typing and office management in the department of commerce was not segregated in the same way as domestic science. A man held the post of department head, several men were teachers and a man managed the reprographics office where teaching materials were reproduced and pupils acted as technical assistants. There girls learned to play roles both as workers and subordinates to male managers.

The craft workshops and domestic science provided services for the school. Domestic science served tea at open evenings and cooked for official school functions and for staff parties. The women teachers were rewarded in the traditional way, with bouquets of flowers. The technical studies department made school furniture. It endured and they were respected. 'If you want to see his monument, look around!' said the head when one of the craft masters left, recalling Christopher Wren's imprint on London.

MODELS FOR GIRLS

The message of the importance for women of domesticity pervades many aspects of school life. I am doubtful whether it can be considered part of a '*hidden*' curriculum (Byrne 1978, p. 110, Llewellyn 1980, p. 49) for the message was often overt and explicit as in the two incidents reported below.

A school assembly School assemblies were held each morning. Pupils gathered in the school hall around three sides of a square. After they had filed into place with their form teachers, the top management of the school, first the deputies and then the head, took their places along the fourth side, clad in academic gowns and mortar boards. Whatever was said at the assembly carried the full symbolic force of the authority of the school.

Assembly began with a prayer. Then came a moral interlude, a presentation by a group of pupils and their form teacher, on a theme which changed weekly. The presentation could be in the form of music, film, poetry reading or drama of some kind, for example, the theme of death was illustrated by a reading from D. H. Lawrence describing a funeral. This was accompanied by a film of decay in an inner city centre.

The week in question the theme was 'the future'. Six children, four boys and two girls, came forward in turn to stand within a wooden frame and speak about their hopes for the future. An atmosphere of a television interview was conjured up: the children spoke clearly and the presentation was dramatic. The first to speak was a boy who said he had just signed for Arsenal. He hoped to become a famous footballer. The second, a girl, said she was learning to be a secretary: she hoped to become secretary to the mayor. Next came a scientist in a white coat; he was hoping to find a cure for cancer. Then came a girl, dressed in white. It was, she said, her wedding day and she was looking forward to becoming a wife and mother. Another girl stepped forward and presented her with a bouquet. A boy followed her, a politician just elected to parliament and looking forward to serving his constituents faithfully. Finally (the form teacher taught religious education) a white-robed boy stepped into the frame. He was, he said, taking us back in time several hundred years; he was St Paul and he was looking forward to preaching the Christian gospel. The headteacher added little. He thanked the group and finished with a prayer and the usual words 'Let us take these thoughts with us into the day'. The marked lack of ambition on the part of the girls, the stress on domesticity, their numerical under-representation were all accepted as a symbolic representation of their future. Practically no comment was made by the staff, neither by the women nor the men.

The message of domesticity and limited occupational ambition could not be clearer. In so far as women teachers are involved in presenting such messages or in failing to question them, they are seen as implicitly supporting them and themselves become victims of the subordination they purvey to their girl pupils.

The humanities wedding The humanities wedding was a mock marriage conducted between two pupils by a real clergyman in a mock-up of a church wedding with teachers standing in as parents of the bride and groom. The ceremony was followed by a mock wedding breakfast complete with cutting of the cake and speeches from the bride's father, groom and best man. It all took place in the school hall. The headteacher gave his official authoritative blessing by looking on from the balcony.

It was a popular event with pupils and staff alike. It touched a deep chord with many of the girls who themselves hoped to be married in church and in white. It was seen as a release from normal lessons. For the staff it was an occasion for much jocularity; apparently ridicule was the only way they could cope with the event. Only a few teachers from religious education and domestic science treated the event seriously throughout.

Ostensibly the humanities wedding was about the responsibilities of marriage for both girls and boys: it was generally thought that the pupils took both sexual relations and marriage too lightly. The ceremony followed lessons on different types of marriage in different parts of the world. But rather than being used to examine marriage in our society critically, it became an exhibition of the right and proper way to do things in our own world.

The effect of the event was to glamorize and dramatize the role of marriage for girls. Marriage in our society marks a more significant change in status for women than it does for men. A wedding day is 'the bride's day'. 'This is my happy day, this is the day I will remember the day I'm dying . . .' as the popular song goes. The wedding was directed much more towards girls than boys. The bride was the centre of attraction, dressed in a genuine white bride's dress complete with headdress and bouquet; her attendants were in bridesmaids' dresses borrowed from family and staff. The women acting as mothers had borrowed hats for the occasion. The men in contrast were merely more tidy than usual in the regulation male teacher's dress of jacket, trousers, shirt and tie, but with a suit rather than a sports jacket. Girls, rather than boys, had been involved in preparing the 'wedding breakfast,' baking a rich fruit cake, learning how to set the table for a wedding feast and preparing floral decorations for the mock altar and the dining table.

The humanities wedding dramatically set the seal of official educational school approval on marriage as a goal for adolescent girls. Concern was shown throughout about the 'proper' way of doing things, the dress, the service itself, the etiquette of the breakfast. It gave messages to boys as well as girls of the 'proper' family role of women in our society.

The 'best man's' speech referred to the male image of football and to the female images of preoccupation with appearance and of motherhood as a normal consequence of marriage. 'I've not felt so proud since the day Scunthorpe beat Hull', he said and 'I never thought Jane would get married because I never thought she would risk getting fat'.

The event keyed into existing romantic aspirations of schoolgirls. At the tired end of term and end of year it was an easy and friendly way for teachers to communicate with their pupils. Yet it was an exploitation of the girls' aspirations rather than a genuine educational exercise. It shows teachers and the school acting as agents in the reproduction of a male-dominated culture where the ideology holds woman's true vocation to be that of wife (Shaw 1976).

Discipline, control and the macho image

Within the school a small number of teachers confront a large number of pupils who are compelled to attend. This raises problems of discipline and control. A number of different mechanisms are brought into play to ensure teachers remain in control. The major one is breaking down the number of pupils in time and space, timetabling lessons and assigning groups of pupils to particular locations at particular times. There is also a system of rewards in terms of academic achievement in that those pupils who co-operate with teachers have a greater likelihood of exam success. For some pupils interaction with and approval of the adult world of teachers is a reward in itself. This is especially true when set in a sexual context. Much interaction in our society, both in speech and body language, is couched in terms of sexual banter or flirtation. Woman teachers may offer boys the mock excitement of interaction with a sexually mature woman; men teachers offer girls the excitement of the attention of an adult male. Teachers themselves manipulate the sexual content of these relationships in order to attract the attention of or exert influence and control over their adolescent pupils (Wolpe 1984). As one woman bluntly put it 'You use your sex'.

Formally, authority was exercised by the headteacher and delegated through heads of departmental and pastoral units. These heads had access to formal authorities in the community, to educational welfare officers, to social workers and to the police. The image carried by formal authority in the school was that of the middle-class law-abiding male citizen clad in jacket, trousers, shirt and tie. Informally there was another powerful and pervasive source of authority, underpinning but independent of the formal system, and that was the threat of physical force. Its image was that of the strong, powerful male, a macho image. And its main physical location was in the craft workshops and the male physical education department. But it spread through the school in a network of 'heavies', men who would exert or threaten to exert force on recalcitrant boys. Each pastoral unit had its 'heavy' in addition to, or as part of, the formal network of authority. The pinnacle of the macho system was a strong, powerfully built deputy head with a reputation of being able to get confessions out of pupils by means of a Sherlock Holmes style of questioning and deduction. He was the focus of discipline problems in the school. He was part of a male group of teachers including several from boys' physical education, who met informally to train at weight lifting. It was said that men teachers coming new into a school were advised to establish a reputation for toughness during the first lesson by knocking down one of the lads. Women, even when provoked, rarely handled even the smaller boys. One who reported losing her temper and doing so had a sudden moment of panic when she realized the boy might be stronger than her. She resolved never to put herself in a similar situation.

The disciplinary power of the macho image lay in its dual force, first as a positive attraction, the macho hero to which girls as well as boys were attracted, second as a threat to actual physical force against boys, and probably fantasized about by girls. There was a strong sexual element in the attraction for girls of the macho image. It showed clearly when, after one of the girls' heroes brought his wife and young children into school thereby proclaiming himself as a family man, the girls dropped him and transferred their attachment to a younger, less well-known man, but a bachelor.

The headteacher refused to use corporal punishment and one reason he gave was that by stressing physical rather than moral force, it put women teachers at a disadvantage. The macho element in discipline although it was entirely informal had precisely this effect. In practice women became dependent on men for disciplining difficult pupils. A woman teacher described how one particular boy who had defied her authority had been sought out by a male member of staff, taken on his own to a quiet corner at the back of the school and threatened. The threat carried double force because the boy hero-worshipped the member of staff on account of his prowess at football. Moreover, because women as a category lacked the aura of strength and potential to inflict physical damage, they were considered in this respect to be less suitable than men for posts of authority. Women teachers tended to concur with this view; most of the women in the school thought that men, because of their greater strength, were more appropriate than women as headteachers. (Stanworth (1981, pp. 29–30) has an interesting account of pupils' perceptions of gender in relation to authority and discipline.)

The image of the macho man and the domestic, family-oriented woman complement one another. The organization of subject teaching by gender ensured a strong focus in the school for each of these images. Women in traditional domestic and office subjects were willing agents in the reproduction of these images. The humanities wedding shows how teachers in other subjects may be drawn by pressures both within and without the school to join in purveying domestic and family images. I would argue that when women teach, formally or informally, seriously or in jest, overtly or covertly, in support of the inherent domesticity of women, their inferiority and the irrelevance to them of occupational qualifications, they thereby undermine their own status as professionals. The same arguments about domestic and family values and interests can be applied equally to women teachers as to any other women. The incorporation of such teaching practices is a powerful factor in the maintenance within the school of the stereotype of the 'woman teacher' (National Union of Teachers 1980). This stereotype pictures her as a secondary earner within the family, as less committed to her job, and as having no wish to incur the further responsibilities which go with promotion to department or pastoral headships. For most women the stereotype was acceptable as a means of accommodating professional achievement with a focus on the domestic. To some teachers however, older single woman already in posts of authority, the stereotype was clearly inapplicable. And to an increasing number of young women whom I have called the new career woman, it was unacceptable. How and at what point did such teachers challenge the stereotype?

Challenges to the culture

The traditional challenge of women teachers to male domination within the school has been for themselves to attain positions of authority. The traditional cultural response to this has been twofold. The first is the exclusion of such women from key areas of school management. The second is ridicule. Such is the typical response to women who occupy the position of senior mistress or woman deputy, the highest position which women usually reach in mixed-sex secondary schools. For all secondary schools, including single-sex, 4.4 per cent of woman teachers were deputy head/senior mistress, 0.9 per cent head. For men the figures were 4.5 per cent deputy head, 3.4 per cent head (Department of Education and Science 1976). Senior mistresses are usually excluded from timetabling, a crucial management exercise which controls who is able to study which subject. Instead women deputies were usually assigned peripheral duties such as girls' discipline colloquially known as in charge of 'knickers' or the 'lavatory chain'. With some fight they could carve an influential niche for themselves, for example, supervising student teachers coming to the school, but they rarely got involved in central management. The whole post of senior mistress/woman deputy thus becomes derogated. There were, in the school I studied, petty indicators of this such as the listing of the senior mistress as second of the three deputies even though she had been there the longest (the names were not in alphabetical order).

Within the school there were five women teachers holding posts at scale three or above. Without exception they were the butt of jokes: one because of her devotion to her aged mother and to her dog; another for acting as a special constable; a third for frequent absence, a fourth for 'flapping' and a fifth for having unspecified 'hang-ups'. In all cases there was an implied lowering of competence, but in only one case did there appear any justification for this.

Women at the bottom of the career ladder who might be hoping for advancement were also subject to a range of comment and joking which stressed their role as women rather than teachers and which indirectly challenged their competence. There was a lot of sexual banter directed to women's appearance, their make-up, dress, body measurements etc. Even older women were not allowed to forget their sex but subjected to comments about size and weight. The kitchen sink featured: Any small mistake might be greeted by the cry 'Back to the kitchen sink!' Childbearing featured: 'Get your husband to lie on you and you could be out of here in nine months time!' said one ambitious young man to a young woman in competition with him for a scale post. Another tack used by men to control women's ambition was remorseless joking about women's supposed inferiority, their small brain size, their weaker muscle power etc.

MORAL AUTHORITY VERSUS MACHO POWER

Women in the school, as I have explained, tended to rely on men and in particular macho power when they had disciplinary problems with boys. Sometimes however, they rejected macho power but used instead their own moral authority. Such an incident occurred while I was at the school. It was quite unplanned and occurred in response to a critical disciplinary situation, but it was nonetheless a challenge to macho power as a disciplinary resource.

Some boys passed by as a PE teacher was giving a dance lesson to a group of girls. The music was playing. 'Stick your finger up your bum! Stick your finger up your bum!' the boys sang to its rhythm. The teacher could not let the boys get away with this. She took them to the office of the macho deputy. 'You're nowt but a bairn for telling on us' they taunted her. To her dismay the deputy was out of his office. She thought rapidly. She could take them to one of the other deputies; she would get an apology but it would mean very little because they neither admired nor feared the other deputies. Suddenly she decided she would handle the matter herself. Quickly she took the boys back to the class with her. As soon as she got there she turned to the girls. 'Girls', she said 'these boys have something to say to you'. And she herself told the boys to apologize for their rudeness. They did so. 'They'll hate me for making them do that' she said, 'but I couldn't let them get away with it'.

The incident shows the way male structures of authority and macho power combine to make women's dependence on men almost automatic. It suggests the difficulty of challenging such a system. It was only the temporary absence of the macho deputy which forced the teacher's hand and allowed her to reveal to herself her own latent moral authority. Usually she taught in the PE department where there were nearly always men ready and willing to take over any disciplinary problems. Indeed, men were often eager to avenge women teachers who were insulted by boys. A man who caught a boy trying to put his hand up the skirt of a teacher as she went upstairs boasted how he immediately took the boy by the collar and marched him into the nearest room, straight into the blackboard. 'His eyes stuck right out of his head. I thought I'd killed him,' said the teacher.

CHALLENGING THE STEREOTYPE – THE 'NEW CAREER WOMEN'

The images of women current in the school culture supported a stereotype of the woman teacher which showed her at a disadvantage professionally compared with men. The stereotype can be thought of in two ways. First women were defined primarily in domestic terms as wives and mothers. Women teachers therefore might be expected to marry, when married to take time out of teaching to bear and rear children, and then if they returned, to be less committed to the job, putting their family first and being unwilling to contribute to work after school hours. Second, they may be expected to behave in a conventionally feminine way, to pay attention to their appearance and to dress in a traditionally feminine way, to be occupationally unambitious, to be more decorous in their manners and less firm and abrasive than men, and to be dependent on men for keeping control.

Some women teachers who were keen to get promotion considered this stereotype to be detrimental to their prospects and deliberately set out to distance themselves from it, and to make sure that other teachers, especially in management positions were aware of their distance.

One example of such distancing occurred with a young teacher who deeply resented the explicit and implicit controls placed on her behaviour not only in her contacts with pupils and in her dress but also in the school staffroom. She became incensed when a deputy head approached her in the staffroom while she was having a private conversation with another teacher, talking, laughing and incidentally swearing. The deputy admonished her. She turned to him. 'Oh piss off!' she said. 'It's nothing to do with you!' It was a brave effort. Later she was called to the office to account for herself. She stuck to her right to behave as she wished in the staffroom. Yet she found herself apologizing for having spoken to him in a way which offended him, even though he had provoked the incident.

About one third of the women in this school were clear in their own minds that they wanted promotion. Some of them were aware of the way in which the stereotype of women as wife/mother disadvantaged them. Some challenged the idea of family first by making it quite clear they saw no reasons for conflict between the demands of their professional and married lives. Some distanced themselves from the stereotype by publicly rejecting the idea of marriage, or if married of having children.

Half of those who rejected stereotypes were unmarried: two were firmly decided against marrying; one thought it very unlikely and in any case intended to support herself. The others thought it likely they would marry but intended to continue teaching. Of the married teachers, none presented herself in conventional wifely terms. This was made clear through staffroom conversations which covered matters such as shared responsibility for housework and taking turns moving to new jobs. One teacher showed her horror of conventional life in the suburbs by poking fun at the housewives 'behind their lace curtains' who came to the door each morning to wave their husbands off and wish them a good day then meeting one another later for coffee. 'Thank God I've got a job' was her comment 'I couldn't live like that'.

None of these 'career women' had any children. Five had firmly decided they did not intend to have any. One was dithering. By the time the research was complete she had decided against but another had 'fallen'. Women who did not want children tended to make their views publicly known. One talked graphically about smelly babies who made even the walls of rooms smell and about 'yucky' children. Women thought the headteacher was influenced in the decisions he made about promotion by possible pregnancy. 'He's always afraid when we're coming up to about thirty that we're going to rush off and breed' as one teacher said. Some women, therefore, made a point of telling the head directly that they had no intention of becoming pregnant, so that this possibility should not interfere with the possibility of their promotion.

I have called these young women teachers the 'new career women'. None was over thirty. All were of an age to have been influenced as students by the various strands of the Women's Movement and by recent changes in the position of women in employment and in law. They differed from the 'old career women', those women who had become career teachers in default of marriage or in the event of widowhood. And they differed from those married women teachers who, conventionally, put the demands of children, husband and home before their jobs.

Conclusion

In this chapter I have looked at certain features of the organization of subject teaching in the school and at a range of events drawn from a morning assembly, from class teaching, from staffroom interactions. They have been analysed in terms of a range of beliefs and values about the position in society of men and women, of boys and girls, beliefs and values which are a basic part of the culture of the school. I have looked also at some of the responses of women teachers to the way they are defined and controlled by this heavily male-dominated culture, and at some of the protests and challenges they made within it.

How useful is this approach for understanding and for trying to change the position of women and girls within the mixed-sex secondary school?

First it shows the interrelatedness of different facets of the culture; it shows how the macho male focus on striving and ambition for boys complements the domestic, family-centred, service-work focus for girls, and how the macho male sexual image is strongly related to the fact that authority and discipline, both formal and informal, lie largely in the hands of men. And, most important, it shows that the way in which women teachers treat girls is related to the way women teachers view themselves, and to the way they are viewed by men teachers including the male management hierarchy.

In the second place it points up tensions and contradictions within the culture. It is at these points that social change is taking place, and hence where interventions directed towards creating greater opportunities for girls and for women are most likely to be useful. The main area of tension lies between the professional ethic which values teachers independently of their sex, and the dominant sexual stereotypes of the school which rate the woman teacher as less than the man. The main point of tension was among the younger women teachers, the new career women, who seemed deliberately to reject the stereotype of 'family first and teacher second'. These were women who perceived quite clearly that gender was likely to be an obstacle to their own promotion, but most failed to perceive the extent to which the school discriminated against girls educationally, or the part they themselves played in this discrimination.

References

Byrne, E. 1978. *Women and education*, London, Tavistock.
Department of Education and Science 1976. *Statistics of education*, Vol. 4, London, HMSO.

Llewellyn, M. 1980. 'Studying girls at school: the implications of confusion', in Deem, R. (ed), *Schooling for women's work*, London, Routledge and Kegan Paul.

National Union of Teachers 1980. *Promotion and the woman teacher*, London, National Union of Teachers.

Shaw, J. 1976. 'Finishing school: some implications of sex-segregated education', in Barker, D. L., Allen, S. (ed.), *Sexual divisions and society: process and change*, London, Tavistock.

Stanworth, M. 1981. *Gender and schooling: a study of sexual divisions in the classroom*, London, Womens' Research and Resources Centre.

Titmuss, R. 1958. *Essays on 'the welfare state'*, London, Unwin.

Whyte, J. 1981. 'Sex typing in schools', in Kelly, A. (ed), *The missing half*, Manchester, Manchester University Press.

Wolpe, A-M. 1984. Unpublished paper read at University of Hull.

18 It's nothing personal: class opposition to the curriculum

David Coulby

In this chapter David Coulby looks at the value accorded to working-class interests in the curriculum. He examines the extent to which schools are analogous to a workplace with an alienated workforce in control of neither their labour nor its products. He looks at the way the expression of aspects of working-class behaviour may be seen as subversive and how disruption may occur as a reassertion of class identity. He goes on to consider the class basis of school knowledge and suggests that the elevation of working-class experience and knowledge to an appropriate place in the curriculum is one of the necessary starting points for reducing disaffection and hence disruption.

Disruption in schools tends to conjure up a multitude of nefarious activities. At one extreme are horrific anecdotes of systematic bullying, violence against teachers and arson. At the other are teachers whose hackles rise at the sight of a bar of chewing gum or the unfastened top button of a shirt. Probably the bulk of what teachers perceive to be disruptive, the kind of activity which wears them down and which makes the presentation of their curriculum almost impossible, rarely falls at either extreme. Activity which interrupts lessons – horseplay, inappropriate talking or shouting out, rudeness to the teacher – may constitute the more daily annoyances of classroom disruption. To this must be added acts of violence, so rarely serious or even seriously intended, against other pupils and acts of vandalism, particularly against the property or fabric of the school. Much of this activity is interpreted by teachers, as indeed it may be intended by pupils, as a challenge to their authority or, more nebulously, that of the school.

Many beginning or trainee teachers are surprised by the apparently anarchic and unkind behaviour of pupils. They feel some commitment to the pupils and they may feel closer in terms of age and personal style to them than they do the senior members of the school's hierarchy. They tend to internalize the challenge to authority and worry that the children do not like them personally when their efforts at friendliness are rejected. It may be difficult to see any rationality or coherence in the activities of those pupils who engage in disruption, or of those others who passively allow apparently interesting lessons to be repeatedly ruined and their own chances of examination success probably impeded. In such circumstances explanations of disruption which focus on the psychopathologies of individual children can seem attractive. Thus pupils are seen to engage in disruptive activity because they are 'disturbed' or 'hyperactive' or 'maladjusted'. A short step from this is the invention of the category of 'disruptive pupils'. At this point the range of explanation becomes hopelessly circular: pupils disrupt lessons because they are disruptive pupils.

These accounts preclude seeing the pupils as dissatisfied with or disaffected from aspects of the curriculum. The focus cannot be shifted from the individual pupil. The other elements in the disruptive episode, the peer group, the teacher's style, the curriculum of the lesson, the organization of the classroom and the school, are excluded from analysis. Yet one advantage of emphasizing a connection between disruption and disaffection rather than disruption and pathology is that it allows for an analysis of classroom events which may lead to a wider range of strategies for reducing disaffection and, perhaps, disruption.

The teacher–pupil relationship

An oversimplified starting point might be that in general pupils are working-class whilst teachers are middle-class. It is possible, though, to see the similarities between schools and factories or businesses with the pupils as workers being ordered about by the teachers who seem like bosses. Further, it is not unknown for teachers in urban schools to return to the tranquillity of more leafy districts each evening. But teachers work for their living too and the majority of them are far from well-paid. Whilst some of them may deny any allegiance to the working class there are very few of them who would qualify as major owners of wealth. A more rigorous, though highly schematic, use of the concept of class sees the middle class as being those who own and/or control the means of production (factories, businesses, etc.), and the working class as those who have to sell their labour to gain a livelihood. Within this categorization very few teachers would be included in the middle class nor would many pupils, though some would.

To argue that schools are middle-class institutions or that they operate largely in the interest of this class is not to make any classification of the personnel of schools. It is to insist rather that it is the middle class who, in the main, benefit from the operation of educational institutions. State schools, through their examination system, stratify pupils for their appropriate place in the workforce. They also tend to inculcate pupils into an ideology, the major component of which is that the existing social and economic relations are the best, if not the only, ones possible. That working-class teachers find themselves transmitting middle-class ideology to working-class pupils is one of the structural ironies of their jobs with which many of them struggle with some perseverance.

The concept of class suggested above has only two categories: it is, then, not a very sophisticated instrument for classifying those pupils who are perceived by their teachers to indulge in disruptive activity. Ford *et al* (1982) used the Registrar General's classification of social class when they carried out their research into the social origins of London schoolchildren referred as being maladjusted. These children may represent the more extreme versions of disruption mentioned in the opening section, but the results are nevertheless illuminating. Almost all of the referred pupils came from categories IV and V, the skilled and unskilled labourers. Ford and colleagues conclude that 'It is a most remarkable and interesting piece of information that, in these areas at least, middle- and upper-class children do not become maladjusted' (Ford, Mongon and Whelan 1982, p. 136). From this it is perhaps possible to generalize that those pupils who engage most frequently in disruptive behaviour have social backgrounds which are working-class not only in a Marxist sense, but also in the sense that they are predominantly from families where wage-earners do manual work.

It is this section of the working class which perhaps comes closest to the everyday understanding of the concept. Part of this understanding is that there are specific forms of familial, social and recreational behaviour associated with this section of the working class. Regional variations do not necessarily conceal the common elements generated by similar patterns of poverty and oppression. *Andy Capp* or *EastEnders* offer regional stereotypes of working-class culture – male-dominated, beer drinking, footballing, pigeon-fancying, violent etc. Whilst rejecting these stereotypes it is apparent that different classes, both in Marxist terms and those of the Registrar General, do have differing forms of familial and social behaviour. In discussing working-class recreational culture, then, or middle-class forms of knowledge it is necessary to be aware of the level of generalization which is being employed and of the solidity of the social practices to which these generalizations refer.

Under the capitalist system of production and distribution the worker is forced to sell his or her labour in order to earn a wage. This involves the sacrifice of autonomy in the important area of work. Personal objectives or criteria of fulfilment must be subordinated to the requirements of the system of production and distribution. The worker in such a system may be said to be alienated. Indeed she or he is alienated from both the *products* of his or her labour and the *process* of the work itself. Since workers need to sell their labour and since they have no control over the conditions, hours, social or material organization of their work, they are alienated from the process. Since the product is not designed by them and since they may play only a small and trivial part in its manufacture (bolting on the wheel of a car, say, or typing a letter written by someone else) and since it will be sold in order to make a profit for the employer the worker is also alienated from the product.

It has been suggested that pupils are similarly alienated from both the process and the product of their schoolwork. The process may seem as oppressive as the capitalist workplace: their conditions of work, their movement and behaviour are regulated and beyond their control; their curricular material is externally defined, organized and assessed. The product (often schoolwork in exercise books and ultimately marks) may seem even more trivial and meaningless than many of the products of capitalist enterprise. Thus, although teachers are not bosses in the sense of belonging to the bourgeoisie they may appear like bosses to many pupils and often even behave like bosses because of their structural position.

WORKING-CLASS ACTIVITY AND SCHOOL VALUES

Workers may resist their alienation and oppression by collective organization and action. Pupil unions were a feature of the late 1960s and pupil strikes do occur (see Chapter 27). But workers may also resist by less purposive or coherent behaviour, by messing about, taking long breaks, mistreating employers' equipment. In this way they attempt to regain at least partial control over their own time and over their process of labour. Children and young people in schools likewise attempt to gain control over their own time and activity by messing about or 'bunking off'. There is rather more here than a similarity or a correspondence of resistance between the school and the workplace. The forms of resistance in schools may to a certain extent represent a working-class cultural pattern derived from experience at the workplace (Willis 1977).

This position may seem remote from the exigencies of the disrupted classroom. However, if some of the aspects of working-class culture are examined it may be possible to relate them to some of the components of disruptive behaviour. One element of working-class culture is a high regard for quick wit, particularly in spoken repartee. This may take the form of jokes or backchat. Humour is not an exclusively working-class preserve, but there is a particular form of wit, often personal and derogatory, sometimes antagonistic, tending to focus on people's weaknesses, idiosyncracies or inadequacies, which is readily identifiable as being a product and pursuit of this class. Working-class culture also tends to place value on physical strength, skill and finesse. This may be seen in its male-oriented, macho presentation in a predilection for physical sports such as football or boxing. It can also be seen in the more everyday physical contact of mucking about. Working-class culture may also value collective, co-operative activity rather than the individualistic, competitive ethos so commonly found in schools.

These forms of working-class activity can all too easily be construed as disruptive in schools. Humour that focuses on the personal characteristics of teachers or that leads to pride and skill in 'answering back' can simply be interpreted as a challenge to authority. (As a teacher I once foolishly addressed a pupil with a remark along the lines of: 'Come on, Jones. Who shook your cage?' To which I received the swift reply: 'Who opened yours?' The resulting laughter did little for my *amour propre* or for my authority with the class.)

Physical boisterousness in the classroom can easily be interpreted as violence, impoliteness and vandalism. Finally the collective nature of working-class activity is a very threatening phenomenon when it takes the form of a class united in opposition to their teacher. This aspect of solidarity is perhaps a different way of perceiving the collusion of the mass of pupils in what appears to be the disruptive activity of only a few. These three aspects of working-class activity, then, are likely to be perceived as disruptive when they occur in schools since they interrupt the flow of lessons, challenge the authority of teachers and schools and tend to wear down teachers. However, by placing these activities in their cultural and potentially resistant context, it might be possible for teachers to acknowledge that they are not necessarily irrational or the product of some individual 'disturbance'.

The pupils may be asserting aspects of their own culture in a setting which they perceive as hostile or dismissive of it. Insofar as the teachers are the representatives of, or at least the images of, the bosses the pupils may be resisting their subordinate position and their alienation from process and product. One way of understanding aspects of classroom disruption is as an attempt by the powerless to reappropriate some areas of schooling. It does not overthrow the structures of schooling, any more than western workers have yet overthrown the structures of capitalism, but it does challenge them at some of their weak spots as well as providing light relief along the way.

The argument of this section has concentrated largely on activities associated more with boys than girls. Willis's research focused almost exclusively on boys. Boys are more frequently perceived by teachers as engaging in disruption. Other chapters in this book examine in some detail issues surrounding sexism and disruption. A parallel argument here may be briefly suggested. The culture of working-class young women involves, among other things, fashion, pop-music and romanticized fictional accounts of the man–woman relationship. Some schools do endeavour to keep themselves sanitized from such activities. However, usually their intrusion into school is perceived as less of a threat to teachers than the vigorous activities of boys and schools may actively encourage such passive pursuits for girls (see Chapter 16).

The types of explanation which focus on individuals and their imputed 'disturbance' tend to transform characteristic social class activity into deviance. An aspect of this view is to see the 'problems' of individuals as emanating from their home backgrounds. This reduces the issue of class to one of family background and places the responsibility for disruptive or 'resistant' behaviour outside the context in which it occurs, thereby ignoring the social class relations of the school. It may be the conventional explanations rather than the disruptive activity which lacks coherence and rationality.

Working-class children and school knowledge

The second argument of this chapter concerns the class-based nature of the knowledge selected for the school curriculum. Just as aspects of the school curriculum are discussed elsewhere in this book as being based on racist and sexist assumptions about knowledge, it is possible also to reveal the ways in which the curriculum is infused with specific class values and traditions. The knowledge selected for the school curriculum reflects that more commonly found and valued in middle-class than in working-class backgrounds. It serves to advantage middle-class children who find that school knowledge is something with which they are familiar beyond school. It also serves to legitimate middle-class knowledge by replicating and evaluating it whilst undermining working-class forms of knowledge by ignoring or denigrating them. This can be seen most glaringly in the difference between the language of many working-class children and the language in which much of school business is conducted. Working-class children can encounter language at school with which at best, they are unfamiliar and which, at worst, they may find incomprehensible and threatening. Their own language may be criticized in terms of its grammatical structure or its spoken accent. The long debate about the relative merits of working-class family language and that of the school is now no longer conducted in deficit terms but the mismatch between the two still remains. Middle-class children whose language approximates more closely to that used in school are conversely advantaged. Far from being threatening the language of the school is comfortingly familiar and their everyday accomplishment is rewarded as a school success.

As well as language, the knowledge selected for inclusion in the school curriculum may seem more familiar to pupils with middle-class patterns and backgrounds. Primary school history, for instance, can all too easily become a procession of the careers of rulers, 'great men' and a few token women of substance. At secondary school it is likely to involve wars, inevitably won by the

'English' and the ineluctable spread of European civilization, despite occasional 'mutinies' by intransigent 'natives'. Liberal and nationalistic values are unlikely to be questioned. In so far as geography touches on the third world it will be presented as an area of 'problems' largely caused by climatic factors and the irrationality of the local populations. The role of European and North American nations in the economic fragility of the third world is unlikely to be discussed. Links, in terms of class position, between poor people in the third world and the poor and unemployed in the UK are likely to be studiously avoided. The idea of a world class structure based on a world economic order is reserved for the more select discussions of academe. Links between events in Johannesburg, Kingston, Brixton or Belfast will probably not be explored.

English language in schools is often the systematic enforcement of the written and spoken modes of the middle class at the expense of the linguistic and dialectical diversity of the communities in which the schools operate. English literature is often concerned with the domestic passions or grandiose aspirations of middle-class and aristocratic protagonists. Although it is a subject which often appeals to girls, women writers are likely to be seen as romantic, just as black and third world writers are seen as an exotic periphery. Working-class or black families are perceived in the context of 'problems', or as the salt of the earth. At the centre of the syllabus, dwarfing the rest of world literature, stands white, male, Shakespeare who, whatever the general nature of his appeal in his day, now symbolizes the cultural aspirations of the middle class.

Science is presented as the product of the male Western mind. Its debt to Islamic traditions is as infrequently mentioned as its inseparable connection, in the West, with military developments. It leads to the activities of professional (commercial or military) scientists rather than to the encouragement of wider curiosity about humanity, nature and their interaction. Working-class history, culture, forms of solidarity and ranges of explanation are either denigrated or ignored. Parallel arguments could be made to reveal the racism and sexism latent in the curriculum (see Chapters 16 and 20). The working class appears in the school curriculum as an object of concern and pity, a social problem, a dangerous mob or an empty space.

Of course, this is not invariably the case. Many teachers and schools have made considerable efforts to gain an accepted place in the curriculum for working-class experience and knowledge and I will discuss, briefly, two such schools in the following chapter. There is a continuous strand of work which has recognized and supported the class interests of pupils. Chris Searle is a well-known example. Working in secondary schools in the East End of London he encouraged children to write stories and poems about their own experiences in the area. He taught them about the working-class struggles that had taken place in East London and encouraged them to find out and write about international working-class struggles (Searle 1973; 1977). Searle is an example of a teacher who has struggled successfully with the structural position in which his job placed him. Teachers as well as pupils can engage in resistant activity. Nevertheless, there was much opposition to Searle's early work at Sir John Cass School and he eventually left after a struggle with the school authorities. A strong sense of class identity is exercised in this section of a poem by Paul Sharp from Bethnal Green who was twelve when he wrote it:

> The East End is all cluttered up
> Not much space, just lots of muck
> There is a park every 30 miles
> Rubbish tips there's piles and piles
> The West End is just space and space
> Rubbish there! There's not a trace!
> Houses big, gardens wide
> Like a football pitch inside
> In the East End unemployment's so high
> Thousands and thousands
> Nearly touches the sky
> In the West End the odd thousand or so,
> They've got all the money, they've got all the dough
> So you can see who's better off
> Nice big steak or a pig's trough.
>
> Paul Sharp 1984

It is not only the content of the school curriculum but also its organization which seems to give preference to middle-class forms of knowledge. In most schools the curriculum is stratified so that elite subjects such as science, maths and English are seen as being more valuable than other practical subjects such as gardening or craft, design and technology. It is those subjects associated with working-class skills and occupations which form the least valued strata. Those pupils who are perceived as most able are the ones likely to follow the elite subjects: those who do not succeed in school may be directed towards the less valuable practical options.

Concluding remarks

Pupils who do not learn sufficiently quickly to read and write are often the ones who, spurred on by frustration and boredom, engage most enthusiastically in disruptive activity (Coulby and Harper, 1985). The present stratification of the curriculum and the whole notion of ability and intelligence work against working-class pupils in that they are perceived to under-achieve by not learning middle-class knowledge and values. If the knowledge taught paid adequate respect to working-class culture and experience, there would be far less likelihood of working-class pupils failing to come to grips with it.

When working-class experience and values do not penetrate the school curriculum, disruption may be seen as a defiant statement of those values as is also argued in this book about the disaffection of black pupils and girls. The implication is that disaffection – and thus, probably, disruption – could be reduced by curriculum change. Reducing classroom disruption is a considerable task which necessitates changes in the ways pupils are grouped, their days organized, their work set and evaluated. The curriculum needs to reflect the wide diversity of experience and values which children bring into schools. Working-class language, values and activities need to be incorporated as areas for potential success at school. The curriculum needs to be opened up for negotiation with pupils and their parents (Coulby, 1985). Such negotiation would need to cover all aspects of the curriculum and all phases of education. A curriculum revitalized along these lines might well be one which would play a major part in the reduction of disaffection. More positively it might be one in which working-class pupils could experience success in schools.

References

Coulby, D. 1985. 'Some notes on cultural relativism – curriculum planning in a multi-cultural society', in Slade, I. (ed.), *Managing curricula: a comparative perspective*, London, LACE.

Coulby, D. and Harper, T. 1985. *Preventing classroom disruption: policy, practice and evaluation in urban schools*, London, Croom Helm.

Ford, J., Mongon, D. and Whelan, M. 1982. *Special education and social control: invisible disasters*, London, Routledge & Kegan Paul.

Searle, C. (ed.), 1973. *Stepney words I & II*, London, Reality Press.

Searle, C. (ed.), 1977. *The world in a classroom*, London, Writers and Readers.

Sharp, P. 1984, in Searle, C. (ed.), *Our city*, London, Young World Books, 20–21.

Willis, P. 1977. *Learning to labour*, Farnborough, Saxon House.

19　Changing urban schools
David Coulby

In this chapter David Coulby takes a brief look at two urban schools which have been successful in their attempts to prevent disaffection and disruption through the development of inclusive curricula and the creation of an atmosphere in the school which enables pupils and teachers to develop a mutual respect. Both are situated within the ILEA where the series of central initiatives on anti-sexism, anti-racism and anti-classism have themselves met with varying degress of resistance from the schools. In both the schools described here the push and the resources from the authority have coincided with a commitment on the part of staff to make the reforms work.

One of the themes this book explores, is the link between disaffection with curricula and the level of disruption within a school. There is an implication that a high degree of disruption should lead schools to examine their own practices and curricula rather than simply blaming their pupils. Nevertheless, I am aware that when people ask 'How do you get rid of classroom disruption?', they may have a pupil in mind whose behaviour is so outrageous that they think I must be a clown if I believe that teachers can do anything to change it. I consider that teachers do need to be, and can be, armed with survival skills for dealing with and avoiding such situations or for coping with classes of disaffected pupils where disruption is barely contained. However my general answer to the question, 'How do you get rid of classroom disruption?' is to suggest that it is better to approach a solution to disaffection through curricula reform than retreat from a solution because of the disruption of pupils. By developing rich, varied, stimulating curricula, which involve the pupils, whatever their ability, teachers can often afford to reduce the stress on behaviour. When children or young people are active, interested and learning, when their culture, families and values are seen to be respected, when their work is appreciated by teachers and displayed in the classroom, there is considerably less likelihood that they will engage in disruptive activity. When teachers have positive things to say about children's work instead of negative things about children's behaviour the atmosphere of classrooms can be altered.

Of course it is easier to talk about inclusive curricula than to develop them. In this chapter I want to give a glimpse of two schools where a visit provides powerful evidence that inner city areas can provide an education environment fit for their pupils.

Argyle Primary School

The three hundred children at Argyle School share sixteen languages, the main one being Bengali. Many of the children are housed with their families in local hotels and there are traveller children from a nearby camp. Some families are political refugees, others are studying at London University. Most of the families are working-class.

When headteachers are asked about developments in their schools they frequently find it easiest to refer back to the way things were when they arrived. Barbara Allan, for instance, referred to a remedial class of third and fourth year juniors. These pupils had given up and their negative behaviour seemed linked to their placement in a labelled class where there was no praise for their work and little stimulation. This situation was changed dramatically after introducing a no-withdrawal policy. Assistance is now given in the mainstream classroom by support teachers working alongside the class teacher. They may team teach or the support teacher may take a small group. This is also the model for community language and English as a second language teaching.

After Barbara Allan came to the school, she tried to appoint new staff who shared her ideas about curricular diversity. As I was introduced to a teacher at Argyle, the headteacher remarked, 'We don't have any disaffected children left since you arrived'. The children in this class were all eagerly working; some had spread out into the hall, lying on the floor in small groups inventing number games.

Another main component of developing change at Argyle School has been in-service training. It is school-based and school-focused. It seeks to draw on the expertise within the school as well as using outside speakers. Practical sessions and workshops ensure that it actually feeds into practice in the classroom. Topics have included the development of school policies on language, anti-racism and English as a second language. By involving all the staff in the same programme, the sessions become an opportunity to share good ideas and problems. They provide a chance for staff to work out common policies and to develop a sense of cohesion.

The contribution of parents to Argyle is encouraged in their first communication; a booklet called *Welcome to Argyle School*. It is written in English, Bengali and Chinese and is illustrated with children's drawings. It emphasizes that parents are always welcome to visit and they can come and discuss any aspect of their child. It also adds, 'The staff will be grateful for any help you can offer – e.g. mending equipment, hearing children read, helping with cooking, accompanying groups of children on educational visits, talking with children for whom English is not their mother tongue etc.' Parents provide real support with community languages, helping with writing notices for the school, and preparing community language reading material. Parents are often invited to class assemblies. The multilingual welcoming signs in the school and in the classrooms are more than a mere token: they are an indication of the close relationship between the parents and the school.

The environment of the school and the classrooms reflects the richness and diversity of the curricula. On the walls of the reception class it is not only the 'best' products which are displayed. The work of all pupils is valued through the mass of carefully presented and labelled display. There is a writing table with materials and illustrations in Bengali and English. Displays are labelled in a variety of languages. There is a stock of folders for the books the children will take home. The children work enthusiastically and methodically. In another reception class a group of Bengali girls are contentedly banging away on a carpentry bench.

The curricula draws on the linguistic and cultural diversity of the pupils. Obviously English as a second language work is important but the schools also uses language teachers to collaborate with the families in the development of the children's community languages. The cultural diversity of the children is brought into the curriculum by topic work. The headteacher provides an example:

> In one top junior class a ten year old Nigerian boy who had recently come to this country and had previously shown little interest or enthusiasm for collaborative work or class discussion was able to talk about his experiences when discussing the differences in climate and weather in different parts of the world. His previous schooling had been in a highly structured missionary school and although his English was very good, the class teacher had not until then, realized how articulate he was.

Handwriting was one surprising area where cultural diversity made a positive contribution. For many pupils English is a completely new script. When the teacher saw the high standard of scriptwriting that some children could produce in Chinese, Bengali, Arabic etc., they decided that better presentation should be expected of the children writing in English. A new policy on written work emphasized presentation as well as planning, writing and negotiated revision of texts. As the presentation improved so did the quality of the work which the children produced.

The wish to avoid both 'remedial' groups and the whole 'remedial' concept led to a change in reading policy. A structured reading scheme which tended to encourage competitiveness was abandoned. Now the headteacher says: 'Our reading scheme is a library'. Apart from a wide and careful selection of books, stories on tapes, often made by the teachers, allow the children to read and listen together in small groups. Mother tongue books and dual language books are also used. These are particularly important for taking home to share with families who can speak little English. All children are encouraged to take books home.

Barbara Allan recognizes that Argyle benefits from the resourcing policies of the ILEA which allow the school to develop a store of materials and to have floating support teachers. English as a second language and community language development are supported through the provision of part-time teachers. ILEA's equal opportunities policies have provided a focus for curriculum development and staff discussion in the school. The implementation of bilingual strategies, anti-racist policies and a multicultural curriculum is encouraged. The section of Argyle School's Anti-Racist Policy which deals with curriculum illustrates what this entails:

1 We will continue to create an atmosphere which reflects the multicultural character of our school through such things as display, music, celebration of festivals, etc.
2 Our curriculum must be enriched by using experiences children bring to the classroom and ensuring that their cultures and religions are understood and valued.
3 Anti-racist teaching must be included in the curriculum.
4 Assemblies should set the tone by giving equal value and respect to all the religious groupings in the school. We acknowledge the right for everyone to worship or not in their own way.

The approach to behaviour problems at Argyle is one which insists that discipline is not the main item on the school agenda. Nevertheless, there is a code of conduct for the school. This is brief and simple and, characteristically, is shared with parents. *Welcome to Argyle School* states:

> We strive to maintain standards of behaviour and discipline from the beginning of school life. Children are expected to:
>
> 1 Show respect for each other's social and racial backgrounds.
> 2 Be aware that they are representatives of the school within the community and behaviour should be orderly and controlled both inside and outside school.
> 3 Be helpful and respectful to all staff whether teaching or non-teaching.
> Parents are expected to support the school in the above policy.

A clear explicit code without any unnecessary and hidden regulations helps to minimize confrontation.

Argyle is not an isolated example of good practice nor is it a 'show school.' It contains examples of developments which are occurring in many urban schools. However, experience there does provide support for the idea that pupil's behaviour in school can be changed by altering the grouping arrangements, the teaching style and the curriculum. The staff have opted to construct as far as they are able, a non-elitist, multicultural curriculum and find that there is little disaffection at their school.

Lilian Baylis Community School

There are just under six hundred secondary age pupils on role at Lilian Baylis and about seventy-five per cent of them are black. Situated in the middle of a housing estate, its buildings are open to community involvement on the one hand and unwelcome intruders on the other. The headteacher arrived after the school had been formed by amalgamating separate boys' and girls' schools into one co-educational establishment with a new headteacher. At that point the school was suffering an absence of identity and from huge monthly bills for the replacement of windows. The head and deputies have supported changes in the physical fabric of the school and in its curricula. Of considerable impact is the fact that in a relatively small comprehensive school it is possible for them to know nearly all the pupils by name. There is no streaming or segregation within the school.

The appearance of the inside and outside of the building is important at Lilian Baylis. Outside there are trees and lots of flowers. The head stresses the importance of making the site look attractive and of talking to the pupils about it. She considers that this helps them appreciate the school and reduces the possibility of vandalism. Inside the school a relaxed informal style is encouraged with carpets and the use of furniture that can be easily stacked and rearranged.

As at Argyle, in-service training is an important aspect of the running of the school and is again based on the premises. It takes two forms. There are regular meetings of departments, year tutors, and the whole staff during school time. There is also a mixed-ability adviser. This is a scale-three teacher whose obligatory class-contact time involves six out of twenty-four periods. He spends the rest of his time working in collaboration with heads of department on the diversification of curricula. This includes working alongside class teachers in a cooperative teaching and consultative role.

This following extract from a note from the headteacher to heads of department concerning first year classes clearly indicates the high standards which are expected in mixed-ability work:

Can you let us know if you are happy on all these dimensions:

1 The operation of mixed ability teaching in the classroom, e.g. (a) Is the task appropriate? (b) Is the task clearly explained and understood? Are suitable extensive materials for able pupils in use? (c) Is there sequential development of the task?

2 The pace of the lesson, e.g., (a) How quickly does it start? (b) How does it end? (c) How many activities are undertaken to stimulate pupils by listening, group work, individual explanation, emphasis in oral skills, etc.?

3 Homework – is it being set and completed on time?

A third year pupil commented on the curriculum: 'In my old school lessons were a bit easy. But I can manage the work here. We can always ask the teacher questions.' The mixed-ability advisor himself is convinced of the link between what children are taught and the way they behave in class: 'If the most able pupils and the least able pupils are both stretched and occupied then you will get less disruption.'

The school is involved in two special initiatives. It is one of the twenty schools in the ILEA involved in the development of annual statements of achievement for pupils. It is also one of the schools involved in the first phase of ILEA's grand plan to improve secondary schools (the Hargreaves programme). For this initiative they have had to break down curricula into half-term 'modules' in each subject area. In doing so the curriculum is made pupil-sized. Pupils can see what it is for and what they are trying to learn. An example of one such unit which contributes to a *CSE course* in office practice is given below.

5th Year – term 1   September/October

IMPROVING SECONDARY SCHOOLS (ONE CREDIT)

Unit titles
    (a) The banking system and petty cash
    (b) 'Advanced' keyboard skills

Length
6/7 weeks – 3 hours per week

Aims/Objectives
Students should be able at the end of the unit to:
    1 Describe, compare and contrast services offered by the main commercial banks.
    2 Record petty cash transactions and restore Imprest.
    3 Complete relevant 'work' assignments.

Content
    A Bank accounts, statements, giro credit, paying-in slip, standing orders, direct debits and other major services offered to customers – both private individuals and business people.

B Recording of petty cash, why petty cash, Imprest system.
C 'Advanced' keyboard skills including typing letters from manuscript and basic correction signs.
D All students will have 'Mock' CSE assignments to complete.

Anti-racism, anti-sexism and anti-classism are not merely ritualistically acknowledged, they are principles which underly the social relations of the school and the process of curriculum development. They are seen as a single approach to developing the self-worth of all pupils. Home ecomonics is compulsory for boys and girls and PE is mixed and competition is not stressed although competitive teams do play in extra-curricular clubs. Whilst posters against apartheid or uranium mining in Namibia decorate the walls, pupils are encouraged to gain a thorough knowledge of such topics. In social studies, for example, a group of pupils studied apartheid in South Africa. After doing some reading and research four pupils, both black and white, visited South Africa House to carry out an interview with officials. On the way out they were heckled by anti-apartheid demonstrators. The pupils stuck up for themselves and insisted that they were gathering information, wanted to try to understand as many points of view as possible, and had attempted to get into dialogue with the South African officials.

This example runs contrary to the well publicized aspersion that there is bias inherent in these curriculum approaches. Another example of penetrating but impartial investigation can be seen in a fifth year social studies project on social class. In the course of learning about differences between upper-, middle- and working-classes, the young people were taken on a visit to Harrods. They wrote up diaries as if they were members of each of three classes. They then took current issues – such as the nuclear power plant disaster in the Ukraine – and worked out the reactions of representatives of each class.

The struggles of ordinary people to find and keep their homes, for example, can become a project in humanities and the effect is to integrate the knowledge of these young people into the curriculum and to accept its legitimate value. Obviously raising complex issues such as class or racism has its pitfalls. It is easy to lapse into stereotypes, and to be really educative the teachers have to allow views to be expressed which they may find unpalatable. However, the curriculum material here provides pupils with the opportunity to reflect on their own experience and to contextualize it within the wider structures of society. It allows them to participate imaginatively in a wide range of views. Such objectives are vital components of a lively and demanding curriculum.

When I first spoke to the headteacher, she had told me that the way to reduce disaffection in schools was by 'flowers and trees and love'. One of the teachers used more familiar educational language: 'It is a combination of environment, teacher attitude and the curriculum'. These three points do seem to suggest positive policies whereby disruption and disaffection can be reduced in urban schools. The policies of Lilian Baylis School on the environment and the curriculum have been briefly outlined above. Teacher attitudes may be slower to change but a pupil compared Lilian Baylis with her previous school in these terms: 'I think the teachers are kinder. They give you a fair hearing. Here they talk it over. They don't just blame you. They hear both sides.'

20 A question of interest: tackling racism in the curriculum

Europe Singh

In this chapter Europe Singh describes the work of the Inner London Education Authority's Anti-Racist Strategies Team. In devising anti-racist policies the initial concern of schools was strictly with racist incidents. But the painstaking work of the group has begun to reveal the institutional racism embodied in school textbooks, syllabuses and the assumptions behind courses. Challenging the racism of schooling lays bare, too, the interests that are served by the way the curriculum is currently presented.

In September 1983 after much struggle, the Inner London Education Authority seconded four teachers, two secondary and two primary, to develop anti-racist strategies for ILEA schools and colleges. Admittedly two primary teachers and two secondary teachers were not much in terms of catering for the needs of the largest LEA in the country but it marked a sharp break with the hitherto unquestioned philosophy of multicultural education.

For us multicultural education rested on two false premises. Firstly it assumed that the underachievement of black children stemmed from the lack of a cultural identity and that this produced a negative self-image. This we would describe as the victim-centred approach to underachievement. What was required to redress this, argued the multiculturalists, was cultural reinforcement and the presentation of positive images. The second underlying error was that the racism of white children stemmed from an ignorance of the cultures of black people. 'They didn't understand us.' Again the remedy suggested was an exposure to a diversity of cultures. The resulting practice of multiculturalism, too often, boiled down to one-off celebrations of religious festivals, international evenings and steel bands.

Whilst not underestimating the need to redress the 'negative images' of black people projected by a racist society and by the nature of schooling in that society, we strongly believe that the emphasis on culture was worse than diversionary, it was positively dangerous. Not only does multiculturalism place a straightjacket on 'cultures' – denying any cultural dynamics – it also validated all cultures without question including the so-called 'majority' culture for which Sir Keith Joseph pleaded when he resigned as Secretary of State for Education. This is a culture which celebrates the glories of empire and the triumphs of Britain's military past.

We feel, however, that the underachievement of black children and the unchallenged racism of white children stem from this culture itself and the social structures which support and reproduce it. To the extent that it is transmitted in school, the racism of white pupils and the alienation of black pupils will continue. Gill and Singh 1987)

Initially we were engaged along with the Multi-ethnic Inspectorate, Divisional

Coordinators, and others in assisting schools in developing anti-racist policies. The authority had issued guidelines, suggested a detailed process of consultation and had set deadlines for all schools, colleges and other ILEA establishments to produce an anti-racist policy. The policies, with a few exceptions, concentrated on dealing with racist incidents in each particular establishment. The issues of institutionalized racism in the educational system, though often mentioned, were in the main neither understood nor addressed.

Many of our first contacts with groups of teachers, especially at school staff meetings produced defensiveness and hostility. Teachers would insist, and many more silently agree, that racism was not a problem for them, their school, their curriculum, their pastoral structure, etc.: 'There's no problem here, we treat them all the same!.' There were others who were sure we were making a mountain out of a molehill. Church schools in particular would insist that all their pupils were 'equal in the eyes of God' and were treated accordingly.

One of our first tasks was to counter the notion that schools existed in a vacuum. The idea that racism was something that happened elsewhere and that what happened outside the school gates, sometimes literally, was none of the schools concern. There are echoes of this even in the Swann Report (Department of Education and Science 1985), or Professor Bikhu Parekh writing after its publication (Parekh 1985).

We collected newspaper clippings and reports from a whole range of publications that showed the pervasive nature of racism in Britain in the 1980s; from employment to the provision of ante-natal care, from immigration controls to policing. We produced these as a handout (Gill and Singh 1986) and as a set of cards for group discussions. They were used to great effect to stimulate an analysis of the link between individual acts of racism, institutional practices and state policies. We also asked teachers to consider what the school's silence on these issues might mean to students both black and white. We explored the school changes required to challenge these aspects of racism.

Often participants would register shock at the level and diversity of racism in Britain. For example, one card read:

Therapy
Electro Convulsive Therapy (ECT) may be used on people diagnosed as 'depressives'.

70% of those diagnosed as depressives are women, 39% of black patients receiving ECT had not been diagnosed as depressed, compared to 16% of the whites receiving ECT.

Black patients are also more likely than whites to have at least six consecutive ECT treatments.

'Black patients appear... to be perceived by the staff as in greater need of physical treatment than the white British born . . . there appear to be assumptions that:

(a) ECT is suitable for non-depressive reactions in black patients.
(b) Black patients require more ECT.
(c) Intramuscular medication is more efficacious in black patients.
– from research carried out at a hospital in East London.

R. Littlewood & S. Cross. 'Ethnic minorities and psychiatric services', Sociology of Health and Illness Vol.2, No.2. July 1980.

and another:

Lawful Killing
Winston Rose, a black man, died while police were attempting to take him to a mental hospital. He had a history of mental stress, but no history of violence.

Twelve police officers were involved in Rose's apprehension; some had gone to Rose's house believing that they were looking for an escaped criminal, others thought that he was violent.

Rose died of asphyxiation, having choked on his own vomit after being held in a strangle hold by police.

Police stopped a passing ambulance to try to revive him but the ambulance workers were unable to release his hands from the handcuffs as one of the police had driven off with the keys.

An inquest jury returned a verdict of lawful killing.

Mind Out, December 1981.

The issues raised by such reports were very real to many of the schools in Inner London. Pupils experienced harassment on housing estates and between school and home – something that often had roots in the school playground. The school had to consider the effect of this treatment on the performance of black pupils and how to counter it. Why was this anti-social behaviour of some white pupils, which was silently condoned by many others, not being challenged? Could the school continue to support this state of affairs by its silence and inaction?

Reports on racist policing raised questions not only of police involvement with schools, now a controversial issue in Inner London (Advisory committee on police in schools 1985), but also of the ways in which criminal stereotypes, especially of the black mugger, fed the fears and anxieties of teachers. Did this affect not only assessment, placement in special units, discipline, but also the very way in which white teachers related to black (mainly Afro-Caribbean in this case) pupils?

Out of these exercises and others a series of workshops developed which eventually formed a weekend course for teachers and others involved in education. From the outset we rejected the approach of racism awareness as simply guilt delving. Rather we attempted to give participants an analysis of racism in terms of historical, political and economic dimensions and also to get them to focus on concrete strategies for action in the school. We made it clear at the beginning of the course that we had no illusions about schools being able to eradicate racism. We had to ensure that schools did not condone or reinforce it and develop ways for teachers to challenge it. An examination of the curriculum became an increasing focus of our work.

Institutionalized racism in schools

Institutionalized racism in schools takes many forms. One manifestation of this is the number of black staff in a school in an area with a significant proportion of black people in residence: there might be lots of black cleaners but no black school keepers, and a few black teachers at the lowest level. Another manifestation might be that in a school where the majority of students are black there are no black governors. However, by far the most pernicious and widespread manifestations of institutionalized racism in the school system are reflected in two ways. Firstly by the way the assessment and grading systems in schools label black children's abilities and behaviour and result, in particular, in referral to special units. Secondly by the reinforcing of racist ideas through the curriculum and the hidden curriculum both by commission and omission.

For us the underachievement of groups of black children and the inculcation of racist attitudes amongst white children were very much linked, as Milner (1983) describes, to socialization of all children into a racist society and culture against a background of structured inequality. We felt that the school curriculum, both hidden and overt, was an important part of that process of socialization.

CHILDREN'S READING SCHEMES AND RESOURCES FOR PRIMARY AND EARLY YEARS

Two of our team involved themselves with groups of teachers in looking at texts for early years and other non-written resources. The work of the ILEA Primary Curriculum Development Team in analysing the ten most popular reading schemes in ILEA's schools was a very powerful beginning for the work. One member of the team went on to examine toys, nursery home-corners, even comics written for very young children.

Topic work A group of primary teachers came together to look at topic work in their schools. A survey was carried out of the books that were used in ILEA primary schools for history, geography, and science teaching. These books were then examined critically for their racist content. A set of guidelines for examining texts was devised and circulated. Members of this group went on to develop topic webs and listed suggestions suitable for reference materials for teachers. The result of their work are soon to be published by the Association for Curriculum Development.

The following examples were collected by Olive Moore for the Primary Topic Work Group. One popular illustrated Atlas gave the following information about South Africa:

COUNTRIES OF THE WORLD

Southern Africa
The main countries in southern Africa are Angola, Zambia, Zimbabwe, Botswana, Mozambique, South-West Africa and the Republic of South Africa.

In the north of the area, there are tropical grasslands. In Zimbabwe cattle rearing is important. There are also many mineral mines. Zimbabwe exports gold and asbestos. In Zambia there are large copper and zinc mines. An important railway runs through Angola. It takes the copper from the mines in Shaba province in Zaire to the port of Lobito on the coast.

South-West Africa, which is also called Namibia, and Botswana are much drier countries. The long and narrow Kalahari Desert is in Botswana. There are many mines in Botswana and South-West Africa which produce diamonds, nickel and tin.

The Republic of South Africa is the most southerly country in Africa. The population is about 24 million. Of these over 15 million are Bantu Africans, 4 million are Europeans and over 5 million are Asians. There are many racial problems in South Africa.

Farming and cattle raising are important in South Africa, but it is also a mining country. Gold mines around Johannesburg employ many people. Diamonds are exported from Kimberley. There are also iron, copper, and asbestos mines. Johannesburg is the largest city in South Africa.

Dicks ed. 1982, p. 94

To describe the situation in South Africa in such bland terms is to give the impression that, apart from some mutual antagonism between 'races' everything is fine. Of course, nothing is mentioned about the continued occupation of Namibia by South Africa.

Another school book had this to say of the Mexican character:

THE MEXICAN CHARACTER

The Indian and Spanish heritage
The typical Mexican has a dual character. He or she inherits Indian stoicism, patience, fatalism, and silence, together with the pride, arrogance, and generosity of the Spaniard.

Courtesy is natural to both races, and no people are more graceful and polite than the Mexicans. Visitors are charmed by the friendly, genial welcome they meet everywhere. Nothing is too much trouble to please a guest, and the kindness and hospitality can be overwhelming.

Mexicans are proud of their long, eventful and historical heritage, and archaeologists are constantly making further discoveries, adding to their knowledge of a brilliant past.

The Mexicans are a dignified people. The poorest somehow manage to appear neat and clean on fiesta days, and children are proudly displayed in spotless if oftmended clothes. The national characteristic of gracious good manners gives to the humblest Mexican the style of a grandee.

A contempt for death
All Saints Day is know as the Day of the Dead in Mexico. It is a feast day on which families go to the cemeteries to have parties. Food and drinks are offered to the departed relatives. Bakers sell specially made 'death bread' decorated with skulls of icing, and sugar coffins, which are eagerly eaten in large quantities amidst the graves.

Young men commonly demonstrate their *machismo* – a kind of boastful manly pride – in the thick traffic roaring down city avenues. Darting into the path of hurtling cars they make 'passes' like those of bull-fighters, defying drivers to run them down and usually escape violent death only by an inch or two. Others, at Acapulco, make hair raising dives from a very high rocky cliff, plunging into a narrow crevice just as a surging wave thunders in for barely enough depth of water.

Machismo tends to make some Mexicans more prone to violence. Mild disputes may very quickly erupt into angry struggles. Insults, real or imagined, can lead to the use of guns and knives. Mexico's very high murder rate is undoubtedly a result of this acceptance of blood and death as part of life.

Time is different in Mexico
Mexicans are a hard-working people, quite unlike the popular image of idlers dozing in the sun under their broad sombreros. Long hours in fields, offices, shops, factories, and building sites, leave little time for long siestas in the afternoons.

But even for the most up-to-date Mexicans, time has not quite the same meaning as it has for us. The plumber who says 'Eleven o'clock tomorrow morning without fail' will often turn up on time a week or a month later. *Mañana* means tomorrow, but in Mexico it can really be just another day.

(Howard 1976, p. 12)

Not only are the 'attributes' of the Mexican ridiculously contradictory, apparently justified by the word 'dual', but the whole piece transmits this notion of human types, as if the behaviour of Mexicans is hereditary. This fits snugly with the racist ideas developed by sociobiology. It also supports the notion of 'hot-blooded', 'violent' natives of South America. Partly in response to such criticisms Macdonald have allowed the series, of which this is a part, to go out of print and are planning a revised series.

A third school book described the benevolence of plantation owning companies:

Tropical plantations
Plantations... are very well-organized. The companies who own these employ experts to help them grow as much sugar as possible. Experts test the soils to see which fertilizers are needed, set up irrigation schemes, spray pesticides to kill off insects and other pests, and experiment to find the cheapest and best methods of growing better crops.

The plantation companies also try to look after their workers. They provide houses, good roads, schools, clinics, churches and other amenities. Thriving plantations like these can be seen in many parts of the world.

(Sauvain 1983, p. 8)

SECONDARY GEOGRAPHY

The Association for Curriculum Development in Geography was started by one of my colleagues, Dawn Gill, in response to the Schools Council's refusal to publish her critique of geography syllabuses (Gill 1987), in particular their own syllabus, Geography for the Young School Leaver (GYSL). The dispute turned into a battle both with the GYSL organizers (incidentally GYSL is one of the few democratically inclined school syllabus bodies) and more fiercely with Nelson's who published the GYSL materials. (See Gill 1987).

Nelson brought out new materials but these were often just glossier. For example, the following extract is from *Patterns in Development* (Bale 1982). It gives a sanitized history of the European conquest of South America. It is written from the perspective of the colonizers and no alternative view is presented. We are expected to identify with the economic interests of the planters:

Colonial history of Guyana
Spanish navigators *traced the coastline* of South America and Orinoco in 1500. The native people were closely related to the people of the Caribbean islands and they lived by hunting, fishing and farming. European adventurers, *searching* for the legendary city of El Borado, *explored* the area during the sixteenth and seventeenth centuries and *this led to the establishment of* several trading posts on many rivers like the Pomeroon. At these posts bartering between traders and the native people took place. *Later, settlers planted* tobacco, cotton, coffee and sugar.

In 1621 *Holland granted* the Dutch West Indian Company a charter *giving it control* of Essequibo. In 1624 the company *was given control* over the areas of Demerara and Berbice. *Plantations, growing mainly sugar, were set up* on the banks of these three rivers. *The plantations needed* a large labour force and attempts were made to force the native people to work on the plantations. These efforts were met with fierce resistance and *there was much bloodshed*. Those native South Americans who were not killed retreated inland into the forest, leaving the coastal areas to the Europeans. *Because labour was so desperately needed*, people *were taken* from West Africa and *brought* to Guyana, where they were force to work as slaves.

(Bale 1982, p. 32)

The Association of Geography Teachers through their journal continue to develop alternative curricula and curriculum materials. For example, they have devised a worksheet on text book analysis for pupils to make them more critical of what they read, have developed passport games, and have examined transnational corporations and ideas about and development from the perspective of 'the South'.

A dispute has rumbled on over the issue of GCSE syllabus revision and still centres around the opposition to the presentation of geographical issues outside of a perspective of global, national and local power relationships. Too many school geographers (the ILEA geography inspectorate included) are still wedded to the safe mono-causal explanations for poverty, starvation and famine, those views popularized by *Blue Peter* and *John Craven's Newsround*: climatic disaster, soil erosion, poor farming methods, etc.

HISTORY

We brought together a group of London history teachers (mainly ILEA and Haringey) to examine the teaching of history in our secondary schools. They have recently formed the Association for Curriculum Development in History and are publishing an in-service training manual for teachers. (Association for curriculum development in history 1987). This document contains an analysis of textbooks, a guide to resources, and some suggestions for good practice in history teaching. They have stated their position as follows:

History teaching is partly responsible for the racism inherent in British society, and it is part of the mechanism by which this racism is perpetuated. Too often in the past and today, what passes as education in History has been little more than a distorted account of Europe's involvement with the rest of the world, and a celebration of 'great' men, 'great' wars, and the growth of capitalism. An examination of the contents pages of books which purport to be about World History frequently reveals an exceedingly Eurocentric world view; examination syllabuses in history, too, carry the implicit suggestion that the interaction of 'great' white men is the only history there is. The perspective of the colonised and oppressed peoples of the world – black people and women, workers and peasants – are seldom recorded for posterity, and where they are, these records are rarely presented as valid content in history lessons in British schools.

'British' history – the history of the industrial revolution, for example – is presented in a vacuum, as if it took place in isolation from the plantation economy of the Caribbean which provided the wealth for Britain's railways and factories. No mention is made of the destruction of the Indian cotton industry, which took place in order that the cotton industry of Lancashire could be assured of a market. No mention is made of the colonies which provided the raw materials for Britain's industrial development. 'British' history is part of a history of colonialism and imperialism. School history textbooks and syllabuses fail to make this point.

History, more than any other school subject, has been responsible for misrepresenting Britain's imperial past as glorious and beneficial for all. Its contribution to the perpetuation of racist notions is perhaps its most distinctive quality. It is in an analysis of history textbooks and syllabuses that the notion of political neutrality in education becomes most obviously and starkly a lie. The analysis of the subject's role in mediating racist and imperialist ideologies is imperative if educators are to tackle the racism inherent in British society.

(Association for curriculum development 1985, p. 10)

SCIENCE

The Association for Curriculum Development in Science arose, once again, out of a network of science teachers committed to anti-racist teaching. It began with many theoretical discussions about science, science education and anti-racism. The first task was to examine the notion of the neutrality of science. This was obviously a fiction in an area like human biology, the history of the study of which is riddled with justifications for race and class superiority. (See Gould 1984) The word 'race' itself was an ideological formulation fundamental to the theoretical validation of imperialism, colonialism and slavery. The fact that skin colour is an insignificant difference between human beings in genetic terms has not lessened the commonsense view of 'race' as a biological category. It is used as if it were a legitimate term in most human biology textbooks. Why are these ideas not discussed openly in school science lessons? Why does the 'commonsense' biology of 'race' go unchallenged?

Many science teachers like to think of their subject as unencumbered by political issues. But the science of nutrition, for example, is hardly neutral if it omits the global politics of food. The history of the appearance of certain food in the Western diet, e.g. sugar, must be as relevant to an understanding of the subject as the web of interests that prevent changes in dietary habits that lead to better health (Lindsay 1985).

In an overall sense, the move towards an anti-racist science curriculum is the move away from 'anti-social' science. Science as it is commonly presented in public and taught in schools makes a differentiation between theory and practice. Technology is perceived as separate from science. The theories of atomic physics in school, for example, bear no relation to the problems of nuclear power (waste disposal, Sellafield, Chernobyl, etc.) nor to nuclear weaponry. Plant biology is divorced from ecology, the over-use of fertilizers and the green revolution. Research depends on funding and prestige not on the solving of human problems. Nowhere is this more stark than in medicine, where drug research is related to drug profits. Whilst there is an explosion of drugs supposedly alleviating western diseases such as cancer and arthritis, there are far fewer attempts to find cures for malaria, Bilhartsia and other diseases prevalent in the Third World. (See Young and Levidow 1986).

MATHEMATICS

The Association for Curriculum Change in Mathematics as the group is now called, is composed of teachers, ILEA mathematics centre workers, FE lecturers and one maths education magazine editor. We rejected the multicultural token-ism of doing one lesson on 'Rangoli patterns', or 'Islamic mosaics'. As with the science group, our first major problem was convincing maths colleagues in schools that mathematics was not the pure, neutral, apolitical activity they had for so long assumed it to be.

Historical distortions The hidden curriculum of mathematics quite clearly transmitted the idea that mathematics was a purely Western invention. I myself, trained as a mathematics teacher, had been educated with the idea that a Frenchman called Pascal had been the first to develop the 'triangle' of numbers that now bear his name. I had no idea that the Chinese had been using it at least two centuries before. I thought algebra came from the Greeks and was not aware that the name itself was Arab in origin. (See Zaslavsky 1973, Goonatilake 1984).

Political ideology Another aspect of the hidden curriculum is the political ideology transmitted through texts. My colleague, Dawn Gill, analysed a popular set of mathematics textbooks. Here she takes up the use of interest rates:

> *Examples:* All 'O' level and CSE maths courses include a study of interest rates.
>
> The idea of interest is presented in a political and economic vacuum, outside of a context which would give it meaning.
>
> 'X invests £100 at an annual interest rate of 10%. How much will he have earned in 3 years?'
>
> Questions like this abound in maths textbooks. What does 'interest' signify in a real world context? Is interest really 'earned' income? Who earns it – and who gets it? These questions are never asked.
>
> The interest rates on investment in South Africa are among the highest in the world. The level of malnutrition in the Bantustans is among the highest in the world. The level of infant mortality is one of the highest in the world. High interest – high levels of profit – and low wages are related: they are part and parcel of the economic system in which 'interest' is a meaningful concept. To present 'interest' in isolation, apart from other aspects of the same system is to blinker perceptions and limit comprehen-sion. Maths courses which do this help to foster an acceptance of the political, status quo in a global capitalist economy. This operates to the disadvantage of some countries, and particularly some groups within those countries – while it works to the advantage of others.
>
> (Gill 1986, p.12)

Sometimes the ideology is not as sophisticated. Take this delightful piece from a highly recommended teaching pack on graphs:

Island fires

The little Pacific island of Jalumbah is covered with forest.

The natives who live on Jalumbah are terrified of fire, which would rapidly spread and destroy their island.

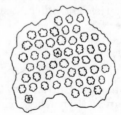

1 Imagine that a tree in the centre of the island accidentally catches fire (marked A).

Sketch a graph to show how you think the fire may spread.

(Swann 1984, p. 40)

Why could this example not have been South Australia or Tasmania, where such an event actually happened? Why is it only these obviously stupid natives on 'Jalumbah' who fear fire?

The use and abuse of statistics People are bombarded daily with all kinds of statistics, some of which are intended to present falsified accounts of what is happening in the world. Wage negotiations are presented in a variety of ways, depending on whether the employer or the union is putting forward statistics. Crime stereotypes are created by the Metropolitan Police, using statistics. It is essential that pupils in British schools are educated in the use and abuse of statistics. Maths course which do not take responsibility for such education are failing to prepare people to understand the world in which they live. The maths curriculum is potentially a powerful tool for anti-racist education. Institutional racism, such as discrimination in housing, health care, employment and in applications of the law can be clearly demonstrated through statistics.

The functioning of the global economy and the extent to which it operates to the advantage of some countries, or groups within countries, can also be explored through maths and statistics. The history of colonialism and imperialism can be examined through trade statistics. The operation of currency markets and commodity markets can be analysed to reveal how some people/countries benefit, and others lose in the struggle to maintain living standards.

Concepts such as area, ratio, percentage, average, median, mode can be taught just as effectively through socially relevant data as through the toy-town examples which currently form the 'subject' content of maths textbooks. Area and ratio, for example, can be studied using data on black/white land ownership in South Africa; 'average' can be studied through income rates at global, national or local scales. 'Percentage' can be studied through an analysis of wage increases for low-paid workers and those whose income is much higher.

As the recent 'Cockcroft Report' states: 'too often, maths is about nothing at all . . .' it may therefore be a boring set of mental exercises which do little or nothing to help students understand anything outside the confines of the classroom. Cockcroft makes a plea for maths to be more interesting and relevant. If this plea were to be taken seriously by maths teachers, then the subject could make a major contribution to pupils' understanding of a racist and sexist society in operation. Understanding is necessary if there is to be any effective challenge to these forms of institutionalized discrimination.

The maths group is in the process of publishing a handbook for teachers containing our discussion paper of history, ideology, statistics, and 'sociomathematics'. We are also about to publish three workpacks of learning materials on: 'International Trade', 'Employment/Unemployment: Race, Gender and Class' and 'Southern Africa'.

Conclusion

Racism is a central issue for schools in the 1980s. It cannot be separated from its production within a class-stratified society. A school cannot affect, directly, the racism that black school-leavers will face in attempting to secure employment any more than it can affect the generally dire employment prospects that face all youngsters. What teachers can and must attempt to do is to ensure that schools do not perpetuate the institutionalized racism of underachievement – whether caused by the assessment process or alienation from racist curricula. They must also ensure that the school does not reinforce but challenges, those racist ideas that white students absorb from the society in which we live. All aspects of school practices and curricula need to come under scrutiny. It is a process for which no expert can hand down a formula, but all those concerned with the school must be engaged in a conscious drive for change.

References

Association for Curriculum Development. 1985. *Racist practice in the secondary school curriculum: the case for anti-racist education*: briefing document, campaign to boycott GCSE. London, Assocation for Curriculum Development.

Association for Curriculum Development in History. 1987. *A guide to anti-racist teaching in history*, London, Association for Curriculum Development in History.

Advisory Committee on police in schools. 1985. *Policing schools*, London, Advisory committee on police in schools, PO Box 447, London, E29 PS.

Bale, J. 1982. *Patterns in development*, London, Nelson.

Department of Education and Science. 1985. *Education for All: the report of the committee of inquiry into the education of children from ethnic minority groups*, London, HMSO.

Gill, D. 1986. Political ideology in maths textbooks, *maths teaching* No. 114 p. 12

Gill, D. 1987. What's taught in geography? A critique of Geography for the Young School Leaver, in Booth, T., Potts, P., Swann, E., eds. *Curricula for all: preventing difficulties in learning*, Oxford, Blackwell.

Gill, D., Singh, E. 1986. *No racism here – we treat them all the same*, London, Association for Curriculum Development, PO Box 563, London N16 8XD.

Gill, D., Singh, E. 1987. *A beginner's guide to anti-racist education*, London, Association for Curriculum Development.

Gould, S. J. 1984. *The mismeasure of man*, Harmondsworth, Pelican.

Goonatilake, S. 1984. *Aborted discovery: science and creativity in the third world*, London, Zed Press.

Howard, J. 1976. *Mexico*, Macdonald countries series, London, Macdonald.

Lindsay, L. 1985. *Notes on the teaching of nutrition*, London, All London Teachers Against Racism and Fascism.

Milner, D. 1983. *Children and race: ten years on*, London, Ward Lock Educational.

Parekh, B. 1985. 'The gifts of diversity', *Times Educational Supplement*, 29 March, 22–23.

Sauvain, P. 1983. *The developing world*, Hulton new geographies, London, Hulton Educational.

Swann, M. 1984. *The language of graphs*, Shell centre for mathematical education, Nottingham, University of Nottingham.

Young, R., Levidow, L. 1986. *Racist society: racist science*, Association for curriculum development in science, London, Free Association Books. PO Box 563, London N16 3XD.

Zaslavsky, C. 1973. *Africa counts*, Connecticut, Lawrence Hill.

21   A problem in the family: explanations under strain

Jan Reid

When people account for the problems pupils face in school they frequently point to the pupils' homes. In this chapter Jan Reid describes how the personal qualities of parents figure prominently in such explanations. Whilst many people do acknowledge that poverty or poor housing play a part in family stress few of those who pass judgements on families make the imaginative leap to understand the precise effects of material circumstances. This chapter takes a detailed look at the effects of poverty on family life, the bringing up of children and the relationship with welfare services. An accurate understanding of the conditions under which pupils live may be a prerequisite to effectively including them and their families within the school community.

This chapter will focus on children who, in the telling phrase of many social enquiry reports, become 'known to social services', because someone regards the care they are receiving at home to be a matter for concern. The dominant interpretations of the problems these children face, will commonly emphasize parental and family characteristics and events, and will do so in a way that individualises them and sees them as arising in isolation from the wider social pressures within which they are located. Yet there are other crucial aspects of these situations which receive less attention than they deserve: structural, material and organizational factors which are, for the most part, outside the immediate influence of the families concerned. These factors, however, deeply affect their lives, the choices they can make and the room for manoeuvre they have, and may often prove to be highly relevant to understanding why a problem is identified.

While being critical of an approach which emphasizes individual family pathology, I do not wish to imply a crude stance of structural determinism, one which views the individuals concerned as mere clay in the mould of their social circumstances. I recognize the enormous variation in personal resources and characteristics which people bring to situations and in the way they act on them as well as are acted upon. In many ways, the situations I shall describe highlight the tension all of us experience between holding people individually and personally responsible for their actions and attempting to recognize other factors which both limit and enhance individual behaviour. My suggestion is that in many of the circumstances on which I shall focus, notions of individual responsibility and pathology win the day all too readily and without challenge.

I shall not be considering the experience of children and young people who have been found guilty of committing a criminal offence or who are thought to be at risk of doing so, but rather those generally, but not exclusively, younger children who with their families make up the rest of a social services child care workload.

Who are the clients?

Anyone relying entirely on the media for information about social services child care work, could be forgiven for assuming that social workers spend the majority of their working lives dealing with parents who inflict serious, sometimes fatal, injuries on their children. This impression is highly misleading, for only a small proportion of children referred to social services, including those who eventually come into care, are victims of the type of child abuse and neglect that is commonly the subject of news reports and the poster campaigns of some voluntary organizations. For the majority of children who are referred to social services because someone considers they may be 'at risk', the concerns are much more diffuse and unclear. Even if we were to confine ourselves to discussing those children officially recorded on local child abuse registers, we should find, as a growing number of writers have observed, that the range of phenomena now commonly regarded by relevant agencies and some researchers as legitimately coming within the terms 'abuse', 'neglect', and 'at risk of abuse or neglect' is now rather wide and diverse (Sutton 1980, Montgomery 1982, Geach 1983, Parton 1985).

However, social services child care work is by no means limited to those children officially designated in this way. On the contrary, social workers spend a great deal of their time with families whose care and upbringing of the children is regarded by someone as simply not very satisfactory or more vaguely a cause for concern. This is not to suggest that the fate of those smaller numbers of children who do suffer serious injury, neglect or death at the hands of their parents is unimportant, nor that it does not matter that some children live unsatisfactory lives, even if they have not been the victims of serious abuse. Rather, I am attempting to begin to clarify some of the circumstances and characteristics of the majority of children and parents on whom I am focusing in this chapter.

In the main, social services departments are not pro-active in determining which particular families will become their clients, and they rely heavily on referrals from schools, the police, doctors, health visitors, hospitals etc. The influence of these outside agencies is considerable not only because of the role they play in selecting which families merit the attention of social services departments, but also because there is evidence that any pressure they bring to bear at a subsequent stage, will be one of the significant factors which affects social work decision-making in child care cases (DHSS 1985).

It seems almost too obvious to need stating that those who come the way of social services departments, particularly those parents and children who are at risk of being separated from each other, are not drawn representatively from all sectors of the population. They are, of course, predominantly those working-class people living in poor material circumstances. There is now a considerable amount of research on the material and social conditions of the families of children most vulnerable to being received or committed to care for a variety of reasons, and it has been shown that there is an undeniable and clear association between poverty, material deprivation and the risk of children and parents being separated from each other. Indeed, in many cases, childrens' reception into care is triggered by a specific material crisis such as homelessness (Taylor *et al* 1980).

Summarizing some of the available research, Holman argues that separated children are drawn disproportionately from geographical areas of high deprivation, and that they are likely to possess five interrelated features. They are more likely to be the children of single parents, children from large families, children of unskilled manual workers, children from low-income families and children living in inadequate housing. These five features, Holman points out, are themselves associated with poverty and social deprivation (Holman 1980).

For most children who are vulnerable to being separated from their parents, poverty, then, is a necessary but of course not a sufficient condition. Quite clearly, not all children of poor parents are received or committed to care, or even come anywhere near it. Many families do survive intact, and too little is known for certain about the complex array of factors which affect this. However, the fact that some do manage despite the harsh conditions, should not deter us from exploring what it is that makes survival very much more difficult for those children and adults who are our concern. Before doing this, however, I shall review some of the dominant explanations and perceptions of the problems faced by those children and their families, explanations which are to be found embedded in public policy and everyday practices. I shall try to discover what, if any, attention is given to the poor material conditions in which we know so many are living.

Dominant explanations

The conviction that it is the poor themselves who are personally and individually responsible for the problems which cause them so much grief, is one that has been strongly held for a very long time. The explanation, that families are poor because they are personally inadequate, incapable, lacking in skills or simply unwilling to help themselves, is one that has persistently emerged and re-emerged, though the exact form that it has taken and the vigour with which it has been promoted has varied according to the particular historical circumstances. The notion that because of their personal limitations, poor parents will necessarily offer their children inadequate and damaging care and socialization opportunities which will, in turn predispose those children to become the next generation of social deviants is one that has commonly accompanied it (Handler 1973, Clarke 1980).

In the period after the Second World War training for child care work concentrated on personality and relationship problems within the family, often using ideas and methods of intervention borrowed from psychoanalysis or its derivatives. This approach frequently ignored the material and structural context in which personal difficulties occurred, or saw them as someone else's business. There was even marked resistance among some powerful groups within the emerging social work profession in the 1960s and early 1970s, to seeing social work identified with the amelioration of material hardship in any way. It is telling to note that by the early 1970s it was still not uncommon for social work training courses to contain no teaching at all on welfare rights. Those who saw interventions which focused upon clients' material needs and their welfare rights as a priority, were generally regarded as being on the radical fringes of the profession (Case Con 1970, Bond 1971).

This tradition dies very hard indeed not only in social work, but in other professions too. I realize that this statement will appear puzzling to many who feel that there are now growing numbers of social workers, teachers and other practitioners who attend to welfare rights issues and who are not only aware of the harsh conditions in which large numbers of children and their families are living, but also sympathetic to their situation. Equally, there are many who would wish firmly to disassociate themselves from the extremes of an ideology which they see as blaming only the victim. While I recognize this, I would maintain that even those of us who take this stance, often find ourselves in our everyday practice, underestimating or minimizing the possibly intimate and detailed connections between the poor material and social context in which people live, and the child care issues and personal crises which have been identified as a problem. At best, the connection that is sometimes made only goes as far as saying that there are relationships or personal problems exacerbated by poor material conditions, the assumption being that they would have been there anyway and that they are merely made worse by force of circumstance.

In addition, the very familiarity of poor conditions can make them invisible, and the fact that they are commonplace render them unremarkable. One social worker who worked very effectively on welfare rights issues but agreed that he attempted to make no connections at an individual level between poverty and child care problems had this to say: 'All the families on Lane End estate are living on the poverty line. I just don't even register it anymore'.

For those of us who recognize at a general level how debilitating it is to live in poverty for a long period and who feel certain that we must surely absorb that general appreciation into our practice at an individual level, there is a deceptively simple exercise involving social work reports or school records which we can undertake to begin to test out that assumption. For the purposes of the exercise, I do not propose to enter the important debate about the rights and wrongs of recording certain sorts of personal information about children and their families but rather, to use what we know about this process to try to discover what are the dominant values and explanations contained in the files.

I would ask any teacher or social worker practising in an area of social deprivation to go to the office filing cabinet and remove ten sets of records or reports kept on 'problem children' and their families, records to which they have made a contribution. I would ask them to look at these files with a fresh eye and to try to discover what information it was thought important to include and, just as crucially, to leave out. In other words, it is an exercise which begins to make explicit the theory embedded in everyday practice. For the purposes of this chapter, the following five questions might be helpful:

1 Do the records contain any substantial reference to the poor material circumstances in which the family lives?

2 If these factors are recorded, are they given any prominence or are they seen largely as 'useful background', important to note, but of little direct relevance to the 'real problem?'

3 Is there any attempt at all to explore the possible relevance of these conditions to the 'real problem?'

4 What other factors are recorded and what is their implied or explicit relevance to the issues of the upbringing and care of the child?

5 If a note is made about familial or parental characteristics, behaviour or crises, what yardsticks of pathology or normality are being used explicitly or implicitly?

Perhaps a couple of examples relating to the last question might be useful. If it is noted that a child is from a single-parent family, is this because, for example, the practitioner acknowledges the material hardship that often goes along with this status and the consequent spin-offs for the children and adult concerned, or could it be that they uncritically hold the view that the normal well-adjusted family has two parents and that any deviation from that offers an inferior context, *per se*, for the socialization of the child? If it is recorded that the mother goes out to work, is this based, even partially, on the assumption that caring and loving mothers don't?

A great deal of what we record or say about people is done without our paying sufficient attention to the implicit theory we are using. We include or exclude certain material uncritically, as if it is perfectly natural or just self-evidently plain common sense.

Family life in poverty

What is it about living in poverty that makes bringing up children such a problem? How does the structural position of these children and their families make them highly visible and prone to the attention of a variety of state agencies? I shall suggest that such attention exposes them to selective interpretations of their problems and to organizational arrangements which may present them with additional difficulties. There is now a great deal of research which details the effects of poverty on family life (Wilson and Herbert 1978, Townsend 1979, Brown and Madge 1982) and it is only possible here to draw out some aspects of three interrelated strands by way of illustration: I shall focus on income, housing and health.

It has been estimated that there are now around 3.7 million children living at, or close to, the official poverty line in Britain. The income on which they and their parents live means, quite simply, that they cannot afford to pay for all the basic material commodities and services which they need or which someone else requires them to have: adequate food, clothing, footwear, furnishings, domestic appliances, heating, lighting, rent, transport, school uniform etc. Because there is not enough money to go round, they regularly forego these basics. If you buy new shoes, you go short on food. If the gas bill arrives, you miss payment of the rent. There is no margin for error or for unexpected crises and there are no overdraft facilities for families living in poverty. In addition, the things that you buy, work out to be more expensive in the end. If you do not have lump sums of money, you are forced to buy cheap clothing, furnishings and other household goods which wear out quickly and need replacement more often. For the same reasons, you have to buy goods on credit through hire purchase and mail order companies, both of which tend to be more costly. You may find yourself borrowing money to cover items which you had not anticipated needing, and the only credit facilities available to families in poverty come a deal more expensive than the Bank lending rates.

Many families have described how events such as Christmas are a nightmare. Celebrating even in a modest way and getting presents for the children, requires an outlay they simply cannot afford. Kitting a child out for secondary school presents similar problems to which the only solution, once again, is to get into debt or do without (Tunnard 1979).

Surviving in poverty requires enormous efficiency, energy and staying power for you cannot regularly afford the things that make life easier. You have to shop around to find the cheapest items and if you cannot afford the bus fare, you and the children walk. If you don't have the money for the launderette, you wash by hand. You cannot afford to spend money on things which take the edge off your and the childrens' misery or give you a bit of fun – a drink at the pub, a packet of cigarettes, a day in town, a toy which keeps an ill child occupied – or if you do, it is at the direct expense of something else, and often something which you all need. Remember, this affects 3.7 million children!

Families living on low incomes find that their access to decent housing is severely restricted and that they are more likely to be living in poor-quality accommodation and overcrowded conditions, whether in the private or public sector.

Despite legislation which protects some rights of private tenants, there is still a considerable amount of housing in the worst end of the private rented sector, particularly in areas of urban decay, which is substandard and lacking in basic amenities. Damp, structurally unsound accommodation with unsafe heating and lighting and without adequate toilet and washing facilities is still all that is available for many families who have been unable to secure or keep tenancies in the public sector.

However, housing problems are not limited to the private sector. Families in poverty may find themselves in 'hard to let' council accommodation which few people want, in areas which are unpopular. This may happen because a combination of being in urgent need and of having restricted options available, means that these families are not in a position to be choosey. They have to accept what is most quickly available.

Some of this property is 'hard to let' for very good reasons in that design faults and structural problems present enormous difficulties for families living there. A great deal of the housing stock in large urban authorities, consists of that built in the 1960s – high- and low-rise factory-built flats and maisonettes on large open plan estates. Apart from the obvious difficulties of high-rise living and lack of safe outside play space for children, much of this housing has other well documented major structural problems (see for example Family Service Units 1983, City of Birmingham 1985). For example, faults intrinsic to the design, cause condensation to a degree that severe damp is a constant and almost insurmountable problem. Wallpaper will not stay on walls, plaster work rots and furnishings and clothes become mildewed and spoilt very quickly. The only way to keep these effects in any way under control is to have a high level of heating and ventilation in all rooms. Families on low incomes, those most likely to be in such accommodation, simply cannot afford to pay for that level of heating. They may only be able to heat one room inadequately, leaving the rest damp and unhealthy or resorting to unsafe or unsatisfactory forms of heating such as paraffin stoves.

Apart from the fact that it is very grim indeed to live in such spoiled accommodation, apart from the health hazards, and apart from the difficulty of constantly replacing clothing and furnishings, there is the additional problem of the way such situations produce over-crowding. When families cannot make full use of the limited accommodation they have, they are in a very real sense, living in over-crowded conditions.

The association between social class, poverty, and ill health and disability is well documented (see, for example, Townsend and Davidson (eds.) 1982) and while the relationship is undoubtedly complex in some respects, for the purposes of this chapter, it is really only important to recognize that a considerable proportion of the families on whom we are focusing are likely to contain children and adults who suffer persistent and quite often debilitating health problems. Further, it is important to recognize that they are less likely than better-off families to receive the quality of health care they need. In other words, those who need it most, are least likely to get it (Stacey 1977).

When inadequate resources are constantly juggled an unforeseen emergency, even on a small scale, can present a real crisis, and not just a material crisis. While a lack of access to things which others regard as essential is a problem in its own right, it has other equally important repercussions. The impossible choices which people have to make, can be seen to wear them out, to sap their energy and to make them feel that they and their children are outside the common definitions of living a normal life. The fact that people on the outside as well as the inside of those families become accustomed to these features, does not make them any less damaging, debilitating or unacceptable.

BRINGING UP CHILDREN

So what are the direct and indirect effects on the children? They are less likely to have access to things which others take for granted and which they, themselves, see as important: a reasonable choice of toys, clothes, and other possessions, outings, holidays and leisure activities, a safe place to play or a comfortable place to be with friends, the sports equipment you need if you are to be in the school team. Children can be acutely aware of these deficits in their lives and of the embarrassing situations and restrictions which they face as a result. They may learn to deal with them in a variety of ways: resignation, withdrawal from situations where it becomes apparent, stealing, defiance, covering up, taking people on etc. Some of these responses themselves can cause the child additional problems.

While children undoubtedly adapt to their restricted circumstances, they do not always take things lying down and it is often their parents who bear the brunt. Small children cajole and whine to get something they want, older children create a fuss in other ways appropriate to their age and size. Darren, the 13-year-old son of a single woman with three other children, described how he persuaded his mother to buy him new trousers:

.... the others was all ripped ... I looked like a right dosser. The old bag wanted to go down to Jean's second-hand place to get me some. What a show up! I ain't wearing that crap. I wouldn't go so she got us these ones off the market.

The period between Darren's mother's suggesting second-hand trousers and her finally capitulating over new ones, had been filled with a series of rows, threats, counter-threats and mutual accusations.

Parents are often acutely aware of these direct effects on their children. Reviewing current research, Brown and Madge comment that there is abundant evidence of this and point out that many parents emphasize this as being the worst aspect of living in poverty (Brown and Madge 1982).

Apart from the children's lacking the material goods and opportunities which others have, some studies have suggested that parents are very aware indeed that living in poverty affects the upbringing they can offer their children in other crucial ways. Studies which have attempted to research the knowledge, skills and attitudes of poor parents have indicated that they often hold many of the same aspirations for their children and values about their upbringing as much of the rest of the population. However, they are forced by the multi-dimensional problems of living in poverty to lower their expectations and to adopt child rearing practices of which they themselves do not approve (Wilson 1974, Wilson and Herbert 1978).

Bringing up children is an exacting business in the best of circumstances and there can be few parents who have not at times felt themselves stretched beyond their personal capacity to cope, and found themselves behaving towards their children in ways that are shaming. When people bring up children in poverty, those ordinary stresses, difficult at the best of times, are magnified by the enormous restrictions in their lives, restrictions which often continue to exist for a very long period. One single parent on benefit put it this way:

I saw that Conservative MP on the telly who'd tried to live on Social Security for a week. He didn't even manage that and he didn't have kids with him or anything. Any fool can do it for a week. It's when it's for the rest of your bloody life that it's a problem.

People living in poverty experience not one set of problems, bad enough in themselves, but a host of interrelated deprivations, so that merely keeping a head above water requires terrific energy and staying power. Doing all that, and having sufficient personal resources to offer your children what they need in circumstances which render it virtually impossible, is a truly gargantuan task. Coping alone with small children who are persistently ill when your own health is poor or when you are made depressed by the pressures of merely surviving without an end in sight, is an unenviable position for any parent. Doing so in housing conditions which do not allow you to get away from each other, or in an environment which is so unsafe that it presents hazards for children left un-attended even for a few minutes, makes extraordinary demands on people. How understandable that in such circumstances many parents find themselves more short tempered, less consistently sympathetic, more demanding or more lax towards their children than they would otherwise wish to be. How tempting it must be, when you haven't had a break from all that and cannot afford a babysitter, to slip out for half an hour, leaving the children asleep on their own.

How tempting it must be to let small children play outside even though the road is busy and they are not old enough to cope with the dangers of traffic. How easy it must be to hit out too hard when a child has done something that was not so bad, but was just the final straw.

Perhaps a real incident might serve to illustrate how parents can be driven to treating a child more harshly than they would wish by an escalating material crisis:

> A social worker was working with a woman, a single parent with three children aged eight, six and three, who had been living on supplementary benefit for five years. Her already precarious financial position had been exacerbated by a spurious and anonymous allegation that she was cohabiting and this had resulted in her benefit payments being suspended while the matter was investigated by the DHSS. Late in the day that her payments had been reinstated, she telephoned the social worker in a very distressed state to say that she had lost her temper and had hit Jason, the six year old, so hard that his face was marked and swollen. When the social worker visited, the following events were pieced together.
>
> When the mother's benefit was cut off, she had survived for several days, by borrowing small amounts of food and money from neighbours, many of whom were in a similar financial position. She had been angry and desperate about her situation not knowing what the outcome would be and how long it would take the DHSS to make a decision. Jason had developed a middle ear infection and had been off school for four days during which time he had been restless and grizzling, asking for soft drinks, sweets, and more particularly, 'going on' about his mother buying him a pet of some sort. His intermittent hearing loss, caused by persistent infections, had also had the effect of making him seem inattentive and unco-operative when, in reality, he often did not hear what was asked of him.
>
> His mother had felt irritated with him but had managed to contain herself. When she had finally received her benefit payment, she had felt sorry for the boy and had decided to spend the money she owed to the clothing club on a rabbit and a hutch as a surprise. That afternoon she had found him treating the pet unkindly and when she had told him to stop, he had said that he hadn't wanted a rabbit anyway, he really wanted a dog. She had then lost control and had hit him across the face.
>
> A long period of material hardship had been followed by an acute financial crisis, during which she was coping with an ill child, the anxiety of how to manage in the short and the long term, as well as her own sense of injustice at what had happened. She had stretched herself beyond her means to give the child a treat and he had thrown it back in her face.

Not all parents in poverty have the experience of hurting a child in this way but many do have to contend with the knowledge that they are not offering their children a fraction of what they could, were they in improved circumstances. They cope with this knowledge day in, day out and often for protracted periods. I know of no evidence to suggest that this matters less or causes less grief to parents in poverty than it does to anyone else.

EXPERIENCING SOCIAL WORK

I have suggested that bringing up children in poverty is a daunting task, but in addition, I believe that when families come to the attention of a public agency such as social services, further complicating factors come into play. By virtue of being in poverty, families rely more heavily on help from public agencies and are more prone to intervention in a variety of ways. Aspects of their lives come under scrutiny in a fashion that those of others do not, and this does not necessarily result in helpful or overwhelmingly positive outcomes for the children and adults concerned. I recognize that there are, of course, children whose wellbeing has been safeguarded by stringent and careful enquiry into their lives, and that, sadly, there are others who have suffered because of a lack of it. I am not making out a case for non-intervention, but am suggesting that enquiry into and assessment of the care children are receiving at home is extraordinarily difficult for both the families and practitioners involved. If we consider only a handful of the factors which come into play, and there are many more, we begin to see just how complex this process is.

Parents living in poverty may have a constant fear that one of the consequences of the acute financial difficulty may be that their children will be received into care, and indeed, they may know other people to whom this happened. Brown and Madge point out that this is frequently reported and one of the most severe causes of anxiety and desperation for many parents (Brown and Madge 1982). As a result, parents may see social workers and other professionals as extremely powerful people who can make crucially important decisions about them and their children.

In addition, as I have already suggested, their problems may be defined in ways which emphasize certain features and neglect others. In a variety of ways the aspect of their lives which the parents see as difficult and the child-rearing issues they see as crucial, may not always be viewed as central by those with power and responsibility to intervene (Mayer and Timms 1970, DHSS 1985). In reality, there is often very little that the families can do to ensure that their definitions of problems carry any weight at all. Perceptions held about their problems by teachers, social workers, the police, health visitors, doctors etc., will often be recorded and shared with other professionals as part of a formalized assessment procedure, without the families ever having had the opportunity to find out what is being written or said about them, to check its accuracy or to challenge it in any way. Some of the most crucial decisions that can ever be made in the lives of children and their parents may result from these procedures.

Whilst families are sometimes quite mystified by the way social workers and other professionals approach their problems, they may feel that they have to go along with a particular process because they fear the consequences of not co-operating, because they are reliant upon the resources and services which the professional controls or simply because it is very difficult to challenge an apparently articulate person whose status is very much greater than their own.

This set of issues becomes even more important when one recognizes, as many social workers do, that the assessments which they and other professionals make, are hardly the stuff of which an exact science is made. For example, Sutton, in his work on reports to the juvenile court, points out that there is an absence of any relevant knowledge base and that technical issues are inextricably entangled with moral judgements. He suggests, among other things, that the content of these assessments is as likely to depend on unwritten lore and the culture of the workplace as anything else (Sutton 1983). More recent research has also pointed to a lack of use of theory in child care decision making (DHSS 1985).

In addition, the social worker will inevitably be viewing a family in a highly selective way. It is a confident practitioner indeed who can say, with her hand on her heart, 'I know this family well'. What she will be privy to is only a series of snapshots of that family's life, taken from a particular position, with particular concerns uppermost in the minds of both sets of parties in the encounters. There will be whole dimensions of their lives, aspirations, ways of approaching both problems and ordinary events which will never be available to her.

Also, if a social worker or any other professional, is trying to make a judgement about the quality of care offered by the parents to a child, she ought to experience considerable dilemmas about what exactly are the norms she is working to, and what other factors influence this. Establishing yardsticks for what constitutes 'good enough care' is an extremely subjective process and one which is fraught with problems. It is also one with which social workers have to struggle daily in their practice.

A social worker illustrated some aspects of this dilemma with reference to one small incident among many in her practice. She had been working with a single mother with small children, who was coping in poor material conditions. She felt that the woman showed many strengths in relation to her children, and described the care she gave them as 'generally OK, but a bit dodgy sometimes'. The three-year old was admitted to hospital for twenty-four hours after swallowing some hair perming lotion, an event she survived after having a stomach pump. The social worker described her deliberations as follows.

> I didn't know how to record it or even whether I should record it at all. I suppose Sharon shouldn't have left the stuff around but lots of people do. I went to the hospital and there were hoards of kids there who'd swallowed God knows what – things you couldn't even imagine they could get past their lips. I thought the parents who didn't have a social worker, particularly the middle-class ones, would probably get a telling off from the consultant or the sister and that that would be it. But I'd be putting it down on Sharon's file in a way that might be held against her if someone was building up a case bit by bit. It seemed very unfair. On the other hand, if I didn't record it and somebody found out, particularly if anything went wrong later, I'd be for it!

The social worker's deliberations raised two initial points. Firstly, she was unsure whether Sharon's leaving toxic substances round was particularly unusual or indicative of poor parenting, and secondly, the fact that Sharon's had a social worker placed her in the position of being scrutinized in a way that other parents who had done similar things were not. At the end of her statement, she also raised an additional factor which influences social workers in the assessments they make: pressure they constantly feel about what will happen if they make the wrong judgement.

During the past decade, there has been considerable public attention focused on the issues of child abuse and neglect, and there has been a shift in the way such situations are perceived. Occurrences which were once reported in the media as discrete criminal events, are now increasingly portrayed as failures of the welfare system, or, in some cases, failures of particular social workers to protect children effectively (Hartley 1985). While there are undoubtedly some horrific situations which may have been ameliorated or prevented had agencies or practitioners adopted a different approach, many social workers are now left with the unenviable pressure of feeling that they must predict the unpredictable and prevent the unpreventable. Parton has described the preoccupation that social workers and their agencies have with these concerns. Quite simply social workers' day-do-day practice is influenced considerably by their acute awareness of the consequences both for the children and for themselves of having 'another Maria Colwell' on their caseload (Parton 1981). This awareness and pressure inevitably colours the judgements they make about families and affects the procedures they decide to set in motion. Many workers have reported a pressure to 'play safe' and to protect themselves in ways which have unintended and not always positive consequences for the child and family.

Perhaps a final and more detailed case study might serve to pull together the major themes in this section.

In the autumn of 1984, a headteacher referred a family to social services because two of the daughters, aged seven and eight years, were bed wetters and came to school each day smelling strongly of urine. This made them the butt of teasing from other children. It was reported that they had both been seen at the local enuresis clinic but the parents, in the head's view, were apathetic about the problem and seemed unsympathetic to the difficulties it caused the girls in school.

The social worker contacted the clinic, and the doctor there who had seen the girls and their mother twice, said that he, too, had been about to make a referral. He had given the family an enuresis alarm but did not think they had used it. He said that he was also concerned that this might be 'a case of sexual abuse'. He was unable to substantiate this extremely serious suggestion, apart from saying that sometimes enuresis indicated that kind of family disturbance, that the mother had been defensive, and that the girls had looked to her before answering his questions. He may have been associating the latter behaviour with the state of 'frozen watchfulness' which it has been suggested is exhibited by some children who have been abused by parents and are fearful of them. The doctor clearly expected the social worker to call a case conference in line with local child abuse procedures.

When the social worker visited the family, she quickly came to the conclusion that the material conditions in which they were living, made the successful management of the girls' bed wetting virtually impossible. The parents had quite simply given up trying. She noted the following. Both parents had been unemployed and therefore living on state benefit for several years. Their prospects of getting work were not optimistic as they lived in an area with one of the highest rates of unemployment in the country. Much of the furnishings, clothing, bedding etc., which they had accumulated before the father was made redundant were now worn out or in a very poor state. The girls shared a double bed (a fact which made it impossible to monitor the pattern of their enuresis accurately) which was spoiled by their constant wetting. Even if the girls had become dry, they would still have been smelly from sleeping on it. There was only one set of sheets and blankets for each bed in the house, and these were in a poor state of repair. The house was substandard, being damp, having no bathroom and only an outside lavatory. The only source of hot water was an immersion heater over the kitchen sink, but the family could not afford to use this and relied on heating kettles for washes. The only form of heating was an electric fire in the living room. The rest of the house, including the bedrooms, was not only damp but very cold indeed. The mother could only afford to go to the launderette once a week. The two girls shared the bedroom with a younger sister who had been woken by the alarm, as had the rest of the family, on the only occasion that there had been a half-hearted attempt to use it.

The social worker in her initial and subsequent contact with the family found nothing to indicate that the girls were victims of sexual abuse. The mother's account of her interview with the doctor was that she had found him personally unfriendly and that the advice he had given was unhelpful. She had interpreted his separate questioning of the girls as not trusting her word and checking up on her. She also said that she had resented 'being dragged up to the school' to discuss the girls' bed wetting. The social worker did not find the girls overly watchful, merely a little reserved, she thought, in the presence of a stranger, and a little embarrassed at having their bed wetting discussed. This did not appear to be a problem later.

She and the family agreed that their first priority was to improve the material conditions. After that they would tackle the enuresis in its own right. By dint of her knowledge of welfare rights and a considerable degree of guile and energy, the social worker managed to secure from DHSS, from social services and from local trusts, sufficient funds to cover the costs of the following: two single beds with plastic covers for the girls, new bedding, a washing machine, some clothing, additional heating. She also put in an urgent rehousing application supported by her area manager. After this she secured the help of a clinical psychologist who was interested in bed wetting and was prepared to visit the family with her and work out with them a detailed programme geared specifically to the circumstances in which they were living.

It needs to be acknowledged however that while the social worker worked very successfully in this situation and accomplished a great deal both as far as she and the family were concerned, she experienced a considerable degree of anxiety throughout. The fact that the doctor had made an allegation of sexual abuse, no matter how vague and unsubstantiated, placed enormous stress upon her. She said: 'I went back to him twice to ask him to go over things again and he still couldn't come up with anything more concrete. He was quite casual about it in a way. But I kept thinking he was a very experienced man and perhaps he'd just got a very good intuitive sense about these things. Perhaps I'd missed something. I'd never forgive myself if those girls were going through that and I'd been blind to it.'

The material conditions in which the family lived severely restricted their personal lives and the opportunity they had to tackle things that were problematic to both children and adults. These problems were highly visible and could not be hidden from the outside world. Neither could many other features in their lives remain private. Once they were referred to the clinic for help, they began to be subjected to speculative accounts of their lives and highly selective and personally damaging definitions of their difficulties, definitions which did not take into account the things they saw as the greatest problem, and definitions over which they had little control. Although the service they received from the clinic could be said to have been short on attention to detail, they were in a weak position to challenge it. The quality of that service was never on the main agenda for discussion. Rather, the lack of use the parents made of the alarm and also their disaffection with the doctor and his approach, were merely seen, at that stage, as a further indication of their apathy and their unsympathetic and possibly abusive relationship with the girls. Lastly, despite the fact that the social worker's assessment of the difficulties was in many ways, similar to that of the family, despite the fact that she was an experienced and confident woman, a combination of her own professional and personal concern for abused children, the responsibilities of her agency and public concern over child abuse, made it extremely difficult for her to disregard the unsubstantiated allegations of incest made by the doctor. A less experienced and a less competent person might have been tempted to call a child abuse case conference just to be on the safe side and to cover herself and her agency. The implications of such action for the family could have been far-reaching to say the least.

Changing practice

For any individual practitioners, whether they are teachers, social workers, health visitors or doctors, who might want to take into account some of the issues raised in this paper, making even small moves in that direction can often seem a daunting task. They may find that the other powerful ideologies I have described are not only accepted by their colleagues and by policy makers, but that they seem to be built into the very bricks and mortar of the agencies in which they work. Those who press for even marginal changes of emphasis can feel that they are swimming against a very strong tide and are taking on an additional burden at a time when it feels impossible just to manage the routine demands of their work load.

Some of the problems which have been described are clearly outside the influence of individual practitioners and require different sorts of interventions. Quite simply, no social worker or teacher can resolve the problems of structural poverty, the crisis in public sector housing, or stem the rising tide of unemployment. However, as I have tried to show in the case studies, some practitioners do not always fall back on more orthodox assumptions about the nature of peoples' child care difficulties. Some make very valuable attempts to work in ways which address the often neglected issues, and to make use of the room for manoeuvre that they, the children and their parents have.

While a social worker may not be able to create a job for an unemployed person or conjure a house out of thin air, it may nevertheless be important to a family that someone competent checks out that they are getting all their entitlements. It may also matter that someone attempts to understand how the deficit of essential material things affects their lives at very personal and basic levels, and that a person who has considerable power to intervene in their families, does not blame them for the effects and repurcussions of things that are beyond their control, or does not offer explanations of their behaviour which are totally foreign and meaningless to them.

Individual teachers, social workers and other practitioners can also try to take account of the way in which certain sorts of decisions and ways of working can have unintended consequences. Interventions which seem unremarkable to a practitioner because they are the stuff of which everyday practice is made, can have very different, more uncomfortable, more threatening implications for other people in certain circumstances. Some interventions, or disposals, merely because they are located in a particular set of structures, may place the client in a more vulnerable position than is necessary or desirable.

Individual practitioners do have some power over aspects of these events, decisions and ways of working and also a number of choices about how and when to exercise that power. What they can do, compared with things over which they have no control, may appear to them very small fry. To the recipient of the service, it may be that at a crucial point, it matters very much indeed.

References

Bond, N. 1971: 'The case for radical casework', *Social Work Today*, 2, (9).

Brown, M. and Madge, N. 1982. *Despite the welfare state*, London, Heineman Educational Books.

Case Con. 1970. Can-u-Cope, June.

City of Birmingham Housing Department 1985. *Time to stop the rot.*

Clarke, J. 1980. 'Social democratic delinquents and Fabian families in national deviancy conference', *Permissiveness and Control*, London, MacMillan.

Department of Health and Social Security 1985. *Social work decisions in child care*, London, HMSO.

Family Service Units 1983. *Homes fit for people*, London, F.S.U.

Geach, H. 1983. Child abuse registers – a time for change, in Geach, H. and Szwed, E. (eds.), *Providing civil justice for children*, London, Edward Arnold.

Handler, J. 1973. *The coercive social worker*, New York, Rand McNally.

Hartley, P. 1985. *Child abuse, social work and the press*, Warwick Critical Studies (4), Department of Applied Social Studies, University of Warwick.

Holman, R. 1980. *Inequality in child care*, London, Child Poverty Action Group/Family Rights Group.

Mayer, J. E. and Timms N. 1970. *The client speaks*, London, Routledge and Kegan Paul.

Montgomery, S. 1982. 'Problems in the perinatal prediction of child abuse', *British Journal of Social Work* 12, 189–196.

Parton, N. 1981a. 'Caught in the crossfire', *Social work today*, 15 (3).

Parton, N. 1981b. 'Child abuse, social anxiety and welfare', *British Journal of Social Work*, 11, 391–414.

Parton, N. 1985. *The politics of child abuse*, London, MacMillan.

Stacey, M. 1977. 'People who are affected by the inverse care law', *Health and Social Services Journal*, 3rd June.

Sutton, A. 1980. 'Child abuse procedures – are they worth the risk?', *Legal Action Group Bulletin*, May.

Sutton, A. 1983. 'Social enquiry reports to the juvenile courts', in Geach, H. and Szwed, E. (eds.), *Providing civil justice for children*, London, Edward Arnold.

Taylor, L., Lacey, R. and Bracken, D. 1980. *In whose best interests?* London, The Cobden Trust and MIND.

Townsend, P. 1979. *Poverty in the United Kingdom*, London, Penguin Books.

Townsend, P. and Davidson, N. (eds.) 1982. *Inequalities in health*, London, Penguin Books.

Tunnard, J. 1979. *Uniform blues*, London, Child Poverty Action Group.

Wilson, H. 1974. 'Parenting in poverty', *British Journal of Social Work*, 4 (3), 241–254.

Wilson, H. and Herbert, G. W. 1978. *Parents and children in the inner city*, London, Routledge and Kegan Paul.

SECTION 4

Systems of control

22 Lifting up stones: a housemaster's day

John Schostak

In this chapter John Schostak focuses on one aspect of his study described in Chapter 15. For one day he recorded the activities and interactions of a housemaster at Slumptown comprehensive using a radio-microphone. From the transcript of several hundred pages he has edited together an account which illustrates the conflicts between the caring and disciplining aspects of pastoral work. He reveals the subtle distinctions housestaff draw between 'characters' and 'deviants' between cases deserving a sympathetic treatment and others requiring simple disapproval. Contradictions are not just shown in relationship with pupils. For the way this housemaster internalizes aspects of his caring role creates disjunctions in his reactions to other staff and in his identity as a teacher.

'Pastoral care' is a strange and inadequate term. Though perhaps the word 'pastor' from which it is derived has its own double meanings. The notion of the pastor as 'the one who knows what's best for you' is not out of place in the context of the history of modern mass schooling. The conflict between control and care was a recurrent theme during a study of a large, house-based comprehensive school made by the author during March 1982. The tension had practical implications each day leading one housemaster for example, to say:

> .... as a housemaster I'm expected to discipline kids who have misbehaved for other people ... and whom I might be getting on very well with ... apart from that. Now I have got to try and build a relationship which allows that situation to exist. I've got to try and ... kids have got to understand – I try and teach kids that it's my, part of my job sometimes to be nasty to them even though they've not done anything personally to me. Um, and in that sense they've got to identify me with the institution. And when they hurt the institution they hurt me kind of situation. Having said that, I also personally want them to see me ... as somebody that they can trust and somebody that they can uh have a relationship with as a person, as an individual. I don't want to be just part of the institution.
>
> (Schostak 1983, p. 125)

There is a sense in this complaint that the imperative of the organization to discipline pupils undermines the work of the housemaster. Equally, the ideal of pastoral 'care' prescribes behaviours, attitudes and values which are themselves at odds with the goals of the institution. With another housemaster, the hero of this paper, the sense of contradiction is quite overt:

> ... sometimes y' see John, what (the pupils) are telling you is so flaming true and real that you don't want to hear it, because, it's, it's absolutely loaded, loaded with problems. What, what some kids are telling me in not so many words is that they loathe and detest this system that we're forcing them through ... once you start lifting up stones that ... y' know, you're into really serious sort of problems, aren't you, and the ramifications of it for all of us are very serious ... y' know, if, if you were to reflect on the messages that uh ... these kids ... uh, I think more and more (are)

beginning to tell, then they're serious. Very serious indeed. They throw into doubt the whole purpose of what these schools are here for . . .

(Schostak 1983, p. 215)

In order to gain insight into the experience of the house staff this housemaster agreed to be radio miked for a day. The transcript runs to several hundred pages. Here I have concentrated on the dilemma between care and control. The day chosen, was not quite normal since it included 'parents' evening'. The housemaster wore the radio mike until about 2 p.m. when formal school ended. He felt it would intrude upon the confidences and sensitivities of parents. Parents started entering the school from about 2.30, few at first then more as time progressed. After a break, the evening session began about six and ended about 9.30 when a number of teachers and I adjourned to a local pub. I have preserved a sense of the development of the day in this account and interspersed it with my own comments and interpretations.

The day begins

Children stand talking and larking about at the entrance to the houseblock as I pass through and into the housemaster's office. It is a small whitewashed breeze-block box. It feels cramped and is. As I enter, the housemaster George Black and assistant housemistress Freda White (all names fictitious, of course!) are already at work well before the bell. There is a routine busy-ness. George is collecting money from pupils for a trip. Freda is interrogating a pupil to establish the 'truth' as to why she was missing recently on school days:

> *Freda:* An' you're tellin' me that last time you went to doctor's was the fifth of February an' it's now the fourth of March. An' you got six or eight tablets the last time you went?
> *Girl:* Yes.
> *Freda:* Why didn't you go in half term then?
> *Girl:* I don't 'ave to get them all the time, only 'ave to get them when my eye goes up.
> *Freda:* They why can't you go at half-past four? . . . You're missing too much school, pet. Are you taking your exams do you know?
> *Girl:* Supposed to be.
> *Freda:* An' you've done one-and-a-half days this week . . . One-and-a-half days . . . You can go to the doctor's now and be back to me by twenty-past-nine.
> [Girl goes out]
> *George:* I think that's a bit of a try on . . .

One of the major tasks of the housestaff is to ensure that pupils attend lessons and school and that absences are legitimate. They are continually having to interpret, analyse and look for inconsistencies in the stories pupils tell when they account for their whereabouts and intentions. Housestaff become skilled interrogators. For their assessments of *the truth*, they draw upon past experience, images of typical behaviour, community and their own gut feelings. Pupils, consequently, are often placed in the position of being potential liars rather than truth tellers.

More broadly, housestaff are supposed to be the hub of an information system not only of where pupils are and what they are doing but of teachers and the workings of the system. Thus, a moment later the 'phone rings and a passing teacher answers it – it is a request from a parent to speak to a teacher. George supplies the information. At the same time he is looking at the work a pupil is showing to him: 'Very good that. That's more work in there than you've done in your humanities' book for a bit'. A little time for a bit of praise. As George said on another occasion he wished there was more time simply to talk to kids. The boy is instructed to put a good cover on the book and to put it into his tray. At this point the housemaster who shares George's block enters saying they had made 'twenty-five quid' on the previous night's disco. Shortly, the 'phone rings again – it is a parent wanting information on his son's report, wanting to know if he is required at the parents' evening: 'as far as I can remember, you see, there's no problem with Billy's report. You know, there's nothing special I'd want to see you about ... so, uh, you know, he's doing alright, he's satisfactory, so yeah, I think that'd be fine if she'll come and pick it up tonight. Alright?'

The boy returns having put his book away:

Freda: Your report isn't all that startling is it?
Boy: ... it isn't all that good.
Freda: And it won't get any better till you attend every lesson then.
George: Have you got, have you got the work for Miss Jones as well?
Boy: Sir, it's in the house, sir.
George: Why?
Boy: Sir, I forgot it.
George: Amazin' that you could remember mine and forget Miss Jones', isn't it?
Freda: (To another boy) See that hair, it keeps affecting your hearing. No report card, next time ...

The themes of 'checking up', nagging, and surveillance reassert themselves throughout the day.

A major concern which arose throughout the week was the discussion of the likely truancy of a group of girls. The conversation started when a teacher entered saying he hadn't seen a particular girl and decided, 'she's bunking'. There is a continual pooling of information between the teachers in order to identify when *bunking* was actually taking place.

There was a steady flow of individual pupils either to show their report cards or to pay money for the school trip. With each pupil there was usually some other comment to be made about the year report or the way they dressed:

Do you really expect me to believe that? That you've been allowed to come to school today wearin' jeans an' trainin' shoes? ... You've worn them before? Good job I didn't see you, isn't it? Because you can't. That means you're goin' home to get them changed. I don't really know about these shoes either. If you're not going to wear proper shoes you'd better bring me a note back ... '

And there was Jacko. Jacko had recently beaten up a boy during a lesson; (see Schostak 1983a for the incident in detail) and after a period of suspension was now doing detentions as a punishment:

Jacko: Sir, you didn't even see me yesterday. I was doing detention.
George: That's right, yeah, I'd forgotten that. Um ... I can't ... did you do your school detention yesterday?
Jacko: Yeah.

George: You can't do a detention today with it being parents' night. Ah, the next detention then will be tomorrow night with me. Alright? So report to me tomorrow night. All bein' well, Jacko, that will be it then. The sheet will be clean. Alright, so don't forget tomorrow. You miss, tomorrow, of course, I'll have to think of some more...

All these transactions occurred during about the first twenty-five minutes of the morning. Lessons then began.

The lesson

The housemaster is a subject teacher but he is always a housemaster first. It is not unusual for lessons to be interrupted. Thus, there is a tension between duties as a classroom teacher and duties as a housemaster responsible for individual pupils. Teaching in the houseblock immediately in reach of the office, housemasters are always available for 'phone calls and emergencies thus reinforcing the priority given to pastoral matters.

Several pupils had already arrived in his classroom. The chairs and tables, however, had to be set out before lessons could begin:

George: Alan come on... Look, instead of sitting there doing nothin', could be setting the tables out...
Harry: Sir, can I go to the toilet please?
George: No, not yet Harry, we want this room set out first of all.
Neil: Sir, can I leave at ten past sir, I have to go to the dentist.
George: Right, well, it's up to you to remember that... We're startin' a lesson now Andy, not a disco...

The setting up of the tables continued for some minutes. Then George had to signal the beginning of the lesson:

George: Right, can you come and get your seats now girls. You put that away... I am uh waitin' very patiently... Mike... Alan, you can move from there... No... Right, you've got your *Living History* books, now will you open it at page 72... 72... Looking at page 72 for a minute. Yesterday, most of you did finish the writing at the top. But I know for a fact that some of you didn't even though you were kept in for ten minutes.

Shortly, George's lesson is interrupted. The 'phone in his office rings. It is a member of staff at a children's home calling to hear a report on one of their children. This telephone conversation reveals several criteria by which housestaff tended to assess and form opinions on the character of their pupils:

... one of the things is that uh that set uh very few of them are doin' any exams an' 'e's one of them. An' what's happened, the interest level has fallen away remarkably um in his own group – that's the boys in my house – he's lucky in that five of them and there's six in it, are still attending very regularly, you know. But if you take the other part of that set which are from another house... for example, there is uh one boy in today out of seven. And that's fairly consistent you know...

Under these circumstances George feels the boy, Paul, is doing quite well. The tone is informal, knowledgeable, edged with a kind of pessimistic realism concerning Paul's feelings about school:

I've talked to Paul about it, I mean basically, he's never had any great incentive to go to school but I mean, it's even less now it's sort of micky mouse now. So, we can't really be too uh hard and harsh or surprised to be honest.

... The history is, once he learnt to read and write you know, which he could hardly do when he came here in the second year, once he'd cracked that, I mean, that was it as far as he was concerned – his schooling was over, you know. I mean if we look at it academically, it was a total and abysmal failure, you know, but uh, in fact, he's not developed too badly. Given the right sort of company then, you know, reasonable opportunity... Oh, I'm convinced Paul can make it 'cos he's no mug, you know. I don't think he's the sort who would easily get into crime. I think he does, uh think about that, that side, I mean he's prepared to uh... to do some certain things but there's a limit you know... (listens to house parent). Yeah, Yeah. He argues the point a lot now doesn't he but you see, I mean, he's got to assert himself and well, while he reacts badly sometimes you give long enough, he comes round doesn't he? Like he argues an' he does, he does get up your nose a little bit when he's like that. He can be very uh stick his heels an' uh very stubborn... it doesn't last though does it, you know, 'cos basically he isn't a bad lad at all. He wants to be liked and uh popular rather than disliked. So, uh that's a good point...

It seems Paul exhibits and is allowed what might be called a degree of controlled autonomy. On the one hand, his characteristic of standing up against teachers and adults generally brings him into conflict. On the other, this very characteristic allows him to keep his distance from 'bad company' which is counted as a plus.

That Paul takes an anti-school attitude means that George has to place him under surveillance. He agrees to keep an eye on the register 'and if I haven't seen him around for a few days I'll check the register a' I'll let you know'. Paul, of course, is experienced enough to know that he must get his registration mark before absenting himself from lessons. Thus being marked present is no actual guarantee of *being present*.

During this conversation the lesson bell sounds. As George put the phone down a boy from his class entered asking if he could go to the toilet now. The housemaster, like any teacher, is a centre of permissions and prohibitions. The phone rings again. Shortly after this, the boy who earlier had been sent home to change his trousers enters:

Boy: Sir.
George: Wh'...? That looks more like you now. I recognize you now.

It is, of course, a fairly trivial statement. However, since during interviews most pupils had something critical to say of the staff's obsessions with dress it is an important statement to the pupils. It carries the sense that one can only be recognized if one conforms, that wearing alternative clothing brings with it a sense of being a different person, an anti-school image perhaps. One can only be what one is permitted to be.

With such statements, an image of what it is to be a pupil, and by implication, a deviant, is continually reinforced. And the housemaster must inhibit certain deviations. However, being a deviant carries with it an acceptable side if one can achieve the status of being a *character*. A *character* appears to achieve a certain autonomy without being too threatening, maintaining a basic friendliness – rather like Paul, but always an object of the housemaster's function as censor.

George specifically pointed out to me one such pupil in his class when at last he returned to teaching:

> He's a character that one, a case of eggs, him ... Quite good at acting. He was sent to me yesterday for swearing in the classroom. He does that the whole time [laughs]. Usually, when I go in there [indicating his office] when the phone calls, I'll hear him 'You fuckin' bastard', you know, to somebody. It's normal. And that's what, he always does that as well [the boy, Joe, is rocking in his chair], he always rocks on his chair, never has a clue he's doing it. Joe! [Joe sits forward in his chair.]

There is an ironic tension between George's understanding that Joe is acting normally but that this is threatening to teachers who want to create their own normality. His pastoral care can be as much for other teachers as for pupils.

At that moment Freda enters bringing information about one of the group of girls discussed earlier that morning concerning truancy. The girl, Sally, was being placed on a charge of theft. This is a girl who cannot be a *character*, she is in danger of being left to take the consequences:

> *Freda:* I'll get them both down (Sally and her sister) and tell them that I've spoken to (the social worker) today and told them to please tell her her attendance has improved.
> *George:* Yeah.
> *Freda:* But uh one more bunkin' and that's it I'm afraid. It's fair enough isn't It?
> *George:* Of course it is. Well, I mean, I've warned Sally, didn't I?
> *Freda:* Yes.
> *George:* You know, I said I'll, you know, this time I'll wear it but if you do it again then you just ...
> *Freda:* Said, 'I can't give a toss'.
> *George:* Deliberately and openly goin' against ...
> *Freda:* Yeah, since July her attendance is appalling.

The distinction between the 'character' and the deviant is the deliberate oppositional stance, the open attitude of 'I can't give a toss'. It is this that influences the housestaff's attitude towards the pupil and justifies the implied next step of allowing the case to go to the next official level.

Meanwhile, the lesson proceeds. Pupils are beginning to finish their work, several approach wanting confirmation they have finished. George walks around the class for a while as pupils ask him questions – some to do with television programmes. However, he is not fully able to concentrate on the lesson. The phone rings twice more – both calls from parents – and shortly thereafter the lesson period is over. During those long periods when he left the classroom I observed the effects of his leaving. The effect was not as dramatic as other similar occasions with other housemasters. Nevertheless, a large proportion ceased work and commenced conversations and play, including a couple of incidents of play-fighting. Without personal supervision to compel work, work tends to be given up in favour of more social talk. The role of the teacher as censor or inhibitor of activities is implied. The housemaster is also a teacher and hence the pastoral role is coloured by the teacher as censor, as a person who tells, instructs, commands. Pastoral work, focusing upon individual cases necessitated listening, empathy and creating an atmosphere of informality or even permissiveness in order to 'reach' the inidividual. Pastoral work therefore has another set of opposing demands placed upon it.

Back in the office

Housestaff generally had no more than ten hours a week timetabled teaching in order to devote the rest of the time to pastoral work. Such work divided into administration, following up discipline matters, responding to any crisis and liaising with external agencies usually with regard to children in trouble.

As an illustration of the more benign aspect of his work, shortly after George returned to his office a boy enters. He had just walked into school – he'd watched football late last night! Both George and Freda treat him in a fairly lighthearted manner, quite casual. He is clearly a *character:*

> *Freda:* What lesson you missed, Mike?
> *Mike:* Madam, I don't know...
> *Freda:* Oooh!
> *George:* Bet you it was Mr... I was just gonna say I'll bet you a pound it was the headteacher... I'll get a note now [from the headteacher].
> *Freda:* [In a high, ratty voice] 'Mike Jones not in my lessons.'
> *George:* 'Absent from my lesson' (thumbing through timetables)... Yes, it was.

Freda and George mimic the headteacher's tone of voice, implying a set of values different from the lighthearted manner they take towards Mike. It further stands in contrast to the way in which Sheila's truancy was being treated during the earlier part of the morning. She had crossed the threshold from characterhood to deviance. Mike is merely to go to the headteacher to see if there was any homework. In both cases, however, the stance taken towards the pupils is permeated by discipline matters. This is not so in every case as is seen in the next example which occurred soon after Mike left. A number of kids are hanging around the doorway, babbling. Freda asks one of the girls, June, if Sally's sister Alice is in. She was not. A conversation starts concerning a girl, Mary, who is being picked on. June is accused of upsetting Mary again:

> *Freda:* You know that her uncle died the other day.
> *June:* [mentioning glue sniffing] I don't sniff it [but] I smelt it yesterday... we smelt it yesterday, didn't we? Can still smell it on her breath.
> *Freda:* OK June, thanks, but you know, next time she tells you anything come and tell Mr Black or I but don't, try not to pick on her at the moment, she's a bit sensitive, OK?

The focus is upon the individual sensitivities and problems of Mary. June and her friends are asked to make allowances for her individual circumstances. Freda expresses concern, displays her empathy for Mary and asks for similar consideration and empathy to be displayed by the girls. The values are straightforward. However, with other teachers the housestaff may affect a more straightforwardly punitive stance. Pastoral staff rarely challenge their colleagues, explicitly, in their relationship to pupils, although behind their backs criticism is frequently voiced.

Louise had been sent out of the class by her teacher who said she 'was muttering under her voice an' all that.' George tells her to go and wait outside the teacher's classroom which was where the teacher had wanted her to remain. Louise, however, wanted to stay and do some work in the houseblock. Reluctantly she left. After a brief interlude Louise's teacher angrily entered:

> *Teacher:* I've just had a standing battle with Louise ... who has been determined to get the last word. I've been trying to introduce m' lesson, tryin' to get goin,' she's just been carryin' on a conversation then she started hummin' and singing in a high voice. Um, I picked her out and roasted her and then she was still tryin' to get the last word. So, I asked her to leave. An' then I went out the room to find her ...
> *George:* She'd come down 'ere asked if she could work at the houseblock.
> *Teacher:* ... By [the time Louise returned] of course the other one [Louise's friend] had been sent out 'cos she then turned round, started talkin' to somebody else. Then I thought, 'I'm sure there's something wrong 'ere' [laughs]. And they're just takin' not a scrap of notice. I'm gonna give them both punishment. I'm gonna give Louise ten sides [of work to copy], I'm gonna give the other one six sides 'cos I'm absolutely disgusted. I was just wantin' to pass it on to you.

George's responses were short, saying he does not know what they're like as a class 'I don't take them. They're not sent out a lot but I know that they are talkative.' That kind of problem was more for the teacher and not for him to solve. However, he tells the teacher to get the girls to bring the punishment work to him in the morning.

There is no sense in which the attitude of the teacher is challenged. George's quiet matter of fact approach barely suggests the criticism which many times he had expressed to me concerning 'over the top' teachers. There could be no explicit accusation only the fact that: 'They're not sent out a lot but I know that they are talkative.' There are few such reservations, however, with pupils. Just as the teacher leaves, another pupil, Paul (the boy from the children's home), enters having just been sent from his lesson. He felt that since he was hardly ever in the lesson there was little point in him doing a test being set by the teacher because:

> *Paul:* I don't know nothin' at all about it what I'm supposed to do. She just said, 'Well I'm not 'aving you up 'ere, go an' see Mr Black. Sir, can I stay with you?'
> *George:* Alright, well you can stay 'ere anyway. They phoned me from the Home this morning, Paul ... because of you sayin' you didn't seem particularly keen to get to school today after last night. You've had a bit of a, bit of a hump have you?
> *Paul:* Well, I was sick last night an' I said 'I'm goin' over the doctors. I'm gettin' pains now and again.' And they said, 'No, you can go after school'.
> *George:* Well, I thought it was a bit of a grudge you were bearin' about not bein' taken from the disco or somethin.'
> *Paul:* I wasn't bothered about that. I knew they'd come for me sometime. But after 7 o'clock when they never came ...

The initial stance is one which hints at suspicion, albeit carried out in a friendly manner. The boy is questioned about motives in a way a teacher would never be. Paul's reason for wanting to go to the doctor is challenged:

> *George:* ... It's only a con anyway.
> *Paul:* It's not though.
> *George:* It is 'cos if you really needed the doctor you'd be grateful to get there any time.
> *Paul:* If I 'ave this paper I'm not goin' in my own time.
> *George:* That's right, that's right, I'm not going to be ill in my own time, is that what you're saying? 'I will be ill in the school's time?'

Paul: No but last night when I was sick ... I said to one of the staff, 'Can I go to the doctor's?' She said, 'Yeah, you can go tomorrow morning.' When I got up, I says, 'I'm goin' to the doctors ...'
George: You're not sick though are you really?
Paul: Yeah, I was sick last night and I'm gettin' pains now and again. They just say to me 'Oh well, yer can still go to school, go on.'
George: Stomach pains?
Paul: Yeah.
George: ... and that's the system is it? You go to the doctor every time?

George eases in his suspicions. Paul has been characterized as a bit of a 'con-man' (implied as much in the manner George takes towards Paul as in what is stated). As is typical, housestaff work to establish the truth. The pupil, however kindly the voice, is placed in a position of being potentially untrustworthy. The norms and demands of the institution, and the statements of those in authority are placed in a higher regard than those of the child. George signals his slight shifting of stance through the two questions 'stomach pains?' and 'and that's the system is it...?' He never, however, indicates unambiguously that he believes the boy. Paul gives a few more instances of comparable cases and how they were treated differently to him. George rounds off the conversation by asking Paul if he wants to do a job. The job is then explained to him and Paul happily goes off to do it. It seems an emotional compromise has been reached, satisfactory to both. Paul has had his moan, received some individual attention, and goes away 'trusted' to do a job.

Besides these incidents George's morning has involved a discussion with a union representative about the latest pay talks, a discussion with the deputy head about suspected bullying in the fifth year and a discussion with the headteacher concerning a pupil absent from his class and the success of the previous night's disco, a topic which the next door housemaster initiated in order to impress the headteacher:

Housemaster: Well, that's what we've decided to do, to give the customers what they're asking for and to see whether it's valued and whether it's looked after ... 'cos if they start bringing friends or reprobates ... these things tend to fold up.
George: They do.
Headteacher: Sometimes it seems to me that if you could ... give all the girls uh a continuous disco and all the boys a continuous football match ... (laughter from all) ...
George: Well, you could intersperse both with long sessions of hairdressing ... (all laugh).

There is an ambiguous sense of 'put down' – as if entertainment, having fun were inferior activities. Having fun is not on the curriculum. However, making good with the headteacher is – as the other housemaster and headteacher leave another teacher (the union representative) present says quietly to George 'Nowt like blowin' y' own trumpet is there?'.

George's morning ends with a discussion on a cafeteria system to be introduced at dinner time. A union meeting is called for that dinner break. George is worried about the demands it will make on staff and passes what appears to be a sexist comment on four ancillary staff: 'They're supposed to patrol the school at lunch time an' keep good order in the place. Four women there are. There'll be absolutely no authority really so far as the kids are concerned.' He notices noise coming from inside the houseblock. It has been raining and so pupils had come in for shelter. But: 'Hey! Come on . . . out! . . . You lot are smoking in there, now cut it out. You . . . Yes . . . definitely been around too long!. The toilets are then locked and the houseblock entrance is locked. During the period of the union meeting George takes off the radio-mike.

The afternoon

George returns to his office shortly before the bell. As usual the office is crowded, kids hanging around the doorway, chattering. One boy calls over to George, 'Sir, what do you think of Smithy's hair?' Smithy has a ragged haircut not quite punk, not quite anything. George laughs, 'No comment . . . Smithy, where did you get that done?.' He'd done it himself. Such banter, of course, is as important in adult work places as it is in classrooms. It is a temporary suspension of authority relations and most teachers whether in or out of classrooms attempt to foster it.

A similar function is served when George and Freda start talking about the coming parents' evening:

> *George:* Ee I'm knackered. I've only got about another ten hours to go. [Wonders whether he has to do the 'morals talk' – a sex education talk for parents and children] . . . I say there'll only be one or two parents [laughter].
> *Freda:* One or two will pin you against the wall . . .
> *George:* [To me] Tell you what I 'ave been doin', Freda keeps ribbin' me about it, runnin' off at these parents' nights, hidin' for a bit [laughs]. I slide off an' hide . . .
> *Freda:* Yeah . . . an' I'm left behind and by the time [he comes back] . . . I'm speechless, lose my voice. Don't try it tonight I'm not in a very good mood!

Neither have had what could be called a proper break since about 8.45 a.m. Both look tired.

When the bell goes George has to take a 'preparation for independent life' course for fifth years. This involved watching a video film of school leavers undergoing job interviews. After the film the pupils were brought back to the houseblock for a discussion. George sat on one of the desks asking if there were any questions, emphasizing that he was willing to contribute to a discussion. Nobody wanted a discussion. So far as he was concerned, he said to me, if there was to be proper preparation for adult life it entailed being responsible for one's own decisions. It would defeat the purpose, he said, to have insisted on a discussion, that would have taken away their independence. There was still, however, about half-an-hour of the lesson left. George went back to work in his office, (where, at other times he had said, there is always a week's work waiting for him in administration alone). Pupils wanting to leave early would enter, plead for a while and be sent out to wait again. However, he can rarely resist placing a little moral, even ironical, sting in the tail. For example:

Sheila: Sir, what time is it?

George: It's about five minutes yet before you can go.

Sheila: God! [whispered].

George: Before you can be released . . . [Sheila says something] . . . Pardon?

Sheila: It's a cage – we get released.

George: That's a bit like it isn't it, you do feel like that. Do you feel like that, sometimes?

Sheila plus friend: Yeah.

Sheila: The lesson drags on and on and on.

George: That's life though, isn't it? I mean, if you start work it's the same idea, isn't it?

Sheila: I know.

George: You can't just come and go as you please, you know.

Sheila: [Laughing] Um you can at school.

George: You got to be there say at half-past-eight in the morning. You can't run away before half-past-five, you get three-quarters of an hour for your dinner and . . .

Sheila: [Laughing] My brother does . . .

George: Where does he work though what does he do? [He works on a YOP scheme.] Ah, but that's not work though is it?

Sheila: No.

George: It's just not real work. There's no way you could do that working for a real employer . . .

They state that they will be pleased to leave school although they have no work lined up. At last it is time when they can leave this lesson.

Some minutes earlier George had given me an article written by a local headmaster concerning the achievements of his school. George described the contents of the article as 'a load of crap'. He portrayed, instead, a school under siege where pupils rioted, literally, every lunchtime and after school. In his view it is the duty of the pastoral staff, and particularly head and deputy head, to provide a system of surveillance outside classroom hours which serves as a community service: 'to me that's a community job because you're thinking about your neighbours and the neighbourhood, you're thinking about the wider issues and the good order of your lads . . .'. Interestingly, during the previous summer, during the 'street disturbances' (as the Scarman Report in 1981 called them) the pastoral system of this school acted as a forward warning system for the police, able to provide street-wise information through its community-wide contacts as to the likely occurrence and whereabouts of disturbances. Two or three riots involving up to 250 people did occur locally. However, fights involving that sort of number of young people were not untypical. As George went on to say, if one brings young people from different territories and lumps them all together, each territory will have its gangs and there will be trouble. The two schools served two distinct territories and brought them into close proximity. Years ago, he continued, there had been an agreement between the two schools to stagger the end of the school day by ten minutes in order to avoid all the riots and fights that used to occur as the two schools released their pupils. This agreement, he felt was being eroded by the lack of supervision as the rival school's pupils left.

Shortly after the close of lessons parents began to arrive at the office hoping to pick up reports and avoid the crowds and queues of the later afternoon and evening. George took off the radio mike at about 2.50 p.m. feeling that it would be unethical to continue.

Parent's evening

It is a very large hall, each of the houses having their own areas. Parents wait until staff are available in order to talk about their children. There is no sound record of George's work. From the moment of his entrance, even as he walked across the floor he was engaged in conversations with parents about their children. Particularly in the evening most of the parents appear to do more waiting than talking to the staff.

It was a very large turnout. For a while I am cornered by the headteacher proud of the achievement. He considers that the idea of parents coming to collect their reports acts as an incentive. Although, he said, it is often considered that parents in the area 'just don't care, they do care and care a great deal as is witnessed in this turnout'. Teachers, he continued, have to make the effort to build up relations and prove that it is important for them to come in. Teachers have to keep on at children about, 'did your mum come to parent's evening?.' But, he says, 'It's not easy to listen to bad news all the time. In middle-class areas there are not the problems'. And, later as a parent said to me, she found the evening useful, although she did not like all this standing around. She thought it was a good idea collecting the reports. Also, 'you have to come really, else the tutors get on at the kid, "did your parents come last night?".'

Several hundred parents came that evening, and many pupils, a few to help out – pour tea and coffee, collect empty plastic cups, organize displays of work. George had a number of parents who he particularly wished to see, for example, the parents of the girls, Sheila and her friends who had been discussed that day because they were truanting, one of whom had also been caught stealing. One parent came to George to recount how a pupil had pulled her child up by the ears and how that had started a fight. Many come to talk to someone about their problems. Not many parents of course, are given glowing reports of their children. As George said, 'It's hard for the parents to hear so many criticisms...'.

Reference

Schostak, J. 1983. *Maladjusted schooling, deviance, social control and individuality in secondary schooling,* London, The Falmer Press.

23 Who's inside the wooden horse? The role of pastoral care in curriculum change

John Quicke

Pastoral care structures appeared inside most secondary schools following the educational expansion of the sixties. In this chapter John Quicke discusses their influence on the curriculum. Many people saw them as a progressive force, providing a counter-balance to narrow subject specialisms and a focus for initiating curriculum change. However, others argued that they were inherently conservative, that instead of 'pastoralizing' the curriculum such structures served only to control deviant pupils. John Quicke identifies a further irony of the pastoral care story in recent years. Many pastoral staff have embraced the behaviourist or skills-based approach to teaching as well as the values of the 'new vocationalism.' From such a perspective the earlier rhetoric that they should serve to democratize the learning process may sound very hollow indeed.

The term 'pastoral care' was probably first used in print in the fifties (see Lang 1984), to mark the beginning of pastoral care systems which by the early seventies were present in most secondary schools. Of course, the idea that teachers should oversee the well-being and progress of individual pupils was not new but the general emergence of separate staff responsibilities for it were. According to a review of education in the years 1974–5 this formal structure was necessitated by the large size of the reorganized comprehensive schools (DES 1977).

However, probably a more important influence was the gradual disappearance of the general subject teacher in favour of the subject specialist. In many of the old secondary modern schools, as in present-day primary schools, the form teacher had responsibility for teaching a large part of the curriculum to his or her form group. In the comprehensive school it was likely that pupils would be taught by many different teachers, none of whom would get to know the pupils particularly well as individuals. The career interests of teachers displaced by secondary reorganization also played their part. Many teachers in positions of seniority in secondary modern schools were provided with an acceptable niche in the pastoral structure. This structure continued to provide a career route for non-graduate teachers or teachers not strongly qualified in a particular subject area, although some recent evidence suggests that the position is changing (Cook 1983).

The rhetoric of pastoral care

The rhetoric of pastoral care has always been characterized by primarily child-centred aims. Thus an HMI national secondary survey reported that schools considered that pastoral systems had the following aims:

1 attempt to coordinate consideration of the pupil's personal, social and academic development;

219

2 facilitate the development of good relationships between teachers and pupils;
3 try to ensure that each pupil knows and is known by a particular adult;
4 make available relevant information through the development of effective communication and record systems;
5 involve parents and outside agencies in the work of the school, where appropriate;
6 enable someone to respond quickly and appropriately to pupils' problems or indeed to anticipate a problem that might arise;
7 by these means improve the learning of pupils.

(DES 1979, p. 219)

One might expect such a perspective to lead to questioning of the impact of the hidden curriculum and formal curriculum, on the well-being of pupils. Hamblin (1978) refers to the need for 'a carefully planned integration of the pastoral and curricular aspects of the comprehensive school, based on the realization that the true failure of the secondary school lies in the field of learning'. However, in many schools a division of labour has been created by the separate structures. The pastoral care staff find themselves preoccupied with and taking responsibility for problems of discipline and deviance generally. The result is that the pastoral system has been integrated with the academic system only in the sense that a pit prop is integrated with the roof it holds up! It helps to keep the traditional academic system in business and thus supports the status quo. In fact 'pastoralisation' is a term used by Williamson (1980) to describe the process by which those regarded as failures in school are persuaded to accept the system. In such a process deviance and disaffection are located within the characteristics of individual pupils.

Pastoral care in practice

I shall illustrate the issues which have arisen with a description of practice in a secondary school which had a reputation for 'good practice' (see Poppleton *et al* 1983, p. 1). It was a large city comprehensive drawing its pupils from public and private housing estates and from a number of outlying country villages. An attempt had been made to break down the barriers between the pastoral care system and the formal curriculum by incorporating what the school described as 'a guidance programme' into the formal curriculum. This received one timetabled period a week in a week divided into twenty periods. Year tutors had responsibility for both guidance lessons and pastoral care. Form tutors met their classes for twenty-five minute periods every morning and gave one guidance lesson a week. In these periods they were encouraged to do more than just mark registers, by using the time for 'active tutorial' work, for getting to know the children better and dealing with various problems.

The progressiveness of the school's thinking is evident in the emphasis on 'relationships' not ony as part of a hidden curriculum, but as a legitimate part of the formal curriculum. 'Relationships' are perceived as on a par with other reforms of the curriculum such as those involving 'language' policy or technology. Thus when teachers were asked 'where does good practice in pastoral care lie?' they tended to stress qualities like 'being approachable', 'treating children as individuals', 'being a person', 'liking children', 'not ignoring normal children, yet recognizing problems'. As one teacher put it: 'I am a person and I am a great believer that that's what education is all about, inter-relationships between people'.

In the general drift of the rhetoric there thus emerged a commitment to going beyond the deviance-centred approach to a conception which stressed 'relationships' and treating all children as individuals. This embrace of the pastoral rhetoric also resulted in some teachers being critical of the methods and content of traditional academic curricula as these continued to be practised in most parts of the school. One teacher contrasted guidance lessons with traditional subject teaching. It was alleged that in the former, teachers tended to be more reflective and asked themselves 'what am I teaching and why *am* I teaching it?' This contrasted with a 'normal examination class' in, for example, physics and chemistry lessons where there would be no expectation that pupils should 'ask you why you are doing this'. Unlike the rest of the curriculum, guidance involved listening, revealing personal feelings and encouraging moral choices. Another teacher felt that '... we haven't done enough to change the curriculum, to make it relevant and I think a lot of kids find a lot of time they spend in school depressingly irrelevant'.

This school has adopted the rhetoric of a policy which goes beyond that of Hamblin (cited above). Not only is there to be integration of the two curricula but many of the teachers with official responsibilities in pastoral care see themselves as putting forward an *alternative* to the status quo both in relation to traditional processes and traditional content. The processes advocated are more humanistic and the content more 'relevant'. There is every indication of a commitment to practices designed to alter the status quo and calculated to produce a shake up in the way we 'educate' children in schools. The rhetoric is 'progressive' in that it is compatible with a child-centred rather than an institution or subject-centred view of education.

But what of reality? Although the school in question had a good reputation in pastoral care, the staff were clear that they were far from implementing their progressive ideals. For instance, there was some indication that key staff were finding it difficult to escape from narrowly defined pastoral roles. Thus a small observation study of the Year Tutor concluded that: 'the observations do support the 'sceptical' view of pastoral care as being preoccupied with problems of attendance and deviance, more so as one moves from second year to fifth year level' (p. 24). Lack of time seemed to be one of the major constraints. One of the observers commented: 'the year tutor is always rushing to lessons ... The job therefore seems somewhat thankless and certainly demands time in and after school' (p. 21). Not only was there insufficient time for the preventative and curriculum-oriented aspects of the role but it was even a touch and go question as to whether pupils' problems could be dealt with adequately when they were detected at an individual level. The following statement was fairly typical:

> Sometimes through pressure of time and pressure of work ... I don't feel I've done well. I mean sometimes I know that there's something wrong somewhere with that particular child and you don't follow it up and you do get bouts of guilt ... because you do have restrictions on your own ability, time-wise, to do things.
>
> (Poppleton *et al* 1983, p. 59)

As far as curriculum and pedagogy were concerned it was also doubtful if progressive pastoral ideology had penetrated very far. In certain subjects there was an awareness of the importance of 'process' factors, but in the main the traditional disciplines were intact both in form and content. As the principal author concluded:

> But, even in our good schools there is little evidence of the power of pastoral work to penetrate pedagogy and this is unlikely to happen for as long as teachers conceptualize their work wholly in terms of teaching content... The experience of teaching-as-process which the guidance programme provides... has enhanced the teaching of some staff in some subjects but has left others untouched.
>
> (Poppleton *et al* 1983, p. 67)

Thus the evidence seems to suggest that the attempt to implement curriculum and pedagogical innovation via pastoral practice in this school has so far met with only partial success. As to whether the staff would be optimistic or pessimistic about future developments is difficult to estimate. From an observer's viewpoint it is difficult to be other than sceptical. A considerable investment of time and effort has created a good reputation and some improvement in the system, but even so some of the basic goals of progressive pastoral care were a long way from being achieved.

Continuities with the past

Why did the presence of a progressive pastoral ideology fail to alter the learning environment in a significant way? From the responses cited above the answer may seem plain enough. 'Lack of time' was probably the manifestation in teacher consciousness of a whole host of material constraints, such as too many children and too few resources, and there is no doubt that pragmatic and survival concerns played their part in compromising pastoral ideals. But there is another simple explanation: that many teachers were not, in fact, committed to progressive pastoral ideals.

Contradictions in the notion of pastoral care have been handed down in the history of schooling. As Lang (1984) has pointed out it has roots in the systems created by nineteenth-century public school headmasters to instil 'godliness and good learning' into their pupils. The house system was developed to implement these high ideals, although they were transformed or distorted later in the century into the competitive sporting ethos, jingoism and muscular Christianity which many now associate with the public school tradition. There is an important continuity between Victorian perspectives and the preoccupation with deviance of much current pastoral practice.

In one sense then pastoral care seems to have more to do with conformity to social norms than with liberal or progressive education, with socialization in accordance with preconceived notions of what pupil morals should be like rather than pupil autonomy and the development of critical thinking. Thus, in the school under consideration, one teacher summed up guidance lessons as 'private input to all kids about how to behave'. Another interviewee commented: 'You have to make the kids realize that giving is very much a part of taking... they should learn to appreciate what parents and teachers do for them – what's right and what's wrong' (p. 49).

There is no suggestion here of presenting open alternatives to pupils, for example, by encouraging them to consider the alternative view that it is appropriate for them to be angry about how little is done for them at a time of education cuts and mass youth unemployment! Similarly the following statement of aims is difficult to justify from an educational viewpoint:

Preparation for life can't just be done in guidance lessons but the guidance programme has played a large part in reawakening responsibilities. There was a desire to see the guidance curriculum link strengthened by building the idea of service into the broader curriculum. If pupils are going to be unemployed they will be getting money from the State; what will they do in return?

(Poppleton *et al* 1983, p. 81)

The concern of pastoral care with moral welfare and obedience is also illustrated in a case study by Alun Pelleschi (1983) which focuses on pupils' as well as teachers' accounts. The pupil perspective is frequently omitted in studies of pastoral care which seems very strange when you consider the supposed pupil-centred nature of the practices being investigated! The study was of the pastoral system of a coeducational comprehensive school situated in a catchment area which contained a large working-class black population mainly of Asian origin. The school stated two of its aims as 'the development of tolerance, understanding and respect for others,' and 'the meeting of individual needs'. The pastoral system had a role in fulfilling both. The researcher focused on the views of two groups of black girls who tended to reject the pastoral system for a number of reasons. They said they did not know their tutors well enough and lacked trust in members of the pastoral team. It seems that some staff interpreted their 'support and respect for the cultural background of the girls' as implying that they should tell parents about boyfriends when this would have been seen as a private matter for 'white' girls. Such actions had overtones of both racism and sexism. As Pelleschi points out:

By focusing on girls' relationships with boys, a differential treatment of the sexes emerges in which the girls are discouraged by the pastoral staff from developing such relationships, and where there is suspicion of moral danger or of 'going too far', the girls' parents become involved. This does not necessarily follow for the boys. This can be related to a misinterpretation of cultural values to a certain extent as, whilst it is true that boys tend to have more freedom than girls, under Islamic law for instance there should be equal morality for both sides.

(Pelleschi 1983, p. 151)

Intervention on the basis of these interpretations was clearly seen by the girls as an infringement of their personal liberty. When they did have problems, such as being the recipients of racist abuse, teacher intervention was not as sharp or as frequent as they would have liked. Pastoral policy seems to have involved a double system of control on these pupils leading to attempts to make the girls conform to a view of women both in white society and in the filtered notion of the culture of their families.

Pastoral care, 'the new vocationalism' and social skills

Pastoral care may have been a force for progressive change in the curriculum as a whole but it is currently in danger of giving way completely to traditional forms of discipline and control as child-centred education appears to be on the retreat in secondary schools. This is supported by the infiltration of two mutually support-ing and pervasive practices. The first is the 'new vocationalism' in which a greatly increased emphasis is to be placed on the relationship between school and work and, by implication, unemployment. The second is the introduction of skills-based curricula which, frequently, have displaced the emphasis on pupil autonomy in the pastoral curriculum. Paradoxically these have been presented, too, as progressive.

Supporters of the Manpower Services Commission's Technical and Voca-tional Education Initiative (TVEI), a key element in the government's strategy for intervention in the curriculum, claim that pupil participation in many of the schemes is voluntary and that it is open to children of all abilities and to boys and girls equally (Centre for the Study of Comprehensive Schools 1984). Each scheme includes work experience, regular assessment and counselling, a final record of achievement, courses in technical and vocational subject elements which relate to local employment opportunities and access to nationally recog-nized qualifications (see Cohen 1984, McMurray 1986). There is a stress on a negotiated curriculum, with pupils choosing areas of interest, modifying their individual courses and controlling their own learning. But this similarity between progressive pastoral rhetoric and the 'new vocationalism' is only credible if one takes words like 'negotiation' and 'choice' at their face value and out of context. It is difficult to see how the progressive aim of encouraging children of all abilities to participate in 'technology' is compatible with the essentially divisive nature of the concept of different technological levels employed by the MSC.

As the CSCS pamphlet points out some LEAs have emphasized a high-technology approach with courses in electronics, microprocessor control and information technology, whilst others have used the MSC's 'Occupational Training Families' to identify vocational areas – community care, food indus-tries, transport services, retail and distribution and administrative, clerical and office studies. Clearly in some schools where the staff have a strong commitment to the comprehensive principle TVEI might be incorporated in a way which is not divisive, but even in these schools one suspects that progressive track records will be increasingly difficult to maintain in the face of government policy bent on reversing egalitarian reforms. There is an obvious streaming element in the distinction between 'high technology' and 'vocational areas' or what Nigel Lawson (when he was Secretary of State for Employment) referred to as 'no tech' areas, and it is difficult to see what schemes involving the 'occupational training families' have to do with teaching all children an understanding of our technological society.

In short, such initiatives seem to intend a return to a form of schooling which provides 'training' for some and 'education' for others. Amongst the former will be the deviants who require 'extensive pastoral care'. Pastoral care, in the sense of moral training and discipline, is more in tune with these developments.

Whilst progressive pastoral care emphasizes creativity and critical thinking, the new vocationalism is concerned with skills-based learning. Reducing curricu-lar aims to the technical language of skills implies a neutrality which is totally unwarranted. It is as if listening and observational skills for example could be taught in a way which did not involve value judgements or assumptions about the nature of knowledge. The teacher may claim to be teaching relatively uncontroversial technical matters. But since skills must always be taught and practised in relation to specific contexts a failure to explore conflicting interpretations of the context can lead to an unexamined bias. A particularly pertinent example comes from 'Active Tutorial Work' a buzz phrase of pastoral care. In *Active Tutorial Work Book 5* (Baldwin and Wells 1981) the pupils' objectives are described as: 'To develop skills in "political" awareness: Trade Unions' (p. 86) and 'To demonstrate competence in social skills by entertaining visitors from the world of work in order to ascertain information' (p. 88).

The introductory activities are in two phases. The first is called 'Preparing the Ground' and consists of three sections involving class, individual and group work. The second is called 'Preparing for a Visitor' and the aim is that groups should arrive at decisions about how to organize such a visit. The third and final phase is the visit itself followed up by a session in which groups discuss 'what did we learn?' It is clear from an examination of this material that it is not just 'skills' which are being taught. The pupil will learn that knowledge about trade unions is on a par with preparing a curriculum vitae, constructing an interview check list, form filling and other career guidance activities which constitute the rest of the term's work. He or she will also learn that 'political awareness' is a 'skill' which, described thus, does not therefore involve a great deal of reflection or thought and by implication is not something which is connected with the fundamentals of his or her personal existence. The whole effect is to dilute the topic and keep discussion on a superficial level.

There are other obvious biases in the material. In 'Preparing the Ground' an overhead stencil is used consisting of a potted history, in pictures, of work 'before our time' which presents a simplistic, contentious and sexist account of how people, work and economy developed from the times when 'man's (sic) whole life was about surviving' to our present stage where '... machines are replacing men' – the impression being that all this was 'natural' and inevitable and conflict-free.

In 'Preparing for a Visitor', the teacher is advised to suggest to the class that it might be interesting to ask one local trade union leader, one employer, one parent 'to take a standpoint on a worker's loyalty to his family at the time of a dispute' and another 'to take a standpoint on a worker's loyalty to his fellow workers at the time of a dispute'. Presumably the two people are supposed to represent a conflict of loyalties. This of course presupposes that there usually is such a conflict, a view which stems from a particular political position. An alternative view would suggest that there is no such conflict of loyalties because loyalty to fellow workers is not incompatible with loyalty to family – indeed both are part of a wider loyalty to class. From this viewpoint, the teacher's suggestion seems aimed at being divisive.

There certainly is discussion and argument encouraged by this material, but it is located within a framework, the political parameters of which, are unacknowledged. For example, pupils are encouraged to make up their own minds about the advantages and disadvantages of joining a trade union, but there is no such encouragement to make decisions about whether bosses should have the right to use profits in whatever way they wish or whether workers should control the industries in which they work.

Conclusion

Many schools have attempted to address the issues raised by the foregoing analysis. In the first example provided, a serious attempt was being made to alter the social and educational climate of the school by using the pastoral systems and its formal curriculum slot – the guidance programme – as a mechanism for penetrating the traditional curriculum. However, if progressive pastoral care is to achieve its aims, it must disassociate itself from the 'new vocationalism', otherwise its critique of the traditional curriculum will be construed as support for a divided and 'mindless' skills-based system of education.

But this disassociation should clearly not mean throwing out the baby with the bath water! One should remember that it was because of the inadequacies of the traditional academic curriculum that the 'new vocationalism' with its emphasis on 'relevance' and practical skills became so appealing (see Quicke 1985). The world of work and technology are legitimate areas of educational experience and the study of both of them demands the development of imagination and critical thought. The way forward, therefore, is not to retreat from 'relevant' areas but to develop a pastoral and guidance programme which is broadly defined, based on progressive educational principles and integrated into the core curriculum for all pupils.

References

Baldwin, J. and Wells, H. 1981. *Active tutorial work, book 5, the fifth year*, Oxford, Blackwell.
Centre for the Study of Comprehensive Schools 1984. *TVEI: an observers guide*, York CSCS.
Cohen, P. 1984. 'Against the new vocationalism', in Bates, I., Clarke, J., Cohen, P., Finn, D., More, R., Willis, P., *Schooling for the dole?: The new vocationalism*, London, Macmillan.
Cook, G. 1983. *The role of the head of year in the English secondary school*, unpublished M.Ed. Dissertation, University of Sheffield.
Department of Education and Science 1977. *The education system in England and Wales (1974–5)*, London, HMSO.
Department of Education and Science 1979. *Aspects of secondary education in England*, London, HMSO.
Hamblin, D. 1978. *The teacher and pastoral care*, Oxford, Blackwell.
Lang, P. 1984. 'Pastoral care: some reflections on possible influences', in *Pastoral Care in Educatoin*, 2, 2, 136–46.
McMurray, A. 1986. 'TVEI and the comprehensive school: challenge or threat', in Booth, T., Potts, P. and Swann, W., (eds). *Curricula for all: preventing difficulties in learning*, Oxford, Blackwell.
Pelleschi, A. J. 1983. *The part played by the pastoral care system of an inner city school in conjunction with home and peer group factors in the reproduction of the status and role of Asian girls in their social class and ethnic group locations*, unpublished M.Ed. Dissertation, University of Sheffield.
Poppleton, P., Dear, R., Gray, J., Harrison, B., Lindsay, G., Sharples, H. and Thompson, D. 1983. *Aspects of care in schools*, Division of Education, University of Sheffield.
Quicke, J. C. 1985. 'Charting a course for personal and social education', in *Pastoral care in education*, 3, 2, 91–99.
Williamson, D. 1980. '"Pastoral Care" or "Pastoralization"'', in Best, R., Jarvis, C. and Ribbins, P., *Perspectives on pastoral care*, London, Heinemann.

24 Tampax and flowers: an approach to pastoral care?

Jan Sargeant

In this chapter Jan Sargeant casts another light on the question posed in the title of Chapter 23. She argues that in the past women have been directed and channelled into the 'pastoral' side of school life as a means of career development though it is an area which has traditionally offered less status or financial reward than subject heads of department. She goes on to suggest how changes in the nature of pastoral care are making it more like a specialist subject area and more attractive to men seeking promotion who are edging out women from yet another area of responsiblity in schools.

Not so many years ago, I made an appointment with my then head of department to discuss the possibilities of promotion. At the time I was responsible for lower school English, including the organization of a liaison system with our numerous 'feeder' schools. I felt I deserved a scale point for this but I was advised to move into the pastoral area if I was seeking promotion since this was an area more suitable for a woman to pursue than 'academia'. My own suggestion that I should return to college to gain further qualifications was bombarded with well-meant comments along the lines of my possible wish to marry, have children, the difficulty of combining a job and a course . . . the possibilities seemed endless, the problems insurmountable. There seemed nothing for it but to devote myself to pastoral care. After all, if I didn't have the qualifications to be a subject specialist, I had all of the necessities for a people specialist; namely I was a woman and women, as we all know, are expert at recognizing and accommodating other people's needs.

The fact that many of the pastoral posts were low status and did not, in many cases, carry the financial distinction of a scale point, spoke for itself. Yet a number of women had over the years been shunted into these posts as a means of career development. Exactly where the said career developed to was not very clear: in some cases, assistant year tutors on a scale 2, in fewer cases, year tutors on a 3 and in even fewer cases, a deputy headship. In some schools, even now, the woman deputy is still renowned for her ability to gracefully dispense tea, Tampax and sympathy, a role of limited if unstartling clarity. Without the experience of timetabling and curriculum work that the other (male) deputy undertakes, it is hardly surprising that this is the end of the line for many of those who do make it so far.

The pastoral aspect of education is predominantly a caring approach. In his book on the subject, Ben Morris refers to 'the essential caring element' being 'that part of each of us that cares for others'. Women have therefore, in the eyes of many, an important role to play. Have not women been for centuries the carers, the enablers, the nurturers, for children and/or men to fall back on? Isn't it logical that women should be the likeliest candidates to compensate pupils for the 'incompetent mothers' to whom Michael Marland refers in his book, *Pastoral Care* (Marland 1979)? In speaking with a number of women teachers I have come to the conclusion that most of them have long been aware that a pupil's learning difficulties might be a result of her problems at home, and generally what those problems were, even before such things as profiles were invented, making it necessary for the information to be written down.

For many women, the pastoral aspect of school life was merely an extension of their domestic role, but then again, it is traditional for knowledge which already exists to be stolen and made a science of, mystified often by a process of language development, as we shall see later. What is now happening is that the pastoral element is being focused on more and more and as a consequence, is becoming more and more structured. The inroads of bureaucratic patriarchy are making themselves more apparent. In *Educational Institutions: Where Cooperation is called Cheating*, Dale Spender argues, 'Stratification is fundamental to the male view... With this basic premise of inequality hierarchies emerge as a logical social arrangement' (Spender 1980, p. 40). Many schools are now re-organizing their pastoral work into a system, using existing hierarchies and formulating, when necessary, new ones, basing the actual tutor period on Active Tutorial Work.

Active Tutorial Work is the coined name for a system of active learning, based on children working together, often in groups, and even actually talking together. The phrase itself and the terminology which now surrounds it can be intimidating for those teachers who have not been on one of the available courses. In fact, a whole web of words and jargonese has developed around the area of Active Tutorial Work, or A.T.W. as it is known to the initiated. The esoteric use of language has long been a tool used in the power games of professionals: those who hold the power are those who understand the terminology. Those who remain ignorant of such terms as 'deflecting' (that is fending off pertinent questions by posing another) have no access to the sacred pastoral sanctum and therefore remain powerless and excluded. Such terminology has naturally become a useful weapon in the armoury of interview techniques and it is an unprepared candidate who fails nowadays in an interview for a pastoral post to throw in at least some of the jargon associated with a pastoral syllabus. Never mind the quality of care, feel the width of the coursebook!

The educational ideas associated with Active Tutorial Work are not in themselves new. Some teachers, many of them in English and Drama departments, or Junior and Infant schools, have long practised group work, talking and listening skills, dealing with attitudes and personal and social development. The whole idea of an active learning approach, in which children actually participate in the process of education, is nothing new – to some teachers. Others, however, fail to see the relevance or efficacy of such methods in their particular subject area, or perhaps they are frightened by the potential loss of classroom control in such a participatory situation. Perhaps, even, they are unaware of how to structure such sessions effectively – a very real consideration.

Whatever the reasons, it is necessary and vital for all children to be given such exploratory sessions at some time in their education, and it is perhaps only in their 'tutor period' in some schools that such opportunities are made available. For this reason alone, then, Active Tutorial Work can be a valid and valuable area of the school curriculum. At least there is one lesson a week when children can be actively involved in their learning. Then again, if there were less mystification, perhaps more teachers would be willing to use such methods in general day-to-day subject teaching. I see no reason why the skills and relationships fostered in such pastoral work cannot be developed elsewhere, given that a caring approach could be adopted even within the macho confines of a science laboratory. Such developments are now being fostered by the people who run A.T.W. courses but whilst schools are eager and willing to grasp at the lifeboat of a system of developing tutor periods, not many teachers feel easy at the prospect of the methodology being used within their own subject area. Such an approach does, admittedly, threaten the traditional power balance between passive recipient (child/woman) and omniscient subject specialist (teacher/man).

Does the only status it can be afforded have to be based on the rigid patriarchal structure of specialist subjects? And will that subject then adhere to the traditional division of what boys need as opposed to girls? At a course I attended on A.T.W. I was discussing with one teacher the pastoral syllabus at his school. The boys did what he termed a Ph.D. – paper hanging and decorating. The girls did not follow this particular activity. It was not deemed suitable as a 'lot of swearing goes on'. No doubt the girls acquire instead a B.Sc. – Bachelor of Service and Care?

Perhaps as a result of all this structuring and development, more men are becoming involved in the pastoral side of school life. A number of senior posts are now being held by men and one might assume that this could be a response to men's growing awareness of the skills involved in caring and enabling, for so long the traditional provinces of women. On the other hand, altruism may not be the reason.

Their newly kindled interest may be a response to more pressing needs – in a climate of educational recession and less promotional opportunity within subject areas, the pastoral side of school life may be an appealing route to a further scale point. The pastoral area may also be that much more attractive now that it has been rendered more concrete in form. After all, there is more often than not a syllabus to follow; in many schools, the year tutor is seen as a tool for the implementation of discipline, in others, as the career adviser. The 'essential caring element' is perhaps too firmly cast in the feminine role for men to pursue this angle, but if there is a systematic approach, concrete objectives and text books to follow, and a scale point at the end of the rainbow, then this area could be very appealing.

Meetings have been held, committees formed, even a national association founded, all in the name of pastoral education. They all provide a platform for discussion about how pastoral work can be implemented in schools. Yet I see little reason why it should be developed as either a subject on the timetable or as a means of career development for aspiring males. To me and many women, pastoral care is an essential part of the general interaction between any teacher and any pupil in any classroom.

References

Marland, M. 1979. *Pastoral care*, London, Heinemann Educational.

Spender, D. 1980. Educational institutions: where cooperation is called cheating, in Spender, D. and Sarah, E. (eds.), *Learning to lose*, London, The Women's Press.

25 'Smile at him when you ask for the books': transmitting sexuality in school

Shirley Prendergast and Alan Prout

In this chapter Shirley Prendergast and Alan Prout uncover some of the ways in which sexuality, as information, knowledge, experience or behaviour is present in the formal and hidden curriculum. They describe the elaborate, but often implicit, systems of control which shape attitudes towards 'normal' sexuality and also keep male and female pupils in their place. They take a particular look at the messages of sex education films. As a system of control with such ambiguous and hidden features associated with disturbing emotional and social taboos, sexuality provides a focus for 'disruptive' and 'challenging' behaviour in school. The authors illustrate the way an examination of sexuality in school brings to the surface contradictions both about our wider view of sexuality and about the nature of schooling itself.

Mixed secondary schools bring together pupils of both sexes at a time when they are intensely interested and aware of each other, and at a time of rapid physical, sexual and emotional growth. Yet schools must formally restrict and control the expression of sexuality in their pupils as well as educate them about it and for it. Pupils can be almost but not quite adult, legally minors yet often physically and emotionally mature. On the other hand teachers as adults may have private sexual lives of their own, but these lives ideally should not intrude into school, and in particular should not cross the boundaries that keep adults at a distance from the 'child' in their charge. Yet clearly attraction and affection might and do occur and even bridge such boundaries unless restricted and controlled. Sexuality then cannot formally be acknowledged to be operating as a dynamic between pupils and teachers, and has to be limited and contained in how it is seen to operate between pupils. It is thus usually hidden in schooling unless it 'goes too far'. Nevertheless not only does its potential remain, but this very invisibility also makes it more potent a force should pupils or teachers wish to use it as such.

The way in which the young child is considered relatively asexual, or as having an 'infantile sexuality' that gradually matures through latent period into a proper 'adult' sexuality parallels a growing concern to restrict, guide and channel that sexuality into age- and gender-appropriate behaviour for boys and girls. It is suggested that this concern is expressed earlier and more forcefully for boys than it is for girls, but that girls may experience it particularly in the transition to secondary schooling.

Any discussion of sexuality tends to assume that 'normal' sexuality is heterosexual and is primarily directed towards reproduction. Sexual pleasure is rarely mentioned and women are more likely to be portrayed as passive while men are active and in control. In the hidden curriculum of pupils' and teachers' behaviour, men and boys seem more likely to use sexuality aggressively and controllingly than women or girls. Indeed where girls particularly use their sexuality to manipulate or control it may serve in the long term only to confirm

and reinforce their relative powerlessness. While school may not actively promote such sexual behaviours, lack of comment or 'turning a blind eye' may be
tantamount to tacit acceptance.

While all pupils have access to and may be recipients of the expression of
disaffection through sexuality, some groups are more likely than others to use it to
express their individuality, dissent, control and power over processes of schooling
and each other.

In part this chapter may repeat or reaffirm themes touched upon earlier in this
book in Lynn Davies's discussion of deviance and sexism (Chapter 16). Clearly
pupils' sexuality and sexual behaviour is an aspect of gender and one that may be
emphasized in looking at 'disaffection' in school. This is because 'sexuality' is not
a separate category of action but is an aspect of everyday behaviours and events,
in the sense in which we have used it, to lesser or greater degree. It is this
everyday quality that gives sexuality its power – it is both nowhere and
everywhere. Yet sexual knowledge, activity, imagery, suggestion and language,
with their associated baggage of legal constraint, forbidden-ness, secrecy, excitement, pleasure and danger are powerful elements of our culture and ambiguities
about them in the process of schooling enables their expression to serve as a
pressure point around which confrontations can gather.

The sexual curriculum

Throughout the sixties and seventies schools were under pressure, from a number
of different sources, to include sex education in their curriculum. Secondary
schools have increasingly been seen as the place to intervene in a number of
sexual 'problem areas' such as unplanned teenage pregnancies, sexually
transmitted diseases and rising abortion rates (see Reid 1982). On the other
hand, sex education, or particular forms of it, is often seized upon by right-wing
pressure groups who wish to demonstrate a link between 'permissiveness' and
sexual knowledge, decay in moral standards, pornography and the breakdown of
the family. The obligation in the 1980 Education Act for schools to state to
parents their policy on sex education, was, in part, a response to this political
pressure, though its unintended consequence seems to have been to encourage
some schools, sometimes for the first time, to think about or even extend this area
of the curriculum. There has been, in fact, new pressure to constrain such
activities by amendments to the 1986 Education Bill.

But schools are inevitably engaged in more diffuse forms of 'teaching' about
sexuality as part of the hidden curriculum, and some would argue that these
forms are likely to be more significant than formal learning. Walker and Barton
have noted that gender stereotypes in school are reinforced in three ways:
'through the communication of teacher expectations, through classroom practices and through school rituals' (Walker and Barton 1983, p. 6). The evidence
suggests that similar processes facilitate sexual stereotyping. In all primary or
secondary schools there are rules that, directly or indirectly, regulate the degree
to which sexuality can be represented or expressed. Rules about uniform and
dress, changing rooms and cloakrooms, about the sex of the teacher in some
classes and about language are some obvious examples. In primary school the
young child, if she does not already know, learns that boys and girls often play

separately, do not undress or visit the toilet together. They must not touch themselves or others in inappropriate ways and must learn a proper accepted language about when and how to talk about their bodies. These rules and values may be very different from what has already been experienced at home. Lee (1983, p. 125) tells of a case where a four-year old was sent home for using 'rude language.' This turned out to be the correct and proper use of the word 'gina' (vagina). Likewise Walkerdine (1981) notes how a group of small boys of nursery age reduced their teacher to tears by refusing to stop chanting 'willy – willy . . .'

At the level of the hidden curriculum, joking, flirtation, teasing and harassment may all draw upon sexual imagery and ideas and play a part in structuring daily interactions between pupils, teachers, male and female. Davies (1983) and Wolpe (1977) and others have described how pupils, particularly girls may play out a part which involves directing their sexuality for particular objectives and may be supported in this by teachers. Wolpe reports just such an event:

> In addition this teacher defined for the class the manner in which girls should behave when trying to win the favour of a man. Text books for a particular lesson have to be collected from another male, young, equally 'mod' teacher. Mr B. selects one of the prettiest girls in the class (and also one of the cleverest) for this chore and advises her to 'go to Mr A., charm him, use a lovely voice, say thank you Sir, and smile at him when you ask for the books.

> (Wolpe 1977, p. 36)

Between pupils the characterization of girls into 'slags' and 'drags' noted by Cowie and Lees (1981), Willis (1987), Sharpe (1984) and others, and the pressure on them and particularly on boys to prove their heterosexuality, suggests that potent sexual forces can and are manipulated within peer groups in school and out. These aspects will be discussed below.

Nevertheless, because the expression of sexuality in school, appears as routine as its expression outside, it can be represented as a 'natural' background in front of which the 'real' business of school is conducted. Indeed the influence of sexual and romantic interests expressed as more visible and stable heterosexual 'pairing-off' may be something that is welcomed and even accommodated in secondary school. Such relationships appear to begin the long process of splitting and fragmenting group solidarities based on sex, and of course it is these that often are the source from which disruptive and challenging behaviour may be generated and sustained in schooling. Wolpe describes how 'pairing off' of pupils was seen as a normal part of school life, an event to be expected.

Teachers felt that such heterosexual relationships had no adverse effect on school work and did not impinge on the classroom situation at all (Wolpe 1977, p. 32). The undermining of single-sex groups that this heralds may thus have implications for discipline and control in a wider sense. The gradual drawing in and naming of pupils as 'couples' may mark their entry into some more definitive maturing process. Romantic attachments and above all the 'civilizing' influence that girls are seen to exert upon boys mark the start of those processes whereby boys take on the 'proper' male adult role of wage-earner and parent. Nevertheless, 'pairing off' may itself bring its own problems and difficulties. Steven Ball has pointed out that in Beachside Comprehensive, boys and girls preferred to form couples inside their own particular group. For example anti-school girls said that pro-school boys were '. . . "weeds" were not "modern", and did not wear the latest fashion and haircuts. They were not "a laugh", they were too serious, and too involved in doing school work' (Ball 1981, p. 69).

But pro- or anti-school behaviour is not an unambiguous matter, and many pupils see it in their interests to straddle the boundaries between these attitudes and behaviour, for example the 'knife edging' described by Measor and Woods (1984). This kind of behaviour is that which allows pupils to balance being credible and acceptable by their peers against not getting into trouble or challenging the teacher or school authority beyond certain limits. A fine distinction between humour and insult can be one that allows pupils to have a foot in both camps, for example. In these circumstances the meaning of couple-formation may involve subtle interactions and receive contrasting interpretations: on the one hand evidence of a 'domesticizing' process, or on the other 'disaffected' and challenging behaviour.

At what point does sexuality break cover and become defined as such by the school authorities? In general, it appears that teenage pregnancy, early motherhood, abortion, homosexual or very explicit heterosexual behaviour, liaisons between pupils and teachers and obvious or open sexual harassment are issues defined as 'sexual', and are points at which the school may feel the need to intervene. The recent (Autumn 1985) Manchester strike clearly illustrated this as teachers refused to teach pupils who, it was claimed, had written sexually explicit comments about them on the walls of the school thus making public what nevertheless every teacher knows pupils may say privately (see Chapter 3). In this respect sexuality seems to be recognized for the main part, only when it *goes too far*. The effect of this may be to make sexuality an issue in school only when it becomes visible. Yet as we have seen the only ways in which it can become visible are already predefined as 'problems'. This can be seen more clearly in the formal sexual curriculum.

Sex education

The presence and nature of sex education in the school curriculum is strongly influenced by motives other than the simple provision of information (see David 1983). We have referred already to the wider political and social implications and to those we may add ones based on developmental theory such as Piaget and Kohlberg, or psychological theories such as Freud. As the Goldmans suggest in their book *Children's Sexual Thinking:* 'Children are still largely regarded as asexual creatures in thought and behaviour, and childhood remains characterized as the age of innocence unaffected by an interest in sex' (Goldman and Goldman 1982, xv). This idea of innocence, characterized by Freud as 'sexual latency', seems to have shaped ideas about early sex education – pupils are seen as not being 'ready' for sexual knowledge until they near puberty, and that which is done tends to be framed in the analogy with the natural world. The Goldmans (ibid) found that only 50 per cent of their English-speaking sample had had any sex education before the age of twelve. This is despite the availability of a range of appropriate and carefully adapted resources for this age group, as catalogued in Went (1985), for example. The Goldmans found anyway that there appeared to be no latent period of sexuality and children's observation and knowledge of the sexual continued to develop and expand in the primary period between four to eleven, although it might not be marked by the urgency or anxiety of those in, or approaching, puberty. (Indeed, they argue all the more reason to start sex education early.)

For pupils themselves, puberty marks many shifts in the lives of both boys and girls. The transition to secondary school can be seen as a key moment in growing up and involves a reorientation into more instrumental schooling practices. Measor and Woods (1984) document the fears of homosexuality that boys express at this time, both its potential discovery in themselves and as a threat of assault from older boys and male teachers. For girls it may be an even more important moment in the hardening of sexual identity. As we shall discuss below a proper 'maleness' seems insisted upon earlier than 'femaleness' but as Chandler notes, however much a girl may have enjoyed her 'tomboy' years:

> Adolescent girls have little chance of denying their emergent sexuality once they have started to menstruate . . . it seems that for some women this event is greeted with such resentment that its importance has always had to be denied.
>
> (Chandler 1980, p. 27)

The fact that puberty also parallels the start of the drop in girls' achievement relative to boys (although there is evidence that this has begun to change a little) and the marked divergence in subjects chosen, characterized as 'girls into arts' and 'boys into science' is an issue that needs further exploration (Equal Opportunities Commission, 1982, Deem 1978, Whyld 1983).

A careful control of the representation of sexuality in the formal curriculum of secondary schools may go alongside its even more open and pervasive appearance in the informal curriculum of school, such that it may be impossible to ignore. Jones for example documented 'sexual tyranny' in one school in 1982, a mixed comprehensive on the outskirts of London, and reports how visual, verbal and physical harassment of girls and female teachers was always based on sexual characteristics. Girls were called 'cunts', 'slags', 'pros' and 'bitches' while giant penises were drawn on every available surface (Jones 1985, p. 30). Other accounts suggest that this is not unusual in its form although the degree and openness of it may be.

Formal sex education in the first year in secondary school generally brings what is often revealingly called a 'review of the plumbing' usually done in biology: a brief review of the facts of reproduction and some material on puberty including menstruation. In the third and fourth year, pupils usually have more intensive sex education that may, or may not set sexuality in its emotional context as well as providing the routine content of puberty, contraception, sexually transmitted diseases, pregnancy and birth and early parenthood. Our study of sex and parenthood education in secondary schools (Prendergast and Prout 1985) suggested that the input that fourth year pupils received was strongly framed in a reproductive view of sexuality and served to stress issues about how and who controlled reproduction. We analysed some of the most frequently used films in such classes.

MATURITY AND PUBERTY

The onset of puberty was seen as being marked by 'menstruation' for girls and 'becoming fertile' for boys. Whilst nevertheless the pleasure aspect for boys was dampened down the dominant impression was that girls enter a period of embarrassment, the possibility of pain, and 'learning to cope'. The reward of maturity for women seemed to be 'now you are fertile'; the unspoken message was that boys have sex but women have babies. While 'reproduction' was the framework used to describe changing bodies, boys' 'pleasure', since it is part of reproductive behaviour, had to be noted. Women's apparently is not and was therefore entirely left out.

Images of male and female

We found an interesting distinction here between representations of male and female nudity. While diagrams of the human body were often used and male erections can be shown in diagram form there were no photographs of naked men. (Similarly there was an outcry when Jane Cousins, (1978) book *Make it Happy* showed a photograph of a young man with an erection.) The clitoris and its function was usually absent from diagrams and not commented upon. However, because so much of sex education focuses on female reproduction there are many films (and books) showing actual pregnancies, births, breast-feeding and small babies and children being cared for at home. Photographs (in contrast to diagrams) were usually therefore of women. Many of these showed adult women naked and exposed in birth or breast-feeding films. No equivalent images of adult naked men were shown. Many of the images were of women either rather dazed by the pain of labour or romantically breast-feeding (in one case many women were shown naked from the waist up – obviously all with centrally heated homes!). The shift from diagram to photograph seems to signify that as women become mothers they become asexual and therefore can be safely viewed, but that there is no equivalent transition for men (see Kent and Morreau 1984).

Control of Sexuality This was generally located in expert scientific knowledge, either of biology or medicine, and was reinforced by the fact that guest speakers on sexuality or parenthood tended to be health visitors, doctors or school nurses. It often therefore appeared as though all sexuality could be reduced to reproduction – and that all reproduction was under medical control. Since the aspects of reproduction considered were mainly concerned with women's bodies the overall image is one of women controlled by doctors who are mostly male (see Prendergast and Prout 1985a for a discussion of birth films in this respect).

FRAMEWORKS AND CONTEXTS OF SEXUALITY

These films were often placed in a strong preventive framework so that avoiding pregnancy became bound up with avoiding sex. A sense was created that preventive solutions were imposed largely by adults and it was difficult for the actual concerns and interests of pupils to be acknowledged or addressed particularly in any classroom discussion. Sexuality was pictured in terms of stable, often white, middle-class, heterosexual relationships, geared towards the nuclear family in comfortable settings, all of which might be totally unrelated to much of the pupils' actual experiences. The reproductive framework filtered out any recognition that boys and girls, men and women may have different sexual experiences. Homosexuality may be noted but only briefly. Reid (1982, p. 5) says that in 1974–5 'abortion, masturbation and homosexuality were discussed with between 20 and 32 per cent of fifteen- to nineteen-year olds in English secondary schools'. Likewise there was no suggestion of either the very positive or the very negative ways in which our lives may be affected, or the power struggles that may go on between different definitions and uses of sexuality. For example, none of the wider debates around the women's movement, rape, incest or pornography were drawn upon in class discussion and contemporary changes in sexual behaviour tended to be dealt with as examples or irresponsibility and 'falling standards'.

We would suggest that films are a very potent medium in this area and dominate pupils' memory of school sex education (where it is remembered) whatever else might be discussed. Importantly they may convey to pupils and teachers alike that the film and its content is the 'official version' of an area of the curriculum about which many teachers and schools have difficulties in thinking out and expressing a view of their own. 'If there's a school film then it must be OK to show it' was a sentiment heard many times. So such films convey tacit acceptance of the images they present. Two examples from our fieldwork may illustrate this point. A film was shown of several women breast-feeding, over which a male 'doctor' narrated an account of the benefits of breast-feeding. As each new image appeared, dominated by breasts of every shape and size, many very enlarged, the women mostly half dressed, the boys whistled, laughed, cheered and made sexual comments. Amidst all the noise one boy shouted 'Can *we* have a drink now, Miss!?' In another school a birth film was being shown. The camera is pointed directly at the woman's vagina as the baby's head was born. The women's body is distended, strangely coloured, as the baby's head pushes it open. Many boys laughed and called out 'heave!' This is not to argue that all boys consiously meant to devalue women by these responses and in talking afterwards this was, clearly, not the case. What is significant surely, is that the films conveyed a sexual image of women that overlapped with and encouraged and facilitated a *collective* response from boys. They showed women as objects of the camera and our gaze, relatively passive and exposed, their bodies often distorted and ungainly in relation to the stereotyped image, ambiguously poised between the sexual and non-sexual, as women and mothers. Girls watched these films silently; often with digust, and some were angry with the boys. In both cases the messages conveyed must have been reinforced by the teachers' silence, and lack of sensitivity to girls' comments in the discussion afterwards.

Sexual control: aspects of conflict and struggle

The image of 'normal sexuality' that is conveyed in the school setting is a complex one, encompassing both the formal and the hidden curriculum; its scope touches on the family, heterosexuality, proper gender roles, images and control of reproduction. The expression of sexuality in the school setting, however, is not a static and fixed thing. Even if it is largely hidden, it is the subject of constant struggle in and by schools. This may be because, sexuality itself is such a rich and creative source of conflict and contradiction in our society. The conflict between educating pupils about 'normal' sexuality and yet warning them off it until they are beyond the age of consent is reflected in almost any school resource on the topic, as we illustrated above with examples of films. Giving information that will really allow pupils to make choices or sort out their ideas, a true 'educational' purpose, is often in conflict with preventive purposes of controlling pupils' sexuality. Getting a critical purchase on such material is not obvious or easy, and moreover requires that teachers, particularly, *want* to do it.

The messages that may come from school then may often be very contradictory: a rhetorical notion of equality between the sexes may be belied in hundreds of different ways, but the sexual hierarchy of teachers, the value placed on 'female subjects', the space given over to boys' games, and by school uniform. What happens when this 'hidden curriculum' is challenged also suggests that these are fundamental and very touchy topics. Delamont notes how (in 1977–8) a young woman teacher tried to begin a discussion about sex and gender with pupils and teachers in her school. She was asked by the headteacher to stop talking to the girls about sexuality and noted:

> If you discuss explicit aspects of domination with the girls you are immediately viewed as a subversive by the hierarchy here...All radical teachers walk on a tightrope, and feminist teachers trying like me, to create spaces with young women, face a particularly painful and exhausting struggle.
>
> (Delamont 1980, p. 80)

The ways in which boys, in particular, use sexuality to dominate girls is also expressive of particular struggles to which schools may give tacit acceptance by ignoring them. For example, Whyld (quoting from Campbell) notes eleven- to twelve-year-old girls' comments:

> It's as if boys rule us, and there's nothing you can do about it. They get girls in corridors and say 'How big are your tits?' and start feeling them up. It makes you feel sort of terrible about your body.
>
> (Whyld 1983, p. 37)

Sexual language is also deployed to reinforce boys' sexual identity and to keep girls and women in their place. Within the peer group the labelling of girls in negative sexual terms is well recorded – from the 'slags and drags' scale to the 'virgins to lays' typology noted by Wilson (ibid), and serves to remind girls that while any sexual behaviour might get her into trouble, conversely, to be asexual may also have negative consequences. Yet sexual experience in boys raises their esteem, at least for the working-class 'lads' we have the fullest accounts of, as in Willis (1977). For them, early sexual experience was seen as emphasizing masculinity and machismo.

Derogatory names for boys are equally revealing ('pouff' or 'queer' (Cowie and Lees 1981), 'bastard,' 'cunt' or 'wanker' [own observation]). If boys are allowed to be 'sexual,' there is also an overwhelming pressure on them to prove their *heterosexuality*. This anxiety is present in the minds of teachers and parents, from early nursery and infant school, where 'deviant' boys may be called a 'mummy's boy', 'girlish' or 'cissie' – a crushing insult as Browne and France (1985) record when a small boy dressed up in girls' clothes. Tony Booth notes that when he was an educational psychologist he had a boy referred to him 'for playing in the Wendy house too much.' Another Junior age boy was referred in East London as being 'odd.' He liked to talk about the buds and blossom on the trees in spring – he was said to be out of step with the other pupils! [personal communication].

Boys use a sexual language both to dominate girls and define their sexuality and reassert the virility and normality of their own identity. These strategies win symbolic and material space both for those who actively use such strategies, but also for all boys – space to believe that the world can be controlled, and controlled in a particular and elemental way, and also space to talk in class, to play freely, to demand attention. Boys' right to be sexual is not just something tacitly accepted, however, and policed by the threat of violence but is accepted more publicly. For example, Wilson's study of a group of young girls some of whom were officially defined as delinquent, found that:

> Girl offenders were treated differently, according to whether or not they appear to have been sexually active, and moreover one of the latent functions of the Juvenile Court appears to be the reinforcement of the conventional female sex role.

She notes that:

> ...female delinquency is generally assumed to be synonymous with sexual delin-quency. In contrast the sexual behaviour of boys is generally assumed to be immaterial by the Courts.
>
> (Wilson 1978, p. 72)

Boys, then, may use sexuality to express disaffection, while girls are often treated as disaffected if they fail to conform to an image of themselves as feminine but not openly sexual. One way that girls may express disaffection is by appear-ing to totally reject a 'normal' feminine appearance and conformity as in Smith's (1978) study of 'skinhead', 'Hell's Angel' or 'greaser' girls and more recently in the Punk phenomenon.

Likewise Davies (1983) describes how girls exaggerate feminine behaviour to express their identity by behaving as 'super feminine'. They may emphasize stereotyped female behaviours such as flirtation and seductiveness. This may be particularly so in relation to younger male teachers, who may encourage and reinforce such behaviour themselves.

Such display is risky, however, and may incur the penalty of being labelled a 'slag' by both boys and other girls. Passive 'feminine' behaviour, therefore, might seem a safe refuge for girls in respect of their growing sexual expression – what Anyon (1983) has called 'resistance by accommodation'. However, the result of this may be that girls pass through school virtually invisibly, making fewer demands on their teachers, receiving less attention and accepting a sexually stereotyped curriculum. These were the girls described by boys in an 'A' level English class as 'the faceless bunch' in Stanworth's study (1983).

When girls more actively resist or reject sexism itself they may be met with open aggressive action from boys. When what is resisted is both sexist and racist then the full nature of contempt and hatred that may be expressed sexually becomes very clear. The case study of Leila, a half-Turkish girl who at eleven was singled out for 'treatment' by a group of National Front boys shows how the combination of her cultural identity and her resistance, defiance and brightness in class led to a full-scale onslaught including being beaten up and pushed down stairs (Sulieman and Sulieman 1985). Similarly Brah and Minhas describe how

Asian girls are seen either as 'exotic oriental mysteries' or as 'sexual rejects...ugly, smelly, oily-haired pakkis' (1985).

Both boys and girls, then, appear to pay costs as a consequence of challenging sexual roles or in attempting to expand or utilize areas of sexuality for themselves. One could argue that Willis' 'lads' expressed their anger at the class system partly via a particularly aggressive sexuality, which cut them off from certain groups and made them an obvious target for those in authority. Likewise other boys, not belonging to the 'lads' subculture, risked definitions of their sexuality, particularly their heterosexuality by conforming more closely to school-defined goals and behaviours. However, it is suggested here that the relative costs for girls are much higher. Any choice for girls is dictated by images of femininity that can work against her. There is no image for her as an adolescent that positively reaffirms and values her as a sexual being, only the future one as a proper girl-friend, wife or mother. Moreover the question of power is important since these images are actively defined and policed in school largely by boys, although the school may generally share and underpin these values in a more basic sense by its tacit acceptance and passivity in the face of boys' activities. While not all boys are involved, nevertheless, the benefits accrue, indirectly, to most boys. Likewise most girls have to fight the consequences at some level. This may be equally true of relations between male and female teachers.

Conclusion

In this chapter we have outlined some of the ways in which sexuality is manifested in schooling; in images of pupil development, the separation of boys and girls, attitudes to the body, the form and content of sex education, sexual language and harassment etc. It is through these practices that an image of normal sexuality is both promoted and used as a template against which to define deviance. Although sexuality is generally an invisible (though powerful) factor in schooling it can at moments spring into stark outline, usually in the form of 'trouble'. Both of these forms operate to promote certain kinds of behaviour as appropriate and normal. It is precisely this, however, that allows sexuality to be used also for the expression of disaffection.

It is suggested then that sexuality is one site of a struggle between conflicting interests in school. Gender and authority relations find sexual expression in diverse and complex forms. Because of this diversity and complexity, because schools are under contradictory requirements both to educate and control, and above all because these may be at odds with pupils' needs to assert their maturity, individuality, and sexual identity, schools are a particularly rich and creative place to explore, and intervene in, the development of sexuality.

Note

Shirley Prendergast and Alan Prout are Research Associates at the Child Care and Development Group, University of Cambridge. They are currently working on a project on parenthood education in secondary schools funded by the Health Education Council. This chapter represents the views of the authors and not necessarily those of the HEC.

References

Anyon, J. 1983. 'Intersections of gender and class: accommodation and resistance by working-class and affluent females to contradictory sex-role ideologies', *in* Walker, S. and Barton, L. (eds), *Gender, class and education*, Lewes, The Falmer Press.

Ball, S. 1981. *Beachside comprehensive: a case study of secondary schooling*, Cambridge, Cambridge University Press.

Brah, A. and Minhas, R. 1985. 'Structural racism or cultural difference: schooling for Asian girls', in Weiner, G. (ed.), *Just a bunch of girls: feminist approaches to schooling*, Milton Keynes, Open University Press.

Browne, N. and France, P. 1985. 'Only cissies wear dresses: a look at sexist talk in the nursery', in Weiner, G. (ed.) *Just a bunch of girls: feminist approaches to schooling*, Milton Keynes, Open University Press.

Chandler, E. 1980. *Educating Adolescent Girls*, London, Unwin Books.

Cousin, J. 1981. *Make it Happy*, London, Virago.

Cowie, C. and Lees, S. 1981. 'Slags or drags', *Feminist Review* (9), Autumn

David, M. 1983. 'Sex, education and social policy: a new moral economy', *in* Walker, S. and Barton, L., (eds), *Gender, class and education*, Lewes, The Falmer Press.

Davies, L. 1983. 'Gender resistance and power', *in* Walker, S. and Barton, L. (eds.), *Gender, class and education*, Lewes, the Falmer Press.

Deem, R. 1978. *Women and schooling*, London, Routledge and Kegan Paul.

Delamont, S. 1980. *Sex roles and the school*, London, Methuen.

Equal Opportunities Commission, 1982. *Gender and the secondary school curriculum*, EOC Bulletin No. 6, Spring.

Goldman, J. and Goldman, R. 1982. *Children's sexual thinking*, London, Routledge and Kegan Paul.

Jones, C. 1985. 'Sexual tyranny: male violence in a mixed secondary school', *in* Weiner, G., (ed.) *Just a bunch of girls: feminist approaches to schooling*, Milton Keynes, Open University Press.

Kent, S. and Morreau, J. (eds) 1984. *Women's Images of Men*, London, Readers and Writers.

Lee, C. 1983. *The ostrich position: schooling, sex and mystification*, London, Writers and Readers.

Measor, L. and Woods, P. 1984. *Changing schools: Pupil perspectives on transfer to a comprehensive*, Milton Keynes, Open University Press.

Prendergast, S. and Prout, A. 1985a. 'The natural and the personal: reflections on birth films in school,' *British Journal of Sociology of Education*, 6, 2.

Prendergast, S. and Prout, A. 1985b. *Knowing and learning about parenthood*, Report of Education for Parenthood Project, Mimeo. HEC Library.

Reid, D. 1982. 'School sex education and the causes of unintended teenage pregnancies', *Health Education Journal*, *41*, 1. 4–11.

Sharpe, S. 1984. 'Nice girls don't', *New Socialist*, No. 16.

Smith, L. S. 1978. 'Sexist assumptions and female deliquency: an empirical investigation', in Smart, C. and Smart, S. (eds.), *Women, sexuality and social control*, London, Routledge and Kegan Paul.

Stanworth, M. 1983. *Gender and schooling: A study of sexual divisions in the classroom*, Explorations in Feminism Series, London, Hutchinson.

Sulieman, S. and Sulieman, L. 1985. 'Mixed blood – that explains a lot of things: an education in racism and sexism , in Weiner, G. (ed.), *Just a Bunch of Girls*, Milton Keynes, Open University Press.

Walker, S. and Barton, L. 1983. (eds), *Gender, class and education*, Lewes, The Falmer Press.

Walkerdine, V. 1981. Sex, power and pedagogics, in *Screen Education*, 38, 14–26.

Went, D. 1985. *Sex education: some guidelines for teachers*, London, Bell and Hyman.

Whyld, J. (ed), 1983. *Sexism in the secondary curriculum*, London, Harper and Row

Willis, P. 1977. *Learning to labour*, London, Saxon House.

Wilson, D. 1978. 'Sexual codes and conduct: a study of teenage girls', in Smart, C. and Smart, S. (eds.) *Women, sexuality and social control*, London, Routledge and Kegan Paul.

Wolpe, A. 1977. *Some processes in sexist education*, Explorations in Feminism, No. 1, London, WRRC.

26　Keeping schools in line
Len Barton

In this chapter Len Barton indicates some of the trends in education which constrain the freedom of teachers to respond flexibly to pupils. In particular he describes the increasing political control of education by central government through resource cuts and selective funding which are said to have the intention of pushing schools to 'meet the needs of industry.' The contribution of teachers has been further limited, he argues, by the abolition of the schools council, by calls for teacher evaluation, and the contradictory expectations under which they work. Pressures on teachers curtail their abilities to respond positively and effectively to the disaffection of pupils.

Everybody in our society experiences some form of schooling and as a result, education is a topic about which most people feel well qualified to talk. Yet it remains a contentious subject in which conflicting priorities and expectations are frequently expressed. Passions often run high when deeply held views on, for example, issues of standards or discipline are articulated and defended.

The difficulties in understanding the functions of schools within a society are compounded by the varied nature of schools in terms of their ethos, organization and outcomes. The practical and personal implications of this have been vividly described by a teacher who recorded his experience of being a 'relief-teacher' (Loveys 1985). Tensions arose from the range of expectations and demands encountered from heads, colleagues and pupils, as well as from a lack of clear directives from the Local Authority. In a chapter dealing with these contradictions, he says:

> So the relief-teacher is under constant pressure to prove him or herself from one school to the next, but with the *enormous variations* in school policies and head-teachers' expectations, to achieve this requires recourse to a variety of strategies...
> (Loveys 1985, p. 24, my emphasis)

Disputes about schooling are intractable because education is an inevitably political subject. As Maurice Plaskow (1985) has succinctly maintained:

> Anyone who imagines, or plaintively urges that education has nothing to do with policies has to be simple-minded. The investment of a large chunk of national resources into a compulsory and comprehensive education system is a political act. It is based on certain beliefs, assumptions, values and expectations.
> (Plaskow 1985, p. 1)

Politics is about priorities, *power* and who has the ability to devise and implement decisions. In a society and system of education characterized by gross in-equalities of allocation of resources and opportunities, such questions take on particular significance.

Increasing central control

The politics of schooling have become more and more explicit with moves towards greater overt centralized intervention. The Ruskin College speech in Oxford of the Labour Prime Minister, James Callaghan, in 1976, heralded what became known as 'The Great Debate'. This was a call for a re-examination of the purpose and nature of schooling. Some people believe that little was achieved by this means and even question the extent to which open discussion was ever realized. This interpretation seems even more plausible when one begins to appreciate, that this period culminated in the end of educational expansion and the beginning of a new aggressive form of centralized control over expenditure and curricula. Certainly, whatever previous consensus existed between politicians, teachers and others, it began to disintegrate and the demand for more accountability on the part of schools intensified. Such demands were legitimated by criticisms from a wide range of groups including politicians, industrialists and parents. It was alleged that education had failed to respond adequately to a changing industrial scene and to provide the sort of labour force an economically competitive changing world market required. Pressures for accountability were supported by allegations about declining standards in schools, increasing discipline problems, inadequate time being devoted to the basic subjects and the inappropriate nature of teaching methods (Hunter 1981).

With the introduction of a new Conservative government in 1979 the existing pressures were intensified. Policies and practices are now geared towards a much greater central control at all levels of the social system. These changes have taken place at the same time as an apparent ideological celebration of the power of the individual and the denigration of the role of the State in people's everyday affairs. A particular brand of monetarism is being urged and as a result decision-making is increasingly led by financial considerations in all institutions (Kegan 1984). The involvement by the State is not a new thing, but what is new, are the types of control being generated and implemented and the speed with which it is being accomplished (Simon 1984).

Its impact within education is particularly acute and a specific view of education is being established, one that is extemely narrow and excessively instrumental. Thus the quality and effectiveness of work within school is increasingly being judged in terms of how successfully it 'meets the needs of industry' (Finn 1982, 1984). The emphasis on vocationalism is central and in the recent White Paper on 'Better Schools' (1985) in which the future intentions of government for schools are rehearsed, it is clearly stated that: 'It is vital that schools *always* remember that preparation for working life is one of their *principal* functions (my emphasis) (DES 1985, p. 15).

Apart from the narrow view of the nature of school experience that is assumed in this statement, it fails to recognize both the extent and implications of youth unemployment. Increasing numbers of young people are facing a future in which work does not figure at all. In some areas involvement in youth training schemes can be seen as delaying the time when the majority will join the unemployed. Indeed, writers of a major study of youth unemployment in a town in the West Midlands, maintain that we are witnessing the establishment of a 'new social condition'. It is characterized by a wageless and pessimistic youth, who distrust the State, which they see as being '... concerned with regulation and control rather than help and support'. They argue that this is fundamentally a working-class experience (Youth Review Team 1985).

So, this emphasis on vocationalism and work occurs against a back-cloth of frustration on the part of increasing numbers of working-class youth. This increase has been disproportionately greater for black youth. Many young people see school as being of little relevance to their immediate and future lives and the credibility of schools can no longer rest on the promise of a job. A failure to recognize the disaffection arising from increased unemployment is likely to lead to further active or passive disruption of school (see Roberts 1984, Walker and Barton (eds.) 1986).

In the past five years particularly, intervention on the part of government in the field of education has increased enormously. The nature and control of the curriculum, introduction of a new examination system, TVEI and YTS schemes supported by the Manpower Services Commission, the control of Local Authority spending in education, the organization and future evaluation of teacher-education and the demise of the Schools Council, all testify to this trend. Indeed, with regard to the latter event, Maureen O'Connor, the education correspondent for the Guardian states:

> With the death of a representative forum on the curriculum and examinations, power shifted sharply to the centre. Senior civil servants, who had neither understood nor wanted partnership, took control.
>
> (*Guardian* 9.3.85, p. 13)

Thus, there has been a growing attempt to '... ignore, downgrade and progressively to devalue the role of teacher organizations in determining policy...' (Simon 1984, p. 23).

The involvement of the Manpower Services Commission in education has been one of the most striking features of increased centralized control. Its funding is independent of both local authorities and the Department of Education and Science. At a time of public expenditure cuts and rate capping, the large sums of money the Commission has at its disposal are a potent and seductive force in the eyes of many directors of education and school personnel who become caught in a dilemma between satisfying the demands of a powerful sponsor and using the money to meet the locally defined needs (see McMurray 1986).

Demands for greater control and monitoring of standards within school are now finding their expression in calls for a specific form of assessment and evaluation of teachers. Falling school rolls, expenditure cuts, redeployment and redundancy of teachers according to Grace (1985), have produced a climate which is conducive to raising questions about teacher competence. He maintains that such questions serve a number of useful ideological functions:

> In the first place, it diverts attention away from the effects which educational expenditure cuts *per se* are having upon educational standards and achievements by concentrating upon purported teacher deficiencies. In the second place, it legitimates policies for closer control and monitoring by implying that excessive teacher autonomy exists and in the third place it provides a useful 'quality-control' argument to be used in strategies involving the reduction of teacher numbers and of their

training institutions and in decisions involving teacher redeployment and redundancy.

(Grace 1985, p. 4)

The nature of the intervention in teacher education is far-reaching and the changes in the role of the inspectorate, the introduction and decision-making of a government-generated committee like the National Advisory Board for Local Authority Higher Education are already having their impact on the nature of the overall system and provision of teacher education courses.

Higher education generally has also suffered from, for example, cuts in funding resulting in the contraction of subjects offered to students, as well as the types and amount of research being supported and undertaken. There is more ominous interference in connection with teaching content. An editorial in *The Times Higher Educational Supplement* referred to the 'almost totalitarian interference in what is being taught' at certain institutions (*THES* 11.1.1985, 32).

Thus attempts at securing greater control over the nature of provision, including the curriculum, can be seen to be occurring at all levels of the educational system. However, given the inequalities of funding and provisions across, and even within authorities, one recognizes that centralized intervention and the pressure arising from it, may be experienced disproportionately by some teachers. Nor is one arguing that the pressures are all of equal weight or significance in the lives of all teachers, all of the time. What is being suggested is that the cumulative impact on the system generally, makes it increasingly difficult for teachers to be oblivious to such powerful attempts to control the nature of schooling and thus, the work context and conditions of teaching.

The reactions of teachers

A growing body of material from research conducted by acedemic researchers, teacher unions and the inspectorate, gives strong grounds for maintaining that within the teaching body morale is low and stress is on the increase. Little incentive or encouragement is being offered to teachers. In an NUT document entitled *Today's Teacher* the views of numerous teachers are recorded. For example one teacher argued:

> I am expected as a primary teacher to be an expert in all aspects of the curriculum; to be a competent practitioner, up-to-date on current issues, well-read, informed, prepared for change. As areas receive a national 'push' e.g. science, micros, health education, multi-cultural education, language work, mathematics, etc., I must assimilate them in my working week. At the same time, resources diminish, advisers and in-service provision are being cut back, thus denying me the support I need.
>
> (National Union of Teachers 1984, p. 21)

A teacher in Birmingham attempting to inform the readership of a local paper about the nature of teaching maintains that:

> Schools are desperately short of books and materials, which means many hours extra work preparing work sheets. We can find ourselves teaching all our free (i.e. marking/preparation) periods, covering for absent staff and doing duty through breaks and lunchtime. The most energetic find themselves on the point of collapse after a few days of this.

(Sutton 1985)

It would seem that industrial action on the part of many teachers in 1985–6 was an expression of their feelings of lack of support and adequate remuneration, for an increasingly difficult job. This was not merely a concern for personal economic gain; it was also about the quality of the education service for pupils. As a teacher of young pupils with 'special needs' argues:

> I've been conned. The harder we work, the less help we get. The more children we send out successfully, the easier it will be for them to say that we are no longer needed. The more equipment I make, the less they will spend on us. I went on strike because *it isn't only* my salary the government is skimping on. I want a fair deal for the children too, but I'm not prepared to get it for them on my hard work alone... Teachers cannot keep covering over the cracks in the system caused by massive under spending (my emphasis).
>
> (Winter 1985, p. 13)

One result, then, of the recent political push on schools has been that most teachers have become acutely aware of the outside pressures on their schools and the way these affect their work. In particular the role of the headteacher in mediating and transmitting such external forces has sometimes become dramatically apparent to both heads and staff. Headteachers do have a tremendous influence over the nature of communications within school, the ways in which change is resisted or implemented and the general ethos of the institution. They are increasingly involved in the evaluation of teachers' work and do have significant decision-making powers over the appointment and promotion of staff. Headteachers can come to be seen paradoxically as the very originators of all tension and stress. Though to do so is to ignore the significant forces which shape and constrain their actions.

Conclusion

Schools are influenced by a complex interplay of structural, institutional and interpersonal factors. It would be misleading to interpret the analysis of central intervention to imply a one-way, irresistible movement. Attempts to introduce the voucher system, to change the nature of students' grants, to close particular schools and colleges, for example, have been effectively resisted. Equally, teacher autonomy is not only limited by external constraints, it is as Alexander (1984) notes, at least as important to recognize:

> ...the constraints which the teachers themselves impose by virtue of the sort of people they are, what they believe, how they perceive children and so on.
>
> (Alexander 1984, p. 170)

Though clearly the 'sort of people' teachers are is determined, in part, by their own experience of schooling and teaching. Yet teachers are not mindless dupes of the system, they are thinking people, who individually and collectively play a part in constructing the world of schools and the social conditions outside them (see Lawn (ed.), 1985 on the role of the teacher unions). Increasingly, teachers find themselves in an invidious position as expectations increase with regard to their work and resources and encouragements are in short supply. Any critique of teaching or teachers must endeavour to understand the working conditions and constraints with which teachers are attempting to cope. Calls for teachers to understand the disaffection of pupils, cannot be effectively met while teachers themselves experience frustration, insecurity and a general lack of encouragement.

Note

I am grateful to Tony Booth and Martin Lawn for their helpful comments on an earlier draft of this paper.

References

Alexander, R. J. 1984. *Primary education*, London, Holt Education.
DES 1985. *Better Schools*, London, HMSO.
Finn, D. 1982. 'Whose needs? Schooling and the "needs" of industry', in Rees, T. and Atkinson, P. (eds.), *Youth unemployment and state intervention*, London, Routledge and Kegan Paul.
Finn, D. 1984. 'Leaving school and growing up: Work experience in the juvenile labour market', in Bates, I., Clarke, J., Cohne, P., Finn, D., Moore, R., and Willis, P., *Schooling for the dole*, London, Macmillan.
Grace, G. 1985. 'Judging teachers: the social and political contexts of teacher evaluation', in *British Journal of Sociology of Education, 6* 1, 3–16.
Hunter, C. 1981. 'Politicians rule OK? Implication for teacher careers and school management', in Barton, L. and Walker, S. (eds.), *Schools, teachers and teaching*, Lewes, Falmer Press.
Kegan, W. 1984. *Mrs Thatcher's economic experiment*, London, Allen Lane.
Lawn, M. (ed.), 1985. *The politics of teacher unionism*, London, Croom Helm.
Loveys, M. 1985. *A view from the relief teacher: an ethnography of the relief teacher's work*, B.Ed. in-service Hons. Dissertation, Westhill College, Birmingham.
McMurray, A (1986). 'TVEI and the comprehensive school: challenge or threat?', in Booth, T., Potts, P., Swann, W. (eds.), *Curricula for all: preventing difficulties in leaving*, Oxford, Blackwell.
National Union of Teachers 1984. *Today's teacher*, London, N.U.T.
O'Connor, M. 1985. 'A stab in the dark', in *Education Guardian*, 9 March, p. 13.
Plaskow, M. (ed.), 1985. *Life and death of the schools council*, Lewes, Falmer Press.
Roberts, K. 1984. *School leavers and their prospects*, Milton Keynes, Open University Press.
Simon, B. 1984. 'Breaking school rules', in *Marxism Today*, Sept, 19–25.
Spooner, R. 1981. 'On leadership and ethos', in *School Organisation, 12,* 2 107–116.
Sutton, E. F. 1985. Letter in *Birmingham Daily News*, 12 March, p. 18.
Times Higher Education Supplement 1985. 'Sir Keith's easy ride', 11 January, p. 32.
Walker, S. & Barton, L. (eds.), 1986. *Youth, unemployment and schooling*, Milton Keynes, Open University Press.
Winter, S. 1985. 'The enemy within', in *Education Guardian*, 9 April, p. 13.
Youth Review Team 1985. *The social condition of young people in Wolverhampton in 1984*, Wolverhampton Borough Council.

27   Who has the power? Memories of school strikes

Stephen Humphries

When conflicts arise in schools between teachers and pupils they may be a contest between individuals. Often there is need to attempt to keep them that way for a whole group in rowdy opposition is a spectre that is avoided and feared. Yet in all such exchanges there is a recognition that pupils have power which they can use with great effect. In this chapter Stephen Humphries' informants recall the most organized form of opposition to schooling: the pupils' strikes at the end of the last century and the beginning of this. Discontent centred around corporal punishment but there were strikes about school hours, school meals, in support of and against teachers and the celebrated cases of strikes to maintain the place of the school in the community such as that at Burston.

The most dramatic and subversive act of resistance to schooling was the pupils' strike. Recently, a few of these strikes have been rediscovered; for example, the nationwide protest of schoolchildren in 1911[1], the wave of Herefordshire school strikes[2] and the creation of an alternative strike school at the village of Burston, Suffolk, in 1914.[3] However, because such strikes were a source of acute embarrassment to teachers and education authorities, they were often conveniently forgotten and omitted from the pages of punishment books, committee minutes and official school histories, and it is only by listening to the reminiscences of people involved that we can discover the true nature and extent of this type of resistance. By scanning the press and by speaking to and corresponding with elderly people, I have discovered strikes at over a hundred other schools between 1889 and 1939, a few of which continued for periods ranging between several weeks and eighteen months. The memories of former participants are especially valuable, for they reveal a much more complex set of motives than is indicated by contemporary press reports, which normally dismissed school strikes as expressions of ignorance, indiscipline and precocious childish misbehaviour. Although most of the strikes were quickly suppressed, they were not quickly forgotten by the participants. Photographs of the strikers were often displayed in local pubs; stories of strikes were for many years recounted in families, shops and workplaces and this powerful oral tradition occasionally inspired further acts of resistance against authority.[4] For the school strike was essentially a defiant gesture of protest by working-class children and their parents against the authoritarian, bureaucratic and centralized structure of schooling that increasingly wrenched

[1] D. Marson, *Children's strikes in 1911* (Oxford, 1983).

[2] P. Horn, 'The Herefordshire schools strike of 1914', in History of Education Society, *Studies in the local history of education* (Leicester, 1977), pp. 46–52.

[3] B. Edwards, *The Burston school strike* (London, 1974).

[4] This information was obtained from my own interviews and correspondence with many old people throughout Britain who remembered school strikes.

control of education away from the local community and geared its organization to the demands of a capitalist state.

First, we will examine school strikes that were protests against the irregular or excessive infliction of corporal punishment. Such strikes were invariably instigated by pupils and tended to be of extremely short duration, rarely persisting for longer than a week and more commonly collapsing after only a few hours as a result of the coercive action of a combination of schoolteachers, attendance officers and police. This militant activity originated either as an isolated protest against the brutality of an individual teacher or as part of the nationwide wave of school strikes demanding the abolition of corporal punishment that occurred in 1889 and 1911.

Sporadic strikes are extremely difficult to document because teachers, anxious to protect their school's reputation for efficient instruction, often refused to acknowledge the existence of strikes and instead recorded them as instances of extensive truancy. Usually these isolated strikes failed to achieve their aims and resulted only in the severe and summary punishment of the participants, as Les Kenyon, recalling a strike provoked by the caning of an older boy at Gaskell Street school, Bolton, in 1914, remembers:

> I remember going on strike at school . . . over Mr Fernhall giving one of the lads stick, and around fourteen mark then, you see – I were getting ready for leaving. And he were cock at school. He were boss at school. And he'd had stick, he said, for something, for nothing, so he got us all to go on strike. And we went back to school at dinnertime, and then when whistle blew were about a dozen of us went on Mere Hall Park, and we stayed there till Mr Fernhall, Mr Smith and Mr Roshill came to school and brought us all in, and we all got four raps apiece and our name in black book. . . . Soon as they knowed we weren't in class they were all up for us. And soon as we saw 'em, well, we were all shaking. Wonder what we're going to get at t'other end. . . . We got four raps, and we got 'em off Mr Smith in his office, and they were real corkers. You blew your hands when you'd had 'em.[1]

Occasionally, however, strikes such as the following one, which occurred in Manchester in 1924, succeeded in bringing the assaults of assistant teachers on children to the attention of a sympathetic headmaster, who subsequently exercised more rigorous control over the irregular forms of corporal punishment inflicted in their schools.

> One of the boys had been sent out into the corridor for misbehaving, and this teacher come along. 'What are you doing here Hannam?' 'Oh', he said, 'Mr Smith has sent me out 'cos I've been misbehaving myself'. He said, 'Oh, well, you'd better go to the headmaster then, hadn't you?' Well, it wasn't his place to tell him to go to the headmaster, 'cos he wasn't his pupil. Well, this lad wouldn't go, and he [the teacher] thumped him in the stomach, said he was being cheeky. And he was seen by one of the boys in the classroom, and all went on strike over it. First, at lunchtime we went up to the headmaster's office, but he'd gone for lunch, so when I got back (I used to go home for my lunch), the boy that was organizing the strike, he come up to me and said, 'Spence, we're going on strike. Are you with us?' I said, 'Yes, I'm with you, I'm with you'. And we went to the hills . . . we played all sorts of games up on

---

[1] Interview no. E.134, p. 61. Quoted in P. Thompson. 'The war with adults', in T. Vigne (ed.) *Oral History*, vol.3 no. 2 (1975), p. 33.

the hills and kicked a ball about, and we were out for over two hours...And anyway, eventually we agreed to go back, providing there were no repercussions, providing nobody was to get caned or anything. And we went into the headmaster's office. He said, 'Well, I appreciate you boys standing together and working for one another, but you shouldn't take the law into your own hands. You should have come to my office and told me about it.' So I said, 'We did do, but you weren't available. You weren't there.' I remember when we got back into the classroom the teacher said, 'Who was on strike?' So I put my hand up and one or two more. 'So you were one of the heroes, were you, Spencer?' But that teacher never used the cane again. He got admonished for it.[1]

Whereas these isolated protests often passed unrecorded in the official records, the nationwide waves of school strikes in 1889 and 1911 aroused widespread public interest and concern. The 1889 school strikes originated in Hawick, Roxburgh, at the beginning of October and rapidly spread throughout the Scottish lowlands, the Tyneside area and as far south as London, Bristol and Cardiff.[2] The 1911 strike began at Bigyn School, Llanelli, on 5 September, when pupils deserted their classrooms and paraded the streets after a boy was punished for passing around a piece of paper urging his friends to strike.[3] During the following two weeks the strike spread to schools in over sixty major towns and cities throughout Britain.[4]   The rapid diffusion of strikes in both 1889 and 1911 was viewed by most commentators as a consequence of the conformity, gullibility and unlimited capacity for blind imitation of working-class children and youths. This claim was substantiated by the fact that most major school strikes tended to occur at times and places at which parents were engaged in either local or national strike action and by the sensational publicity given to the children's activities by the popular press. Thus, the editor of the *Educational News* in 1911, for example, confidently assured his readers that

> the cause...is easy to find. Men tired of work...strike. 'Striking' conversations are meanwhile carried on in their homes to the detriment of all else. Naturally, children are possessed of powers of...imitation, waiting only to be called into play...Hence 'strikes', being the fashion with adults, become likewise that of the juveniles. The daily press has done much to spread the epidemic; for instead of paying little heed to the pranks of the scholars in one or two towns, has published full details...and a real game of 'Follow the Leader' has been the result.[5]

However, oral evidence indicates a more subversive explanation for school strikes, one that is related to deep-rooted class conflict. The characteristic features of both these major strikes – notably their nationwide scale, the widespread use of pupil pickets and street marches and demonstrations – were all derived from the practices of the emerging labour movement. Interviews clearly

---

[1] Interview no. M.272. Born 1912, Broughton, Manchester, Decorator. Father decorator and glazier.
[2] See *Scotsman*, 9 October 1889, p. 7.
[3] *Llanelli Mercury*, 7 September 1911.
[4] The information for the diffusion of school strikes in 1889 is based upon my own research into local press reports in all the major towns and cities throughout Britian. Information concerning the extent of the 1911 strikes is based primarily upon Marson's *Children's Strikes in 1911* but is supplemented with references to other strikes that I have myself discovered in newspapers and school logbooks.
[5] *Educational News*, September 1911, p. 968.

reveal that working-class children learned strategies of collective bargaining and resistance from the parent culture and practised them at moments when they seemed most likely to succeed – moments when the local working-class community was locked in industrial conflict.[1] And although sensational press reports did indeed act as the principal agency of transmission for information concerning the strikes, most of the participants were inspired by more serious motives than the infantile foolishness and frivolity attributed to them by journalists. For, as Joe Hopwood remembers, the bitter experience of regular canings led many children to resort to strike activity in the hope that it might prove to be as powerful a weapon in the hands of pupils as it was for parents in securing fundamental rights, such as the abolition of corporal punishment.

> The teachers was hard in they days. They did cane you just for a little mistake in your work, you know. I've still got a mark on me finger where the teacher caned me. Well, there was a lot of fathers out on strike in Bristol in 1911. And on my way to school I saw on the content bill outside the newspaper shop: 'The London Schoolchildren on Strike For No Cane'. I run down the lane into the playground an' started it. 'Come on, out on strike! Come on up the top an' see the bill.' And they all see'd it an' there was forty or fifty of us, and we all marched out of St Silas round the other schools to get the others out, singing an' shouting. We were going to get everyone out, then bide out 'til they says, 'No more cane'. But they locked em in by the time we arrived. It didn't work, so then we said, 'Come on, we'll go back'. That was the only time I remember playing truant, on that strike. We thought it might have done good, but it didn't. It done worse. They were just more determined. We got back 'bout twelve an' the headmaster lined us all up, 'Come on, hold 'em out!' an' we 'ad three of the best on the hand.[2]

Although children who despised school work enthusiastically joined the ranks of the strikers, interviews suggest that some strike leaders were in fact successful school pupils or were the sons and daughters of socialists and militant trade unionists. This socialist presence in school strikes was also detected by the popular press – for example, in October 1889, when a correspondent of the *Pall Mall Gazette* noted the four or five hundred boys who marched through the streets in the neighbourhood of Bethnal Green making the street echo with their cries of 'No more cane' were headed by a couple of boys carrying ... red flags and wearing scarlet liberty caps.[3] Indeed, in Dundee, which experienced the most prolonged and disruptive school strikes in Britain in both 1889 and 1911, involving several thousand pupils, the local press suspected that the children's uprising was part of a wider left-wing conspiracy to subvert the social order – a fear clearly expressed in the doom-laden warnings of the *Dundee Advertiser*:

> It has not yet been ascertained through what medium schoolboys received the signal for united action ... Such movements as this do not spring up spontaneously. They are always evidence of a deep conspiracy against social order ... It is perfectly

---

[1] It is significant that the nationwide waves of school strikes in October 1889 and September 1911 occurred in months and years in which industrial conflict was particularly intense, and my research has revealed a close correspondence between the strike action of parents and of pupils in particular localities.

[2] Born, Eastville, Bristol, 1900. Lamplighter. Father, canal boatman.

[3] *Pall Mall Gazette*, 10 October 1889, p. 7.

evident that the schoolboys from Land's End to John o' Groats could not without organization arrange to strike simultaneously. The doom of the Empire must be near at hand if the country is honeycombed...with Secret Societies of schoolchildren...[1]

The contrast between the severe retribution administered by schools and the relatively lenient approach of parents can be seen in the memories of Bernard Dennison, who escaped punishment at home, despite the fact that he was discovered to have concealed his involvement in the strike from his disapproving mother.

> Several women, including my mother, were out in the street talking about the strike, and they asked me if I'd been one of the strikers. I said 'No'. My mother said, 'I thought he wouldn't be a striker'. It seemed I was safe because my mother could give a good hiding if it was necessary. Now the funniest part of the story is that about a fortnight after the strike one of my older brothers, who was a lemonade salesman, served the Rose Bush House and saw a photograph of the strikers which had been taken by the pub landlord, and he had had it enlarged. And there, slap bang in the front row, was one of my brothers, with his head, and shoulders almost into the camera, and I was in the middle of the group. Well, we were cross-examined about the strike, but my brother and I still denied being in it, then my older brother produced the photograph. We were stunned. We couldn't keep our lie any longer, so we had to admit being out on strike. So all our family had a good laugh about how we'd been caught out. But it was different at school. The day after the strike the headmaster had us out one by one and gave us a rap of the cane on each hand, and he had the ringleaders out bent over the desk, and they had to have four strokes across their backsides. And, strange as it may seem, after our sentences were meted out the strike was hardly ever mentioned again.[2]

Interviews suggest that brutal canings acted as an effective deterrent and that the memory of these savage reprisals helped considerably in discouraging any future attempts to stage a nationwide strike. Even Clyde Roberts, a West Indian youth with a local reputation for physical strength and tenacity who led the 1911 school strikes in Cardiff's dockland area, was frightened into submission by the beating he received from his schoolmaster.

> Somalis National [School], in Bute Terrace, I'm going there. And I led 'em out on strike. I led the school out on strike. I was supposed to be the ringleader. So we marched down to North Church Street school, trying to get them out. Anyhow, when we got back, we had a schoolmaster, name was Mr Hobbs, so I got singled out. And he said to me, he said, 'I'm going to put the fear of God into you'. He did. There was a boy [on] each of the arms, legs, over the desk, and he didn't half whack me... He was the only schoolmaster that I can say I was frightened of. I was dead scared of him after that lot.[3]

So far we have focused on school strikes that sought to abolish corporal punishment. There were also a number of strikes that aimed to reduce the

---

[1] *Dundee Advertiser*, 11 October 1889, p. 5.
[2] Letter to author. Born Hull, 1900. Confectionery van salesman. Father, inspector for shipping firm, then egg and butter merchant.
[3] Interview no. E.452, pp. 84–85. Born 1899, Cardiff. Merchant seaman, labourer, later foreman. Father, merchant seaman.

amount of time that children were compelled to spend attending to their lessons by agitating for reduced school hours, extended holidays or a lowering of the school-leaving age. Often these demands, the most common of which were a shortened school day from 10 a.m. to 3 p.m., one free afternoon a week, an eight-week summer vacation and no homework, emerged as subsidiary claims of militants during the nationwide anti-caning strikes of 1889 and 1911.[1] But in a number of instances strikes were staged specifically to achieve a reduction in school hours, and although such demands met with repressive measures similar to those administered to children who wished to abolish the cane, a well-argued case for moderate reform occasionally received a sympathetic hearing. For example, Joseph Proctor, who together with some other members of the St Paul's school football team in Oswaldtwistle, Lancashire, went on strike in 1911, remembers that despite severe chastisement, his headmaster was impressed by his written statement that sport should be played in school hours.

> We read about the strike of schoolboys in the paper, so at dinnertime the elder boys amongst us decided to strike in sympathy. After dinner about twenty of us went parading the streets with a home-made banner that we made out of a placard from a newspaper shop fastened to a broom handle we borrowed from a hardware shop. We never got the chance to go to other schools, though that was our intention, because we were rounded up so quickly and returned to our teacher, Mr Wilson. He gave us three of the best on each hand. Also, we had to stay after school and write an essay on it and our views on strikes. The cane was rarely used at our school and our strike was really for time off lessons twice a week to train for sports. It was mainly sporty types in the football team who were involved. We would have liked to have an hour off in the afternoon because it was after school hours that we played our football matches with other schools. I remember in the essay I had to write I was strongly in favour of sport in school time instead of after school. The headmaster read it and saw me the next day, and I had to rewrite my essay on separate pieces of paper. These were pinned up along the corridor of the school, so my essay must have been pretty good.[2]

The campaign for shorter school hours and the abolition of homework was not simply an expression of the perverse and wilful nature of children, as was assumed by some journalists and educationists. In fact, they can be seen as reasonable and justifiable claims, for homework was often impossible in the gloomy and overcrowded conditions that prevailed in most working-class homes, and the rote learning and regimentation that dominated the school day placed an intolerable burden on many children, already exhausted by the domestic chores, child-minding duties and part-time jobs that were necessary for family survival. Indeed, although most commentators insisted that the strikes should be ruthlessly suppressed, some admitted that they were perhaps a symptom of the psychological 'over-pressure' on children produced by the system of payment by results, whereby pupils were 'crammed' with facts by teachers in preparation for the annual inspection, so that their school would qualify for a government grant.

[1] See D. Marson, *Children's strikes in 1911*, pp. 1–23, and other press reports of the 1889 strikes cited in the footnotes.
[2] Letter to author. Born 1898, Oswaldtwistle, Lancashire, Army, Father, daily farmer.

The disruption caused by the 1889 school strikes was one minor factor that led to abolition of this iniquitous system in the 1890s.[1]

Statutory increases in the school-leaving age were viewed even more seriously as a threat to the domestic economy of the working-class family. The desperation of poor families found expression in April 1914, when children and parents in Bedworth, Exhall and other villages in north-east Warwickshire resorted to strike action in order to resist the local authority's attempts to raise the school-leaving age from thirteen to fourteen. The struggle to assert community control over the duration of children's schooling persisted for several weeks and involved protest meetings, a petition signed by almost 6000 local people and a parentally supported pupils' strike. Militant action occurred in this particular area primarily because there was a huge demand for seasonal child labour in the locality, and to terminate the protest the education authority was forced to make a number of minor concessions, assuring parents that no children aged over thirteen from large families would be immediately prosecuted for non-attendance.[2]

Closely related to the widespread feeling among working-class people that compulsory schooling should not impose severe financial hardship upon families was the belief that free school meals should be provided, particularly in times of economic distress.[3] To achieve this aim a school strike was declared in the villages of Washington and Usworth in County Durham, where in 1917, because of prolonged half-time working in the local pits and high unemployment, many families were reported to be on the verge of starvation. A mass meeting of local miners held on 18 November 1917 unanimously resolved to instruct the children not to attend school until the local authorities implemented the Feeding of Necessitous School Children Act, whereby children suffering from malnutrition were entitled to free meals.[4] The following day over a thousand children from nine local schools responded to the strike call, thus risking corporal punishment, in a spirit of class solidarity that was remarked upon in the local press.

> Those few children who did attend school – mostly the children of officials, shopkeepers and soldiers – were the subject of no little contempt and abuse. Yesterday the writer observed an incident near Usworth station illustrative of this attitude. A group of ragged boys was sitting on a fence, languidly throwing stones at a telegraph post across the way. Down the road came a more respectably dressed youngster across whose shoulders was slung a dilapidated satchel. As he drew near the lads on the fence he crossed to the opposite side of the way and with face half-averted and his hands stuck deep in his pockets, he began to whistle with affected nonchalance. The boys on the fence ceased their assault upon the telegraph post and when he came abreast of them they burst into loud, shrill shouts of abuse. 'Yah!' they cried. 'Blackleg! Blackleg! Scallywag!' The object of their abuse proceeded onwards at a slightly accelerated pace and the boys on the fence with bewildering rapidity hurled a series of questions at his retreating figure. What did he mean by

[1] See, for example, *Educational News*, 5 October 1889, p. 167; 12 October 1889, p. 702; 26 October 1889, pp. 738, 739; *Scotsman*, 9 October 1889, p. 7; *Truth*, 10 October 1889, pp. 640, 641, and 17 October 1889, p. 684.

[2] See *Bedworth Observer*, 8 April 1914, p. 5, and 15 April 1914, p. 5; *Education*, 6 March 1914, p. 141, and 24 April 1914, p. 265.

[3] See, B. Simon, *Education and the Labour Movement* (London, 1965), pp. 133–7, 278–286.

[4] *Sunderland Daily Echo*, 19 November 1917, p. 4, and 21 November 1917, p. 5.

going to school? Hadn't he heard of the Lodge resolution? Was he afraid? Did he think he'd get wrong? Then altogether, 'Cowardly, cowardly-custard!' they yelled.[1]

Confronted by the fierce resistance from parents and children, the authorities conceded defeat on the second day of the strike, and miners' families were awarded increased financial assistance and relief from the Durham County Prince of Wales Fund.[2]

Another way in which pupils and parents sought to assert community control over provided education, was through strikes to support the retention of teachers whose position was threatened by local authority interference, or to press for the dismissal of unpopular or incompetent teachers. The most prolonged and powerful strike action brought by pupils occurred in Herefordshire in 1914, when children supported the country's National Union of Teachers members' militant demands for salary increases. The children's resistance began at the beginning of February, when, in response to the union's strategy of mass resignations, the local education authority appointed new teachers, many of them unqualified, to replace those involved in the dispute. Pupils in towns and villages throughout the country expressed sympathy for their former teachers, who were among the lowest paid in the country, by refusing to be taught by the new members of staff, and seventy schools were forced to close. The most violent scenes occurred at Ledbury Girls' School, where a riot developed in which desks were overturned, and the new headmistress was chased off the premises by a crowd of girls chanting 'Blackleg'. And at Ross, although boys demonstrating in the town in favour of the strike were captured and locked inside the school, they retaliated by vandalizing the classrooms and escaping through some open windows. A bitter conflict ensued, in which the former members of staff enjoyed the enthusiastic support of pupils, parents, school managers and the press, and in the following weeks the Board of Education was forced to intervene to settle the dispute, successfully applying pressure on the Herefordshire education authority to re-instate the teachers and to award substantial salary increases.[3]

Another situation in which pupils and parents occasionally resisted education authority dictates was when economies in local government spending were made by dismissing members of staff considered to be superfluous. Married women were often the prime victims of these education cuts and were discharged indiscriminately on the grounds that they would suffer least personal hardship from the termination of their employment.[4] However, these measures aroused considerable resentment, and a strike was staged at Eastwood Council School, Keighley, Yorkshire, in September 1922 as a protest against the local council's decision to dismiss Mrs Belfield, the headmistress of the girls' department, who had taught in the town for over twenty years. Mrs Belfield had inspired the admiration and affection of the local community through her success in capturing children's interest in learning and through her involvement of parents in a variety

---

[1] Ibid., 21 November 1917, p. 5.
[2] Durham County Chronicle, 23 November 1917, pp. 2, 3.
[3] This account is based on Horn. 'The Herefordshire School Strike of 1914.'
[4] For the background to the dismissal of married treachers in Keighley, Yorkshire, see *Keighley News*, 28 February 1922, p. 8; 8 April 1922, p. 9; 3 June 1922, p. 7; 15 July 1922, p. 13.

of social and educational activities that revolved around the school.[1] The strike was the culmination of several months' agitation by the parents and pupils, who petitioned the local education committee and their Member of Parliament, then, receiving no satisfaction, resolved to strike on the day that the newly appointed headmistress was due to replace Mrs Belfield.[2] Although Mary Slater was just nine years old when the strike occurred, and was therefore only vaguely aware of its precise purpose, her recollections vividly recreate the militant atmosphere, with picketing girls threatening blacklegs with doffers' bumps – an initiation ceremony for young doffers practised in local worsted mills, in which the victim was lifted up by two assailants and banged on her bottom several times.

> It was a well-run school at that time. It was considered one of the good schools, and Mrs Belfield was such a lovely headmistress. She was one of those kind, gentle sort of women. Everybody liked her... Well, there'd been this talk about Mrs Belfield having to leave, but I was too young to bother about what it was all about, and that we'd be going on strike. All I can remember is going to school this particular morning, me and two more girls that I went with. We turned the corner into the street where the school was, Marlborough Street. It was absolutely chock-a-block with scholars, just crowded in the street. All the length of the school was thick with folk, pretty solid, and parents intermingled, mothers not fathers. We got right up to the front, us little ones. We all stood outside, and at the school railings there were quite a few boards tied on. 'We Want Mrs Belfield Back' and things like that, about not coming back 'til Mrs Belfield returned. Then I've just the vaguest recollection of seeing the school door open and somebody push somebody out, and then somebody said, 'What happens if anybody goes in?' And they said, 'Oh t'prefects are in there and they'll give 'em t'doffers bump and shove 'em out'. So this must have been somebody that had gone in that they'd shoved out.[3]

The strike collapsed on the second day, principally because of Mrs Belfield's strong disapproval of the action, the refusal of any boys or members of staff to participate in the protest and the promises made by the new headmistress that she would ensure that her staff did not inflict corporal punishment upon girls for acts of disobedience.[4]

Strikes that demanded the resignation of unpopular and despised teachers were more likely to succeed, for the prospect of prolonged hostility and harassment from pupils and parents was a source of acute embarrassment and concern to both the teacher and the local education authority. Ada Iles recalls one such strike in Fishponds, Bristol, in 1911, which resulted in the transfer of a teacher who was accused of inflicting unjust and unnecessary punishments upon pupils.

> The strike started because of a teacher who was always down on the boys. When one of 'em was messing around in class, instead of finding out who it was an' making that person stop 'alf an 'our, he'd keep the whole class in day after day. Well, there was a miners' strike on, an' George Hesketh said, 'We'll 'ave a strike. We won't go to

---

[1] I am indebted to Ian Dewhirst, Reference Librarian, Keighley Library, for this information, which was obtained from the Eastwood school log book and from the recollections of his mother, a former pupil at the school.

[2] See *Keighley News*, 15 and 29 July 1922; 2 September 1922.

[3] Interview by Ian Dewhirst. Born Keighley, Yorkshire, 1912. Shorthand typist then housewife. Father, book-keeper at joinery works.

[4] See *Keighley News*, 2 September 1922, p. 7; 9 September 1922, p. 7.

school'. George was the ringleader, an' 'im an' about six other boys stopped by the gate an' stopped everybody from going into school for two days. Everybody was standin' outside the school refusing to move, an' they 'ad some talks, an' Education Committee moved this teacher to another school . . . so we'd won an' everyone went back.[1]

The final area of conflict with education authorities was the important issue of the location and organization of schools. Most of these strikes occurred during the inter-war period as a protest against the process of centralization and rationalization promoted by the Hadow Report, by which elementary schools were reorganized into age-segregated units, redesignated as infant, junior and senior schools.[2] The fundamental grievances that provoked these strikes were the local authorities' failure to consult parents or to consider their needs prior to the implementation of reorganization plans, the removal of children from schools situated within the local community to centralized units and, most important, the threat to the health and safety of children who were forced to walk long distances to their new schools, for in areas of economic distress, where many children were deprived of adequate food and clothing, parents were reluctant to allow them to walk several miles to school each day.

This type of school strike was not restricted to rural areas, however, for a number occurred in various towns and cities, where the main issues that provoked militant action were the excessive distances and danger from traffic to which children were exposed in attending reorganized schools. In addition, the transfer of pupils from neighbourhood to centralized schools disrupted the domestic arrangements of the working-class household, as long distances made it difficult for children to return home for a midday meal and restricted the time and energy available for child-minding duties and part-time jobs. Although the number of parents and children involved in these strikes often dwindled when local education committees commenced prosecutions for non-attendance, direct action in both urban and rural areas often won concessions from the authorities, such as the provision of free dinners and bus services, and occasionally resulted in official submission to the strikers' demands. Many of the strikes deserve detailed case studies, which cannot be attempted here; however, one important point that emerges from these protests must be emphasized again. Strikes instigated by parents provide further evidence that children's resistance within schools can best be understood in terms not of generational conflict but rather of a broader class conflict, in which the working-class community became increasingly alienated from, and antagonistic towards, the bureaucratic state schooling system. Indeed, the contemporary press views these strikes precisely in this way, as expressions of a growing conflict between the local community and the school authorities, and there was widespread concern that the militant action of working-class parents would encourage children to follow their example of determined resistance to authority, which might have disastrous consequences. Thus, for example, the East Ham dispute – which extended from July to October 1929, involved hundreds of parents and over a thousand pupils and was only finally

---

[1] Born 1904, Fishponds, Bristol. Bus conductress. Father, bricklayer.
[2] Board of Education, *The Education of the Adolescent, Report of the Consultative Committee* (Hadow Report) (London, 1927)

resolved through central government intervention – provoked *Everybody's Weekly* to comment:

> There has never been a more iniquitous thing than the toleration of strikes by school children. This deplorable practice was begun a few years ago and now, at the least real or fancied wrong, out come the children . . . At present kids treat it as a rare lark. They get an extra holiday, they play at holding meetings, gain notoriety, enjoy hero worship from other children and get their photo in the newspaper. But what of the future? In the unmoulded minds of these children have been sown the seeds of discontent and the idea of active resistance to discipline which will lead to no end of trouble. In most cases they occur at the instigation and with the approval of the parents . . . who . . . should be made punishable by law.[1]

So far we have examined the origins, the nature and the consequences of several interrelated types of school strike. The final form of defence available to parentally supported strikers in their disputes with the education authorities was the formation of an independent strike school. Although this option was theoretically open to all dissatisfied parents, it was rarely attempted or achieved in practice, principally because of the enormous legal and financial difficulties that such action involved for people whose overriding concern was economic survival. However, in two strikes, those at Newmains and Burston, the local working-class community did manage to overcome these formidable obstacles and to establish alternative strike schools; its resistance must be briefly described here, for in many ways the schools represented the most subversive achievement of the school strike.

The Newmains strike began in January 1929, in opposition to the Scottish Education Department's policy of centralization, which in this instance involved the Lanarkshire Education Authority in transferring senior pupils from the mining village of Newmains to Beltanefoot school, Wishaw, over three miles away.[2] For eighteen months over 150 senior pupils and their parents stubbornly refused to comply with this directive, claiming that the long walk was a hazard to health and safety, that it undermined the domestic arrangements of many families and that it was an essentially bureaucratic measure that could easily be avoided by adapting the available space at Newmains school for the purpose.[3] There was a strong feeling that, as one protestor put it, 'the whole basis of the scheme was to provide highly paid posts for specialized teachers'. The professional classes were becoming the 'moochers on the industrial classes'.[4] The strike aroused the support and solidarity of the entire local community. Regular protest meetings and demonstrations were organized; sympathetic strikes of junior pupils at Newmains school and in the surrounding villages of Morningside and Cambusnethan were staged, and senior pupils, acting on parental instructions, occupied their former school after being refused admission.[5] Despite

[1] *Everybody's Weekly*, quoted in *East Ham Echo*, 13 September 1929, p. 2.
[2] See *Glasgow Herald*, 5 April 1929, p. 7.
[3] *Glasgow Herald*, 26 September 1929, p. 8; 30 September, p. 12; 14 October, p. 10.
[4] Mr May, quoted in *Glasgow Herald*, 31 December 1929, p. 10.
[5] *Glasgow Herald*, 25 September 1929, p. 15; 27 September, p. 10; 28 September, p. 10; 29 September, p. 6; 1 October, p. 2.; 2 October, p. 14; *Hamilton Herald and Lanarkshire Weekly News*, 3 October 1929, p. 6; *Glasgow Herald*, 18 March 1930, p. 7.

harassment from the local education authority and successful prosecutions against six parents, the villagers remained resolute, and their protest was finally vindicated in July 1930, when an inquiry by the Scottish Education Department recommended severe modification of the original scheme for the area and permitted first- and second-year senior pupils to remain at Newmains school.[1] One important strategy adopted in the dispute, which enabled parents to evade attendance regulations, to ensure a basic education for their children and to maintain militant action for a long period, was the formation of a strike school, staffed by five volunteers, in the local church hall.[2]

In contrast to the Newmains dispute, the Burston school strike and the pupils' and parents' formation of a strike school has been documented in much more detail. The strike originated as a protest against the dismissal of Kitty and Tom Higdon from their teaching posts in the Suffolk village of Burston in the spring of 1914. The rector and school managers fabricated a number of charges against them, which included the brutal infliction of corporal punishment on two orphan children, who were pressurized into incriminating their teachers. This conspiracy was engineered by a group of local notables who sought to remove the Higdons from the village, for they were socialists and trade union activists, deeply involved in politicizing and unionizing agricultural labourers in the area.[3] However, both pupils and parents in the village were incensed by this victimization, and a strike, in which schoolgirl Violet Potter played a prominent role, was planned for the day on which the Higdons were due to be replaced by new members of staff. In an account written at the time one of the young militants, Emily Wilby, vividly recreates the local community's intense solidarity, its resistance to harrassment by the authorities and its determined efforts to create an alternative strike school.

We came on strike on April 1st, 1914. We came on strike because our governess and master were dismissed from the council school unjustly. The parson got two Barnardo children to say that our governess had caned them and slapped their faces, but we all knew she did not . . . Governess did not know we were going on strike. She brought us all some Easter eggs and oranges the last day we were at the council school. Violet Potter brought a paper to school with all our names on it, and all who were going on strike had to put a cross against their name. Out of seventy-two children, sixty-six came out on strike . . . The next morning the sixty-six children lined up on the Crossways. We all had cards round our necks and paper trimmings. We marched past the Council school . . . Mrs Boulton, the lady at the Post Office, gave us some lemonade and sweets and nuts. She also gave us a large banner and several flags . . . Mr Starr, the Attendance Officer, sent our mothers a paper saying if they did not send their children to school they would be summonsed, but our mothers did not care about the papers; some put them on sticks and waved them . . . One day a policeman went round to twenty houses with summonses because we had not been to school . . . at Court the fine was half-a-crown each . . . The next day our mothers thought we might begin school on the Common while it was fine weather. We had school on the Common a little while, then we went

[1] *Glasgow Herald*, 16 November 1929, p. 7; 14 December, p. 12; 17 December, p. 3; 14 May 1930, p. 8; 5 July, p. 10; 31 July, p. 5.
[2] *Galsgow Herald*, 27 April 1929, p. 9; 21 August, p. 9; 18 January 1930, p. 7.
[3] See Edwards, *The Burston School Strike*, pp. 13–44.

into the very cottage that the Barnardo children had lived in for a year and a half.
Our mothers lent stools, tables, chairs, etc. Mr Ambrose Sandy said we could have
his [carpenter's] shop for a strike school. Sam Sandy came and whitewashed it out
and mended the windows. He put a ladder up so that we could go upstairs. Our
mothers were soon summonsed again . . . Our parents did not have to pay a penny of
the fine. It was all collected on the Green and in the streets.[1]

The villagers' struggle attracted national publicity and became a celebrated
cause of the labour and trade union movement, which contributed funds for the
building of a strike school. Violet Potter, the pupils' strike leader, remembers the
short speech she made when the school was opened in 1918.

I stood on the steps of this school in front of crowds of people at seventeen years of
age, and opened this school. I remember what I said to this day. 'With joy and
thankfulness I declare this school open to be for ever a school of freedom.'[2]

The strike school continued for two decades in opposition to the state system,
bestowing upon the village children a political education that stressed the values
of socialism, internationalism and trade unionism.[3]

To conclude, although strike schools were an extremely rare phenomenon,
they possess a broader significance than their incidence suggests, for they encap-
sulated the demand for community control over education that, on a wider scale,
was intrinsic to all the school strikes we have examined. The school strike was an
expression of the resistance of the local working-class community to the abuse of
fundamental rights by the authoritarian and bureaucratic organization of state
schooling.

[1] Emily Wilby. 'Our School Strike,' quoted in Edwards, *The Burston School Strike*, pp. 116–18.
[2] Violet Porter, quoted in Edwards, *The Burston School Strike*, p. 179.
[3] Edwards, *The Burston School Strike*, pp. 9–12, 112–69.

28 'A proper regard for authority': regulating schools by rights

Peter Newell

'A proper regard for authority' was one of the attributes that the 1986 Education Bill expected headteachers to instil in their pupils. In this chapter Peter Newell suggests that the regulation of the conduct of members of a school community should not reside in the authority of teachers but in the acceptance of a framework of rights binding on all school members. He discusses the extent to which schools conform to the Articles of the European Convention for the Protection of Human Rights, mentions the rights of school students upheld by courts in the USA and gives an account of the way the White Lion Street Free School, of which he was a founder, attempted to base the relationships of adults and young people there on an agreed set of principles.

A framework of rights

In March 1984, the European Parliament adopted a resolution on freedom of education which amongst other laudable and uncontroversial statements insisted that: 'The school system must comply with the relevant provisions of the European Convention for the Protection of Human Rights and Fundamental Freedoms.'[1]

In March 1985, the Committee of Ministers of the Council of Europe recommended to member states (including the UK) that:

> Democracy is best learned in a democratic setting where participation is encouraged, where views can be expressed openly and discussed, where there is freedom of expression for pupils and teachers, and where there is freedom and justice.... The study of human rights in schools should lead to an understanding of, and sympathy for, the concepts of justice, equality, freedom, peace, dignity, rights and democracy. Such understandings should be both cognitive and based on experience and feelings...'[2]

Apparently unaware of its involvement and commitment to these Euro-moves, in 1986 the Government has busied itself with introducing a new Education Bill,[3] which could well have been about promoting all these high ideals; instead, among its provisions is one which will prohibit anyone under 18 being appointed as a school governor (currently in 1986, hundreds of fifteen-, sixteen- and seventeen-year olds are fulfilling this role in secondary schools in many parts of the

---

[1] Resolution on 'Freedom of Education in the European Community,' passed by the European Parliament, 14 March 1984.
[2] Recommendation NoR(85)7 of the Committee of Ministers of the Council of Europe to member States on the teaching and learning about human rights in schools, adopted by the Committee of Ministers, 14 May 1985. Council of Europe Directorate of Information, BP431, R6 F-67006, Strasbourg Cedex France.
[3] Education Bill 1986 London HMSO. This is due to receive royal assent in November 1986.

country).[1] Another provision gives the head teacher the role of determining measures.

> which may include the making of rules and provisions for enforcing them, to be taken with a view to:
> 1 promoting among pupils self-discipline and a proper regard for authority;
> 2 encouraging good behaviour on the part of pupils;
> 3 securing that the standard or behaviour of pupils is acceptable; and
> 4 otherwise regulating the conduct of pupils.

Is it surprising that the Government has also found it necessary to write into the Bill a reserve power for local education authorities, who in some circumstances will be able 'to take such steps as they consider are required to prevent the breakdown, or continuing breakdown, of discipline at the school?'

In the UK, successive governments have consistently reiterated their commitment to respecting the European Convention of Human Rights[2]; it is a Convention with no age limit, and its protection certainly doesn't – or shouldn't – stop at the school gates, as the European Parliament confirmed.

Yet how many schools have considered the articles in the Convention in relation to their own aims and practices? How many local education authorities have thought of incorporating some of the rights and freedoms guaranteed in the Convention into revised articles of government? And how much legitimate disaffection would disappear if they did so, and provided their students with enforceable procedures to safeguard their rights and freedoms?

In 1981, a small group of people from the Children's Legal Centre, the Advisory Centre for Education and some London local community law centres met to discuss how best to start a debate on developing more democratic structures in schools. A paper[3] proposing a framework of rights and responsibilities for all members of the school community, systematic methods for consultation and participation, and a grievance procedure for settling disputes and conflicts was circulated to a sample of secondary schools. A letter (sent, perhaps misguidedly in the circumstances, to The Headteacher) emphasized that:

> We believe schools could become more constructive and educative places if they were able to adopt agreed frameworks of rights and responsibilities, and procedures not only for resolving conflicts but also for determining policies and the limits of individual choice. The purpose is not simply to develop sets of safeguards against unfair treatment, but to develop procedures which students take seriously and are excited by – which are in themselves an educational experience.

We quoted the Schools Council's discussion paper, *The Practical Curriculum*[4]:

> Some values, like democracy, tolerance and responsibility, grow only with experience of them ... The way a school organizes its staff and pupils and its formal

---

[1] Information published in Advisory Centre for Education *Bulletin*, July/August 1985, No. 6.
[2] European Convention for the Protection of Human Rights and Fundamental Freedoms (available from Council of Europe – see above).
[3] Charter of Students' Rights and Responsibilities, drafted by Children's Legal Centre, Advisory Centre for Education etc., 1981, unpublished.
[4] The schools council working paper 70 *The Practical Curriculum:* a report from the Schools Council London, Methuen Educational 1981.

rules says a great deal about its real values and attitudes. Schools need to practise what they seek to promote.

(We were three years ahead of the Council of Europe's Committee of Ministers – otherwise we would have quoted them as well). The circulated paper (which, incidentally, received minimal response) looked at some of the articles of the European Convention in relation to the structure and day-to-day running of schools. For example, Freedom from Discrimination (Article 14):

> The enjoyment of the rights and freedoms set forth in this Convention shall be secured without discrimination on any ground such as sex, race, colour, language, religion, political or other opinion, national or social origin, association with a national minority, property, birth or other status.

While positive action to combat sexism and racism may increasingly be built into individual schools' aims and curriculum (in some places even on an authority-wide basis), positive action for young students with disabilities still means compulsory segregation for around 150,000 of them. Discrimination by ability – streaming? Setting? Eleven-plus selection? The Assisted Places Scheme? Distribution of funds within schools, and between schools, and the increased dependence of an officially free system of state education on parental funding all mean discrimination in the right to education. A Council of Europe Directive[1] has attempted to do something to limit discrimination on the grounds of language – yet by 1981 only two per cent of UK school students whose first language is not English had integrated teaching in their language and culture of origin.[2]

Freedom of Expression (Article 10):

> Everyone has the right to freedom of expression. This right shall include freedom to hold opinions and to receive and impart information and ideas without interference by public authority and regardless of frontiers . . .

Freedom of Assembly (Article 11):

> Everyone has the right to freedom of peaceful assembly and to freedom of association with others, including the right to form and to join trade unions for the protection of [his or her] interests . . .

Where are school students' rights to free speech and assembly? Rights to form political and social organizations, to have notice board space, distribute printed material, have space and facilities for meetings etc? A sixteen-year-old Birmingham school student wrote to the Children's Legal Centre in 1985:[3]

> Recently a friend and I approached our headmaster about the subject of establishing a CND group within the school. We were told that under the Education Act of 1944, we could not start a political group of any kind unless there was an equal and opposite group established. It seems unlikely to me that anyone would want to start

---

[1] Council of European Communities Directive on education of children and migrant workers (Directive 77/486/EEC).

[2] Report on Implementation of Directive 77/486/EEC, COM(84)54 Final, EEC 1984; European Communities' Information Office, 8 Storey's Gate, London, SW1P 3AT.

[3] Letter published in Childright, January 1986 No. 23, Children's Legal Centre, 20 Compton Terrace, London, N1 2UN.

a 'Let's have a nuclear war' group anyway . . . There exists in our school a Christian Union, but not as yet an Atheist Union, or one for any other religion . . .

(Incidentally, while the 1944 Act does nothing in particular to protect school students' rights to freedom of expression and assembly, it certainly does not limit them either in the way suggested by this headteacher's misinformation.)

Remember the National Union of School Students, born in the heady days of 1968 and all that, dead by the early seventies, with many individual school branches proscribed on formation? Then there are all those cases of exclusion from school on grounds of unacceptable clothes, hair length, jewellery or badges, including – again – CND.

A note of caution – before school student readers lay down the book to rush off their applications alleging breaches of the Convention to the European Human Rights Commission in Strasbourg, they should note a recent Commission decision[1] which suggests, sadly, a less than robust defence of their independent rights to freedom of expression. An application by a mother of two children living in Brierly Hill, West Midlands was rejected (declared inadmissible) in March 1986: it alleged that school uniform requirements and the harassment resulting from infringement of the rules breached the family's rights under the Convention, interfering with private and family life and the children's rights to express themselves and with a peaceful enjoyment of their possessions. The Commission rejected a comparison with the requirement for prisoners to wear prison clothes (already found to be in breach of the Convention): '. . . the conditions pertaining to penal institutions are totally distinct from the facts of the present case . . .' It also found:

> . . . that although the right to freedom of expression may include the right of a person to express his ideas through the way he dresses, it has not been established on the facts of the case that the applicant's children have been prevented from expressing a particular opinion or idea by means of their clothing. Further any rules regarding children only affect the children during their attendance at school and they remain at liberty to express themselves as they wish outside.

While the Commission's argument clearly leaves room for further applications by those who have been forbidden at school to 'express a particular opinion or idea by means of their clothing', it also seems to hint, extraordinarily, that schools can be a 'no-go' area for human rights – in conflict with common sense and the European Parliament's edict.

Freedom of thought (Article 9):

> Everyone has the right to freedom of thought, conscience and religion; this right includes freedom to change [his or her] religion or belief and freedom, either alone or in community with others and in public or private, to manifest his religion or belief, in worship, teaching, practice and observance . . .

In how many schools are young people directly involved in the organization and content of the curriculum? And how about compulsory acts of worship and religious education? Parents – but not young people – have a right of withdrawal,

---

[1] European Commission of Human Rights: decision as to admissibility of application No 11674/85 by *Barbara Stevens v UK*.

but does anyone seriously believe that the legal provisions in the 1944 Act really square with a right to freedom of religion without discrimination, as the Convention guarantees? The Swann Report[1] (*Education for All* 1985) is the first heavy official document to suggest that the hallowed relationship between the established churches and the state in education is deeply discriminatory. The fact that these provisions are no longer observed in many schools, and that the Government – intent on preserving the relationship with the churches – turns a blind eye to this particular form of massive institutional disobedience, does nothing to uphold the principles in the Convention.

The Right to Privacy (Article 8):

> Everyone has the right to respect for his private and family life, his home and his correspondence...

Does the endless circulation of 'confidential' reports, transfer forms, inquiry forms, and referrals without consent to outside agencies – child guidance, social services, health services, careers, even the police, respect young people's privacy? What about compulsory assessment and examinations? The 1981 (Special) Education Act[2] has new rights for parents to involvement, consultation, even access to some professional reports – but where are any rights for young people? When the Data Protection Act was going through Parliament, giving the subjects of computer-stored personal information rights of access, a Government minister reassured members that although young people are clearly the 'subjects' of Statements of Special Educational Needs, any exceptional provision in the Act would ensure that parents and not young people would have a right of access if education authorities should start to computerize such things.[3]

Even apparently trivial and well-intentioned suggestions that children should write essays about 'what I did in the holidays' can as part of a compulsory and generally unnegotiable curriculum, become a gross invasion of a young person's, and a family's privacy. At a much cruder level, many boarding schools censor young people's correspondence and limit their rights to make private phone calls. And at an absurd level, one headteacher refused to allow a boy at a junior school to eat a chocolate bar included as part of his packed lunch (the head wrote to parents: 'It would be most helpful to the continued upholding of a reasonable regulation if chocolate confectionery could be completely avoided'). After five months and the involvement of a solicitor for the family, it was established that 'the contents of packed lunches are ultimately a matter for parents'. The head continues to impose a policy that children must not bring sweets or chocolate to school...[4]

Freedom from Degrading Treatment (Article 3):

> No one shall be subjected to torture or degrading treatment or punishment.

Corporal punishment may be on the way out, thanks partly at least to the European Convention and the courage and persistence of parents and young

---

[1] Swann Report, *Education for All*; report of the committee of inquiry into the education of children from ethnic minority groups, London HMSO 1985.
[2] Education Act 1981, London HMSO.
[3] Data Protection Act 1984, London HMSO.
[4] Children's Legal Centre, advice titles.

people who have pursued their cases through the lengthy and intimidating procedures at Strasbourg, fighting a Government which will have poured literally millions of pounds into defending teachers' rights to hit children. But let no one think that most schools have renounced its use willingly; by 1986, just 32 our of 125 English, Welsh and Scottish local education authorities had banned the cane and the tawse in the schools they controlled (church schools remain a law unto themselves). Recent surveys in authorities which still permit beatings show that between 40 and 60 per cent of primary schools and 80 per cent of secondary schools retain the option to beat.[1] The fortuitous fashion in which Parliament voted, in 1986, to end corporal punishment in state maintained schools is described in the introduction to this book.

Inhuman and degrading treatment does not, of coures, stop at beating. At the extreme, solitary confinement (described by the polite euphemisms of 'time out' or 'seclusion') is in use in some special schools. To a few, apparently, unacceptable sanctions cease to be sanctions when they form part of a behaviour modification programme.

BACKING FROM THE US COURTS

In the United States, appeals to the Constitution have led to genuine progress for students' rights in schools. A celebrated judgement of the Supreme Court (in the 1969 Tinker case[2]), upholding the right of school students to wear black arm bands in protest at US involvement in Vietnam, insisted that:

> It can hardly be argued that either students or teachers shed their constitutional rights to freedom of speech or expression at the schoolhouse gate. This has been the unmistakable holding of this court for almost 50 years.

A lower court in Texas made a similar point somewhat bluntly in 1971:

> Are we really to believe that the appearance of a few long-haired males will topple the pillars of the educational structure of our public schools? If so then fragile indeed is that structure.[3]

At least one state – California – has passed a statute guaranteeing school students the right upheld in *Tinker*:

> Students of the public schools have the right to exercise free expression including, but not limited to, the use of bulletin boards, the distribution of printed materials or petitions, and the wearing of buttons, badges and other insignia, except that expression which is obscene, libelous or slanderous according to current legal standards, or which so incites students as to create a clear and present danger of the commission of unlawful acts on school premises, or the violation of lawful school regulations, or the substantial disruption of the orderly operation of the school shall be prohibited.[4]

---

[1] *STOPP News*, quarterly bulletin of the Society of Teachers Opposed to Physical Punishment, Spring 1986, Vol. 2 No. 2, 18 Victoria Park Square, London, E2 9PB.

[2] *Tinker v Des Moines Independent School District*, 393 US 503 (1969).

[3] *Watson v Thompson*, 321 F Supp 394 (ED Tex 1971).

[4] Details of this statute end of above two cases are given in *The rights of students – an American civil liberties union handbook*, revised edition 1977, Avon Books.

School districts, like the San Francisco Unified School District, have detailed manuals[1] listing students positive rights and responsibilities and explaining the framework of appeals boards etc. designed to ensure that rights are not violated.

In the UK, such developments are still more or less unthinkable, and the current (1986) Education Bill seems to be moving backwards in protecting arbitrary powers of headteachers and authorities.

Disaffection is surely a reasonable, even healthy response to institutions which deny participation and remove basic rights.

Principles at White Lion

One – albeit small and unusual – school which has attempted over its fourteen-year existence to work towards a constitution which respects children's and parents' rights is the White Lion Street Free School, in Islington, North London. An all-age alternative community school in an area of poor housing and general depression, it was one of a brief rash of 'free' schools founded in the early nineteen seventies – free in the sense of no compulsory activities or curriculum and in the sense of no fees. While the building – leased from Islington Council – was being done up by volunteers in the summer of 1972, a handout was prepared to explain to curious local children and parents the aims of White Lion:

> The school will be free in two ways: there will be no fees; the children will be free to learn what they want to learn – so long as it does not interfere with anyone else. It will be their decision, in the first place, that they want to come to the school, and it will be largely up to them to decide when they come. They will also have an equal say with adults in how the school is run.

Children of all ages were to be admitted to the school:

> It must be their decision as well as their parents that they want to come. The maximum the school could hold is about 50 and anyone in this area of Islington will be admitted – space permitting.

A fear that White Lion would be swamped by older disaffected school students led to some fudging of this non-selective policy early on, but by 1977, any child who applied was accepted. The school's principles attempted to respect workers' rights too – hence the non-hierarchical structure, equal pay etc.

The only legal status open to the school when it was founded was that of independent school, but from the beginning the aim was to set a precedent of state funding for a locally-accountable alternative school, and yearly applications were made to the Inner London Education Authority; with equal regularity they were rejected, despite remarkable expressions of local and national support.

In December 1980, the school published the fifth in a series of bulletins[2] on its development:

> We hope that this Bulletin will give heart to people around the world and encourage them to carry on struggling for the things we believe in . . . We believe that the kind

---

[1] *Students' rights and responsibilities manual*, San Francisco Unified School Distribt.
[2] *White Lion Street Free School Bulletin*, Nos. 2–5, 1973–1980 (published by the school, 57 White Lion Street, London, N1).

of thing we are doing here ought to be repeated in every other community. We have not found any need to compromise any of the founding principles of the free school (except being open all the time, as explained in Bulletin 4). We remain wholly democratic. All decisions are made at meetings, open to all and at which all are equal. The school allows adults no power over kids or each other. All jobs are shared. No learning is compulsory. Children are free to choose their own programmes. No repressive ideology moulds, explicitly or implicitly, our curriculum. There are no compulsory lessons or classes . . . Workers have no power over kids and do not use punishment. Above all physical punishment is forbidden. Any worker striking a child must resign immediately.

On the back of Bulletin 5, the school's principles of operation were printed, with a preamble stating:

While the school aims to be flexible and informal, in the first five years certain principles of operation have been agreed which those working in the school are expected to accept and which cannot be changed except by unanimous decision by both the (school) meeting and the meeting of the Council (the council of the company, registered as a charity, which founded the school).

In 1982, the school's annual application to the ILEA for funding was successful; the statement of principles formed part of the application (see Appendix) and a report from the Education Officer (Peter Newsam – now [1986] chair of the Commission for Racial Equality) to the Schools sub-committee stated:

The free school has described its aim as: 'to teach people from the earliest age that they have the right and ability to exercise control over their own lives. To this end it puts into practice three central principles:
1 children, with parents and social workers, should have full and democratic control over their school;
2 effective learning takes place only when the learner chooses the conditions of his or her learning; and
3 the curriculum is a matter for negotiation between adults (who have ideas of what is worth learning) and children (who have ideas of what they want to know).'

The report concluded:

It will be seen from the objectives . . . that the free school has developed an alternative approach to educational provision which may have important lessons for the maintained sector.

So the free school gave up its independent status, and went into ILEA. The company and charity remained, to receive funds and employ those workers not employed by the Authority. Unable to found a new 'county' school, and unwilling to help a voluntary school (just when it was staving off the formation of some other less ideologically attractive ones), the Authority fell back on the legal fiction adopted for the rash of little units set up for 'disaffected' students: the free school students are for legal (but no other) purposes on the roll of nearby primary and secondary schools. Naturally enough, those who had been involved in the school feared that the autonomy of the school meeting and the basic principles of White Lion might in time be threatened by the size, power and momentum of the Authority; in practice there has been no sign of this. The agreement stated:

Mindful of the Authority's wish that the WLSFS centre retains the traditions of the free school, those responsibilities which normally would fall to the head and staff of a maintained school will remain under the control of the school meeting.

The Authority has scrupulously observed the agreement. But the status of the school's principles remains uncertain; a working party of workers and ex-workers produced a refined draft of the original code by consensus during 1985 which is reproduced as the appendix to this chapter. It has been adopted formally by the council of the founding company, but not by the current workers.

It proved impossible to resolve fundamental differences of opinion over such issues as the right of children and parents to an equal say in decision-making, and whether the school should have a catchment area, and be selective or non-selective within it. The council for the company referred the dispute to the Authority early in 1986.

Appendix

WHITE LION FREE SCHOOL: PRINCIPLES OF OPERATION

Preamble

The White Lion Street Free School sets out to meet the social and educational needs of those attending the school and their families. It also seeks to be a resource for the local community.

The following principles, which provide a charter of rights and duties for users of the school and those who work in it, have been adopted by the subscribers to First London Free School Ltd, and must be accepted by those working in the school.

They can only be amended following a unanimous proposal from the school community endorsed at the annual general meeting or a special general meeting of First London Free School Ltd.

PRINCIPLES

1 Decision-making shall be democratic. There shall be regular meetings, normally weekly, with an open agenda and open to all attending the school, part- and full-time workers and parents of children attending. These shall be the main decision-making meetings of the school. When consensus fails, decisions may be put to a vote.

   Decisions shall not be valid if they: violate one or more of these principles of operation; threaten the long-term stability, financial viability or legality of the school.

   In case of disagreement over interpretation of these limitations on the power of the meeting, or of the principles, the matter shall be referred to the subscribers to First London Free School Ltd.

2 Children will be encouraged but never forced to take part in learning activities.

3 In the operation and activities of the school, there shall be no discrimination against a member of the school community on the grounds of race, colour, sex, language, religion, political or other opinion, national or social origin, cultural beliefs or practices, property, educational attainment, disability, birth or any other basis whatsoever.

4 Only children who live within the school's catchment area – currently a circle of 1000 metres radius – are eligible to join the school. The free school has a current capacity of 50 school-age children. The size of the school's catchment area and its capacity may be changed subject to the agreement of the subscribers to London Free School Ltd.

Both parents and child must be fully informed about the free school, and both must express a wish to join.

If at any point there are more applicants than places available, places will be allocated in order of date of original application of those eligible, except that priority will be given to brothers and sisters of children already attending the free school.

These are the arrangements for admission to the free school: there shall be no selection based on race, colour, sex, language, religion, political or other opinion, national or social origin, family status, cultural beliefs or practices, property, educational attainment, disability or any other basis whatsoever.

5 The individual right of members of the school community to freedom of thought, conscience and religion shall be respected. Political action may be taken according to personal belief but never in the name of the school without the unanimous agreement of the school meeting.

6 The school shall not charge fees for its basic activities, and it aims to ensure that no child attending shall be prevented by financial hardship from using the school's resources.

7 Full-time workers shall be paid equally, and part-timers on a pro-rata basis. Additional allowances may be agreed depending on workers' personal circumstances.

8 Money earned by workers through promoting the ideas embodied in the school shall be paid to the school.

9 The workers shall work collectively in a non-hierarchical way, and shall encourage full involvement of children and parents.

10 Paid and voluntary workers must agree that they will not hit children or use physical violence. If they do, they will resign immediately and the parents of the child/children concerned will be told what happened. The school recognizes that there are times when mild physical restraint may be needed in order to prevent children and/or adults hurting themselves or others.

The school community shall commit itself to finding and using non-violent ways of resolving conflicts.

11 Punishment, including expulsion, shall be avoided. This is not to prevent positive measures being used to protect people and their ability to make full use of the school, and to recover or replace stolen or damaged property without violating the legal rights of individuals.

12 All records and reports about children, their parents and others shall be shown to the subjects of them, who shall also have the right to challenge and if necessary correct anything in them. The persons about whom the report is written shall have the right to control who else sees it.

13 Workers shall not consult agencies outside the school (e.g. child guidance, social services etc.) about a named child without the child's informed consent or about other family members without their consent.

Workers shall press for attendance and representation of children and families at case conferences and other meetings. They shall not attend meetings with outside agencies at which children and/or their families may be discussed unless the child/family is also present, or has given an informed consent to the involvement of the worker in the meeting. (If a child is unable to give an informed consent, their parents' consent must be obtained, unless to do so will place the child in immediate danger.)

List of contributors

Len Barton is a principal lecturer in education at Bristol Polytechnic.

Tony Booth is a lecturer in education at the Open University.

Stewart Butterfield is headteacher of a school in Haringey.

David Coulby is head of teaching studies at North London Polytechnic.

Sheila Cunnison is an honorary research fellow at Humberside College of Higher Education.

Lynn Davies is a lecturer in education at the University of Birmingham.

Rob Grunsell was formerly co-ordinator of the Disruption in Schools Project, and is currently manager of a community recreation centre.

Di Hesketh is a teacher in Cambridge.

Stephen Humphries is a writer and broadcaster with a special interest in social history and oral tradition.

Rod Ling is a counsellor at King's School, Birmingham.

Mel Lloyd-Smith is a lecturer in education at the University of Warwick.

Dennis Mongon is an advisory teacher with the Inner London Education Authority.

Peter Newell works at the Children's Legal Centre and was a founder of the White Lion Free School.

Shirley Prendergast is a research associate at the Child Care and Development Group, University of Cambridge.

Alan Prout is a research associate at the Child Care and Development Group, University of Cambridge.

John Quicke is a lecturer in education at the University of Sheffield.

Jan Reid is a lecturer in applied social studies, University of Warwick.

Jan Sargeant is an ex-English teacher, now a freelance writer.

John Schostak is a lecturer in special needs at the University of East Anglia.

Europe Singh is a member of the anti-racist strategies team, Inner London Education Authority.

Neil Toppin was formerly headteacher, St. Augustine's community school, Glasgow.

Mike Vernon is a former secondary teacher.

Cecile Wright is a lecturer in education at Sheffield University.

INDEX

275